Politics, Gender, and Concepts

A critique of concepts has been central to feminist scholarship since its inception. However, while gender scholars have identified the analytical gaps in existing social science concepts, few have systematically mapped out a gendered approach to issues in political analysis and theory development. This volume addresses this important gap in the literature by exploring the methodology of concept construction and critique, which is a crucial step to disciplined empirical analysis, research design, causal explanations, and testing hypotheses. Leading gender and politics scholars use a common framework to discuss methodological issues in some of the core concepts of feminist research in political science, including representation, democracy, welfare state governance, and political participation. This is an invaluable work for researchers and students in women's studies and political science.

Gary Goertz teaches political science at the University of Arizona. He is the author or coauthor of seven books and over forty articles on issues of international politics, methodology, and conflict studies, including *Contexts of International Politics* (Cambridge, 1994).

Amy G. Mazur is Professor in the Department of Political Science at Washington State University. Focusing her research on comparative feminist policy issues, she has published numerous book chapters and articles and is author or editor of four books, including *Theorizing Feminist Policy* (2002).

Politics, Gender, and Concepts

Theory and Methodology

Edited by

Gary Goertz

and

Amy G. Mazur

CAMBRIDGE UNIVERSITY PRESS
Cambridge, New York, Melbourne, Madrid, Cape Town, Singapore, São Paulo, Delhi

Cambridge University Press
The Edinburgh Building, Cambridge CB2 8RU, UK

Published in the United States of America by Cambridge University Press, New York

www.cambridge.org
Information on this title: www.cambridge.org/9780521723428

First published 2008

Printed in the United Kingdom at the University Press, Cambridge

A catalogue record for this publication is available from the British Library

Library of Congress Cataloging in Publication data
Goertz, Gary, 1953–
Politics, gender and concepts / Gary Goertz, Amy G. Mazur.
    p.   cm.
Includes bibliographical references and index.
ISBN 978-0-521-89776-1 (hardback)
1. Women–Government policy.   2. Women in politics.   3. Feminism.
I. Mazur, Amy.   II. Title.
HQ1236.G55   2008
306.201 – dc22   2008023547

ISBN 978-0-521-89776-1 hardback
ISBN 978-0-521-72342-8 paperback

Contents

Part I   Gendering concepts

Part II   Gender-specific concepts

Figures

Tables

Notes on contributors

Karen Celis has been Assistant Professor at the Department of Business Adminis-tration and Public Management of the University College Ghent since 2004. Her research and publications focus on the political representation of women and on state feminism. Besides a book on gender, politics, and policy in Belgium (with Petra Meier, 2006) she has (published and forthcoming) articles in the *Journal of Women, Politics and Policy*, *Representation*, *Parliamentary Affairs*, and *Res Publica*, and book chapters in J. Outshoorn and J. Kantola (eds.), *Changing State Feminism: Women's Policy Agencies Confront Shifting Institutional Terrain* (with Petra Meier, 2007); J. Magone (ed.) *Regional Institutions and Governance in the European Union. Subnational Actors in the New Millennium* (with Alison Woodward, 2003); D. Stetson (ed.) *Abortion Politics, Women's Movements and the Democratic State: A Comparative Study of State Feminism* (2001).

Georgia Duerst-Lahti is Professor of Political Science and a faculty member of the Women's and Gender Studies Program at Beloit College. Her research interests center on the gendering of political institutions and on gender in campaigns. Recent contributions include a book, coauthored with Cathy M. Johnson and Noelle Norton, entitled *Creating Gender: The Sexual Politics of Welfare Policy* (2007) and a chapter on masculinity on the campaign trail for Lori Han and Caroline Heldman (eds.), *Rethinking Madame President* (2007). Her research appears in several journals, including *Sex Roles*, *Women and Politics*, and *Political Science Quarterly*. Her best-known work con-tinues to be *Gender Power, Leadership, and Governance*, with Rita Mae Kelly (1995). She has been elected as President of the Midwest Women's Caucus for Political Science and the President of the national Women's Caucus for Political Science, and has served on the Executive Council of the Midwest Political Science Association and on the Committee on the Status of Women of the American Political Science Association.

Gary Goertz is Professor of Political Science at the University of Arizona. He is the author or coauthor of five books and over twenty-five articles on issues of international institutions, methodology, and conflict studies, including *Contexts of International Politics* (1994), *War and Peace in International Rivalry* (with Paul Diehl, 2000), and *International Norms and Decision Making: A Punctuated Equilibrium*

Model (2003). The topic of necessary conditions, their theory and methodology, has also been a research agenda item for a number of years. He is coeditor of the anthology *Necessary Conditions: Theory, Methodology, and Applications* (with Harvey Starr, 2003). His most recent methodological work deals with the construction of concepts: *Social Science Concepts: A User's Guide* (2005). He is editor of a special issue of the journal *Political Analysis* entitled "Causal complexity and qualitative methods" (2006).

Dorothy E. McBride (formerly Stetson) is Emeritus Professor of Political Science at Florida Atlantic University, where she was a founder of the women's studies program. She is coconvener (with Amy G. Mazur) of the Research Network on Gender, Politics and the State (RNGS), an international group of scholars engaged in the study of women's movements and state feminism in postindustrial democracies. She is author of *Abortion in the United States: A Reference Handbook* (2008) and *Women's Rights in the USA: Policy Conflict and Gender Roles* (3rd edn., 2004) and has published articles in *Politics & Gender, Political Research Quarterly, French Politics* and *Women & Politics*. She co-edited *Comparative State Feminism* (with Amy G. Mazur, 1995) and was editor and contributing author of *Abortion Politics, Women's Movements and the Democratic State: A Comparative Study of State Feminism* (2001). She has been a Fulbright Senior Fellow in France and received research grants from the National Science Foundation. During 2006–8 she was visiting scholar at the University of Washington.

Amy G. Mazur is Professor in the Department of Political Science at Washington State University. Her research and teaching interests focus on comparative feminist policy issues with a particular emphasis on France. She is coeditor of *Political Research Quarterly*. Her books include *Comparative State Feminism* (editor, with Dorothy McBride Stetson, 1995); *Gender Bias and the State: Symbolic Reform at Work in Fifth Republic France* (1995); *State Feminism, Women's Movements, and Job Training: Making Democracies Work in the Global Economy* (editor, 2001); and *Theorizing Feminist Policy* (2002). She has published articles in *Political Research Quarterly, French Politics and Society, Policy Studies Journal, West European Politics, European Journal of Political Research, European Political Science, Review of Policy Research, Contemporary French Civilization, French Politics, Travail, Genre et Société* and *EspacesTemps*. She is coconvener of the Research Network on Gender Politics and the State and convener of the French Politics Group of the APSA. In 2007–8, she was a visiting professor at Sciences Po-Paris, and in Fall 2001 she was the Marie-Jahoda Professor of International Feminist Studies at Ruhr University, Bochum, and a Havens Center Visiting Scholar at the University of Wisconsin in Spring 2003. In 2005–6 she was an expert for the United Nations for the Expert Group Meeting on Equal Participation of Women and Men in Decision-making Processes and rapporteur of the final meeting report. She has received research grants from the National Science Foundation, the European Science Foundation, and the French Ministry of Social Affairs.

Pamela Paxton is Associate Professor of Sociology and Political Science at Ohio State University. She is the coauthor of *Women, Politics, and Power* (2007) and over thirty articles covering topics that include women in politics and the link between social capital and democracy. Representative articles include "Detection and determinants of bias in subjective measures" (1998); "Women's suffrage in the measurement of democracy: problems of operationalization" (2000); "Subjective measures of liberal democracy" (2000); "Women's political representation: the importance of ideology" (2003); and "The international women's movement and women's political representation, 1893–2003" (2006). She has received several research grants from the National Science Foundation, most recently to study women in politics.

Diane Sainsbury is Professor Emerita, formerly Lars Hiereta Professor of Political Science, Stockholm University, Sweden. She is author of *Gender, Equality and Welfare States* (Cambridge University Press, 1996), "Gender and the making of welfare states: Norway and Sweden", *Social Politics* (2001) and "Social welfare policies and gender," *International Encyclopedia of the Social and Behavioral Sciences* (2001); editor of *Gendering Welfare States* (1994) and *Gender and Welfare State Regimes* (1999); and coeditor of *State Feminism and Political Representation* (Cambridge University Press, 2005). Her most recent articles include "Migrants' social rights, ethnicity and welfare regimes," *Journal of Social Policy* (2005) and "Immigrants' social rights in comparative perspective: welfare regimes, forms of immigration and immigration policy regimes," *Journal of European Social Policy* (2006). She is also a contributing author to *The Feminization of Poverty in Rich Countries: An International Phenomenon?* (forthcoming).

Kathleen Staudt, PhD (University of Wisconsin, 1976) is Professor of Political Science and Director of the Center for Civic Engagement at the University of Texas at El Paso. At the global frontlines – the international border with Mexico – she has published four books that connect international and comparative politics; the most recent is *Violence and Activism at the Border: Gender, Fear, and Everyday Life in Ciudad Juarez* (2008). Staudt published earlier books and articles on women, advocacy administration, and institutional resistance to women's programs (1982, 1985). With other feminist scholars, she coedited pioneering books on women and the state (1987, 1988).

Georgina Waylen is Reader in Politics at the University of Sheffield, UK. She has researched and published on many aspects of gender and politics, including transitions to democracy and gendered political economy. As well as articles in a range of journals such as *World Politics, Review of International Studies, Journal of Latin American Studies,* and *Comparative Political Studies,* she is the author of *Gender in Third World Politics* (1996) and *Engendering Transitions* (2007), and the coeditor of *Gender, Politics and the State* (1998), *Towards a Gendered Political Economy* (2000), and *Global Governance: Feminist Perspectives* (2008). She is currently an associate editor of *Politics and Gender.*

S. Laurel Weldon is Associate Professor of Political Science at Purdue University. She has published a book (*Protest, Policy and the Problem of Violence Against Women* [2002]) and articles on gender politics in the *Journal of Politics, Political Research Quarterly, Perspectives, Politics and Gender,* and the *International Journal of Feminist Politics.* She serves on the Council of the Midwest Political Science Association as well as the APSA's Committee on the Status of Women in the Professions. She is currently Chair of the Alice Paul Committee for the women's caucus of the APSA (awarding recognition to the best dissertation prospectus on women and politics) and is Newsletter Editor for the APSA's women and politics research section. In 2007, Professor Weldon became a Fellow in the Center for Behavioral and Social Sciences at Purdue, working on a project on intersectionality and the welfare state. She is currently writing a book on social movements and representation as well as developing (with Mala Htun of the New School) a seventy-country database on women's rights with support from the Political Science program of the NSF.

Acknowledgments

This book is a collective effort on a variety of levels. It builds from a host of scholarly work on concept formation and gender and politics across a variety of sub-areas of political science. We hope we have fully recognized the scholars who have contributed to this body of work in the pages that follow. More specifically, we would like to recognize the collaborative spirit of all of the contributors, who respected the structure of the guidelines, followed the timeline of the project, and most importantly brought an incredibly rich and deep knowledge of their areas of expertise to the project. Without their dedication and cooperation this book would never have seen the light of day. Two panels cosponsored by the Women and Politics and Qualitative Methods Divisions of the American Political Science Association in 2005 and 2006 gave us the crucial forum to develop and fine-tune the book as a group.

Shirin Rai provided us with priceless advice throughout the entire project. We would also like to thank Karen Beckwith, Lisa Baldez, Mala Htun, David Collier, Joni Lovenduski, and Birgit Sauer for their input at various stages of the project. The comments of the anonymous reviewers also greatly strengthened the final manuscript. Our respective departments at Washington State University and Arizona State University furnished us with the all-important infrastructure and support for the completion of this book as well. It has been a distinct pleasure to work with John Haslam at Cambridge University Press, whose enthusiasm for the book made our jobs a delight from beginning to end.

December 1, 2007   Amy G. Mazur and Gary Goertz

1 Introduction

Amy G. Mazur and Gary Goertz

Gender and politics researchers have been developing new and exciting concepts and modifying existing concepts since the late 1980s. Their goal has been to make research on politics better account for the realities of gender as a complex process and in doing so to make our theories and studies more accurate and scientifically meaningful; or as we say in the trade, gendering political science. Gender scholars have identified the analytical gaps in existing social science concepts, have suggested how to better incorporate gender into those concepts, and have developed new gender-specific concepts. These reflections on concepts, however, are not systematically assembled in one location. Much work is a fugitive literature, hidden in long research papers, in hard to find specialized research articles, or in chapters buried in edited books. The aim of this book is to assemble expert gender researchers to map out some of the major concepts of current politics and gender research, concepts on which they have spent a good portion of their careers working. While by no means making the claim to cover all concepts, some of the most central concepts in political science and gender and politics research are treated – democracy, representation, the welfare state, governance, development, gender ideology, intersectionality, women's movements/feminism, and state feminism.[1]

It is important to take note of this book's use of the concept of gender itself. Reflecting current scholarship,[2] the authors treat gender as a complex process that involves the social construction of men's and women's identities in relation to each other. In some of the research covered in this book, gender is used as a synonym for biological sex. For example, in the chapters on

---

[1] The Appendix describes a website for this book. The website provides a place and a forum for information about concepts not covered by chapters in this anthology. We also see this website as a resource for classroom use; many of these concepts could be assigned as classroom exercises.

[2] See for example the series of articles on the "Concept of gender" in *Politics & Gender* 2005 (1.1).

democracy and representation, the focus is on women's roles in politics. The operating premise of this book, however, takes to heart Joan Scott's initial call (1986) for using the complex version of "gender as a category of analysis" as well as the lead of the plethora of gender and politics research that has taken gender seriously since. Many of the chapters discuss in detail what it means to treat gender as a category for analysis, as well as presenting the vast literature on gender; see in particular Georgia Duerst-Lahti's chapter on gender ideology. All of the authors clearly state how they use the notion of gender in their conceptual discussions.

Given what we see as the fundamental link between concepts, research, data collection, and theory-building, we develop a set of ten concept construction guidelines, to be followed by all researchers interested in producing scientifically meaningful studies. The guidelines are presented in chapter 2, and the authors in this volume follow them in their specific concept discussions. The guidelines were developed in the context of their application by the authors in this volume. In other words, the lessons learned from the complexities and challenges of conceptualizing gender and politics concepts are used to create better approaches to concept construction more generally speaking. The guidelines presented in chapter 2, therefore, reflect how the intersection between feminist and nonfeminist analysis, embodied by this book more generally, can strengthen our tools for the analysis of any and all political science concepts.

Thus, this volume represents a marriage between a systematic concern for concept formation found in much political science research outside of gender (e.g. Sartori 1970, Collier and Mahon 1993, Adcock and Collier 2001) and the feminist-oriented study of gender and politics that has as its goal to identify the gender/sex-specific patterns of politics and the often inherently gender-biased nature of political science analysis.[3] The editors themselves reflect this marriage. Gary Goertz does not work on gender, but he has done extensive work on qualitative methods in general and the methodology of concepts in particular. Amy Mazur has worked extensively in the gender and politics field in general, and has devoted special attention to conceptual developments in this area (see her chapters with McBride). We believe that the confrontation of the general methodology of concepts with the specific concerns of gender and politics scholars will provide benefits and insights to both sides.

---

[3] For more on core analytical meanings of feminism see Mazur (2002). The chapters on women's movements and state feminism discuss in more detail operational definitions of feminism.

The collective outcome of this volume, we hope, is to move gender and politics research and the field of political science forward toward better analysis and science. In other words, the systematic treatment of gender and politics concepts that follows has the potential to improve the practice of political analysis itself. In this chapter, we first provide the rationale for a book on gender and politics concepts, discussing why it is important to take a systematic and international approach to mapping concepts. Next, we discuss the two major strategies that have been pursued by gender and politics researchers to address gender issues in the development and application of concepts. In the last section, we present our plan and approach by showing how these two strategies structure the book as well as different ways of grouping the chapters with regard to methodological approaches and theory-building.

Why focus on concepts and methods in gender and politics research in a comparative/international perspective?

The beginning of major new research agendas always involves significant attention to and debate about concepts. It is no coincidence that over 150 years ago, J. S. Mill began his famous *System of Logic*, a foundational treatise on the methods of social science analysis, with a long discussion of "names." Names, better known as concepts, allow us to understand and analyze the world in a systematic way through identifying a set of phenomena and providing us with categories for researching and explaining it. Ultimately, sound concept construction leads us to develop better theories about the complex world around us and evaluate those theories using empirical evidence.

It is thus not surprising that as researchers have increasingly turned their attention to gender as a complex social phenomenon, they are immediately concerned with concepts. A critique of concepts has been central to feminist scientific literature since its inception (Hawkesworth 2006). The concern for concept analysis and the recent turn toward its applications in research among gender and politics scholars is exemplified by the fact that the new journal *Politics & Gender* – the journal of the American Political Science Association's Division of Women and Politics Research – devoted its first discussion forum to the concept of gender.

Despite the centrality of concept analysis in the gender and politics literature, there is little work that provides systematic guidelines, examples, and the methodology for the construction and use of concepts in empirically based

theory-building. Some work has taken a normative theoretical approach identifying the weaknesses in thinking on politics from a feminist perspective and
identifying new theoretical approaches (e.g. Squires 1999). Other studies identify a single concept to study in both theoretical and empirical terms either
by a single author (e.g. Siim 2000, Sainsbury 1999) or a series of contributors
(e.g. McBride Stetson and Mazur 1995, Sainsbury 1994, Parpart, Rai, and
Staudt 2002). Phillips (1998) republishes some of the most important pieces
on concept development in gender and politics from both empirical and normative perspectives. Hobson, Lewis, and Siim (2002) bring together a group
of scholars to examine a series of concepts specific to the social policy and
welfare state literature and to assess the "contested" nature of the concepts for
feminist analysis. Ackerly, Stern, and True (2006) discuss feminist approaches
to methodology in International Relations, without mentioning the word
concept. But nothing in this literature provides systematic procedures for the
construction, critique, and use of concepts.

Work that focuses on the methodology of concepts has done little to provide
meaningful guidance to gender and politics research either. While much work
has recently turned its attention to the principles of good concept formation
in political analysis (e.g. Brady and Collier 2004, Goertz 2005, and Collier
and Mahon 1993) none of the books in this area has placed a central focus
on gender. Only Goertz 2005 specifically focuses on gender as an issue in
concept formation through the "gendering welfare state" literature. Like the
divide between quantitative and qualitative analysis, therefore, there is a divide
between feminist and nonfeminist research on concepts. This book is an
attempt to bridge this second divide, with advantages to be gained by both
sides.

To address the feminist/nonfeminist divide, we explicitly link work on concepts and gender to larger literatures on methodology, measurement, and
research design. We feel that the way researchers on gender have dealt with
conceptual problems can inform the larger debate about methodology. Conversely, explicit comparisons with other work on concept formation and measurement can have important implications for work on gender. Importantly,
we stress the intimate ties between conceptualization and theory. One cannot
construct or evaluate concepts without considering the implicit causal arguments embedded in them. To discuss concepts without considering how they
are used in practice, in categorization, in case selection, in operationalization,
etc., means only half the job is done.

We use the term "methodology" in a large sense to cover epistemological
approaches, research design, and the tools of data collection and analysis. It

can be qualitative, such as Sartori's classic article on conceptual stretching (1970), or statistical, as in Bollen's work on democracy (e.g. 1980). In short, methodology means in this volume a wide range of considerations ranging from theory to concrete empirical analysis.

Feminist scholars, those interested in showing how the social construction of sex-based hierarchies play out in the social and political realm, have "problematized" – often in a highly critical fashion – many concepts central to feminist research ever since such research first became prominent in the 1980s. For many, rethinking concepts from a critical feminist perspective was an essential first step in any research enterprise. Many of these analyses were informed by normative feminist theory. Given the breadth of the critical literature, this volume focuses less on the shortfalls in concepts and more on systematizing good procedures and methodology for developing, evaluating, and using concepts in gender-oriented analysis. Over time, feminist scholars have redefined old concepts and introduced new ones to improve the analysis of gender overall. What is lacking in the literature is guidance on concept development and application, in other words the methodology of gender and concepts. What we propose here, for students, researchers, and theorists, is a manual on how to develop and apply gender and politics concepts in comparative theory and empirical research. As such, this book is an essential step in the ongoing research cycle of gender and politics and political science more broadly speaking.

This book takes a decisively comparative and international approach to concepts. Thinking about concepts must include how well the concept "travels" (Sartori 1970) to a variety of cultural and national contexts. To be sure, there is a strong tradition of gender and politics research within individual countries. In the USA, the gender, women, and politics enterprise is a boom industry with obvious practical implications for citizens, activists, and policy practitioners. Thinking about conceptualizing gender and politics from a scientific perspective necessarily implies more cross-national, cross-sectoral, and cross-temporal approaches, and hence takes a comparative eye – a viewpoint that is taken to heart by all of our contributors in their chapters and in their research as well as in the essence of the concept guidelines.

It is also interesting to note that much of the nonfeminist work on concept formation is done in the context of comparative political analysis. A central issue raised in the comparative development and use of gender and politics concepts is Sartori's (1970) "concept traveling." That is, whether concepts can be developed and used in empirical analysis across a variety of national settings. In the infancy of the study of gender and politics, scholars taking a comparative approach asserted that the feminist conceptual analysis was ethnocentric, tending to reflect the Anglo-American context. Indeed, many of the early feminist theorists came from the USA or the UK. Conceptual analysis in gender and politics, as a result, increasingly has focused on how to develop concepts that can be applied in a variety of national settings across the globe.

This volume takes seriously these efforts to develop and apply concepts that travel not only across national boundaries, but also across all levels of state and civil society – local, subnational, national, international and transnational – and across time. Recently, feminist analysts (e.g. Hawkesworth 2006) have asserted that to include the complex notion of gender is necessarily to deal with issues of diversity between cultures, classes, ages, etc., and many chapters make this point. In addition, one of the ten guidelines proposed in chapter 2 and followed by each author covers how to make concepts better travel across cultural and temporal contexts. Thus, although some of the chapters deal with concepts that have been developed either in or for the context of western postindustrial democracies – democracy, representation, the welfare state, women's movements, and state feminism – they all deal with the issue of how to make the concepts applicable to a diversity of cultural and national settings, often outside of the West. In addition, the chapters on governance, development, gender ideology, and intersectionality bring cultural diversity in, both within and across national borders, as a major operating requirement.

This volume is then a methodological reflection on the development of a large body of work that has sought to "gender" political science analysis by systematically introducing gender dimensions into established concepts and gender concepts into the study of politics. The goal of gendering has been to improve the explanatory power of empirical theory-building that uses core concepts as well as the very process of concept formation itself. Political scientists who gender concepts assert that research, methodology, and theory-building that ignore gender as a complex analytical concept are not good science. Thus, by intersecting the methodology of concepts with gender and politics scholarship, this volume's ultimate aim is better social science.

Introducing gender to concepts: gendering existing concepts and developing new gender-specific concepts

A major common theoretical and methodological operation in the gender and politics literature involves the "gendering" of existing central concepts. By this we mean taking an existing concept and introducing gender, as a complex concept, into the concept analysis. As many examples illustrate, the gender bias often does not lie on the surface, but lies hidden. Gendering means bringing out and making explicit hidden biases and assumptions in standard conceptualizations. Most scholars reject the "add women and stir" way of introducing gender considerations into the analysis, where sex is added as an additional variable or the analysis examines women as an afterthought. Adding is only one of the many ways gender can be inserted. If one is sticking to mathematical metaphors, multiplication is another. Besides, adding is not always a simple task. To continue with the implicit cooking metaphor, to add salt to a dessert is not a minor modification. If one thinks in terms of catalysts, combining hydrogen with oxygen produces something quite different.

The "add gender and stir" metaphor suggests that the result of the addition of gender is minor. However, the key issue is what happens to the mix after stirring: if the mixture blows up, then the addition of gender is of importance. The key questions are "How does one insert gender?" and "What results?" Adding gender can have catalytic effects that radically transform the original mixture into something quite new. Pamela Paxton's chapter in particular shows how, by just adding a relatively simple variable of women's suffrage to categorizing democratic systems, the whole enterprise of regime classifications changes significantly. This then means that one needs to revisit the theories that explain democratization. For example, one might relativize the role played by labor unions and upgrade the importance of other social actors.

An illustration of what happens when a more complex notion of gender is folded into the mix comes from feminist scholarship on the welfare state, taken up in Diane Sainsbury's chapter. Classic conceptions of the welfare state involved no gender component (e.g. Esping-Andersen 1990). The traditional, and implicit, view was from the perspective of the industrial worker with a nonworking wife and children. Gendering the welfare state involved bringing in new dimensions to the concept to deal with the special concerns of women as mothers, workers, and caregivers (e.g. Orloff 1993 and Sainsbury 1994, 1996). A very prominent concept of the welfare state was developed by Esping-Andersen (1990). Orloff identifies the concept's three (complex) dimensions:

A first fundamental dimension concerns the range, or domain, of human needs that are satisfied by social policy instead of by the market.
A second dimension of policy regimes is stratification . . . This is the question about who benefits from the policies of the welfare state.
The third dimension deals with the extent to which the welfare state creates "citizenship rights" and result in the "decommodification" of goods and services. (1993: 318)

In her very influential critique, Orloff inserts two new dimensions into the concept of the welfare state:

Thus, the decommodification dimension must be supplemented with a new analytic dimension that taps into the extent to which states promote or discourage women's paid employment – the right to be commodified. I call this fourth dimension of welfare-state regimes access to paid work. (1993: 318)

If decommodification is important because it frees wage earners from the compulsion of participating in the market, a parallel dimension is needed to indicate the ability of those who do most of the domestic and caring work – almost all women – to form and maintain autonomous households, that is, to survive and support their children without having to marry to gain access to breadwinners' income. (1993: 319)

The insertion of these two dimensions has very wide-ranging ramifications for data-gathering and theory. Among other things it can radically call into question the extent of the welfare state and contest various theories of its formation. It provides the beginning of a massive research agenda on the topic (for a survey see Pierson 2000).

Another approach to gendering is to "adjectivize" the concept. The welfare state example illustrates how the name remains constant – still a "welfare state" – but the content does not. A second option is to add an adjective to an existing concept. The term "women's (social) movement," also covered in this volume, illustrates how an adjective, "women's," is attached to an existing concept, "social movement." Classic logic requires that definitions be stated in necessary and sufficient condition terms (see any philosophical logic textbook, e.g. Copi and Cohen 1990). To affix an adjective means to add a new dimension to the list. It must be a necessary condition like all the other dimensions. In set terms, then, the adjectivized concept must be a subset of the original concept.

It is worth noting that "women's movement" drops the "social." Here there is an implicit theoretical link to the concept of social movement. The dropping of the "social" is not necessarily merely for convenience; it may reflect some serious theoretical concerns. McBride and Mazur in their chapter argue that women's movements are not a subset of all social movements, and this is why the chapter is in the part of the book on gender-specific new concepts. One way to suggest that women's movements are not just a subset is to take "social" out of the name. While "movement" still implies linkages to social movements, taking "social" out does suggest that it is not merely a subset relationship.

In summary, gendering can have wide-ranging methodological and theoretical influences on concepts. Because the concepts change, case selection can change and the results of previous empirical analyses can easily be called into question. One needs to consider how gender is being inserted and think about the theoretical and methodological consequences of such insertions. Chapters in the book deal with the gendering of democracy, representation, the welfare state, governance, and development.

A second common theoretical and methodological thread consists of the development of new concepts. These new concepts typically tap an unrecognized gender phenomenon that is of central importance to the understanding of political behavior. For example, comparative gender and policy scholars began to use the concept "state feminism" in the 1980s to better understand how the contemporary state in western democracies has dealt with new demands for women's rights and gender equality (e.g., McBride Stetson and Mazur 1995). Chapters in this volume illustrate how some of the major new concepts specific to gender have been developed and applied. These include gender ideology, intersectionality, women's movements/feminism, and state feminism.

Core to all concept analysis in the gender and politics literature is that of complexity. The existence of debates regarding standpoint theory and intersectionality, where gender is juxtaposed and intertwined with other group identities and systems of exclusion, illustrates that core concepts in the literature are complex ones. Typically, gender scholars reject simple additive views, the "add women and stir approach," often implicit in most methodology courses. Students and researchers need models and tools to think about and model complex concepts. While not pretending to be exhaustive, the volume provides some methodological tools for constructing complex concepts. Each chapter deals with the complexity issue. Each shows how scholars have worked to incorporate complexity in terms of additional dimensions, typical of the gendering operation, as well as the relationship between dimensions, a key issue in the chapter on intersectionality.

The approach and plan of the book

In the rest of the book, gender and politics experts use the ten guidelines presented in chapter 2 to discuss nine different concepts. Classic and core concepts in political science that have been gendered are covered in the first part of the book – democracy, representation, the welfare state, governance, and development. New concepts that have become common currency in gender and politics research are in the second part of the book – gender ideology, intersectionality, women's movements/feminism and state feminism. In Part I, we start with the widely discussed concept of democracy, in the chapter by Pamela Paxton; move to a related concept, representation, in that by Karen Celis, and then to three other state-specific concepts – the welfare state (Diane Sainsbury), governance (Georgina Waylen), and development (Kathleen Staudt). The gender-specific concepts begin with what is also one of the most general, gender ideology (Georgia Duerst-Lahti), followed by another new but quite general concept, intersectionality (Laurel Weldon). Moving down the ladder of generality, Dorothy McBride and Amy Mazur present first a chapter on women's movements and feminism and then one on state feminism.

We do not include a separate chapter on gender, since each chapter shows how gender is brought in, and the chapter on gender ideology provides a thorough and up-to-date discussion of current usages of gender. Feminism, another core concept to gender and politics analysis, is also not treated in a separate chapter. The chapters on gender ideology, women's movements, and state feminism take head-on what is often identified as a contested concept (e.g. Beasley 1999).

It is obviously impossible within the confines of one anthology to cover all concepts relevant to gender and politics scholars, such as power. We present additional important gender and politics concepts not covered in this book on a separate website. The Appendix briefly describes the website. We see it as a place to describe other interesting concepts for gender and politics scholars, and provide some suggested reading on these concepts. We see this site as one where readers, teachers, and students can propose new entries. It can also serve the classroom as a source of inspiration and assignments.

Unlike feminism and gender, democracy, one of the core concepts in political science with dozens of articles devoted to conceptualization and measurement, is treated separately by Pamela Paxton in the first concept chapter (chapter 3). Less than a comprehensive treatment of the highly complex and expansive concept, the chapter concentrates on how to gender current classifications of democratic regimes in comparative politics scholarship. The issue of democracy is taken up in many of the other chapters in the book as well. Karen Celis treats the representation side of democracy in her chapter, and normative issues of democratic performance are broached in the chapter on governance, development, and state feminism. The chapters on the welfare state, women's movements, and state feminism also are set against the backdrop of understanding gender politics in democratic regimes, focusing on the issue of how to make stable democracies more democratic. Thus, democracy is in many ways at the analytical center of this book.

It is important to note the interconnections and overlaps between the chapters, not only through the overarching concept of democracy, but also through the normative issues of how to make government more responsive to women, feminist demands, and gender equality. Representation, for example, reemerges in chapters on women's movement and state feminism, and issues related to women's movements are touched upon in most of the chapters. On some level, most of the chapters deal with the state through a focus on specific governing structures like parliaments or bureaucratic agencies, policy outcomes and content, or broader notions of governance.

As was already pointed out, gendering political science is relatively new on the academic scene. As a result, many of the concepts treated in this book are in their infancy. Georgia Duerst-Lahti presents a brand new concept, feminalism – yes feminalism – in her chapter on gender ideology, and Laurel Weldon presents her own approach on the relatively new concept of intersectionality – intersectionality plus, versus intersectionality only. Governance, even before gendering, is quite a new concept and one difficult to operationalize, as Georgina Waylen points out. Efforts to gender it, therefore, are quite early and uneven. The concept of "state feminism" is also relatively new – at least the current usage as an alliance of women's movements and women's policy agencies – and so is not as widely accepted as other gender-specific concepts. Indeed, as many of the authors assert, their interpretations of how the concept is operationalized are by no means the only approaches, nor do their approaches represent a consensus. State feminism and women's movements, for example, remain quite contested concepts and, as a result, the proposals made in these chapters for a more unified approach may be questioned by many researchers.

Other concepts included in the book are more established, and so efforts to gender them are quite clear-cut and less controversial. This is the case with the chapters on democracy, representation, and the welfare state. At the same time, even with these more established concepts, efforts to gender are quite recent and underdeveloped. In many chapters the authors have developed proposals, presented here for the first time, for the next steps in conceptualization; see the chapters on governance, development, gender ideology, and intersectionality in particular. Kathleen Staudt suggests that the core concept of development should be abandoned altogether. All chapters share a fresh approach to conceptualization that is in the process of constant evolution. In other words, thinking about gender and concepts is a bit like shooting at a moving target.

A final consideration to make about the chapters in this book before moving on is the issue of epistemological approach. While the book as a whole takes a less critical approach to conceptualizing than much feminist analysis, focusing on issues of operationalization for empirical analysis and theory-building, gender and politics research more generally is not all empirically oriented.[4] Arguably less than other areas of women's studies, gender and politics work is only partially influenced by postmodern approaches to scholarship that eschew categories, hypothesis-testing, and the systematic cumulation of knowledge, and where all formal scientific knowledge is politically suspect. The interpretive turn in analysis, with its focus on microbehavior, storylines and participant observation, among other things, is found in political science and more specifically in gender and politics research. Many feminist analysts are particularly interested in social constructivism, which assumes that political phenomena do not exist but are socially constructed. A postmodern approach also seeks to analyze directly the implications of research for political action and politics more generally.

This book does not claim to represent the full range of feminist approaches to analysis; it is decidedly more empirical than postmodern. At the same time, not all of the authors embrace a purely neopositivist approach to research as empirical observation and hypothesis-testing. Waylen, Staudt, and Duerst-Lahti in particular are more representative of the interpretivist and social constructivist approaches in feminist analysis. Indeed, they are the most critical of the guidelines in their chapters. Issues of praxis are raised more solidly in these chapters as well. They all examine what shifting scholarly conceptualization means for political action for practitioners and advocates, as well as for research. Paxton, Celis, Sainsbury, Weldon, Mazur and McBride are more solidly in the neopositivist camp, placing issues of theory-building and validity at the center of their analyses and addressing at a secondary level the implications of conceptualizing for political actors and feminist change.

We invite the reader first to examine the guidelines in chapter 2 and then move through the chapters in the order presented. At the same time, each chapter was designed to stand alone. The concept chapters could be read

---

[4] For an excellent recent analysis of feminist approaches in the social sciences see Hawkesworth (2006), and for a presentation of different approaches in the social sciences see Moses and Knutsen (2007).

separately from the guidelines chapter, although it would be helpful to glance at least at the summary of the ten guidelines in Table 2.1. Indeed, many readers will come to this book interested in a particular concept. Reading all of the chapters together, however, gives the reader a comprehensive picture of the current state of conceptualization in gender and politics.

2 Mapping gender and politics concepts: ten guidelines

Gary Goertz and Amy G. Mazur

Concepts play a variety of roles in the research enterprise; they appear in scope conditions, case selection, contextual, independent, and dependent variables. Systematic data collection typically involves multiple concepts; what data are collected, the units and the scope of the data. The validity and usefulness of much research thus rest on the solidity of its conceptual foundations. Concepts are ultimately important because without them we would have empty theories and causal explanations. Concept analysis, (de)construction, and usage are of special importance to gender and politics scholars. Many gender research projects begin by attacking the "taken-for-granted" character of key social science relationships. This often involves bringing out the gender bias built into – but hidden – in the core of concepts. In this way much gender research is *foundational* in character: it explores the basic gender biases embedded in widely used concepts of political analysis.

While feminist scholars have continually engaged in concept criticism, concept reformulation, and concept creation, there has been no attempt, that we are aware of, to synthesize a set of methodologies for such endeavors. This chapter, and the volume as a whole, present a set of coherent guidelines for dealing with concepts.

More generally, courses on quantitative methods and research design based on statistical principles often devote little or no attention to the methodology of concepts. While sections devoted to measurement are common, there is rarely much on concept methodology. King, Keohane, and Verba (1994) is quite symptomatic of this neglect; they say little about concepts or measurement. Qualitative methods courses typically include discussions of classics by Sartori and Collier, but do not provide a unified methodological approach to concepts. Books on feminist methodology tend not to deal with the topic of concepts either (e.g. Ackerly, Stern, and True 2006).

Table 2.1 List of Guidelines

Context Guideline:	What is the theoretical, historical, cultural, and geographic background context for the concept?
Traveling Guideline:	Does the concept travel well to other temporal or cultural areas?
Causal Relationships Guideline:	How do causal relationships work *within* and *between* concepts?
Naming Guideline:	What is the accepted name of the concept? Why and how does it differ from others in its semantic field?
Negation Guideline:	What is the negation, absence, or opposite of the basic concept?
Zones Guideline:	Is there a gray zone? Is it an ideal-type concept?
Dimensions Guideline:	What are the dimensions or defining characteristics of the concept?
Necessity Guideline:	Are any dimensions necessary?
Interdependence Guideline:	What is the interdependence between dimensions?
Operationalization Guideline:	How is the concept operationalized?

This chapter presents ten systematic and interrelated guidelines for creating, evaluating, and modifying concepts that are applicable to concepts in general.[1] Table 2.1 provides a summary of the guidelines, and the rest of the chapter discusses each one in more detail. While we focus on the concerns of gender scholars, we find that these "special" concerns are in fact applicable to virtually all social science concepts. It is in fact to the credit of gender scholars that they make these important concerns more visible to the political science community as a whole. While gender scholars have pressed certain concerns more strongly, they should not be considered, for that reason, less important in other areas of political science. As the chapters of this volume illustrate, most of the concepts we examine are used in much of political science that is not concerned with gender analysis at all.

The guidelines focus in particular on the key theoretical and causal issues at the core of concept analysis. There are plenty of textbooks that deal with quantitative measurement; what is lacking is how theoretical and causal issues play a role before getting to quantitative data and numeric measurement. Several of the first few guidelines deal with how concepts are connected to theoretical and analytic concerns. For example, changing the welfare state (see Diane Sainsbury's chapter in this volume), as a dependent variable, to include gender dimensions like caring, moves the Netherlands from an advanced welfare state to an average one. This then has implications for theories that

---

[1] Some of these guidelines are based on Goertz's (2005) book on concept formation, but others are new. Special thanks goes to Dorothy McBride for her useful feedback on the guidelines.

explain the welfare state, which in turn may mean bringing in new explanatory variables to get the new dependent variable right. It is important to note that while the guidelines are presented in numerical order, it is not crucial to apply them in a particular stepwise fashion suggested by the numbering. As the chapters in this volume show, they can be taken in a variety of orders and in different combinations as well.

The middle set of guidelines deals extensively with how theoretical concerns play out *inside* of concepts or with concept structure. Most political science concepts are big, complex, and multidimensional in nature. Core to concept design are the nature of and relationships between the internal parts of concepts. One needs to justify theoretically much of the internal content and organization of concepts.

The final set of guidelines deals more with the specifics and mechanics of concept construction and application. Measurement *per se* in our approach is clearly secondary to theoretical and causal analysis. We do nevertheless provide some methodological guidelines for moving toward operationalization and eventually dealing with quantitative data. We stress that one needs to conduct extensive theoretical analysis of the structure of the concept and how it relates to the larger research project before dealing with quantitative indicators, operationalization, data collection, and other similar activities.

The guidelines here can also be used reflectively to think about the "concept of a concept" (Adcock 1998). There are various options and synonyms that can be used, such as "names" (J. S. Mill's choice), "definitions" (R. Robinson 1950), or, in a more quantitative vein, "variables." In much social constructivist, critical, or postmodernist theory, the word "concept" does not in fact appear. To take a relevant comparison, Ackerly, Stern, and True's volume on feminist methodologies (2006) does not use the word "concept" much at all (there is no index entry). To find what we are discussing one has to go to the index entry "ontology."[2] Ontology deals with what things *are*, as indicated by the verb "to be." To ask "What *is* a democracy?" is to ask about ontology. For example, Ackerly *et al.* basically talk about concepts in these terms: "We use *ontology* to mean an understanding of the world; for instance, what constitute relevant units of analysis (i.e., individuals, genders, states, classes, ethnicities) and whether the world and these units are constant or dynamic and able to be

---

[2] Even here the volume has only a few entries, so in that sense there is very little overlap between this volume and that one.

changed through, *inter alia*, research" (2006: 6). So in that sense our guidelines are about developing good ontologies.

As we outline the ten guidelines in this chapter, we draw on the various chapters of this volume as examples. While the contributors analyze a set of diverse concepts, these guidelines provide a framework that unifies the volume as a whole. As the saying goes, "the proof of the pudding is in the eating." We take a pragmatic attitude toward the guidelines; they are good if they are useful in producing good – or at least better – concepts. They are good if they help scholars and students think more clearly about their concepts and how they are used in various aspects of a research project. By the end of the volume readers can evaluate for themselves the validity and usefulness of the framework.

For each guideline, we identify the principal action, a set of questions to answer to cover the guideline, an in-depth discussion for the guideline's rationale and application in concept formation, and how the guideline relates to the other guidelines. We provide examples to illustrate each guideline, for the most part from the concepts covered in this book. Table 2.1 presents a summary list of the guidelines and questions.

Context Guideline

What is the theoretical, historical, cultural, and geographic background context for the concept?

All research projects begin framed by a historical, theoretical, and substantive background. There are dominant uses of a given concept that have been formed over time because of various normative, empirical, and theoretical concerns. Adcock and Collier (2001) call this the "background level," the first level of concept construction (which is followed by the "systematized concept," and then "indicators and scores for cases"). When criticizing a standard concept or constructing a new one, it is crucial to be explicit about this background level. The new or modified concept will always stand in contrast to standard or common ones.[3]

---

[3] We do not mean to suggest by the use of "standard" that is there is no controversy about concepts. Indeed, discussion of concepts in gender and politics research is often framed in terms of the lack of consensus over concepts (e.g. Beasley 1999; Hobson, Lewis, and Siim 2002). We do believe that in most cases there is a good-sized substantive core about which there is not much conflict. Sometimes that concept is defined by widely used datasets, and as such is resistant to change in practice.

One needs to situate the new or revised concept against its intellectual and methodological background. This is particularly crucial when revising concepts to explicitly include gender dimensions. Many concepts are not explicitly but implicitly gendered. For example, the concept of democracy *per se* is not usually gendered, but the way it is operationalized often is.

Diane Sainsbury's discussion of the concept of welfare state in this volume shows how gender analysis often appears on the scene after a long history of concept development. The welfare state originated – at least the name did – in Britain during World War II. The early phase of this research illustrates how concept analysis is controversial and important in the early history of a concept. One signal of this is the debate over terminology (see the Naming Guideline); the field eventually settled on "welfare state" but there were prominent arguments for names such as "social service state."

For the welfare state, as typical of the history of many concepts, content stabilized after the initial period, that is, during the 1970s. As Sainsbury notes, much changed in terms of methodology and theory, but the concept itself was relatively stable. It can be argued that it was gender analysis that disrupted the stability of the welfare state concept. By adding new dimensions to the concept (see the Dimensions Guideline) and critiquing existing dimensions, the 1990s saw a brand new research agenda on the welfare state emerge.

Karen Celis's analysis of the concept of representation also illustrates how gender critiques have led to an explosion of new work on representation. While the welfare state literature kept the name, the new content of representation has been signaled by adding adjectives to "representation," such as "substantive," "group," or "descriptive." As with the welfare state, this literature has produced extensive new empirical analyses of, in this case, for example, women as legislators.

All the chapters in various ways show that to gender concepts involves knowing about background against which these revised concepts are being developed. One can understand the critiques only by contrast with existing traditions. At the same time, the chapters show that good conceptual revision leads to new theories and empirical analyses impossible within the standard concept.

The Context Guideline is fundamental because a new or revised concept is always in contrast with the existing literature. Its value or interest will not be just in its inherent content but also in the contrast it makes, or does not make, against a background of research and theory.

Traveling Guideline

Does the concept travel well to other temporal or cultural areas?

As one critiques existing concepts or works at constructing new ones, the Traveling Guideline reminds scholars to think about how well the concept will apply to other cultures, countries, and historical periods. Many influential concepts in comparative politics have originated in one country and then have been exported, with more or less success. For example, consociationalism was born in the Netherlands (Lijphart 1977) and then applied to a variety of other countries; pluralism is distinctively American in origin. Amy Mazur and Dorothy McBride, in their analysis of state feminism in this volume, illustrate how a concept which originated in the analysis of Scandinavian countries in the 1980s successfully traveled to other OECD countries in the 1990s.

This kind of traveling works well in part because it is tapping an unrecognized phenomenon. Once scholars begin to see it in country X and they begin to look for it in country Y, and often they find it. However, what they find in country Y is often not exactly what was occurring in country X. This then leads to a better overall concept, which now travels well.

This kind of traveling often means the *expansion* of the concept. It is perhaps natural to associate the Traveling Guideline with Sartori's influential analysis of conceptual "stretching" (1970). Both deal with including more countries or units under a concept. However, we think traveling works exactly the *opposite* of what Sartori proposed for stretching. Sartori suggested that a concept could be made to travel by reducing the number of dimensions (see the Dimensions Guideline, and Goertz 2005: ch. 3 for more details); for example, if concept X has three defining dimensions, making it a two-dimension concept will stretch it but also make it travel further.

We think that traveling as done by gender scholars in particular – and many comparative scholars in general – makes concepts travel by *adding* dimensions. As researchers looked at state feminism in different countries, they saw that it did not always work as it does in Scandinavia. They then expanded the concept to cover these cases. As a result the concept travels better because it takes into account differences between ways in which the state can be used to promote a feminist agenda.

Kathleen Staudt's analysis of the concept of development in this volume illustrates how traveling operates as well. Classically, development was seen basically in economic terms, (GDP per capita). Much of the overall critique of the concept – gendered and otherwise – added new social, health, etc., dimensions to the concept. For example, to be a developed country is to be a healthy one. This meant practically looking at statistics of particular relevance to women, especially problems dealing with maternity and children, notably high-risk groups.

The reconceptualization of development in terms of quality of life and human well-being illustrates the potential for theoretical "blowback" as a consequence of concept revision. Once researchers began to think about development in poorer countries, this could then lead to a reevaluation of development rankings among wealthy countries. For example, the USA usually ranks quite high in GDP per capita. Once development is also defined by other social, educational, and health dimensions, the USA becomes a middle-ranking developed country.

A valid and robust concept will usually have dimensions which stress scope and generalization, core to social science. The Traveling Guideline focuses on the sensitivity to cross-temporal, cross-cultural, and cross-national specificities.

Causal Relationships Guideline

How do causal relationships work within and between concepts?

J. S. Mill began his *System of Logic* with a discussion of names because they are what give theories, propositions, and causal mechanisms a good deal of their substance. We are interested in concepts and their dimensions exactly because they play a large role in causal mechanisms and hypotheses. This guideline, then, is about causal relationships between concepts. Of course, this is why most scholars are interested in concepts: they play a central role in causal hypotheses, models, theories, and mechanisms. Causal relationships play a key role in concept development. One needs to consider how causal relationships work *within* and *between* concepts.

When constructing, modifying, or using a concept, it is absolutely crucial to keep in mind the theoretical and explanatory context. This comes out most clearly when the concept in question is a dependent variable. It is quite possible, and even quite likely, that a gendered dependent variable will require some important modifications on the independent variable, explanatory factors, side of the equation. For example, by including factors like childcare into the concept of the welfare state, we require theories to explain the presence or absence of this dimension. One can no longer just focus on the importance of industrial labor unions. In short, by gendering the dependent variable you almost guarantee that you will have to gender some of the independent variables.

Pamela Paxton, in her discussion of the concept of democracy, illustrates how this works. Virtually no quantitative measures use the vote for women as a criterion for being a democracy. Paxton shows that the inclusion of women into measures of democracy can have radical implications for theories of democracy. Suddenly the dates of democratization shift for many countries, Switzerland being the most extreme, at over 100 years. It is not obvious that the theory that worked well to explain Switzerland's democratization in 1848 is the one that explains its democratization in 1971. She notes that including women's suffrage would dramatically increase the importance of international factors and norms; these factors are typically downplayed by comparative politics scholars who emphasize domestic determinants. It is no accident that Moore (1966) stressed the importance of the bourgeoisie, and Rueschemeyer, Stephens, and Stephens (1992) the working class: these independent variables are closely linked to how they define democracy to begin with.

Since the concepts that often concern social scientists include a variety of moving parts, one needs to consider the possibility of causal relationships *between* parts: this means causal relationships inside concepts. Often one needs to decide whether to build in causal hypotheses or leave them outside the concept and hence make the concept more open to empirical analysis. For example, Tickner makes the following claims about war and gender: "Feminists have sought to better understand a neglected but constitutive feature of war – why it has been primarily a male activity, and what the causal and constitutive implications of this are for women's political roles." (2006: 24).

One might not want to think of war as constituted in a gendered fashion, because this then makes it more difficult to study the empirical and causal connections between war and gender. So one might want to keep war as conventionally defined in terms of battle-related deaths and then explore the causal linkages between war and gender (e.g. Goldstein 2001).

In contrast, the chapter on state feminism illustrates how one can build causal relationships into the concept. The concept of state feminism is about the relationships between women's movements and women's policy agencies. State feminism exists when these two factors work together to produce policy change. This is clearly a causal relationship within a concept. The concept then is about a causal mechanism of its parts. Women-friendly policy outcomes could arise via various causal pathways, such as cooptation, but that kind of state feminism exists only when a particular causal path occurs. While it is obvious that individual concepts combine as independent variables to constitute causal mechanisms, it is not often realized that causal mechanisms also occur within concepts. Hernes, in one of the first works on the topic, describes state feminism in these causal terms: "a variety of public policies and organizational measures, designed partly to solve general social and economic problems, partly to respond to women's demands" (1987: 11).

In short, one needs to think about how the concept and its dimensions interact with theoretical concerns. How is the concept going to be used: as an independent or as a dependent variable? What are the roles that the dimensions play in causal mechanisms? While it is easy to be caught up in the complexities of concept development, it must be kept in mind that this is only one step of a research agenda. We develop concepts not for their own sake but because they play a key role in larger theoretical and empirical enterprises.

Naming Guideline

What is the accepted name of the concept? Why and how does it differ from others in its semantic field?

It is important to consider carefully the question of terminology before making a decision about how to "name" a concept. Naming has a major influence in how the new or modified concept will be received. Naming or developing a terminology is often crucial because it invokes the history and (ab)usage of the concept. Roughly, one has three options in developing new concepts: (1) keep the name but change the substance; (2) choose a new name; or (3) hyphenate or "adjectivize" that concept. Each has its advantages and disadvantages.

For example, one often has the choice between "women," "feminist," and "gender." A journal entitled "Feminism and Politics" suggests a different kind of content than one entitled "Gender and Politics." The choice of one or the other is not an innocent one. Georgia Duerst-Lahti, in her chapter, describes many of the key issues with regard to gender names and terminology. Early on, scholars distinguished between sex and gender. Most languages provide ready-made gender distinctions which have to be dealt with, but which may prove problematic for political analysis. In particular, much work has highlighted contrasting pairs (see the Negation Guideline) such as male–female, matriarchy–patriarchy. With so much historical and political baggage, it is not obvious what to do. Duerst-Lahti argues that it makes sense to use new terms to move the discussion forward and introduces the new notion of "feminalism" as one pole of gender ideology. The choice between new and old terminology is never easy or clear-cut. Even among existing names there are choices, each with advantages and disadvantages, such as "women" versus "gender."

Names can easily become an overtly political issue. If a conflict is defined as a civil war or a genocide, many political consequences follow. The World Bank now has many policies dealing with "indigenous peoples." Important policy consequences follow when a group receives that categorization. One need only consider the political history of "negro," "black," "of color," and "African-American" to realize the importance of names. So in addition to the standard meaning and usage of terms, gendering often means choosing between more or less politicized terms.

Keeping the name but changing the substance is often a good choice when the critique itself fits well with the standard concept. These kinds of "friendly amendments" draw on relatively strong consensus about the standard concept. The evolution of the concept "democracy" illustrates this nicely. Early views, such as that of Schumpeter (1942), focused on elections and government structure. Since then it has proved quite natural to add civil rights as part of the concept (e.g., Freedom House and polity democracy concepts). Pamela Paxton's chapter in this volume illustrates this practice. Very few – outside religious extremists of various sorts – would contest the belief that women should have the right to vote. There is no reason for Paxton to want to change the name because most would understand democracy to include women's right to vote. The same is true of the welfare state; while gender scholars have proposed important modifications, none has really challenged the name itself.

The second option is to hyphenate or add an adjective to a standard concept. This signals a link to a standard concept yet mentions some new aspect. Particularly in gender and politics work, it is tempting, perhaps too tempting, simply to add terms such as "women" or "feminist" to the standard name to signal the nature of the new concept. As we discuss below, this has its traps as well.

Karen Celis's chapter on the concept of representation illustrates how concepts and adjectives often work together. Many concepts have a long history, and representation belongs to this group. Political representatives have been around for centuries. In addition, to "represent" brings with it meanings from art history. As such, much of the development of the theory of representation is symbolized by the adjectives used. In the case of representation, one finds major distinctions denoted by "formal," "symbolic," "group," "descriptive," and "substantive" (see Celis's Table 4.1). For example, a key issue in democratic theory involves substantive representation of individuals and groups. Because they have many common interests based on their roles in families and the labor force, as well as on their biological sex (e.g. pregnancy), one can discuss the extent to which women's interests are represented in legislatures. This then leads to questions about whether women representatives are more fit to represent women than are men.

Another example is "gender violence" (e.g. Weldon 2002a, 2006a). Here we see the operation of adding a modifying name to a standard concept. The concept focuses on forms of violence that occur particularly often to women, such as rape or domestic violence. For this concept there is some variation on names. The United Nations in most of its documents uses "violence against women." Often one is choosing between some common usage and a name which may be more theoretically acceptable. There is no easy answer as to which horn of the dilemma to sit on, but we stress that one needs to think seriously about the question.

The third option is to create a concept *de novo*. This practice has the advantage of providing a clean slate and no historical baggage. If successful, it can have a very large payoff for the author. To get a new concept accepted means to have had significant intellectual influence on a research community. Conversely, such success is rare and often the proliferation of terminology inhibits progress; often such special terminology means that the work does not connect with the larger research community. We suspect that the new concept option works best when it is tapping a new phenomenon (not that the phenomenon is necessarily new, but notice has not been taken of it).

"State feminism" illustrates well the creation of new concepts. Much of the literature on gender and politics originally took place against a background of work on social movements, which saw groups contesting government policies. State feminism in contrast looked at the activities of government-based agencies and structures formally charged with the advancement of women's rights and status or gender equality. Prior to 1995, the concept had been used mostly by Scandinavian scholars to describe public policies that promote gender equality. It was with the publication of a study of women's policy offices in postindustrial democracies (Mazur and McBride 1996) and the ensuing ten-year-long study of women's policy offices by RNGS that the notion of state feminism became associated with the phenomenon of women's policy agencies. The concept of state feminism has gained a certain acceptance because it focuses on an important phenomenon not recognized earlier.

The Naming Guideline shows up in the next section, dealing with the Negation Guideline. Often one needs to analyze the name given to the negation of the concept under analysis. For example, there is no consensus on the name of the opposite of democracy. Is it authoritarian rule, or dictatorship, or simply nondemocracy? Issues of naming also arise in the Dimensions Guideline. The various parts of a complex concept need names, and the considerations discussed here apply just as well to the parts of concepts as to the overall concept itself.

In short, one must think seriously about the terminology used. Different names bring up different associations. One needs to explore why and how the name relates to others in its semantic field. The relationship between the new name and its semantic, theoretical, and empirical field is signaled by the terms used. One need not remind gender scholars that terminology decisions are also political ones. One does not want to be bound by history and usage, and yet introducing new terms has its own problems. The key recommendation is to think seriously about the various repercussions when making terminology decisions.

Negation Guideline

What is the negation, absence, or opposite of the basic concept?

Typically, research starts with a focus on a particular phenomenon represented by a concept, such as the welfare state. We call this the positive pole of the concept. Crucial to concept formation is the opposite, negation, or absence of that positive pole, such as the nonwelfare state. Sometimes the negation presents different options with major ramifications for theory and research design. For example, is the opposite of "war" denoted by "peace" or by "nonwar?"

The lack of symmetry between the positive and negative pole runs deep through the gender and politics literature. Often the visible – and often normatively valued – pole has masculine traits or characteristics. A very common issue of analysis is the supposed dichotomies where one pole is associated with women and the other with men, such as nature–nurture and public–private. The Negation Guideline requires one to be attentive to these issues.

Much of the literature on dichotomies stresses how problematic they are. We agree completely with much of this analysis. However, we also stress that one must develop the negation as a fundamental part of concept analysis and construction. The positive pole is typically the phenomenon to be explained and the central empirical and theoretical focus of the analysis. Therefore, it is crucial to ask specifically about the negative pole and its relationship to the positive. There must be a constructive analysis of the proper negation.

The previous guideline focused on naming and terminology. One potential way to deal with negative pole problems is simply to define the negative pole as the negation of the positive; for instance, masculine = not feminine. This procedure gives a clear, logical relationship between positive and negative. The big disadvantage of this procedure is that it potentially includes many phenomena that one might want in the negation of the positive pole. There may be many traits that are "not feminine" but that one would not want to call masculine.

The concept of development covered by Kathleen Staudt in this volume illustrates a key tricky issue when dealing with the negative pole. There is sometimes a strong tension between the principal object of study (the positive pole) and what dominates the literature or the real world. The real concern with development is with *less* developed countries. So in terms of the guidelines this is the positive pole; the developed countries become the negative pole in development studies.

This tension is standard in the gender analysis of concepts. As the Context Guideline discussed, one is introducing gender factors into, typically, a well-established concept. There is thus, almost by definition, an inevitable conflict between the positive pole as defined by the background context, and the positive pole as defined by the gender scholar. Thus gender analysis is a big example of what is often a good research strategy in general. Since most of mainstream literature is looking at the positive, the negative pole is insufficiently studied. Hence, there is much to be gained theoretically and empirically by an intensive investigation of the negative of what the standard literature deals with.

By looking at both sides of the coin in a more balanced way, new insights can be made for the mainstream concept. For example, by focusing on poverty and less developed countries we develop new criteria for evaluating developed countries. What used to be very developed countries come to be seen as less developed because of the new criteria introduced by looking at poor countries.

Laurel Weldon's chapter on intersectionality illustrates how gender itself has fallen into the trap of focusing too much on the positive pole. As Weldon makes clear, the focus of the intersectionality literature has been on race and gender, particularly on women of color. The argument is that there are causal mechanism patterns of behavior, problems specific to women of color. The Negation Guideline says that one needs to contrast that group with its negation. What is interesting about the intersectionality case is that the negation is three groups: (1) African-Americans, (2) women, and (3) white men. We know African-American women are distinctive only by contrasting them with all three of these groups. Often the contrast is made only within the group of women, indicating how white women and women of color differ; but the Negation Guideline says that one also needs to consider black men versus black women, and the extreme contrast with white men.

The names given to the positive and negative poles often signal a variety of problems that need to be explicitly addressed when making or criticizing concepts. While everyone more or less agrees on democracy as the positive pole, the opposite of democracy has a variety of potential names: totalitarian rule, authoritarian rule, dictatorship. Historically, it was monarchy versus democracy. Goertz (2005) shows that this can lead to important differences in coding actual cases. For example, Freedom House and polity virtually always agree on the democracy cases, but there is much more divergence when coding at the nondemocratic end of the spectrum. In short, the reliability – and probably validity – of their democracy concepts are much higher than their authoritarian concepts. This is because students of democracy have not focused their attention enough on the negative pole.

While much of theory can get by without an explicit consideration of the negative pole, case selection cannot. For purposes of research design and case selection, one almost always needs to contrast cases. Most students are aware of the problems of selecting on the dependent variable, that is selection on the positive pole. This is a problem in comparative research exactly because in the concept formation stage the negative pole has not been explicitly analyzed. If one wants to look at state feminism one needs to contrast countries and policies where state feminism is not present.

One of the major lessons from the research on gender and politics, along with race, has been to focus attention on the neglected "other." Many concepts are implicitly defined via contrasts. Good concept construction and critique involve making those contrasts explicit and justifying them.

Zones Guideline

Is there a gray zone? Is it an ideal-type concept?
One of the ongoing debates in the methodology literature, particularly among comparativists, is whether a concept is dichotomous or not. We think

it is better to ask about the existence or not of important "zones" in conceptualization. One key zone is the gray zone: if a concept is dichotomous, it has no gray zone. Another zone is the positive or negative pole: are there cases at these poles, or are we dealing with an ideal type?

Much of the feminist literature has engaged the issue of dichotomies, such as nature–nurture and public–private arguing that they have little theoretical or empirical utility; there is an important gray zone. In contrast, those who use qualitative methods often prefer qualitative dichotomies. We reformulate this as a question about whether conceptually one can talk about the gray zone. Dichotomous concepts deny the existence of a gray zone. Continuous concepts incorporate a gray zone and often suggest that important phenomena occur in that area. As Georgia Duerst-Lahti shows in her chapter, much work on gender and sex deals with the dichotomous versus continuous issue. Many assert that biological sex is dichotomous and gender is continuous – "Sex, defined as a biological division, is situated at one of the parameters while gender, defined as the social construction of biological sex, is at the other. Whilst sex is a dichotomous variable, gender is a continuum of feminine/masculine differences (Lovenduski *et al.* 2006: 267)." More recently, as Duerst-Lahti shows, feminist scholars have conceptualized biological sex in continuous terms, arguing that sex and gender are conceptualized in quite similar ways in terms of this guideline.

Much of the qualitative methods literature on concepts, notably Sartori (1984), draws heavily on philosophical views on concepts. The classic, Aristotelian, view of concepts says that one scientifically defines a concept using necessary and sufficient conditions. Here all dimensions must be present; the absence of any one dimension excludes the case. Traditional logic is dichotomous, true or false; there are no propositions which are half true. As a consequence, Sartori has vigorously spoken out (e.g. 1984) against "degreeism," the notion that all concepts are a matter of degree. This is one reason why those using qualitative methods have had a strong tendency to think of concepts in dichotomous terms.

In contrast, we suggest that one should start with a continuous view of concepts. To use the metaphor of colors, one should always keep in mind the possibility that things may not be only black or white but can also be gray. In this sense we think that much of the feminist critique of dichotomous categorization is completely on target. There are many theoretical and practical reasons for starting with a view that includes a gray zone. For example, many "marginal" cases are likely to lie exactly there.

It is quite easy to confound two separate issues when dealing with this problem: the conceptual and the empirical. The theoretical or conceptual question is whether or not it makes sense for the concept in question to have a gray zone. For example, if there are six characteristics of being feminine, does it make sense to say that someone who only has three of them is half or weakly feminine? Is it possible for someone identified as a butch to wear Prada?

Democracy is a concept where the battle between dichotomous and continuous concepts has been mostly extensively played out. Many, if not most, comparativists see the concept of democracy as dichotomous (e.g. Sartori 1984; Przeworski *et al.* 2000). To say that a country is 50 percent democracy makes no sense: you are in or you are out. In contrast, most numeric, quantitative measures of democracy imply a continuous view of democracy. For example, the polity democracy measure runs from −10 to 10, so values around zero might correspond to countries that are weakly democratic, or equivalently, weakly authoritarian.

The fundamental problem is that for any complex concept with multiple dimensions one must decide what to do when an object has some but not all of the characteristics of the concept. The classic necessary and sufficient condition model says that if you are missing one, you do not fall under the concept. However, it is also easy to say that if the phenomenon has half the characteristics, it is a gray case of the concept.

In addition to complex concepts, the objects being studied are often complex, which leads to gray zone codings. For example, one categorizes whole countries as democratic or authoritarian. The polity and Freedom House data code the United States in 1950 as maximally democratic. However, it is very clear that a big part of the country, namely the South, was not democratic. Historically, many European countries had power-sharing between the monarch and the parliament (e.g., the UK and Germany). It makes sense to put such countries in the gray zone.

One empirical issue deals with the impact of the frequency of finding gray zone cases and whether that should or should not influence the concept itself. It is not a good idea in general to let the likelihood of actually finding examples in the gray zone greatly influence the concept itself. There may in empirical fact be few gray zone cases, but that is not a reason to make the concept itself dichotomous.

In fact, dichotomizing in these situations hinders good and interesting research. The relative absence of gray zone cases often poses a very interesting theoretical and empirical question. If one defines away that area, the research does not "see" it, because it is not in the conceptual repertoire. If one sees biological sex to be dichotomous, one cannot easily see transsexuals. Similarly, it is hard to imagine democratic transitions (a huge area of research) without some notion of weakly democratic states.

In short, one needs to openly confront the question of the existence of the gray zone. Much of the research agenda will be shaped by the answer to this question. The ability to frame theoretical and empirical hypotheses will be directly as well as indirectly affected. Our recommendation is always to start with a gray zone conception, and to make the concept dichotomous only when there are strong theoretical or practical reasons. Also, it is quite easy to go from continuous to dichotomous (this is done all the time with continuous measures of democracy), but much harder to go backward.

Going back to at least Max Weber, social scientists have constructed "ideal type" concepts (1952). While there is some philosophical literature on this topic, it has received virtually no attention from social science methodologists. An ideal-type concept by definition means that the zone near the positive pole or ideal type has few empirical examples. Dahl's view on democracy (e.g. 1956, 1998) illustrates nicely an ideal type in political science. He very explicitly sees democracy as something that will never be achieved in practice, at least by nation-states. He doubly emphasizes this by giving the name "polyarchy" to those government systems that get closest to the democracy ideal. One might then specifically think about the zone near the positive pole and the possibility of finding empirical cases in this region. Thus, the Zones Guideline, in addition to being concerned about the gray zone, is also concerned about the zone near the positive pole and the possibility of finding empirical cases there.

Both the welfare state (Sainsbury: this volume) and democracy (Paxton: this volume) illustrate the central importance of the gray zone and ideal-type zones to gendering concepts. One consequence of gendering a concept is to move cases around, often dramatically, on the scale from the positive to the negative pole. If the concept does not have an ideal type or gray zone, it becomes problematic as to where these cases are to go. Often, once a concept is gendered, some cases will move from the extreme positive pole to the gray zone. Paxton shows that many countries that are typically coded as maximum democracies by the polity or Freedom House measures move into the gray zone once women's suffrage is included. If there were no gray zone – if the variable were dichotomous – the scholar would be faced with a difficult choice between coding, say, Switzerland as an authoritarian or a democratic country; in reality it is partially democratic. The same is true of the welfare state, once one begins to include gender components, countries are likely to move; to

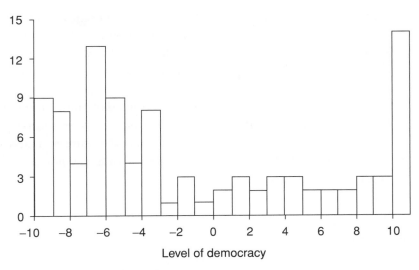

Figure 2.1   Concepts and ideal types: polity democracy measure

stick with Switzerland, it moves from a marginal welfare state to a low-level welfare state.

Gender analysis not only can move countries down but implies the need to have room at the top to move countries up. When one adds dimensions (see the Dimensions Guideline), this implicitly extends the scale in the ideal type direction. To be a high-level democracy or welfare state now requires a country to meet new gender-relevant conditions. Looking at Figure 2.1, if we extend the scale so that there are levels above 10 we imply that countries coded as 10 are much closer to the gray zone, while at the same time some of the countries that are coded as 10 will now be coded at higher levels.

We have stressed how concept development and criticism lead to new theories and new research agendas. Once you have a gray zone you need a theory to explain why some countries are located there. Once you have a theory of a "more" ideal welfare state, you can explain why some states are in that zone. If the concept does not provide a conceptual space for this, it is very hard to ask these new research questions.

In general, we recommend designing concepts with an eye to having few cases at the extremes. The reason is that big spikes at the extremes suggest that the scale really should go further and that there is possibly significant variation within the spike. The polity concept/measure of democracy illustrates how this can be a problem. As Figure 2.1 shows, there is a large spike at the maximum level democracy (10 on the polity scale). In contrast to Dahl, the polity measure finds a lot of country-years with maximally democratic regimes. Such a spike should raise suspicions. It is analogous to an exam where 20 percent of the students get a perfect score. One might suspect that the exam was too easy, and that there is a lot variation in performance hidden in that 20 percent of perfect scores.

In summary, there are often important zones that one needs to think about. Dichotomous concepts imply that there are no gray cases. Ideal-type concepts imply there are no empirical cases at the pole. We suggest that as a starting point one should allow for gray zone cases and that one should not have many cases at either pole.

Dimensions Guideline

What are the dimensions or defining characteristics of the concept?

Many, if not most, concepts that social scientists deal with are complex. Managing this complexity constitutes a major challenge for concept development and analysis. One aspect of concept complexity involves what we call the "dimensions" of the concept. This can be thought of in terms of defining characteristics or traits. Aristotle famously defined human beings as "featherless bipeds." The key point for this guideline is that one needs to develop and defend a list of such defining characteristics. A first step in constructing a good concept is to list the defining characteristics clearly. While this might seem obvious, it is quite rare to see an explicit list of characteristics (outside of quantitative measures, where the methodology forces one to do this). For example, Schmitter offered a very famous conceptualization of corporatism:

Corporatism can be defined as a system of interest representation in which the constituent units are organized into a limited number of singular, compulsory, noncompetitive, hierarchically ordered and functionally differentiated categories, recognized or licensed (if not created) by the state and granted a deliberate representational monopoly within their respective categories in exchange for observing certain controls on their selection of leaders and articulation of demands and supports. (1974: 93–4)

To work with this concept, one needs to unpack it into its constituent parts, such as "noncompetitive," "hierarchically ordered," and "functionally differentiated categories." This unpacking is important, since definitions often have a lot of moving parts, as illustrated by Schmitter. In some cases words may be synonyms; there are adjectival constructions; there are subclauses. One needs to dissect such concepts to reveal the main component parts.

Georgina Waylen's discussion of the concept of governance in her chapter illustrates that the dimensions themselves are (big) concepts in their own right. Governance includes as dimensions "state," "markets," and "networks." Clearly one could apply all the guidelines of this chapter to these dimensions of governance. While perhaps an extreme example, all the dimensions of the concepts discussed in this volume are important individually as concepts.

The "concept within a concept" problem illustrates well the particular poverty of quantitative concept strategies based on indicators and measurement. In this perspective, indicators are often a hodgepodge of different things which may or may not cover all the theoretical dimensions to the concept. In addition, they are typically chosen on pragmatic grounds of data availability, whereas, as we have seen, the dimensions of concepts are actually key theoretical components.

We suggest that all major social science concepts have multiple theoretical dimensions. Because they are complex constructions, we need to unpack each part and justify its role in the concept structure. This means providing a rationale for the importance of each dimension. Why choose these features as opposed to others? Concepts are often built up inductively from cases. Most objects have a huge number of characteristics. One must defend the traits selected as important for some theoretical or empirical reason. So listing the dimensions in a definition is never sufficient: one must justify these dimensions on theoretical and empirical grounds.

To gender a concept can mean adding new dimensions to an existing concept. As Diane Sainsbury notes in her chapter on the welfare state, much of the gendering has been via new dimensions. A major addition has been dimensions dealing with "caring" work (e.g., with children and the elderly), which is often performed by women. The standard welfare state focused on paid work usually done in offices or factories, hence typically by men. The gendered welfare state includes other types of work as well.

The new dimensions of the welfare state also include new groups not covered in the standard concept. Notably, single women and mothers were poorly covered – if at all – in the standard concept. Many of these dimensions stress the extent to which the welfare state revolves around individuals or families. Not surprisingly, we see new names to indicate these new dimensions, such as "defamilialization." As the Zones Guideline suggested, these new dimensions lead to a reevaluation of the relative rankings of countries. Once more dimensions are added, the rankings of countries can vary, sometimes dramatically, depending on concept construction (see the Necessity Guideline). If a country scores very low on the new guidelines it can move into the gray zone. By definition, the new dimensions extend the scale and make it more ideal type in character.

A second way gender can be introduced is by gendering the existing dimensions of a concept. Sticking to the welfare state, welfare state compensation – for instance, pensions – can be introduced for unpaid as well as paid work. Given the heavy concentration of women in this area, this makes the concept much more sensitive to women's interests.

Three common rationales used to defend the choice of dimensions are (1) functional, (2) causal, and (3) empirical coverage. Functional characteristics often appear in concepts related to organizations and institutions. The chosen dimension is somehow key to the working of the institution. Dimensions may play key roles in causal hypotheses of interest to a research community. In particular, causal mechanisms often use dimensions to explicate the process by which causes produce their effects. This is most obviously the case when the concept is used as an independent variable in some hypothesis. For example, in the women's policy office project conducted by the RNGS network, the characteristics of the women's movement is a major potential explanation of, or independent variable for, the success of women's policy agencies. As the chapter on women's movements and feminisms argues, the crucial nature of this concept in the study, as well as the difficulty of identifying precisely what we are studying when we examine women's movements, has led the group to spend a great deal of effort and time defining the dimensions of this concept. Finally, new dimensions tap the identified empirical phenomena not covered under the standard. The gendered welfare state deals with groups and work that just did not fit the concept as it was first used: one needs to be concerned with all kinds of work and people in all kinds of family situations.

We do not pretend that functional, causal, or empirical rationales exhaust the universe of possible rationales for choosing dimensions. The Dimensions Guideline stresses (1) that one needs to explicitly list defining characteristics, and (2) that one needs to provide some empirical or theoretical rationale for the dimension's importance.

Necessity Guideline

Are any dimensions necessary?

One structural question deals with the crucial nature of the dimensions. In the classical view of concepts (as exemplified by Sartori's work), *all* dimensions are necessary. So, if there are five dimensions to the concept, each must be present for the phenomenon to be included. Democracy is one concept where most scholars have used all necessary dimensions (e.g. Dahl 1956 and 1998, Przeworski *et al.* 2000). Concepts that are used to gather data typically, and implicitly, employ necessary dimensions. The list of dimensions is such that the phenomenon must satisfy them all to become part of the dataset.

Dorothy McBride and Amy Mazur in their chapter on the concept of "women's movements" illustrate how one often needs to ask about the necessary character of some dimensions; for instance, "Can men be in women's movements?" This is just another way of asking about the necessity of women. Similarly, they are very explicit about what is necessary for "women's movement discourse" when they state that "To be identified as women's movement discourse, all three of these elements must be present: identity with women as a group; explicitly gendered language about women; and representation of women as women in public life" (p. 230).

The view that all dimensions are necessary (and jointly sufficient) is historically what philosophers have demanded for proper, good, and complete definitions of concepts. And before developments in mathematical logic in the twentieth century, it went unchallenged, and remains the default for most social scientists when dealing with concepts, particularly in a qualitative setting.

The most common alternative to a necessary structure to construct concepts uses the "family resemblance" strategy.[4] This works from the idea that various dimensions represent features of *similarity*, just as members of a biological family have various physical and mental traits in common. The more features present, the closer to the positive pole; the fewer, the closer to the negative pole.

Most quantitative measurement models implement a family resemblance strategy. Typically one adds or takes the mean of the values of the various dimensions. This is almost certainly the case if the dimensions are ordinal, interval, or ratio variables (i.e. nondichotomous variables).

These two approaches have important implications for the Zones Guideline. Family resemblance concepts naturally yield a gray zone. If one has 10 dimensions, then the natural resemblance runs from 0/10 to 10/10, and the region around 5/10 easily becomes the gray zone. In contrast, the necessary dimension view is typically associated with dichotomous dimensions: it is a pretty much all-or-nothing procedure. Modern logic has provided ways

---

[4] See Goertz (2005: ch. 2) for details.

around this, but they have certainly not penetrated philosophical textbooks or social science practice (Goertz 2005).

The methodology for determining necessary dimensions usually works via counterfactuals. Once one has listed all the dimensions of a concept – the Dimensions Guideline – one can usefully ask if they are necessary dimensions. Then the question is: if dimension X is absent, does the case fall under the concept? If the answer is yes, the dimension is a necessary one. For example, communist countries had elections, but because the selection of candidates was controlled by the government, those elections were meaningless. There may be competition between candidates, but if women are not allowed to vote, the country is not democratic.

Karen Celis's discussion of representation illustrates the logic of determining nonnecessary dimensions. She says:

> None of the dimensions described above – formal participation, descriptive or substantive representation – are essential to representation (Necessity Guideline). A representative can be imposed on me, but still represent me if she takes my interests to heart. I can acknowledge a person to be my formal representative, even if he neither looks like me, nor acts for me, or even if he harms my interests. (p. 80)

So how does one achieve representation – the positive pole of the concept – according to Celis?

> However, since the essence of representation is the making present of the absent, the represented has to be made present by the representative in at least one way, be it formally, descriptively, symbolically, *or* substantively. (p. 80)

Thus, there are *multiple* ways that one can be represented. This is common in family resemblance concepts. One can call this the "many roads to Rome" way of doing things. There are various substitutable ways to get to the positive pole. This approach has important implications for the Dimensions Guideline. One then needs to list *all* the roads to Rome (or at least the important ones). The theoretical and empirical issues then in the Dimensions Guideline will revolve around the arguments about the existence of various paths to the positive pole.

In terms of paths, then, the necessary dimensions approach is a one-path structure. If all dimensions must be present, there is only one way to the positive pole. In contrast, there are many ways to the negative pole. Take Przeworski *et al.*'s (2000) view of democracy with four necessary dimensions, there is one way to be a democracy but fifteen ways to be a nondemocracy. In contrast with the "roads to Rome" approach, there are many ways to get

Table 2.2 Possible structures for the concept "mother"

| | DIMENSIONS | | | | | |
	Female	Nurture	Birth	Genetic	Step	RULE
Necessary	N	N	N	N	N	All necessary
Family resemblance	F	F	F	F	F	3 of 5 necessary
Hybrid	N	N	F	F	F	2 necessary + 1 of 3 others

Key: N = necessary, F = family

to the positive pole but only one way to get to the negative (score zero on all causal paths).

The concept of "mother" has been an important example in discussions of concepts (e.g. Lakoff 1987, Collier and Mahon 1993), and illustrates well the different approaches to necessary dimensions. Collier and Mahon give a variety of potential defining characteristics of "mother": (1) female, (2) provides 50 percent of genetic makeup, (3) gives birth to child, (4) provides nurturance, and (5) married to other caregiver (i.e. stepmother). One might reject a necessary approach which makes female a necessary condition for being a mother. One could adopt the family resemblance approach and only require, say, any three of these five characteristics in order for someone to be categorized as a mother.

Table 2.2 illustrates ways to include or not include necessary dimensions in the concept "mother". The classic view requires that all five be present for an individual to be considered a mother.[5] The family resemblance approach does not require a specific dimension but does require that at least three dimensions be present.[6] Hybrid concepts combine the two strategies. So, in Table 2.2, to be a mother one must be a female and provide nurturance, but in addition must have at least one of characteristics (3), (4), and (5) (providing 50 percent of genetic makeup; having given birth to a child; and being a step-parent).

One potential and easy to commit error is to conceptualize a dimension as necessary, but then to find in empirical applications that there are a few rare cases where the dimension is not present. There is a strong tendency then to

---

[5] Formally, this might look like: $Y = (E_1 * E_2) * (w_1 D_1 + w_2 D_2 + \dots)$, where E_i are the necessary dimensions.

[6] The family resemblance approach underlies most quantitative methodologies that are additive. A typical quantitative model looks something like $Y = w_1 D_1 + w_2 D_2 + \dots$ If Y is large enough, the case falls into the concept category. This formalization also illustrates how natural it would be in a quantitative setting to gives weights, w_i, to the dimensions D_i.

say that in fact the dimension is not necessary. We do not – or at least should not – expect the fit between our theories and empirical realities to be perfect. A few counterexamples alone should not prevent a heavy weight like necessity from being applied to important dimensions.

The Dimensions Guideline stressed the importance of giving a list of characteristics that constitute a concept. The Necessity Guideline emphasizes that one needs to think about the relative importance of the various dimensions. It is perhaps unlikely that all dimensions are of equal importance. For example, among the five characteristics of being a mother some might be more important than others. For example, many might suggest that providing nurturance is more important than being married to the father. While it might not be essential, one can increase its weighting *vis-à-vis* the "married to the father" characteristic.

In summary, one needs to think about the relative weight of the various dimensions. One way to give weight is to make a dimension essential. However, one can also give unequal weights to dimensions in the family resemblance approach as well. Hybrid weighting is also possible, as we have seen with the mother concept. Often the default is equal weighting; we think this is often not a good idea. Even if the unequal weights are somewhat arbitrary, it is still better than the equally arbitrary – and often harder to justify – equal weights.

Interdependence Guideline

What is the interdependence between dimensions?

The Dimensions Guideline says that one should clearly list the important dimensions of a concept. The Necessity Guideline continues in this vein with a recommendation to evaluate the importance or necessity of each dimension. The Interdependence Guideline naturally follows with a recommendation to look at interdependencies, interactions, synergies, etc., between dimensions.

Interdependencies play a central role in the concept of development and human well-being, as Kathleen Staudt points out in this volume. To have a good quality of life usually means scoring relatively high on many dimensions. For example, low or bad nutrition as a child has impacts on other areas of functioning. Education enables people to use resources more efficiently and to acquire them. One of the well-established facts in the literature on happiness is that it is not highly correlated with wealth. As Sen has forcefully argued, freedom is central to human well-being; much of family, social, and religious life hinges on having the freedom to make decisions and then the capacity to implement them.

Laurel Weldon's chapter on intersectionality is special in this volume because it is about a concept that itself concerns the complex relationships between concepts. Of particular interest in the gender and politics literature are the interactions between race, ethnicity, class, and gender. As the intersectionality label indicates, many feel that one cannot just add race and gender, but rather that there are specificities to that interaction.

We have seen above that the classic view of concepts defines them via logic and set theory (necessary and sufficient conditions and subsetting). The term "intersectionality" itself clearly makes reference to the set theoretic operation of intersection. In a typical quantitative analysis this would become an interaction term. By definition the intersection of two sets means an observation belongs to both sets.

The immediate and obvious interpretation of intersectionality for those who use regression analysis is as a simple interaction term where the impact of each independent variable on the dependent variable is conceptualized as a multiplicative, interactive variable. This is one possible way in which dimensions can have interdependencies. But, as Weldon's chapter discusses, some scholars argue that the concept means more than or other than just an interaction term. It is important nevertheless to see a simple interaction term as one possible way in which dimensions have dependencies.

Applying the Negation Guideline in this context can be useful. Much of the focus in the gender literature is on the race–gender relationship. In particular, interest has focused on the African-American–woman intersection. The negation of this involves the complete negation, namely white–man, along with the partial negations of white–woman, and African-American–man. To argue that intersectionality means more than simple interaction, one needs to show how some or all of these possibilities have very different properties or implications for theory or methodology.

In the classic form, concepts are defined via necessary and sufficient conditions. This itself means there are interactions between dimensions. The definition of a necessary condition itself means that it must be present, so all necessary dimensions must be present. In short, one has an interaction term between all of the dimensions. In contrast, the family resemblance model has few, if any, interactions between dimensions. It is fundamentally an additive procedure. In the current context it is important that if one uses necessary dimensions, interactions occur between dimensions by definition. There is no need to introduce them separately. One way to signal interdependencies is via making some dimensions necessary.

As discussed above in the Causal Relationships Guideline, interdependencies between dimensions often have a causal character; often they involve a causal mechanism of some sort. The concept of state feminism consists of a causal mechanism producing policy change. If that causal mechanism does not exist, state feminism is not present.

In summary, one needs to think about the interdependencies between dimensions. One simple model is that of the quantitative, interaction term. The literature on intersectionality suggests that dependencies can be more complex. It is always useful to look at all potential interactions between dimensions, not just the privileged ones; for instance, African-American–woman.

Operationalization Guideline

How is the concept operationalized?

Typically the concepts that interest gender scholars in particular, and social scientists in general, are abstract in nature. Frequently, it is not very clear at all how to connect the abstract concept with empirical data-gathering. The Operationalization Guideline argues that one must give specific attention to how to connect abstract concepts with empirical data, behavior, and practices.

One way causal relationships matter within concepts is via the Operationalization Guideline. Traditionally, quantitative methods for concepts, developed in sociology, psychology, and educational testing, see the indicators as *causal effects* of the concept. For example, intelligence (concept of interest) causes one to answer test questions (indicators) correctly. This can be called the "disease–symptom" model of concepts: the disease causes the symptoms. Less well known would be models where the indicators are the cause of the concept (Bollen and Lennox 1991). Finally, Goertz (2005) argues that in many cases the dimensions (not the indicators) *constitute* the concept in the ontological, and noncausal, sense of the word (see Wendt 1999: ch. 3 for similar ideas).

As discussed in the Dimensions Guideline, abstract concepts are in fact constituted by various dimensions which themselves are often quite abstract. The question then arises whether operationalization should be based on the concept or on its constitutive dimensions. Standard quantitative practice is to have various indicators for the concept itself. One gathers indicators of a particular concept or phenomenon and then aggregates these indicators or uses some data reduction technique like factor analysis.

We suggest that it is better practice to focus operationalization on the dimensions and not on the overall concept. If one gathers indicators for the overall concept, it becomes extremely difficult, if not impossible, to apply the Necessity and Interdependence Guidelines. If one does develop indicators ignoring the dimensions, there must be some argument explicitly made about the dimensions. Almost by default, then, there is an assumption of no interdependence between dimensions. This must be justified. In practice it is the nature of the dimensions that usually suggests the operational indicators in any case. So we think that attaching indicators to dimensions will in fact be the natural thing to do.

Usually the researcher works with dimensions or concepts that are quite abstract and that cut a fairly wide swathe across space and time. The Traveling Guideline is where the concept shows real concern for local specificities of culture and history. Here one can think seriously about the multiple ways in which various countries, cultures, and time periods have embodied the general dimensions of the concept, what Sartori first referred to as "conceptual stretching" in his 1970 article that has become a classic.

A second, related, way to make concepts or dimensions travel is to think in terms of functional equivalence. For example, the Sen-Nussbaum view (Nussbaum 1993) of the concept of "human well-being" involves a series of physical, sociological, and psychological necessary dimensions. Physical dimensions include factors like food and health. These are necessary dimensions, since without them human well-being is low. To make their concept travel they allow a variety of functionally equivalent ways to achieve each dimension of well-being. There are many ways to get sufficient food, health, and so on. This is absolutely core to the concept of development, because all scholars want the development concept to travel throughout the vast expanses of the less developed world.

The key notion is that there are various practices (or indicators) that are basically equivalent ways of fulfilling a given dimension. Basically, one has the problem of translation. For example, if one is conducting a cross-national survey (e.g. the Eurobarometer), one needs to translate the "same" question into different languages for use in different national contexts. The goal is to have equivalent questions in each language and/or country. Another example comes from the chapter on state feminism. The notion of women's policy agencies can actually mean a range of different structures, depending on the setting – equal opportunity agencies with a gender remit, gender equality agencies, ministries of women's status, and so on. One cannot do operationalization without paying very close attention to the Traveling Guideline.

It is easy to think of operationalization as a rather technical – hence less important – guideline. Paxton's chapter on democracy illustrates that even attention to this guideline can have major theoretical and empirical consequences. She notes that no one contests that a full democracy should include the vote for women. However, in practice – that is, operationalization – no one includes this. Once one genders the operationalization of democracy, the ranking of countries on a democracy scale shifts dramatically, and the point at which states become democracies often changes by decades. The saying goes that the devil is in the detail: the Operationalization Guideline stresses that much mischief goes on behind the scenes in many quantitative measures. A focus on the operationalization details can result in major challenges to many empirical findings.

Conclusion

While we do not pretend that these guidelines exhaust all the relevant considerations when thinking about, evaluating, or developing concepts, we do think that they do go a long way towards providing a systematic framework for thinking about concepts. Many of the problems we see in the literature dealing with concepts result from the failure to consider one of the guidelines.

While we have discussed these ten guidelines using examples from this volume, it is quite clear to us that they apply to all social science concepts. While some might see the gender and politics literature as being less developed methodologically, there are a number of guidelines that we think the gender and politics literature has been much more aware of than more established empirical research. In particular, the attention to issues of intersectionality is something quantitative research has begun to notice in the increasing emphasis on interaction terms. However, the theoretical and conceptual implications of intersectionality have not always been drawn out. Similarly with the gray zone. This remains a big point of debate in comparative politics, with perhaps the majority holding to the traditional dichotomous view. Here too gender scholars have realized the theoretical and empirical importance of those who live in the margins of class, race, and gender.

We hope that the guidelines outlined here and the extensive analysis of concepts provided by the authors of the chapters will inspire gender and nongender scholars to think more deeply about how they use concepts to select cases, to describe the world, and to explain how the world works.

PART I

GENDERING CONCEPTS

3   Gendering democracy

Pamela Paxton

The concept of democracy has a long history of attention to definition and measurement. Numerous definitions have been proposed and refined (e.g. Schumpeter 1942, Sartori 1987, Dahl 1971, Schmitter and Karl 1991, Bollen 1990, Przeworski, Alvarez, Zhebub, and Limongi 2000). And many measures of democracy have been created for use in empirical research (e.g. Gastil 1978, Bollen 1998, Jaggers and Gurr 1995, Alvarez, Cheibub, Limongi, and Przeworski 1996, Vanhanen 2000). Attention to definition and measurement is critical as social scientists seek to understand the determinants and consequences of liberal democracy (e.g. Burkhart and Lewis-Beck 1994) and practitioners attempt to spread democracy around the world (USAID 1997, Finkel, Perez, Linan, and Seligson 2007). Both this policy and academic work presupposes the accuracy of measures of democracy. Despite the amount of ink spilled on definitions of democracy, little attention is generally paid to gender in discussions of the concept (Waylen 1994, Pateman 1989). And although measures of democracy are frequently critiqued (e.g. Bollen and Paxton 2000, Mainwaring *et al.* 2001, Munck and Verkuilen 2002, Bowman, Lehoucq, and Mahoney 2005), gender is rarely explicitly considered in measurement (Paxton 2000).

In this chapter, I demonstrate that although one could argue that the concept of democracy is gendered in principle, women are not actually included in practice. That is, although definitions are generally inclusive, requiring all adults of a certain geographic area to have certain political privileges, measures of democracy often fail to include women as political participants. Evidence of the misalignment between conceptual and operational definitions is presented for six running examples including classic studies such as

I gratefully acknowledge the support of the National Science Foundation (SES-0318367, SES-0549973, and GER-9554569) and the Mershon Center at the Ohio State University. Portions of this chapter are based on my previous publication, "Women's suffrage in the measurement of democracy: problems of operationalization," *Studies in Comparative International Development* 35 (2000), pp. 92–111.

Lipset 1959, Huntington 1991, and Rueschemeyer, Stephens, and Stephens 1992; more recent work such as Reich 2002; and in a commonly used measure of democracy – Polity IV (Jaggers and Gurr 1995). The extent of the problem is demonstrated with reference to a variety of other studies including Mainwaring 1993, Alvarez *et al.* 1996, and Mainwaring *et al.* 2001.

The chapter continues by discussing the implications of including women, in principle and in practice, into our concept of democracy. I argue that the decision to exclude women from measurements of democracy can affect three areas of research: (1) descriptions of the emergence of democracy, (2) estimates of the age or regional prevalence of democracy, and (3) understanding the causes of democratization. Upon investigation, it becomes clear that oversights like excluding women's suffrage are more likely to result when democracy is measured as a dichotomy. Thus, I illustrate that the "gray zone" (Goertz and Mazur, this volume) is particularly important to women when defining and measuring democracy. Gender can be incorporated more naturally when democracy is measured on a graded scale. The conclusion raises final questions about inclusion and representation in the measurement of democracy.

Before continuing, it is important to note my use of the term "gender" in this chapter. Because many measures of democracy continue to exclude women, sometimes quite explicitly, the concept falls behind other concepts, such as development, in meeting even basic attempts to incorporate women. Thus, my focus on gender in this chapter is on a first step – simple inclusion of 50 percent of a population in definition and measurement.

Context Guideline: definitions of democracy

Understanding how women are, and are not, incorporated into the concept of democracy requires careful attention to its definition. Democracy has traditionally been seen with at least two dimensions: competition and participation. Almost all subsequent definitions of democracy derive from Dahl's (1971: 4) classic distinction between contestation/competition and participation/inclusion. Contestation requires that at least some members of the political system can "contest the conduct of the government" though regular and open elections (Dahl 1971: 4). Contestation is not concerned with the numbers of individuals who participate, only in the procedures used to determine leaders. Therefore, definitions of democracy that focus only on contestation are labeled procedural definitions and concern themselves only with competition and opposition among elites (Schumpeter 1942; Przeworski, Alvarez, Zhebub, and Limongi 2000).

Dahl's second dimension, participation, is also central to most definitions of democracy. Dahl (1971: 2) argues that a democratic regime is "completely or almost completely responsive to all its citizens." Following this lead, contemporary scholars' definitions of democracy typically involve some discussion of universal suffrage. These definitions are generally inclusive, requiring all adults of a certain geographic area to have certain political privileges. For example, Diamond, Linz, and Lipset (1990: 6-7) explain that "democracy . . . denotes . . . a 'highly inclusive' level of political participation in the selection of leaders and policies, at least through regular and fair elections, such that no major (adult) social group is excluded."

A third common dimension, civil liberties, can be described as the freedom to express a variety of political opinions in any media and the freedom to form and to participate in any political group. Civil liberties include freedom of speech and freedom to organize.

Naming Guideline: women are implicitly part of the definition of democracy

As noted above, definitions of democracy stress the importance of universal suffrage and participation of all major social groups. Across definitions, democratic participation is seen to include "adults" (Schmitter and Karl 1991: 77), "the people" (Vanhanen 2000: 252), and the "nonelite" (Bollen 1990: 9). This criterion implies, though it does not directly state, that women should be included. As a major social group, comprising 50 percent of a typical adult population, women are clearly part of a universal suffrage requirement.

Consider the way that women are implicitly (or at times explicitly) included in the following definitions of democracy (emphasis added in each):

Democracy "permits the *largest possible part of the population* to influence . . . decisions" (Lipset 1959: 71).

Democracy provides "*all citizens* with both the opportunity to participate in the governing process, as manifested by *universal adult suffrage* and free and fair elections" (Muller 1988: 65).

A government is democratic when "its most powerful collective decision-makers are selected through fair, honest and periodic elections in which candidates freely compete for votes and in which *virtually all the adult population is eligible to vote* . . . To the extent, for instance, that a political system denies voting participation to part of its society – as the South African system did to the 70 percent of its population that was black, *as Switzerland did to the 50 percent of its population that was female*, or as the United States did to the 10 percent of its population that were southern blacks – it is undemocratic" (Huntington 1991: 7).

"Regular, free and fair elections of representatives with *universal and equal suffrage.*" Democracy "means nothing if it does not entail rule or participation in rule by the many" (Rueschemeyer, Stephens, and Stephens 1992: 43, 41).

"No country can be considered democratic if national executive and legislative authority are not subject to meaningful competition via multiparty elections and no major, adult social group is excluded" (Reich 2002: 7)

Such inclusive definitions are echoed in the quantitative datasets that provide measures of democracy, such as the Polity measure of democracy. In articulating the definition of democracy behind the Polity measure, Jaggers and Gurr (1995: 471) explain that there are "three essential, interdependent elements of democracy." Using Diamond, Linz, and Lipset (1988), the authors go on to describe the first element, political competition, as

the presence of institutions and procedures through which citizens can express effective preferences about alternative political policies and leaders. This is accomplished through the establishment of regular and meaningful competition among individuals and organized groups, *an inclusive degree of political participation* in the selection of leaders and policies, and a level of political liberties sufficient to ensure the integrity of democratic participation.

Like other definitions of democracy, therefore, Jaggers and Gurr include participation in their definition (although they fold it under their larger concept of competition).

Some have argued that in operationalizing this definition of democracy, the Polity dataset omits participation (Munck and Verkuilen 2002). But Marshall, Gurr, Davenport, and Jaggers (2002: 41) argue strongly that the Polity measure is indeed intended to capture participation. They maintain that two components of their measure, "competitiveness of political participation" and "regulation of political participation," measure participation. Their discussion implies that the Polity measure includes formal voting procedures as well as other aspects of participation beyond that single dimension (Marshall, Gurr, Davenport, and Jaggers 2002: 42).

Gendering democracy, therefore, does not require a new name for the concept or adding an adjective (Collier and Adcock 1999). Democracy as a concept already includes women, at least implicitly, as part of the adult social groups that must not be excluded from participation. In no definition is sex considered a valid reason for exclusion from the political process.

Dimensions Guideline: the necessity of participation

What becomes clear from the discussion so far is that the incorporation of women requires that the participation dimension be included in the concept of democracy. Although most definitions of democracy do include participation as a fundamental dimension, procedural definitions do not, focusing instead solely on contestation among elites (Schumpeter 1942, Przeworski, Alvarez, Zhebub, and Limongi 2000). Narrow procedural definitions of democracy make it more difficult to address the inclusion of women (Waylen 1994: 331). Traditionally women have not been political elites, so it follows that a focus on such elites will exclude women.[1]

Interestingly, the participation dimension is so fundamentally important to democratic theorists that suffrage is addressed even by authors using a procedural definition. For example, Alvarez, Cheibub, Limongi, and Przeworski (1996: 5) argue that their post-World War II measure does not need to consider participation, as suffage is now taken for granted. The urge to justify the exclusion of participation suggests that participation is viewed as fundamental, even among procedural thinkers. And as illustrated in the definitions above, as long as participation is included as a dimension of democracy, women should be included, at least implicitly.

Negation Guideline

There is no single, clear, opposite of democracy (Goertz 2005). The negative of democracy can be a variety of distinct concepts – authoritarianism, totalitarianism, and so on. But investigating discussions of democracy's opposite make it clear that lack of participation is usually an important part of the negative. For example, autocracy is the opposite of democracy in the Polity

---

[1] Narrow, proceduralist definitions such as those used by Przeworski, Alvarez, Zhebub and Limongi (2000) are critiqued for being "subminimal" in multiple ways (e.g. Mainwaring *et al.* 2001: 41).

series and is defined in terms of participation. Jaggers and Gurr (1995: 471) explain: "in mature form, autocracies *sharply restrict or suppress political participation*." Similarly, answering "no" to the question "Is the present national government (including executive and legislative authority) selected on the basis of competitive, multiparty elections, in which no major (adult) social group is excluded?" moves a country away from classification as a democracy, according to Reich (2002: 20), and toward either authoritarian or semi-democratic status. In both cases it is clear that lack of political participation is at least one important component of the negative pole of the concept of democracy.

Operationalization Guideline: women removed

To this point, the Context, Naming, Dimensions, and Negation Guidelines all suggest the importance of participation, and therefore of women, to the concept of democracy. As 50 percent of a typical adult population, women are a "major social group" that must be included under typical conceptualizations of democracy.

But there is a significant problem with women's inclusion in the concept of democracy. It appears when we consider the Operationalization Guideline. In brief, in the process of *measuring* democracy, women, specifically women's suffrage, are often deliberately excluded or simply overlooked. Measures commonly use male suffrage as the sole indicator of a country's transition to democracy. Or the achievement of female suffrage will not change a country's score on a graded measure of democracy. Thus, many measures of democracy do not match theoretical definitions, making for poor concept-measure consistency (Goertz 2005: 95). In this section, I outline the problem in a number of studies and a commonly used graded measure of democracy.

To understand the inclusion or exclusion of women, it is important first to recognize that the measurement of democracy can take one of three forms: (1) specifying the date when a country completed its transition to democracy (e.g. country A made the transition to democracy in 1950);[2] (2) measuring the stability of democracy over some time period (e.g. country A has been a democracy for twelve years); and (3) measuring the level of democracy in any single year (e.g. country A rated 88 out of 100 in its level of democracy

---

[2] See O'Donnell and Schmitter (1986: ch. 2) for a discussion of transitions and related terms.

in 1985). As I demonstrate in this section, operationalization problems occur in all three types of measures.

Examples of the discrepancy in transition or stability measures

Sometimes women mysteriously disappear from measurement. For example, in his classic study, Lipset measures democracy by the "uninterrupted continuation of political democracy since World War I" (1959: 73). Many of the countries Lipset lists as democracies, however (e.g. Belgium, the United States, Canada, the United Kingdom, Sweden, Switzerland) gave suffrage to women some time after World War I. Lipset therefore excludes female participation from his measure of democracy. He does not address how or why the discrepancy with his definition occurred.

More frequently, the removal of women from consideration in a measure of democracy is explicitly justified by an author. In this case, typically some additional rule is added during operationalization that happens to exclude women. For example, Muller operationalizes democracy with four requirements, of which the third is most important: "at least approximately a majority of the adult population has the right to vote" (1988: 54). This operationalization moves away from universal suffrage to an approximate majority. Given that many of his relevant transition dates are in the nineteenth century, this redefinition of universal suffrage allows Muller to measure a transition to democracy when "universal manhood suffrage was instituted (giving approximately a majority of the population the right to vote)" (1988: 56). Ultimately, women are excluded from Muller's measurement, although they were included in his definition. Notably, by using the phrase "approximately a majority of the adult population" Muller is able to exclude women from his measurement without ever actually mentioning gender.

Huntington takes a similar tack, although he is more explicit about operationalization based on gender. He gives "two reasonable major criteria for when nineteenth-century political systems achieved minimal democratic qualifications in the context of that century" (1991: 16). Although Huntington's earlier discussion explicitly described societies with male-only suffrage as undemocratic, one of these operational criteria is that "*50 percent of adult males* are eligible to vote." The operationalization of his definition using this criterion leads to a voting population made up of only 25 percent of a typical adult population. And it allows countries to transition to democracy without female suffrage.

The most extended justification for a gendered discrepancy between definition and measurement appears in Rueschemeyer, Stephens, and Stephens (1992). As explanation for the exclusion of women from measurement, they claim that gender relations were "far less important in the known histories of democratization" (1992: 48). Instead, they assert that what is important for measuring democracy is that participation transcend class lines. As further arguments for excluding women, they note that less blood was shed for women's inclusion, and that women's political inclusion did not give rise to regime changes designed to reexclude them.[3] These arguments for the exclusion of women are used again by Reich in his justification for removing female suffrage from his operationalization of democracy. Reich explains:

In the coding algorithm, there was one exception to the clause that democratic elections could not exclude any major adult social group: countries that established universal male suffrage with competitive multiparty elections before the Second World War were considered democratic... This concession to historical context is made because the notion of gender equality with regard to political citizenship was not widely applied until the early 20th century, even in countries where political institutions conformed to democratic practices in all other respects. In addition, as Rueschemeyer, Stephens, and Stephens argue, the electoral inclusion of women did not dramatically alter electoral politics or institutional characteristics in countries that had previously excluded women from political participation. (2002: 19)

Before continuing, it is important to point out that each of these arguments for women's exclusion poses problems. First, one reason why women are "far less important" in the known history of democratization may be that by focusing on male suffrage and class rather than on gender divisions, scholars have made them so. In addition, including a cause (much blood being shed) or a consequence (regime changes to reexclude the included group) in the measurement of democracy moves away from most definitions.

What is the extent of the definition/measurement discrepancy? What difference does excluding women make? Omitting women can shift transition dates to democracy far from what they would be under a more valid operationalization. In Table 3.1, to illustrate the extent of these changes, I implement a very simple technique – I modify various authors' measurements to match their

---

[3] It should be noted that by basing their measurement decision on class participation rather than full inclusion and concluding that the working class plays a decisive role in democratization, it is possible that Rueschemeyer, Stephens, and Stephens's conclusion may have been built into their measurement decision.

definitions.[4] That is, I change the date for a country's transition to democracy if there is a gap between the date given by the author and the date when women gained suffrage. If a country is scored as achieving democracy *before* women gained suffrage, I change its transition date to the date when women gained suffrage. If the original transition date is *after* the date of female suffrage, then no change is made. For example, when discussing Muller, I change the United States from a transition date of 1870 (before women gained suffrage) to 1920 (when women gained suffrage). I do not change Italy, listed as transitioning to democracy in 1946, because women gained suffrage there in 1945. This is the most simple and basic modification to the concept of democracy possible. Indeed, it really can be considered simply "sexing" the concept of democracy – the straightforward inclusion of a biological group.

Table 3.1 demonstrates that the inclusion of women into measures of democracy changes transition dates, sometimes only slightly and sometimes dramatically. For example, France's transition date would change by over 60 years in Muller's and Rueschemeyer, Stephens and Stephens's analyses.[5]

Examples of the discrepancy in graded measures

Other measures of democracy consider the *level* of democracy in particular years. It would seem that graded measures of democracy would more easily and naturally incorporate female suffrage. But here too we see discrepancies between definition and measurement when gender is considered. In this section I focus on the discrepancy in the most widely utilized measure of democracy – the Polity measure of democracy (Jaggers and Gurr 1995). Polity's popularity likely stems from its large cross-national and temporal coverage; the measure covers over 150 countries and begins in the nineteenth century.

---

[4] An earlier version of this table appeared in Paxton (2000). That paper used Sivard (1985) for suffrage dates, and some of those dates were incorrect by referencing the year women could first stand for office, or in listing dates of restricted female suffrage. Table 3.1 presents correct dates of female suffrage based on Paxton, Green, and Hughes (2006).

[5] There are a variety of other adult social groups that have also been excluded from democratic participation in the past, and these are important to consider in the measurement of democracy in their own right. But interestingly, a quick perusal of democracy measures suggests that race, at least, appears to be better included in the measurement of democracy, at least in countries such as the United States or South Africa. Rueschemeyer, Stephens, and Stephens, for example, do not score the USA as a full democracy until 1965, addressing not only *de jure* racial restrictions on voting but *de facto* restrictions. Similarly, South Africa is typically viewed as nondemocratic until the end of the apartheid system in 1994.

Table 3.1 Comparison of transition dates of democracy to female suffrage

	Author's transition date	Date of female suffrage	Difference in years
Lipset			
Belgium	1918	1948	30
Ireland	1918	1928	10
Luxemberg	1918	1919	1
Netherlands	1918	1919	1
Sweden	1918	1919	1
Switzerland	1918	1971	53
United Kingdom	1918	1928	10
United States	1918	1920	2
Muller			
Australia	1892	1902	10
Belgium	1919	1948	29
Canada	1898	1918	20
France	1875	1944	69
India	1947	1950	3
Netherlands	1918	1919	1
New Zealand	1879	1893	14
Sweden	1917	1919	2
United Kingdom	1918	1928	10
United States	1870	1920	50
Uruguay	1919	1932	13
Rueschemeyer, Stephens, and Stephens			
Argentina	1912–30	1947	25
Britain	1918	1928	10
France	1877	1944	67
Italy	1919	1945	26
Switzerland	1848	1971	123
Uruguay	1919–33	1932	13
Venezuela	1945–8	1946	1
Reich			
Australia	1901	1902	1
Belgium	1919	1948	29
Czechoslovakia	1918	1920	2
France	1849–51, 1891–1940	1944	51
Ireland	1922	1928	6
Netherlands	1917	1919	2
Norway	1898	1913	15
Sweden	1917	1919	2
Switzerland	1848	1971	123
United Kingdom	1885	1928	43
United States	1870	1920	50
Uruguay	1918–33	1932	14

Table 3.2 Comparison of Polity with dates of female suffrage

Country	First year high democracy	Date of women's suffrage	discrepancy[a]
Australia	1901	1902	1
Belgium	1919	1948	24
Canada	1888	1918	30
Costa Rica	1890	1949	59
France	1898	1944	40
Greece	1870	1952	82
Ireland	1921	1928	7
Netherlands	1917	1919	2
New Zealand	1857	1893	35
Norway	1898	1913	15
Sweden	1917	1919	2
Switzerland	1848	1971	123
United Kingdom	1901	1928	27
United States	1809	1920	105

[a] Discrepancy between the date of women's suffrage and the Polity first year of high democracy cannot always be determined by simple subtraction. For example, between 1865 and 1870, the United States is coded as 9,1 and is therefore not a "high democracy" in those years by the definition used here.

As discussed above, Polity uses an inclusive definition of democracy. Despite the asserted importance of participation to the Polity measure, however (Marshall, Gurr, Davenport, and Jaggers 2002: 41), the measure does not incorporate women. This appears most obviously to a causal observer in the scores for Switzerland, which receives a perfect 10 on the Polity democracy/autocracy scale from 1848 to the present. The fact that women did not achieve suffrage in Switzerland until 1971 suggests a definition/measurement inconsistency in Polity.

Using the simple procedure for including women outlined above, Table 3.2 presents a list of countries that Polity scores as "high democracies" before women achieved suffrage. I define "high democracy" as a score of 8 or greater on democracy, and a score of 0 on autocracy. Comparing years of high democracy to the date women achieved suffrage, Table 3.2 demonstrates that the discrepancy for the United States and Switzerland is over 100 years, for Greece it is 82 years, and for Costa Rica 59. The average discrepancy across the countries listed is 41 years.

The lack of attention to female suffrage means that large changes in the electorate of a given country do not register in the Polity scale. For example, consider Figure 3.1, which tracks the growth in Great Britain's electorate over

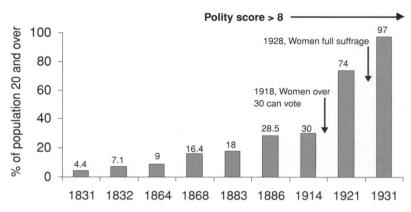

Figure 3.1   Great Britain's electorate, 1831–1931
Sources: Dahl 1998: 24; Paxton, Hughes, and Green 2006; Polity IV Project

a 100-year period. From 1901 on, Great Britain is classified by Polity as a high democracy, with a score of 8 (Great Britain receives a perfect 10 score from 1922 forward). But the lack of variation in the Polity score after 1901 masks substantial change in the size of the electorate. In 1918, women over thirty years of age were allowed to vote. This change led to a large jump in the size of the electorate between 1914 (30 percent) and 1921 (74 percent). The next jump, between 1921 and 1931 (to 97 percent), is due to women's receipt of full and unrestricted suffrage in 1928. Before and after this time, Polity scores Great Britain as a high democracy. (In fact, the change in the Polity score from 8 to 10 in 1922 corresponds to neither suffrage gain.) An individual looking at Figure 3.1 would likely assess the changes in 1921 and 1931 as the most important in the graph. Yet those changes are not reflected in the Polity measure.

In sum, if we investigate the correspondence between definitions of democracy and measurement, we see substantial mismatches in measures of transition dates, measures of the stability of democracy, and continuous measures of democracy. Sometimes the omission is explicit and deliberate, as in Huntington's allowance of differential measurement in the nineteenth century. At other times it is not clear how women fell out in the transition from definition to measure.

Just about the only measures that do not have this problem are those that are recent enough to measure democracy after female suffrage was achieved in almost every country of the world (see Paxton, Hughes, and Green 2006). There, operationalization raises fewer obvious gender issues because women have now gained suffrage in most countries of the world. But researchers need to be careful even in recent time periods. Alvarez, Cheibub, Limongi, and Przeworski (1996: 5) explain that because they consider the period after World War II, suffrage can be taken for granted and their measure does not need to consider participation. But some of the countries in their sample, such as Switzerland and Greece, did not grant women suffrage until after World War II. Similarly, remember that Huntington argues that his measurement decision to exclude women (and 50 percent of men) is reasonable for time periods before 1900. But Huntington continues to score countries without female suffrage as democracies well into the twentieth century. Examples include Switzerland, Botswana, Fiji, and Guyana.

Zones Guideline: gendering democracy through the "gray zone"

How then are we to ensure that democracy is gendered – that definitions *and* measures of democracy include women? In this task the "gray zone" becomes very important (Goertz and Mazur, this volume). Despite the problems with the Polity measure documented above, measures of the level of democracy (e.g. Gastil 1978, Bollen 1998) should not suffer from measurement problems to the same extent as dichotomous measures. Graded measures allow women's participation to be one piece of an overall measure of democracy.

But dichotomous measures remain prevalent in democratic scholarship (e.g. Alvarez, Cheibub, and Limongi 1996). As Muller (1995: 991) notes, "classification of states into democracies versus nondemocracies is a generally accepted procedure for analyses of democratization." Huntington (1991: 11) turns this into an even stronger claim: that the transition from a nondemocratic regime to a democratic one can be identified "by a single relatively clear and widely accepted criterion." As this chapter has shown, however, in practice that criterion translates into male suffrage. And if it does, there is no recourse for the inclusion of women in a dichotomous measure.

We need to further recognize that strict dichotomous codings are likely to lead to measurement error *across* studies. As an example, compare the coding of the United States transition to democracy across various studies. Muller, Huntington, and Rueschemeyer, Stephens, and Stephens each provide different dates for the transition to democracy in the United States. Huntington places the USA as a democracy in 1828, while Muller claims it was not a democracy until 1865. Rueschemeyer, Stephens, and Stephens do not score the USA as a full democracy until 1965. These different dates create a 137-year measurement difference. The confusion is erased if we think of transitions to democracy in continuous terms – the United States was simply at different stages of democracy on those dates. In 1828, property requirements were relaxed; in 1865, universal male suffrage was instituted; in 1920, female suffrage was introduced; and in 1965, nearly universal suffrage with no literacy requirements was achieved.

Thus, researchers should carefully consider the Zones Guideline – that we should take a more graded view of democracy. Dichotomous transition dates explain movement across important thresholds, but these thresholds could be multiple and successive. A serial measure of democratic transition that incorporated more than a single criterion would result in sharper differentiation and allow measurement to more closely approximate commonly accepted definitions.[6] Collier and Levitsky (1997: 437–42) explain that "diminished subtypes" of democracy, such as male democracies, would allow that the instance is less than fully democratic. Indeed, Dahl (1989: 235) labels countries that exclude women "male polyarchies." This procedure would help highlight when an object has "some but not all of the characteristics of the concept" (Goertz and Mazur, this volume).

Traveling Guideline: one consequence of women's exclusion

As is apparent from the discussion above, some authors, such as Samuel Huntington, have responded to the issue of women's suffrage by arguing for retrospective definitions of democracy that are different from modern definitions. Indeed, Mainwaring *et al.* (2001: 40) ask "whether scholars should use international standards for a given period (we call this a retrospective standard) or today's international standards." They ultimately argue for retrospective standards, in which countries can be defined as democratic based on the standards of the era. This definition leads to a measure of democracy stressing adult male suffrage in periods "until shortly after World War II." Mainwaring 1993: 201 pushes the date forward further, arguing that we should only switch over to including women in "recent decades" because before then some nations that were usually considered democracies excluded

---

[6] Bollen and Jackman (1989) present additional benefits accrued by considering democracy to be continuous rather than dichotomous. Collier and Adcock (1999) discuss the debate over dichotomies versus graded measures thoroughly and impartially. See Sartori (1984) for a defense of dichotomous measurement against "degreeism."

women. This means he is likely thinking of 1971, when the last western country allowed women to vote.[7])

There are two problems with allowing the definition of democracy to vary across time periods without acknowledging a diminished subtype. First, definitions of relevant time periods could vary widely, introducing inconsistency across definitions and measures. Put another way, *when should* women be included in the definition of democracy? When the first country granted women suffrage (1893)? The end of World War I (16 countries had female suffrage)? When women in the United States achieved suffrage (1920)? The end of World War II (58 countries had female suffrage)? When the United Nations encouraged women's political rights in its 1953 Convention on the Political Rights of Women? When the last western country finally allowed women to vote (1971)?

The second problem with using retrospective standards is that such definitions do not meet the Traveling Guideline and consequently disallow longitudinal research and an ability to track the growth in democracy over time. If democracy is defined, and therefore measured, in terms relative to a particular time period, then researchers can only compare across countries at that given time point. Instead, we must have definitions and measures that are consistent across both space *and* time. Gendering democracy means that the concept will better travel across time. Of course, the argument that context was uniquely different in the twentieth century also continues the longstanding tradition of excluding women when referencing the individual (Pateman 1989: 219).

Developing concepts that travel across time as well as space is increasingly important with the development of longitudinal data and methods. Scholars must recognize that our theories of democracy are likely to be very different if we use a constant measure of democracy across time, rather than a measure with different criteria for early, middle, and later periods.

Causal Relationships Guideline: more implications of gendering democracy

If we take the argument of this chapter seriously, then understanding the acquisition of women's suffrage becomes important as a significant stage in

---

[7] Some of the definitional and measurement decisions in the literature appear designed to maintain Switzerland's status as a longstanding democratic country. But scholars of democracy do need to recognize that Switzerland did not grant women suffrage until 1971, and in fact the last Swiss canton had to be forced by the courts to allow women to vote in 1990. By any definition of democracy that includes participation, Switzerland was not a democracy before 1971.

a country's overall attainment of democracy. In this section, I argue that the decision to exclude women's suffrage from measurements of democracy therefore affects three areas of research: (1) descriptions of the emergence of democracy, (2) estimating the age and regional prevalence of democracy, and (3) understanding the causes of democratization.

The emergence of democracy

Addressing consequences of women's suffrage on democracy, Paxton (2000) investigated Huntington's "waves" of democracy (Huntington 1991). Huntington hypothesizes that there have been a number of "waves" and "reverse waves" of democracy since the mid-1800s. A wave of democracy entails many nondemocracies transitioning to democracy within a specified time period, while simultaneously few democracies become nondemocracies. In a reverse wave, the opposite is true. Figure 3.2a presents Huntington's summary of the waves of democracy. The darker bands correspond to waves of democratization, while the gray bands represent reversals of democratization (reverse waves). The picture, including the dates of the waves, provides a typical representation of the perceived history of democracy.[8]

Since Huntington's measurement excludes women, Paxton (2000) respecified Huntington's transition dates according to the method described above. The inclusion of women produces changes in the shape and timing of the historical waves of democracy. Figure 3.2b displays the revised waves.

This modified measure does not provide as much support for the idea of waves of democracy. Huntington's original conceptualization shows three distinct waves of democracy with reverse waves in between. When women are included, the shape and dates of the waves change and some of the countries move from one wave to another. As pointed out by Paxton (2000), the major changes are as follows. (1) Many of the countries are delayed in becoming democracies until the second time period. For example, Belgium moves from the first wave to the second wave. (2) The magnitude of the revised first wave is cut in half compared to Huntington's first wave. Only 16 countries

---

[8] To understand how to read the diagram, follow the progression of a single country, such as Austria. Austria is in a group of ten countries that Huntington places in the first wave (as evidenced by the black bar in front of their group during that time period). During the first reverse wave, Austria and the other countries in its group lost democratic status (as evidenced by the gray bar). They then regained it during the second wave of democracy (the black bar returns) and retained it through the end of the measurement period. Alternatively, Australia is in a group of countries that Huntington places in the first wave, that remained democratic throughout the entire period.

Huntington's (1991:14) figure

Category	Number of countries	First wave 1828 1926	First reverse 1922– 1942	Second wave 1943– 1962	Second reverse 1958– 1975	Third wave 1974–
Sudan Suriname	2					
Bulgaria El Salvador Guatemala Haiti Honduras Mongolia Namibia Nicaragua Panama Romania Senegal	11					
Burma Fiji Ghana Guyana Indonesia Lebanon	6					
Nigeria	1					
Bolivia Brazil Ecuador India South Korea Pakistan Peru Philippines Turkey	9					
Botswana Gambia Israel Jamaica Malaysia Malta Sri Lanka Trinidad and Tobago Venezuela	9					
East Germany Poland Portugal Spain	4					
Argentina Czechoslovakia Greece Hungary Uruguay	5					
Austria Belgium Colombia Denmark France West Germany Italy Japan Netherlands Norway	10					
Chile	1					
Australia Canada Finland Iceland Ireland New Zealand Sweden Switzerland United Kingdom United States	10					

Figure 3.2 Comparison of waves of democracy with and without women's suffrage (cont. overleaf)

make up the revised first wave, compared to Huntington's original 30. (3) The revised first wave covers a much shorter time period, beginning in 1893 rather than 1828. (4) The revised second wave increases in size – the revised wave has 34 countries compared to the original 25 countries. (5) The first

Figure revised to incorporate women's suffrage

Category	Number of countries	First wave 1893–1931	First reverse 1922–1942	Second wave 1943–1966	Second reverse 1958–1975	Third wave 1971–
Bulgaria El Salvador Guatemala Haiti Honduras Mongolia Namibia Nicaragua Panama Romania Senegal Sudan Suriname	13					
East Germany Portugal	2					
Botswana Switzerland	2					
Burma Ghana Guyana Indonesia Lebanon	5					
Nigeria	1					
Bolivia Brazil Ecuador India South Korea Pakistan Peru Philippines Turkey	9					
Gambia Israel Jamaica Malaysia Malta Sri Lanka Trinidad and Tobago Venezuela	8					
Belgium Colombia France West Germany Italy Japan	6					
Argentina Greece Hungary Uruguay	4					
Chile	1					
Poland Spain	2					
Czechoslovakia	1					
Austria Denmark Netherlands Norway	4					
Australia Canada Finland Iceland Ireland New Zealand Sweden United Kingdom United States	9					

Figure 3.2 (cont.)

reverse wave is much smaller (7 countries compared to 19) and appears now to be simply a function of wartime occupation. In sum, the revised figure, simply by including women's suffrage, no longer offers strong support for Huntington's conception of waves of democracy. The revision indicates a long, continuous democratization period from 1893 to 1958, with only war-related reversals.

The age and regional prevalence of democracy

As a second consequence, consider how the inclusion of women leads us to different conclusions about the age and regional prevalence of democracy. Most observers tend to stress democracy's ancient pedigree. But Dahl (1998: 3) makes the point that democracy is actually quite young:

Today we have come to assume that democracy must guarantee virtually every adult citizen the right to vote. Yet until about four generations ago – around 1918, or the end of the First World War – in every independent democracy or republic that had ever existed up to then, a good half of all adults had always been excluded from the full rights of citizenship. These were, of course, women. Here, then, is an arresting thought: if we accept universal adult suffrage as a requirement of democracy, there would be some persons in practically every democratic country who would be older than their democratic system of government.

In short, taking women seriously suggests that, contrary to popular perception, nations have not actually had centuries of experience with democracy.

A related point (and one that also addresses the Traveling Guideline) is that the inclusion of women weakens the dominant place of the West in early democratization, since some western industrialized nations did not become female-inclusive democracies until long after other, less developed nations. Consider the mix of industrialized and nonindustrialized nations in the revised second wave of Figure 3.2. In some less industrialized countries, such as Ecuador, Sri Lanka, and Brazil, women gained suffrage around the same time period as in most western industrialized nations. And including women in our measures would mean that western countries such as Belgium, France, and Switzerland reached full levels of participation fifteen to forty years after some less developed countries. Therefore, at least for the participation dimension of democracy, there is not a large time lag between the West and other countries of the world.

The causes of democracy

It is finally important to recognize that, with women excluded, our theories of democratization have largely remained separate from studies of women's suffrage. Put another way, our current understanding of democracy and democratization may be underspecified due to our focus on an exclusionary form of democracy.

To begin, explaining female suffrage will force us to consider whether our theories of democratization (or of the forces that push for democratic inclusion) are universal, holding regardless of the group demanding political power, or whether they are group-specific and differ across different time periods. Female democratization movements could provide valuable tests of our current democratization theories. What hypotheses might we have to revisit once women are incorporated fully into our measure?

But if the processes of women's attainment of suffrage are different than those for men's attainment, then considering women's suffrage may help us formulate *new* theories. Specifically, there is a growing body of research on the attainment of women's suffrage that could inform our larger understanding of democracy and democratization. To begin, domestic social movements are an important piece of the story of women's suffrage. During the latter half of the nineteenth and early twentieth centuries, women struggled to achieve suffrage and eliminate barriers in education, employment, and property ownership (Ferree and Mueller 2004: 584, Chafetz and Dworkin 1986; Kelber 1994). These long, and sometimes bloody, struggles were ultimately successful in many countries. Success depended on movement size, composition, and alliances, as well as the ideology of the movement and its tactics used (see Paxton and Hughes 2007: ch. 2 for a review). For example, the framing and tactics of these movements were very important for eventual democratization in the USA (McCammon, Campbell, Granberg, and Mowery 2001; McCammon and Campbell 2001). Thus, a focus on elites in transitions to democracy (e.g. O'Donnell and Schmitter 1986) means that researchers may not look at the places where women are more likely to be involved – social movements (Waylen 1994).

A focus on women's suffrage also highlights the role of international actors, in that women's political representation has been actively encouraged by powerful international actors like the United Nations (Paxton, Hughes, and Green 2006). For example, during the UN's formation, suffragette Alice Paul and her World Women's Party lobbied for inclusion of the phrase "the equal rights of men and women" in the UN Charter Preamble. Similarly, female delegates from Brazil, the Dominican Republic, and Mexico insisted that a clause affirming equal rights for women be included in the 1945 UN Charter (Galey 1995: 7). After World War II, therefore, global actors like the UN helped define women's suffrage as a taken-for-granted component of national sovereignty (Jayawardena 1986). A focus on international actors helps explain women's acquisition of suffrage in nations without an active women's movement. Indeed, increasing global pressure for the inclusion of women in international politics helps explain women's acquisition of suffrage across a number of states (Paxton, Hughes, and Green 2006, Ramirez, Soysal and Shanahan 1997).

A focus on women's suffrage suggests further that public opinion, not simply elite opinion, matters for democratization. In the case of Switzerland, 1971 was not the first time Swiss voters explored the idea of female suffrage. Women's suffrage was rejected in subnational referendums between 1919 and 1921. And in 1959, a national referendum failed, with 67 percent of Swiss men voting against women's right to vote. To summarize the general point: when we ask what conditions favor democracy, we should also ask whether we would add any if we included women fully into our definitions and measures.

At the very least we need to recognize that our current efforts at assessing explanations are focused on a restrictive form of democratization. Consider Moore's (1966) classic study of the causes of democracy, which measures democracy with a restricted form of male suffrage and finds that the bourgeoisie are the main proponent of democracy. Moore's study is critiqued by Rueschemeyer, Stephens, and Stephens (1992), who argue that one cannot claim that the bourgeoisie was the protagonist for democracy unless *universal* manhood suffrage is ignored. Instead, Rueschemeyer, Stephens, and Stephens measure democracy with general male suffrage and find the working class to be more influential in the push for democracy. Yet, in a manner similar to their own critique of Moore, it can be argued that we can understand the importance of the working class to the inauguration of only an exclusionary form of democracy, involving the enfranchisement of male workers, not democracy as outlined in current theory. So, neither Moore's nor Rueschemeyer, Stephens, and Stephens's explanation for democratization captures full democracy, since they both ignore female suffrage. The entire debate about different class influences on democracy is predicated on the exclusion of women.

Conclusion

Women are implicitly a part of the concept of democracy, just as they were implicitly part of the concept "citizen" (Pateman 1989, Phillips 1991, Young 1990). But like women's actual exclusion from the concept of citizen, if we look carefully at measurement of the concept of democracy, women are not there. In this chapter I documented a prevalent tendency in the literature on democracy and democratization to talk about women in principle but exclude them in practice. This problem occurs in classic studies, in recent studies, and in the most commonly used measure of democracy today. I have also tried to illustrate that the omission of women from our measures is a problem with potentially far-reaching theoretical and practical consequences. When women are included in measures of democracy, the notion of waves of democracy is no longer strongly supported, some countries' transition to full democracy may have come thirty to seventy years after the traditionally accepted date, and the West does not have a hold on early democratization. And, with gendered measurement, we may come to both reassess and expand our explanations of democratization.

It is important to note that some measures of democracy do better match their definitions than others. Bowman, Lehoucq, and Mahoney (2005) are to be especially commended for directly incorporating women's suffrage into their measure. Indeed, their study, codebook, and data can provide a model for other researchers interested in incorporating women's suffrage into measures of democracy. As they state in their Appendix, "We only code Costa Rica a semi-democracy for much of the period before 1948 because women, as in many other countries of the world, were not allowed to vote. Women received the right to vote in 1949." For all five countries measured by the authors, the "content and enforcement of suffrage laws" is addressed and the date of female suffrage is discussed in the coding notes and explicitly included in their measure of democracy (2005: 952).

Forward progress cannot be assumed, however. Importantly, in updating Gasiorwoski's (1996) measure of democracy, Reich (2002) made the explicit decision to exclude women, even though they had been included previously by Gasiorwoski. In brief, Gasiorwoski's (1996) measure of democracy generally meets the minimum criteria of gendered inclusion that countries are not declared democratic before they grant women suffrage (a single mistake is Uruguay). And some attention to women's franchise is apparent in Gasiorwoski's coding notes. But despite the inclusion of women in that measure, Reich, in updating and expanding it, made the decision to exclude women as discussed above.

This chapter suggests that one possible solution to making democracy inclusive is to take the gray zone seriously and grade our measures of democracy. Measures of the transition to democracy tend to treat a "transition" as an isolated event, which implies a single starting date. This forces scholars to make an unnecessarily difficult choice in operationalizing democracy, and this choice has too often led to the neglect of women's suffrage. Instead, the use of graded measures and consideration of the gray zone would facilitate a focus on the multiple steps entailed in democratization. Indeed, as Alvarez, Cheibub, and Limongi (1996: 5) explain, "in most Western European countries, democracy emerged only gradually, in a sequence of steps." Utilizing the gray zone is one way to acknowledge that although countries did make important strides toward democracy in the nineteenth century, *they were not fully there.*

To demonstrate the extent of the problem of women's exclusion, I introduced the smallest possible change into measures of democracy – adding the suffrage of women into measures of democracy. As demonstrated, the consequences were impressive. But we would likely find that these consequences are only the tip of the iceberg if we were to modify measures of democracy further to incorporate women more completely. For example, the full incorporation of women into our understanding of civil liberties might include connecting measures of democracy to measures of women's social rights, such as Humana's (1992) *World Human Rights Guide* or the Cingranelli-Richards (CIRI) measure of women's social rights (2007). Indeed, the CIRI measure's attention to honor killings, dowry deaths, women's freedom to enter and leave relationships, and so on, addresses issues of security important to the civil liberties dimension of democracy. Also important is the CIRI acknowledgment that some countries elevate customary or other laws over the constitution (often in the area of family law). CIRI therefore codes women's social rights based on actual practice, rather than on empty and unenforced constitutional assurances.

Gendering democracy also suggests that we may need to think more fully about the concept of representation in our measures of democracy (see Celis, this volume). Certainly the *de jure* right to participate is quite different from *de facto* informal restrictions that limit actual use of the right to vote or run by women or other groups. Put another way, if certain segments of the population are not included as representatives, does it suggest continuing discrimination that makes a country less democratic? Interestingly, the Bowman, Lehoucq, and Mahoney measure considers whether a "significant portion of the population actually casts ballots." And Cingranelli and Richards (2007) measure women's political rights in part by the level of women's representation in the national legislature. Taking representation seriously has the potential to move us toward the measurement of descriptive as well as formal participation in our measures of democracy. Here, it may be useful to think of "adjective" modifications to the concept of democracy, perhaps making a distinction between "formal democracy" and "descriptive democracy," much as is seen in the representation literature.

But the process of gendering democracy remains at an early stage. In contrast to other concepts where gender is explicitly included in definition *and* measurement, this chapter has demonstrated that talk has been cheap in the democracy arena. Multiple measures of democracy do not meet even minimal requirements of participation and inclusion – leaving out the 50 percent of a typical population that is female. A takeaway message of this chapter is that gendering our concepts requires vigilance at every stage of conceptualization. It is not enough to have women ostensibly included in a stated definition. Researchers must instead investigate women's inclusion in all parts of conceptualization – especially operationalization, which determines the measures that shape our understanding of the world.

Regardless of how it is accomplished, including women will ensure that researchers' measures of democracy match their definitions. When democratic scholars agree to accept definitions of democracy that are inclusive, they must also be prepared to accept the consequences of that definition for their measurement of democracy and its conclusions about the history and causes of democracy. A continuing insistence that women can be written out of our measures of democracy, as they represent an inconvenience to existing theory, measures, or explanations, does a true disservice to our ultimate understanding of democracy.

4 Gendering representation

Karen Celis

The first part of this book clearly illustrates one of the fundamental contributions of feminist and women's studies: revealing the gender bias of so-called objective and neutral concepts (Squires 1999, Bryson 2003). Representation was fated to undergo the same treatment. The gendered dimension of representation is evident regarding the actors; because the represented and the representatives by definition have a sex and a gender, representation is not immune to being structured by hierarchical relations between men and women. However, "gendering representation" is not only concerned with the sex of the bodies, but also focuses on the "what" of representation and examines representatives' acts and claims using a gendered lens (see also Mazur and McBride in this volume). Besides taking into account the sex of the actors involved and the gendered character of representation, "gendering representation" fundamentally questions the way this concept is conceived and formulates conditions for "good" – that is, truly representative – representation (Dovi 2007) and even for democracy as such (see Paxton in this volume). A key contribution of feminist scholars is the rejection of a clear-cut separation of the dimensions of representation, as well as of the hierarchy between them. According to theorists of group representation, descriptive and substantive representation are intertwined, as the former is a prerequisite for the latter. Thereby, feminist analysis of representation complements mainstream political debates revolving around the questions "What is to be represented?" and "What is the relationship between the representative and the represented?"

The following section contextualizes "gendering representation" by providing a short introduction to the concept of "political representation" (Context Guideline). The third section further clarifies the relationship between "gendering representation" and "political representation" and what it implies to insert gender in the latter (Naming Guideline). The fourth section discusses the formal, descriptive/symbolic and substantive dimensions of gendering representation (Dimensions Guideline) and subsequently deals with the necessity of the dimensions and their interdependency (Necessity Guideline and Interdependence Guideline). The fifth section focuses on the positive and the negative poles of these dimensions in terms of sex and gender (Negation Guideline) and the zones between them (Zones Guideline). Subsequently, the chapter's focus shifts toward empirical research and questions regarding operationalizing. The final section contains a brief overview of empirical research on gender and political representation, thereby focusing on the necessity and causal relationship between descriptive and substantive representation (combining the Interdependence, Causal Relationships, and Operationalization Guidelines). Next, it discusses the ability of the research question to travel and suggests a formal operationalization of substantive representation as a master key for traveling across time and space (Operationalization and Traveling Guidelines).

The context of political representation

The concept of "representation" has had different meanings at different times and in different contexts.[1] Etymologically, "representation" derives from the Latin verb *repraesentare*: "to make present (again)." Originally, the term was used most frequently for inanimate objects that were made present (again); for instance, by introducing them or presenting them. It was also applied in artistic settings where actors or art (paintings or sculptures) represented characters, virtues, or ideas. Only later, in the Christian literature and practice of the Middle Ages, was the word used to refer to the embodiment of a collective by a person. In the same period, embryonic institutions of political representation emerged. The advisory councils of popes and kings were broadened in order to include persons from the constituent parts of churches or realms. The role played by these "delegates" evolved from one that was purely administrative and judicial (imposing taxes, applying law to local cases) to one that was more active and negotiational; for instance, by forcing the monarch to meet local demands in return for taxes paid. In the seventeenth century, and more specifically during the English Civil War, representation was interpreted as "acting for others" (agency) and representative institutions were linked with democratic practice and rights. The American and French revolutions that took place during the following century established representation as

---

[1] Pitkin (1969: 1–5); see also McLean (1991, 1996), Eulau (1967), Thomassen (1994).

a universal, democratic right. The nineteenth century witnessed the institutionalization of that right, and from then on much effort was devoted to an accurate formalization of representation.

Although democracy can theoretically exist without representation, representation is firmly imbedded in western liberal democracies (Lijphart 1984; see also Paxton, in this volume). Representation and representatives are seen as indispensable for putting into practice the democratic principle of "government by the people" (Beetham 1992: 41). This makes representation a core concept for political scientists. Additionally, its semantic neighbor "representativeness" (see below) is a central feature in recent debates concerning the democratic level of political institutions and processes (Guinier 1994, Paolino 1995). Nonetheless, there has been disagreement about its nature and definition: "'Representation' is one of the slippery core concepts of political theory" (McLean 1991: 172).

Gendering representation? Naming the concept

Like "gendering democracy" (Paxton, in this volume), "gendering representation" does not introduce a new concept; neither does it add an adjective to an existing "mother category," thereby creating a new subset. Gendering representation is a scientific activity that consists of describing, analyzing, and explaining the gendered nature of the "who" and the "what" of political representation. Representatives, representation, and representativeness are and have always been gendered; gendering representation concerns the investigation of the gendered character of these concepts.

Gendering representation is more than mapping, analyzing, and explaining inclusion and exclusion of sex and gender in (the praxis of) representation. It is also a feminist activity. Ultimately, gendering representation and representativeness aims at improving these concepts and their operationalization; that is, at making them more inclusive and therefore more just and democratic (see also Paxton, in this volume). It adds gendered conditions to representation and representativeness as ideal types regarding the inclusion and exclusion of sex and gender. The underlying rationale is that representation is successful only when it is also representative in terms of sex and gender. It is evident that such critical examinations of representation should not be limited to the categories of sex and gender. For instance, similar investigations can be conducted regarding inclusion and exclusion on the basis of race, age, ethnic background, class, and sexual orientation.

Dimensions of political representation

Reduced to its essence, representation is the making present of something or someone (principal) who is not literally present through an intermediary (agent) (Pitkin 1969: 16). This implies that not only the presence of the represented via the representative is a necessary component of representation, but their absence is too; inclusion and exclusion are inherent aspects of the concept (Judge 1999). Essential to political representation is that a mediating representative or assembly of representatives is set between the citizenry and political decision-making, and therefore it is the antipodal of direct political decision-making (Brennan and Hamlin 1999). Representativeness is an indication of the degree to which the representative (be it a person, an object, or an institution) succeeds in making present the absent that is being represented.

Although useful, this basic definition of representation is not sufficient. It does not give answers to important questions such as: "Why is that mediating person or assembly 'representative'?" "Why are their presence and actions 'representation'?" "What constitutes representation and the representative?" The answers to these pertinent questions refer to formal participation, the identity of the representatives, and their acts (Dimensions Guideline).

Who are the actors?

Representation as a formal participation and as "standing for"

A first component of representation consists of a formal agreement between the representative and the represented (Pitkin 1969: 13; see also Griffiths 1960, Birch 1971, 1993, Braud 1985). Thomas Hobbes's Leviathan is a representative because he is given that authority. The people are bound by the acts of the Leviathan. In this conception, there is no escape from representation (except for not belonging to the people). Others stress that neither the initial act of giving authority nor obedience is crucial in the formal relationship between the representative and the represented. What constitutes the representative and representation is the fact that, as a result of calling the representative into account, the formal agreement can be ended. Although the initial act of handing over authority to the representative is indispensable, if it leads to the represented being regarded as passive "recipients" of the representative acts and commitments an essential part of representation is missed. Subjects must also have control over the representative and not solely the other way around (Pitkin 1972: 232).

The "mandate" – issued by the represented and binding them, limited in scope and/or time, initiated and/or terminated in a characteristic way – is the formal component of political representation. It implies a set of rules and techniques that organizes the input and the output of the process of representation – that is, the election of representatives and information about the preferences of the represented – that are closely linked with legitimacy and efficiency (Hirst 1990, Judge 1999, Sartori 1987). Although representation is much more than structures, regulations, and elections, they are an indispensable part of it.

A second approach to representation focuses on the representatives, on who they are and what they stand for (Pitkin 1969, Griffiths 1960, Birch 1971, 1993, Braud 1985). Descriptive representation stresses the accurate composition of the parliament. Taken together, the representatives mirror the people they represent. Who they are and what they look like are what count. The representatives provide information about the (perceived) desires, views, or interests of the constituents. Therefore, the resembling composition also assures that the representatives *would* act the way the represented would. In this view, direct democracy is the ideal (Brennan and Hamlin 1999).

A specific kind of representation through "standing for" is symbolic representation (Pitkin 1969, Griffiths 1960, Birch 1971, 1993, Braud 1985). A king or a flag represents a nation because of symbolic qualities. Not the resemblance, but the fact that people acknowledge the symbolic quality of an object or a person, is what constitutes representation.

Gendering formal and descriptive representation

Historically, women and men were not considered to have the same capacities to give and receive the authority to represent (Pateman 1988; see also Paxton in this volume). Generally, women were granted the right to vote and to be a candidate later than men. This excluded them for a long time from formal and descriptive participation. Although it was claimed that a woman participated through her father's and subsequently her husband's votes (Sapiro 1981), and an exclusively male parliament represented them symbolically (Mansbridge 1999, Phillips 1995), the absence of the right to vote implied that representatives were not directly accountable to women. Today, women in most countries are fully enfranchised. Nonetheless, in most states women are still underrepresented on a formal and descriptive level, for instance on candidate lists and in assemblies. To counter the lack of representativeness of the political institutions, parity laws and quotas have been applied in progressively more countries to break through barriers hindering women's formal and descriptive participation (Dahlerup 2006, Krook 2004, Meier 2002, Squires 1996). Proponents of descriptive representation point to the importance of role models, to justice and democratic values – there exists no democratic argument to justify male overrepresentation in political decision-making structures – and to the legitimacy of institutions, especially in the case when substantive representation fails (Phillips 1995, M.Williams 1998). The traditional argument against is that it might entail representatives of mediocre quality (Birch 1993, N. Norton 1995).

What and who is represented (and by whom)?

Representation as "acting for"

Formal, symbolic, and descriptive forms of representation do not deal with a crucial aspect of representation, notably "what is going on during representation" (Pitkin 1969: 9). That is the domain of representation as "acting for." Substantive representation is about what representatives do: "acting in the interest of the represented, in a manner responsive to them" (Pitkin 1972: 209). This conception of representation places the subject and the relationship between the representative and the represented in the center of attention. What is to be represented? How is the principal represented? Who decides on what is in the interest of the represented: the representative or the represented? Depending on the answers to these questions, the representative sees his/her role as a trustee (independent from the represented) or as a delegate (with no independency). Not only were these questions dealt with by theorists, but also there exists a rich body of empirical research (Thomassen 1994).

Edmund Burke is well known for his plea for the representative as a trustee. In his view, parliament is a forum where the interests of the constituencies are formulated by the representatives and subsequently reconciled as the "general interest." Since the represented are absent in parliament, they do not know what is the "general interest," and thus their own interests either. Burke's ideas are children of their time. Representation was, as in the Middle Ages, territorially based and interests mainly material. The extension of the right to vote, which made the object of representing "the people" and not merely the economic interests of a territory, called for a different representative role.

Nonetheless, representation of territorial and material interests is still an element of political representation (Judge 1999).

The representative's position with regard to the represented should not be considered static, absolute, and polarized (Pitkin 1969, Judge 1999, Eulau *et al.* 1978, Sobolewski 1968). A representative can behave as a trustee or a delegate and also as a "politico" expressing both orientations, either simultaneously or serially (Eulau *et al.* 1978: 119). A representative's behavior is determined by "metapolitical" considerations concerning, for instance, the nature of the issues and the capacities of both the representatives and the represented: representatives will act as trustees when they are considered to be superior in wisdom and experience to the represented, and political problems are supposed to have a clear and objective solution that can be defined through a rational investigation; representatives will act as delegates when representatives and the represented are considered to have equal capacities and when political issues are more linked with personal preferences, thereby making objective, rational deliberation inapt (Pitkin 1969: 19–21). Moreover, the representative's acts and activities are based primarily on the judgment of the party and not on her/his own opinions or on those of the electorate (Pitkin 1972: 215; Judge 1999, Sobolewski 1968). The "constituency" of the representative is plural and consists of concentric circles: the nation or the territory, the political party, and functional groups (Fenno 1978).

Recently, the debate regarding "What is represented?" and more specifically the trustee position is taken one step further by scholars such as Mansbridge[2] (1998, 2003) and Saward (2006), who consider "creative" acts to be fundamental aspects of representation. "Anticipatory representation" (Mansbridge 1998, 2003) is motivated by winning future voters and is based on what the representative thinks the voter of the next election will prefer. In my view, this implies that, to a certain extent, the interests of the represented are a creation by which the representative hopes to please the future voter, who will in turn approve the representative's actions by reelecting her/him. The

[2] Jane Mansbridge (1998, 2003) distinguishes four "faces of representation." "Representation by promising" implies that the representative will act for the represented according to what he/she promised during the election. Voters vote for the candidate because of what she/he promises and plans to do. In the case of "introspective" or "gyroscopic representation," by contrast, voters vote for a candidate because they expect the candidate to act in a certain way according to internal principles and convictions. "Surrogate representation" occurs when representation takes place notwithstanding the fact that there exists no formal tie between the representative and the represented (for instance, because they are situated in different constituencies). "Anticipatory representation" is motivated by winning the future voters and is thus based on what the representative thinks the voter in the next election prefers. In this case, voting behavior is based on retrospection.

creative aspect of representation is more explicitly dealt with in Saward's work on political representation. He rejects the assumption often present in the delegate–trustee debate that interests exist prior to their representation; that they are "out there" and can be brought into the representational process. During representation the representative creates the represented, as well as himself/herself and the audience, via "representative claims": "The 'interests' of a constituency have to be 'read in' more than 'read off'; it is an active, creative process, not the passive process of receiving clear signals from below" (Saward 2006: 310). Pushed to its limits, this implies that the represented exists by virtue of the representative, who subsequently seems to become the principal and the represented agent.

Gendering substantive representation

Gendering substantive representation refers to representation of women's interests and gendering the general interest. A crucial evolution in feminist political theory in the 1980s and 1990s concerns the demarcation of "women's interests". In the early 1980s, scholars like Virginia Sapiro, Irene Diamond, and Nancy Hartsock tried to define women's interests (Sapiro 1981; Diamond and Hartsock 1981). According to Sapiro, political women's interests are a consequence of the different social positions that women occupy. More precisely, it is the "private distribution of labor" – that is, the tasks of giving birth to and care for children – that makes women take up different socioeconomic positions than men and that gives them distinct interests (as a group) that are politically "representable." According to Diamond and Hartsock, on the contrary, women's common interests are the consequence not of the division of tasks inside the household but of the gendered division of productive labor (Diamond and Hartsock 1981: 194–6). They prefer the more enclosing terms *wants* and *needs* above the utilitarian vocabulary coinciding with the promotion of interests. They thereby refer to female values, behavior, and psyche that have been determined through two studies on the socialization of women in that period (Rich 1976, Chodorow 1978). The scholars of group representation of the 1990s, on the contrary, keep their distance from an essentialist image of the woman (Phillips 1995, 1998, Young 1997). "That which has to be represented" (women's interests)[3] results from the diversified life experience

---

[3] Phillips uses the terms "interests" and "needs" together. According to Phillips, interests and needs both come forth out of the life experience of women, and together they are what needs to be represented (Phillips 1995: 73). This chapter applies the same enclosing definition of women's interests.

of different groups of women. Women's interests then, are *a priori* undefined, context-related, and subject to evolution.

What is at stake in the case of gendered representation is not only the inclusion of women's interests, but also the gendering of the general interest (Lovenduski 2005a: 19; Stokes 2005: 20; see also McBride and Mazur in this volume). In opposition to Phillips, Iris Marion Young suggests that the link between being a woman and representing women is not about interests and needs, but about social perspectives, in particular the way in which people interpret things and events from within their structural social situation (Young 1997, 2000). Social groups are structured around differences such as gender, race, nationality, and religion, but she stresses that these groups cannot be defined through common interests or through similar opinions. Therefore, women cannot be represented as a group based on such shared interests and opinions. Substantive representation of a social group means representing the social perspective of that group deriving from its structural position in society. It is crucial in a democratic dialogue because in that way it will count for all citizens, provide information about the diversity of social perspectives, and lead to more justice.

A second important evolution in feminist political theory concerns the way in which the relationship between descriptive and substantive representation is perceived. The "critical mass theory" – more precisely the way Drude Dahlerup's statements about the importance of numbers of women were interpreted (Dahlerup 1988, Childs and Krook 2005) – supposed a strong relationship between being female and acting for women: women *will* make a difference if they have the numerical strength. The "politics of presence theory" (Phillips 1995, 1998), on the contrary, does not refer to numbers of women. Furthermore, it contends that the link between women members of parliament and the political representation of women is "half-fastened": the *possibility* that women are represented increases when women are present.[4] According to Phillips, the link between descriptive and substantive representation is based on women's life experiences. It is this structural position in society that causes a specific background of experiences and knowledge (Tamerius 1995). Because of their biology and their roles in society, women have personal experiences that are different from men's as well as a gendered perspective on situations and experiences that are objectively the same. Furthermore, shared experiences and perspectives foster group identification, which in turn fosters

---

[4] A similar argumentation can be found in the work of Anna Jónasdóttir (1988), Melissa Williams (1998), and Jane Mansbridge (1999).

sharing experiences. The latter is also due to socialization and to working in groups and contexts that exclude the other sex.

This shared gendered life experience not only provides "resources" in terms of consciousness and expertise for the substantive representation of women, but also impacts upon their assessment of priority of and engagement for representing women (Tamerius 1995; Phillips 1995). Furthermore, the presence of women also enables a "politics of transformation" (Phillips 1995, 1998). Interests and needs are not external data entered in political decision-making; they take shape during political decision-making. Only in the most optimal circumstances, in particular when a group is systematically present in the process of working out alternatives, is it capable of formulating new subjects and challenging dominant conventions. Young (1994, 2000) also contends that making the social perspective of women present can be achieved only by persons who share the experience that goes with a structural position in society, as the people in this position are sensible to certain subjects, questions, or events. Paraphrasing Mansbridge and Saward: female representatives have specific resources of knowledge and expertise to create the female representative and her interests, and to claim to represent them. These resources can be tapped into when representatives behave as trustees and rely on their own insights and internal principles: what Mansbridge terms "gyroscopic" representation.

Necessity and interdependency of the dimensions

None of the dimensions described above – formal participation, or descriptive or substantive representation – is essential to representation (Necessity Guideline). A representative can be imposed on me, but still represent me if she takes my interests to heart. I can acknowledge a person to be my formal representative, even if he neither looks like me nor acts for me, or even if he harms my interests. However, since the essence of representation is the making present of the absent, the represented has to be made present by the representative in at least one way, be it formally, descriptively, symbolically, *or* substantively. In other words, at least one of these dimensions needs to be present in order to claim that representation takes place. Given the variety of instances in which representation takes place, representation is not an ideal type.

Theoretically, the formal, descriptive/symbolic and substantive dimensions of representation are also not interdependent (Interdependence Guideline). One dimension can occur without the presence of the other dimensions.

For example, a member of parliament who does not look like me and was not elected by me can substantively represent me (for instance, in the case of "surrogate representation"). However, empirical research shows a strong relationship between these dimensions. Formal participation (e.g. as candidates and electorate) often is a prerequisite for descriptive (e.g. female legislators) and substantive representation (e.g. through inclusion of women's issues in the party program). Furthermore, feminist scholars point to the existence of a necessity and causal relationship between descriptive and substantive representation, which will be extensively dealt with in my final section.

Representation versus nonrepresentation, and the zones in between

Until now, I have focused mainly on what representation is or might be. Another way of defining the concept is by drawing its borders by defining the antipodal or negation of representation (Negation Guideline). Within the framework of democracy, direct participation in politics can be seen as the antipodal of representation, which is an indirect way of participating in political decision-making. The antipodal or negation of representation in a more general way is nonrepresentation, in the sense of being excluded from the formal, descriptive/symbolic, or substantive dimension of representation (left column of Table 4.1). For instance, I am not represented by the parliament of my country when I am not involved in electing its members *(Case 1)*, when there are no MPs who look like me *(Case 2)*, act in my interests or harm them *(Case 3)*. Furthermore, exclusion can affect not only the represented but also the representatives. For instance, I can rightly state that I am excluded from representation when I am not allowed to stand for elections and be elected *(Case 1)*, or when I, as a representative, cannot look like the people of a constituency *(Case 2)* or act in their interest *(Case 3)*. Representation of women and gendered representation (right column of Table 4.1) occurs on numerous moments; for instance, when they are enfranchised *(Case 4)*, when female legislators are present in parliament *(Case 5)*, when bills in favor of women are introduced, and when their perspectives on general issues are taken into account *(Case 6)*.

The above list of instances in which representation takes place and when it does not (left and right columns in Table 4.1) does not imply that representation and nonrepresentation constitute an absolute dichotomy. Between the

Table 4.1 Dimensions of representation

	FORMAL		
No formal representation *(Case 1)* +	*Lower* ← →*Higher* *(Case 7)* *(Case 8)*		(Full) formal representation *(Case 4)* +
	DESCRIPTIVE		
No descriptive representation *(Case 2)* +	*Lower* ← →*Higher* *(Case 9)* *(Case 10)*		(Full) descriptive representation *(Case 5)* +
	SUBSTANTIVE		
No substantive representation *(Case 3)* + ↓	*Lower* ← →*Higher* *(Case 11)* *(Case 12)*		(Full) substantive representation *(Case 6)* + ↓
NONREPRESENTATION	DEGREES OF REPRESENTATION		REPRESENTATION IDEAL TYPE

poles of representation and nonrepresentation lies a whole zone of degrees of representativeness[5] (Zones Guideline). Representativeness refers to a continuum between the negative pole "nonrepresentation" and the positive pole "representation" (middle column of Table 4.1). In addition, between the poles of representation and nonrepresentation of women's bodies, ideas, and gendered perspectives, lies a zone of "degrees of representation": the representativeness of the formal, descriptive, and substantive dimension of representation in terms of sex and gender. There exist different degrees to which people can be included in the formal dimension of representation; for instance, in those cases where active and passive suffrage was not granted simultaneously and in the case of plural vote system, where some citizens (male, rich, highly educated, married with children) have more than one vote. Possible positions on the continuum between formal representation and nonrepresentation in terms of sex and gender can also be found in Virginia Sapiro's work on representation of women (1981). She distinguishes three

---

[5] Also, between the poles of direct democracy and indirect or representative democracy, exists a whole range of possibilities that are more direct or indirect; for instance, by combining instruments like referendums and hearings with more traditional channels of decision-making via representatives.

phases in the political representation of women. At first, women were represented by their husbands, as man and woman had become one legal person by marriage *(Case 7)*. The husband was seen as the head of the family and he represented the family's interests (Sapiro 1981: 161). Through the husband's vote, married women were held to be involved as well. During the nineteenth century a second phase started: women obtained the full right to political representation as individual members of the political community. The feminist movement, however, subsequently demanded that women (just as other groups) would not be represented as individuals, but as members of a group *(Case 8)*.

There also exist quantitative and qualitative degrees of descriptive and substantive representativeness (in terms of sex and gender) according to the following: the number of representatives who stand or act for the represented or the number of moments when substantive representation takes place; the quality of descriptive and substantive representatives (measured, for instance, by degree of resemblance, status, power, financial resources, or degree of activity); and the quality of substantive representation (measured, for instance, by range, inclusiveness, degree of congruency with the will of the represented). An example of a position between descriptive representation and nonrepresentation in terms of sex and gender is what Carroll (1984) terms "closet feminists": female politicians who refuse to identify with the women's movement *(Case 9)*. An example of a position closer to the positive side of the continuum can be found in what Dovi (2002, 2007) labels "preferable descriptive representatives" who have "strong mutual relations with the dispossessed groups of historically disadvantaged groups" (Dovi 2002: 729) *(Case 10)*. An intermediate position on the substantive representation–nonrepresentation continuum in terms of sex and gender could be discerned by the extent to which expertise and knowledge were investigated in the representation of women, whereby a "lower" degree of substantive representation implies a low level of expertise and knowledge, for instance in the case of voting for women (Tamerius 1995) *(Case 11)*. Degrees of substantive representation could also be defined by looking at the range of the women's interests represented: a "higher" degree of substantive representation of women is reached when a more diverse group of women is represented (Trimble 1993, 1997, 2000; Celis 2006) *(Case 12)*.

Furthermore, the degree of representation (the representativeness) can not only be measured within each dimension, but also by combining them. On the negative pole of this scale, no dimension is present (left column of Table 4.1, marked in light gray); on the positive side, all three are. Moreover, this way of defining degrees of representation can be combined with degrees of representativeness within each dimension, as described in the above paragraphs. Then an ideal type of representation can be identified[6] (right column of Table 4.1, marked in dark gray), implying: (1) a full and equal formal participation (e.g. the right to vote and stand as a candidate, the absence of a gender bias in all aspects of the electoral system and political culture); (2) descriptive representation of men and women reflecting the composition of society as a whole, thereby assuring that the assembly would act the way the represented would act themselves; and (3) substantive representation including representation of women's interests and the gendering of the general interest. Furthermore, this ideal type is a part of representation in general as an ideal type. "One hundred percent" representative representation can be reached only when representation is "100 percent" representative regarding sex and gender. By extension, it is also fully representative only when, for instance, classes, ethnic minorities, heterosexuals and homosexuals, and the young and the old, are fully formally, descriptively, *and* substantively represented.

Empirical research on gendering representation

Empirical research investigating the gendered dimensions of representation deals with the formal and descriptive participation of women and/or their substantive representation. As mentioned before, the necessity order and causal relationships between these aspects is above all an empirical question (Necessity and Causal Relationships Guidelines). It has been a key question in empirical research regarding political representation of women since the 1970s and still is today, albeit that its theoretical underpinnings evolved and its focus was broadened to include institutions. The long history illustrates a high potential to travel, which, as I will argue, can be increased by avoiding freezing the content of substantive representation (Traveling Guideline).

Research on women's formal, descriptive and substantive representation

Empirical research regarding gendered aspects of formal and descriptive representation focuses on describing the evolution towards full enfranchisement, on mapping the numerical force women and men constitute in politics (e.g. Karam 1998), and on explaining the status quo. Recruitment, selection, and

---

[6] On the contrary, nonrepresentation is not an ideal type, since cases of absence of formal, descriptive, *and* substantive representation are more frequent.

election of candidates cause descriptive underrepresentation of women in politics, parliaments, and governments worldwide (Leyenaar 1997). Not only informal barriers such as political culture and tradition, but also more formal features of electoral systems (i.e. majority systems and open candidate lists) are among the more important explanations for the male dominance in politics (Laver, Leyenaar, Niemöller, and Galligan 1999, Farrell 2006, Caul 1999, Matland 1995). Except for the mechanisms causing the underrepresentation of women, the qualitative dimension of the formal and descriptive participation of women, for instance by taking the status of female representatives into account (e.g. Norton 1995, 2002), is far less developed.

Descriptive representation is not only about the presence and the number of women, but also about whether the representatives *would* act the way women would act themselves. This concern is dealt with in empirical research that investigates the attitudes of female representatives regarding the representation of women's interests and their views on general matters. The most frequently analyzed attitudes in this respect are the recognition of the existence of women's interests (e.g. Skjeie 1998); sensitivity to a responsibility to devote attention to them (e.g. Whip 1991) and to lend priority to them (e.g. Thomas and Welch 2001); and the degree of congruence between the points of view of women members of parliament on the one hand and the female citizens (e.g. Diaz 2005) and women's movement (e.g. Reingold 2000) on the other. According to a number of recent studies, women MPs as a group have a greater potential to represent women (e.g. Whip 1991); these conclusions, however, were not always applicable to all women MPs (e.g. Diaz 2005) or for every attitudinal dimension (e.g. Reingold 2000). It is clear that these attitudes are situated in a gray zone between descriptive and substantive representation, since they are an important prerequisite for "acting for" women, a category that I nevertheless reserve for "acts" as distinguished from "thoughts."

Empirical research about the gendered aspect of substantive representation has traditionally evolved around the question: "Do women represent women?" This link between descriptive and substantive representation of women has been empirically tested since the 1970s. Empirical research on gendered substantive representation mainly focuses on parliaments and on legislative activity: initiating, accompanying, and voting of legislation in favor of women (e.g. Reingold 2000, Swers 2002a, Wolbrecht 2002), and participation in parliamentary debates in favor of women (e.g. Cramer Walsh 2002, Trimble 2000). Some studies confirm the existence of a link between the fact that the representative is a woman and voting for women (e.g. Swers 2002a, 2002b, 2002c), speaking in favor of women (e.g. Cramer Walsh 2002), and working on legislation in favor of women (e.g. O'Regan 2000, Carroll 2001). Other studies discard the existence of such a connection (e.g. Tremblay 1998). These studies also contend that a multitude of political, parliamentary, social, and individual situations hamper the wish to represent women in practice, or interfere with its contents. Party affiliation seems to be the most influential factor (e.g. Purdy 1991, Reingold 2000).

Whether or not a "critical mass" of women MPs influence women's substantive representation has been a main question in empirical research on the necessity and causal relationship between descriptive and substantive representation of women (Childs and Krook 2006, Mackay 2004). The expectation that women are likely to "make a difference" once they constitute a "critical mass" (Kanter 1977, Dahlerup 1988) is a key feature in this research (Childs and Krook 2005, Lovenduski and Norris 2003). Although the theses of Drude Dahlerup were often misinterpreted, and although there exists but little proof for the critical mass effect on substantive representation (Grey 2002, Trimble 1997), it is a powerful argument for claiming more female representatives (Childs and Krook 2005).

The descriptive "presence of women" can be conceived in an individual way, as most scholars do, but also in structural terms. In the field of substantive representation, the recent "institutionalist turn" implies investigating the role played by women's policy agencies and the women's movement (see Mazur and McBride, and McBride and Mazur, in this volume). Here also, the main questions are whether or not, and in what way, the presence of these institutions (descriptive level) fosters the substantive representation of women. Research on state feminism explains under what circumstances women's policy agencies are successful in advancing the goals of the women's movement (Lovenduski 2006; Mazur 2001; McBride Stetson and Mazur 1995; Outshoorn 2004; McBride Stetson 2001; Squires and Wickham-Jones 2004; Franceschet and Krook 2005). Women's movements and women's policy agencies might even be more effective in gendering substantive representation than female legislators are; institutional change and mobilization subsequently become more important than increasing the number of descriptive representatives in parliament (Weldon 2002b).

Making the concept travel

The research regarding descriptive and substantive representation has long been predominantly Anglo-American and mainly focused on the USA and Western Europe. Nevertheless, gendering representation is clearly able to travel through time (as became clear in the overview above), but also through space, and to adapt itself to specific political contexts. Questions regarding the participation of women in the formal and descriptive dimensions of representation, and as to whether descriptive representation (in the form of individuals or institutions) enhances substantive representation, are relevant and possible in each political system in which descriptive representation occurs. They are taken into account in recent research on democratization processes in Russia, East Central Europe, Latin America, and South Africa (Waylen 2007; Nechemias, 1994; Matland and Montgomery 2005), and on the enlargement of the European Union to include East Central European nations (Galligan, Clavero, and Calloni 2007). Also, Latin America is obvious research territory, given the widespread use of gender quotas and the installation of women's policy agencies (Htun and Jones 2002, Taylor-Robinson 2005, Franceshet 2005, Stoffel 2008; Zetterberg 2008).

The fact that the research tradition only recently broadened its geographical gaze tells more about the differences in interests of the political science communities than about the possibility of investigating the gendered aspects of representational practices. Nevertheless, the western geographical roots of the research tradition, especially in the case of the substantive representation of women, might hinder the concept from traveling. Substantive representation of women was often operationalized in such a way that it reflected the needs, interests, and concerns of western women, feminists, and women's movements. Investigating the substantive representation of women in political and cultural contexts other than American and Western European needs to take these other contexts into account. This can be done by applying a formal operationalization of substantive representation that would not only make the empirical research more apt to travel and suited for comparison across time and space, but would also solve problems that existing empirical research faces with regard to recent theoretical premises.

In the major part of the research relating to the active parliamentary representation of women by female MPs, as well as the role women's policy agencies play in the substantive representation of women, a thematic selection of women's interests was made in advance, and subsequently used to measure activity in favor of women. The (large or limited) thematic selection carried out by various empirical researches generally takes two forms. First, the thematic selection often contains subjects concerning the traditional roles of women and/or subjects with a clear feminist accent. A second thematic operationalization that one finds in many researches consists of selecting a number of current themes of the women's movement. To illustrate this, I concentrate on the operationalization of women's issues in research regarding the parliamentary representation of women. Nevertheless, the discussion and conclusion also apply, for instance, to state feminism research by RNGS, also partially featuring a thematic approach to substantive representation (e.g. abortion, prostitution, job training, and political representation) (Mazur and McBride in this volume).

Traditional and feminist women's interests

In their research about the impact of female representatives on the representation of women, Dodson and Carroll (1995) included women's rights bills that, on the one hand, relate directly to women or have a feminist undertone, and, on the other hand, laws concerning women's traditional arenas of interest, which relate to the role of women as "dispensers of care" inside the family as well as in society, and to themes such as healthcare and education. In more recent research, one also often finds an operationalization of women's interests in a similar "double" way (e.g. Reingold 2000, Cramer Walsh 2002, O'Regan 2000, Carroll 2001, Meyer 2003, Taylor-Robinson and Heath 2003). Christina Wolbrecht (2002), for instance, investigated women's rights legislation concerning job possibilities, salary equality, women's health, abortion rights, and education, to assess whether female representatives in the House of Representatives from 1953 to 1992 were responsible for the growth and the diversification of women's rights. Wolbrecht concluded that women MPs proposed more of these laws and were most active in proposing new subjects and new policy solutions.

The thematic demarcation of women's interests in empirical research raises some problems. First, although the content of women's interests has not been without discussion since the 1980s, the selection of women's interests is rarely accounted for. In addition, a reflection on the possible consequences of the inclusion and exclusion of issues on the research results is mostly absent. Second, when including "traditional" women's interests, they are sometimes interpreted so widely that the link with women's interests is almost lost. It is hardly sustainable to consider every theme related to children and family (Cramer Walsh 2002, Carroll 2001) as a women's interest. These themes can, of course, given the traditional role of women, contain a gender dimension, but that does not *per se* apply to every theme regarding children or family.

The main problem with the illustrated thematic delimitation of what one considers in the research as women's interest is that it tends to "freeze" or essentialize women and their interests and to deny diversity among women. It also hinders the research question from traveling to different political contexts and time periods. Furthermore, a thematic demarcation does not keep pace with the previously described evolution on the theoretical level that actually distances itself from an essentialist female identity. Therefore, it does not seem to be an interesting trail for future empirical research that wants to connect with the more recent theory about female representatives and the representation of women (see also Celis, Childs, Kantola, and Krook 2008).

Interests of the women's movement

A second thematic operationalization consists in selecting a number of current themes of the women's movement. In some cases, researchers select one or more current feminist themes; in other cases, they start from an overview of program or attention points of a specific women's network or organization. As opposed to thematic operationalization as described above, researchers avoid the subjective manipulation of the selection – and thus also in a certain way the definition – of women's interests (e.g. Dolan 1997, Swers 2002a, 2002b, 2002c). In this case, the selection is left to an external actor: the women's movement or a women's network. Burrell (1994), for instance, based her research on the themes of the chart of the National Women's Political Caucus: equal representation in the National Commission for Neighborhoods tax reduction for childcare facilities, flexible hours for federal civil servants, family planning, federal abortion subsidies, rise of minimum salaries, and gay rights. Based on the voting behavior of these subjects, Burrell showed that in the period from 1987 to 1999, women supported these laws more than men.

The generalization of the program of the women's movement, even though it avoids a subjective selection by the researcher and even though it leads to a very large palette of involved women's interests, is, however, facing three limits. First, as a method of operationalizing women's interests and substantive representation of women, it supposes the existence of a women's movement that is able to formulate claims. This might not be the case in nondemocratic states, and thus this operationalization might hinder traveling to other political contexts. A second objection is that the total population of women is not backing the demands of the women's movement (Sawer 2000). In other words, the representation of feminist interests cannot be identified without problems with the representation of women's interests. Third, the feminist program taken into consideration is mostly reduced to its leftist-progressive variety (an exception being Swers 2002a, 2002b, 2002c; regarding the variety in the women's movements see McBride and Mazur in this volume). The diversity of points of view and visions of the feminist movement is mostly neither recognized nor translated into the research. Karen Offen (2000: 21–2) distinguishes two threads in (European) feminism, in particular a relational and an individual current. The relational feminist current strives to a gendered but equal organization of social relations between sexes and stresses complementarities, equality as "equal value," and the partnership between men and women as the foundation for society. The individualist feminist current, on the other hand, gives the individual and the equality between individuals a central place. The strong focus on the latter in the empirical research tradition causes the researched themes to be only a partial reflection of the demands of the women's movement and therefore an even worse reflection of the interests of all female citizens. And again, the latter and the first point of critique make clear that this form of operationalization might not be suited for traveling to other cultural and temporal contexts.

An open and formal operationalization of women's interests

The empirical research tradition does not travel well. Furthermore, there exists a discrepancy with the recent theories formed about "women representing women" that give a lot of space to diversity and evolution within women's interests, and wish to avoid the essentialization of women. Taking into account the diverse and changing character of women's interests and its theoretical *a priori* "undefinability" is what empirical research will best achieve if it does not determine the content of women's interests in advance. The concrete outline of women's interests therefore also has to be a subject for study. In other words, the research on the relationship between descriptive and substantive representation is only a second research step following the study of the content of substantive representation of women as such. Next to the advantage of a better connection with the theory, this operationalization could also be a master key enabling the research on the substantive representation of women to travel across cultural and temporal contexts and become apt for cross-cultural and historical comparisons.

Theoretically, this can be done in two ways. The first way would be to trace exhaustively what women themselves consider as their interests and to check afterwards what the relationship is between the representation of these interests and the sex of the representatives. This option immediately creates many new problems: among others, its size, the methodology to be used to map women's interests, and – again – the changing character of women's interests. A second way to operationalize the research that enables one to take the theoretically *a priori* undefinable character of women's interests into account consists in using a formal definition of substantive representation of women that does not make claims regarding the content. A formal delimitation of "what has to be represented" dismisses the researcher of the task to carry out an "essentializating" selection. Such an operationalization or research step can be found in research by Reingold (1992), Trimble (1993, 1997, 2000), Childs (2001, 2004), Bratton (2002), Wängnerud (2000), and Celis (2006).

Reingold (1992) used a very large operationalization of women's interests in her research, notably that which politicians themselves pointed out as being women's interests. Trimble (1993, 1997, 2000) based her research on the Hansard Index, a written copy of the debates in the Canadian Parliament, accessible through keywords. Each time an MP referred to women, their lives, or their political needs, this was encoded under the keyword "women." She could thus also draw conclusions concerning the activities of men and women MPs regarding gendering the apparently gender-neutral legislation. This seems very relevant, given the current theories that indeed point out the possibility that women can have, concerning any subject whatsoever, a potentially different experience and thus a specific interest or perspective. Furthermore, the approach made comparisons between men and women MPs possible, which is also indispensable to making statements concerning the specific contribution of women MPs to the substantive representation of women.

Not delimiting women's interests in advance and, on the contrary, leaving it to the representatives, are things one also finds in research that describes the perception of the contribution of female representatives to the representation of women. Sarah Childs (2001, 2004) did in-depth interviews with 34 of the 65 "new intake" women of the Labour MPs in the first three months after the 1997 General Election in Britain. Half of the interviewed Labour women stated that their presence allowed the expression of women's interests concerning such themes as violence on women, childcare, education, equal chances, and employment.

Lena Wängnerud (2000) and Kathleen Bratton (2002) also apply a formal definition of (the representation of) women's interests. However, they have a different view on the operationalization used by Trimble, Reingold, and Childs because they fix the object of the representation of women's interests. Bratton defines women's interest legislation as "bills that may decrease gender discrimination or alleviate the effects of such discrimination and those that are intended to improve the socioeconomic status of women" (2002: 123). According to the definition of Wängnerud, women's interests have to contain three elements: (1) the recognition of women as a social category; (2) the recognition of a power unbalance between men and women; and (3) the wish to implement a policy that increases the autonomy of female citizens. Although discrimination and autonomy are broad concepts, they connect with a rather equality-oriented, individualistic vision of "what is in the interest of women." A similar approach thus again contains the danger that the diversity among women will not be taken into account.

In my own research on the representation of women in the Belgian Parliament, I used a formal operationalization that strongly follows the one used by Trimble and Reingold (Celis 2006). I operationalized "representing women ('s interests)" as follows: "to denounce a situation that is disadvantageous for women, to formulate a proposal to improve the situation of women or to claim a right for women with the same goal." I mapped such interventions between 1900 and 1979, during the most central political debates in the Belgian Parliament: the budget debates in the Lower House. Through this formal definition, I obtained a view on what the MPs themselves considered as women's interests, which contained a wide variety of women's interests as well as perspectives on what was in the interest of women. Subsequently, I compared the parliamentarily represented women's interests with the series of demands of various women's movements. This operationalization allowed me, first, to obtain an indication of whether and to what extent the parliamentary representation of women connected to what "women themselves" wished, and, second, to detect a specific contribution of women MPs – notably, they broadened the dominant vision of what was "in the interest of women" and realized a higher congruence between parliamentary substantive representation of women and the way "women themselves" perceived their interests. Although the formal approach also has a number of disadvantages – mainly capturing only explicit claims that were considered appropriate in the specific context – its main advantage entails not giving an essentialist content to the substantive representation of women and respects the theoretical assumption that women's interests are *a priori* undefined, context-related, and subject to evolution.

Conclusion

Gendering representation is a feminist research praxis that describes, analyzes, and explains the gendered dimensions of political representation. Its central question regards the inclusion and exclusion of women and gender in various dimensions of representation; namely, formal participation, and descriptive and substantive representation. The aim of gendering representation lies also in enhancing the inclusiveness of the concept of political presentation and its praxis in terms of sex and gender.

A key contribution to the latter ambition is the theory linking descriptive and substantive representation: descriptive representativeness possibly furthers substantive representativeness. Whether that is actually the case is an empirical question. Empirical research is challenged, though, by theoretical evolutions in respect of the diverse character of women's interests and gendered perspectives. A formal operationalization of substantive representation meets these demands. Besides the advantage of synchronizing empirical research and recent theories about representation, applying a formal operationalization will make the research question more apt to travel to other cultural and temporal arenas and application in a wide range of political and cultural contexts. Longitudinal and international comparative research can in turn broaden our knowledge about the content, actors, sites, and contexts of substantive representation across time and space (Celis, Childs, Kantola, and Krook 2008).

5 Gendering the welfare state

Diane Sainsbury

The concept of the welfare state can trace its origins to World War II and the politics of persuasion. After an interlude of consensus the welfare state became the source of political controversy and continual debate. Despite this, or perhaps because of it, welfare state research stands out as one of the most productive areas in comparative political analysis in the accumulation of social science knowledge. The research has often been problem-or question-driven (Pierson 2000), and a major strength has been its political and social relevance. Simultaneously, many prominent scholars in the field have lamented the sorry condition of the welfare state as a social science concept, noting that "the welfare state . . . has generally received scant conceptual attention" (Esping-Andersen 1990: 18). Thus it is not entirely surprising that the conceptual venture of gendering the welfare state has concentrated on incorporating gender into the comparative analysis of welfare states rather than reformulating the concept itself. Nevertheless, gendering comparative welfare state research has altered the concept of the welfare state.

This chapter begins with an examination of the concept of the welfare state, using several of the guidelines discussed in chapter 2; the purpose of this introduction is to present the concept prior to its gendering. The next section discusses what is meant by gendering and presents different analytical strategies to gender the welfare state. A major argument here is that gendering the welfare state has been a much more complex conceptual enterprise than solely adding on to the existing concept. The third section focuses on the Operationalization Guideline. It illustrates how the specification of the concept dimensions growing out of the efforts to gender the welfare state has affected their operationalizations in empirical research. The concluding discussion deals with how gendering the analysis has modified the concept of the welfare state and the research agenda.

The concept of the welfare state

The guidelines presented in chapter 2 are not only valuable as an aid in formulating new concepts; they are also useful in revealing the limitations of existing concepts. The Context, Naming, Negation, Zones, and Dimensions Guidelines point to a number of problematic aspects of the early formulation of the welfare state concept and the scholarship it generated.

The term "welfare state" was first coined in Britain during World War II. By contrasting the welfare state with the Nazi warfare state, it was used to bolster morale and provide a vision of postwar reform. Thus the term itself was the result not of intellectual inquiry but of a political act. Influential researchers have also shied away from the welfare state, preferring other names. Among those who were partial to other names was William Beveridge, the major architect of British postwar reforms. He preferred the "social service state" (Flora and Heidenheimer 1981: 20), which highlighted the innovative aspects of the reforms. Richard Titmuss was skeptical of "the indefinable abstraction 'The Welfare State'" (1968: 124), but even so, his most influential book of the 1950s was entitled *Essays on "The Welfare State"* (1958). Instead, he favored "social policy"; and several American scholars, including Hugh Heclo (1974: 2) and Theda Skocpol, followed in his footsteps. Besides objecting to the abstract nature of the welfare state, Titmuss worried about a problem related to the Negation Guideline – the concentration on the positive pole. He was concerned that the name "welfare state" assumed that state policies contributed to people's welfare, and he argued that policies required careful empirical analysis to determine the nature of their outcomes.

Despite its political baggage and several scholars' discomfort with the name, the welfare state captured an important political phenomenon – the increasing involvement of the state in social provision. The reforms in many countries immediately after the war, along with the subsequent expansion of social programs, attracted the attention of scholars, who transformed the term into a concept. By the 1960s, the welfare state had become an established social science concept, as witnessed by its inclusion in the *International Encyclopedia of the Social Sciences* (Girvetz 1968).

Early efforts to systematize the concept of the welfare state focused on specifying the goals or purposes of state intervention and its forms. The necessary dimension of the concept was state responsibility in providing for citizens' well-being; and the secondary level dimensions consisted of types of social programs and policy goals. The goals ranged from security, equity, and equality to self-development. The instruments consisted of a social minimum; social protection from the risks of old age, sickness and disability, and unemployment; and provision of services, such as education, healthcare and personal services – or a combination of all three, as in Asa Briggs's formulation (1961). Alternatively, researchers provided a laundry list of the policy areas forming the core of the welfare state (e.g. Girvetz 1968).

The joining up of "the state" and "welfare" suggested a research agenda where the welfare state was both the independent and the dependent variable. In the first case, the research problem was the impact of the welfare state, and in particular the redistributive effects of welfare state policies (Titmuss 1958). The second research problem was to explain the rise of the welfare state, and this was the focus of much of the early scholarship.

The early classics emphasized either political or economic explanations of the development of the welfare state. In *Citizenship and Social Class*, T. H. Marshall (1950) stressed a political explanation embodied in the process of rights extension – the evolution from civil rights to political rights and ultimately social rights on the basis of citizenship. He also formulated his now famous definition of social citizenship as "the whole range from the right to a modicum of economic welfare and security to the right to share to the full in the social heritage and to live the life of a civilised being according to the standards prevailing in society" (1950: 11). Conversely, other social scientists, including Harold Wilensky and Charles Lebeaux in *Industrial Society and Social Welfare* (1958), viewed the emergence of the welfare state as the functional response to economic development and, in particular, industrialization. A difficulty in Marshall's explanation was the existence of ambitious social programs in predemocratic states and the communist countries, while the industrialization thesis covered these cases.

A generic notion of the welfare state and an emphasis on commonalities informed much of the early scholarship. In terms of the Operationalization Guideline, it was generally assumed that all countries which had introduced major reforms expanding the state's involvement in social provision represented the welfare state. Accordingly, all cases clustered in the zone near the positive pole. This was possible because of the generalized specifications of the welfare state, and many scholars classified a country as a welfare state if it met one or two of the specifications.

Nor were cross-national variations considered a matter of importance. In fact, the conceptual process made this difficult. The welfare state was specified in terms of its defining properties, which were not conceptualized as dimensions of variation. For example, researchers frequently designated a specific goal as intrinsic to the welfare state, ruling out the possibility that goals or purposes could be a welfare state variation. Furthermore, the most useful distinctions in the literature were framed as variations within a country rather than cross-national differences. Initially the residual/institutional distinction was formulated as coexisting conceptions of social welfare in the United States. The residual conception viewed social welfare as an emergency measure to meet human needs when there was a failure in the natural channels of welfare: the family and the market. In the institutional view, social welfare was "the organized system of social services and institutions, designed to aid individuals and groups to attain satisfying standards of life and health" (Wilensky and Lebeaux 1965: 138–40, 147, at 139). Similarly, when Richard Titmuss presented his three models of social policy – the residual, the work performance, and the institutional models – he did not link them to specific countries (1974: 30–2). He stressed that the models represented different criteria for making policy choices involving distributive justice; and later in his discussion Titmuss used the experiences of the UK to illustrate all three models, although he also exemplified the residual model with contemporary developments in the USA.

The comparativist turn

The 1970s witnessed a major reorientation, which can be described as a comparativist turn; and the research problems became the *causes* and *consequences* of welfare state variations. Efforts to explain the rise of the welfare state had produced accounts of many nations' experiences. As a result, the problematic nature of generalizing the development of the welfare state on the basis of a single country's experience became increasingly clear, as did the variety of trajectories and outcomes across countries. The focus of scholarship shifted to comparing welfare states, conceptualizing types of welfare states and dimensions of variation, and theorizing the causes of welfare state variations. The comparativist turn also entailed the analysis of large N's using quantitative techniques. In terms of the guidelines in chapter 2, there was a shift in the prominence given to the Dimensions, Causal Relationships, and Operationalization Guidelines.

Two main approaches have been used in conceptualizing types of welfare states and dimensions of variations. The first has examined a specific country or set of countries with the purpose of describing its/their distinctive features (e.g. Furniss and Tilton 1977, Rainwater *et al.* 1986; Esping-Andersen and Korpi 1987). A problematic aspect of this approach, besides the issue of

broader applicability, is that these features might actually constitute dimensions of variation. The second approach has identified dimensions of variations based on contrasting ideal types, either polar opposites (Mishra 1977,
Korpi 1980) or trichotomies (Esping-Andersen 1990, Scharpf and Schmidt
2000: 11). This approach resulted in a richer specification of the dimensions
of the welfare state compared to previous formulations.

In constructing his influential welfare state regime typology, Gøsta Esping-
Andersen combined both approaches. His major dimensions of variations
were: decommodification (independence from the market) through social
rights; the system of stratification produced by social rights; the relationship
between the state, market, and family in the provision of welfare; and the welfare state's impact on employment. However, each regime type was specified
by its distinctive features. The causal mechanisms underpinning the regime
types consisted of the nature of class mobilization, class political coalition
structures, and the historical legacy of regime institutionalization (class and
ideological preferences and political behavior) (1990: 29–33). Importantly,
the typology's dimensions of variation were primarily welfare state outcomes,
which represented a departure from earlier models where the dimensions were
often policies or policy attributes.

The explanatory reorientation involved synthesis, the development of new
theoretical perspectives, and attention to additional factors so that consideration gravitated increasingly toward political determinants. Scholars constructed analytical frameworks that brought together economic, social structural, and political factors (Flora and Heidenheimer 1981: ch. 2; Uusitalo
1984; Flora 1986).[1] Among the major political explanations was the development of the power resources perspective highlighting class mobilization and
organization (Wilensky 1975, Stephens 1979, Korpi 1980), class coalitions
(Esping-Andersen 1985), and the constellation of parties and the partisan
composition of the executive (Cameron 1978, Korpi 1980). Policies themselves
became an explanatory variable; policy attributes affected popular support
(Wilensky 1975; Korpi 1980) and policy legacies shaped future policy options
(Heclo 1974). Increasing importance was also assigned to state structures –
centralization versus decentralization and the capacities of bureaucracies
(Heidenheimer 1973, Heclo 1974, Wilensky 1975, Cameron 1978, Ashford
1986, Skocpol and Amenta 1986). Researchers also resurrected values and

---

[1] For a graphic illustration of differences over time concerning the incorporation of political factors in
explanatory frameworks, compare Wilensky and Lebeaux (1965: 230) and Uusitalo (1984: 411).

ideologies (Furniss and Tilton 1977, Ashford 1986), which had been eclipsed by economic and functional explanations.

The growing prominence of quantitative comparisons involving large N's to test the strength of alternative explanations also required the development of numerical indicators of the concept and the explanatory variables, elevating the attention given to operationalizations. In these analyses the standard indicator of the welfare state was social spending as a percentage of the GDP, initially social security expenditures (Wilensky 1975). The welfare state concept underpinning most of the quantitative studies highlighted social insurance programs and especially pensions, which were the costliest (see Goertz 2005: 46, 59).

The traveling capacity of the concept has been considerable, even though the welfare state both as a term and as a concept grew out of British experience. Almost immediately it was applied to all industrialized nations – both capitalist democracies and communist countries. Ironically, as the comparativist turn gained momentum, the communist countries moved into the background; the ascendancy of political explanations meant that researchers usually selected only the capitalist democracies, where politics could come into play. This practice also delayed the inclusion of Spain, Portugal, and Greece in comparative welfare state studies. Since the 1990s the geographical reach of the concept has extended to new democracies in the Mediterranean and Eastern Europe, the newly industrializing countries and the developing countries (Esping-Andersen 1996; Mkandawire 2004). In traveling to the developing countries, specific concept dimensions regain relevance; the place of health services and education has been restored, in line with the thinking of Beveridge, Marshall, and Titmuss.

What aspects of the concept and its common operationalizations precluded the gendering of welfare state research? The concept has focused on the state–market nexus and the scope of state responsibility for social provision. Several dimensions of the welfare state were conceptualized in terms of more or less state intervention, such as social spending, scope of program coverage, or benefit levels. Likewise, the ideological dimension had to do with state intervention and the principles of distributive justice; and the public and private spheres referred to the state and the market. Ever since the emergence of the industrialization thesis, paid work and programs to protect workers from market risks have been central, and the development of the power resources perspective privileged class and class relations. Esping-Andersen's elevation of decommodification to a welfare state dimension reinforced the centrality of work and social insurance schemes, since decommodification assumes the prior commodification of labor. Data availability and operationalizations additionally strengthened this emphasis. Social security statistics and data on social expenditures and public revenues, compiled by the International Labour Organization and Organisation for Economic Co-operation and Development, were readily available; while severe data limitations existed for other social programs and services. A typical operationalization has been to measure the social rights of the standard production worker as reflected in social insurance benefits (Korpi 1989, Esping-Andersen 1990). Data considerations contributed to a narrowing of the core policy areas of the welfare state over the years. Increasingly the welfare state was equated with income maintenance programs. In short, the theorizing that shaped the concept of the welfare state and the conduct of welfare state research crowded out a consideration of the family as a provider of welfare and gender relations. The task of gendering the welfare state was even more difficult because much of the theorizing was implicitly gendered in that it was rooted in men's experiences and men were the center of analysis.

Strategies to gender comparative welfare state research

Around 1990, several feminist scholars identified a major gap in welfare state research. Most feminist studies were limited to a single nation upon which the analysts drew universal conclusions, and there was a general neglect of the importance of national contexts as a variable. As a result, country specificities were conceived as intrinsic features of the welfare state rather than welfare state variations. By contrast, mainstream comparative research focused on welfare state variations, but gender was missing from its analyses. This realization triggered a major intellectual venture and discussion on how to gender comparative welfare state research. It was also accompanied by a major shift in the understanding of what gendering entailed. Initially, feminist scholarship on the welfare state had sought to bring gender into the analysis by focusing on women and their relationship to the welfare state. This approach was increasingly replaced by a strategy based on gender as a relational category where the inquiry explicitly dealt with both women and men (O'Connor 1996). Interest focused on how gender relations were inscribed in welfare state policies and conversely how policies were a force in patterning gender relations.

Three major strategies to gender comparative welfare state research immediately suggested themselves: the utilization of existing constructs to analyze gender and the welfare state; refashioning constructs to enable a meaningful analysis of gender; and the development of new analytical frameworks and concept dimensions. Debate and differences have revolved around two broad approaches: whether to highlight gender separately and devise new analytical constructs, or to build gender into existing frameworks. Both approaches have gendered the welfare state by inserting gender into the existing dimensions of the concept and constructing new dimensions.

Highlighting gender separately

Many feminist scholars have concentrated on formulating new frameworks that focus on gender. They were wary of mainstream schemes and concepts because they were implicitly gendered by making the male the norm. A major thrust was to devise gendered typologies and gender-sensitive dimensions of variation. Gender relations were the point of departure; and in much of their theorizing, the causal mechanism was gender relations. This led them to emphasize the gender division of labor and its key components – care and paid work.

The gender division of labor

Among the first efforts to bring gender relations into the comparative analysis of welfare states was the work of Jane Lewis (1992), together with Ilona Ostner (1991, 1994). They constructed a typology based on the gender division of labor typified by the breadwinner model, where men are family providers and women are homemakers and caregivers. In developing their typology, they singled out women's treatment in the social security and tax systems, the level of social service provision, especially childcare, and married women's position in the labor market. In effect, they inserted gender into the existing dimensions of the welfare state having to do with social security programs by calling attention to how the gender division of labor affected women's ability to claim benefits in their own right; but they also extended the core of welfare state provision to childcare.

The typology distinguished between the strong breadwinner model (Britain, Ireland, Germany, and the Netherlands), the moderate breadwinner model (France), and the weak breadwinner model (Sweden), later dubbed the dual breadwinner model or the dual earner model. Of major importance was that their analyses revealed that there were variations in the strength of the breadwinner model across welfare states, and their classification of countries deviated from the clustering of countries in Esping-Andersen's regime typology. A problematic feature, however, was the existence of a single underlying dimension of variation to capture gender relations in welfare states and the assumption that the male breadwinner model underpinned the policies of all countries. Nor did the typology tap the effect of policies on the situation of single mothers, which sharply differed across strong breadwinner states (Hobson 1994). Later, Lewis and Ostner (1994) acknowledged that too many countries with dissimilar policies fitted into the category of strong breadwinner states.

Diane Sainsbury's strategy (1994, 1996) consisted of specifying a set of dimensions of variation, using two polar opposites – the breadwinner model and the individual model of social policy. Thus, in contrast to Lewis and Ostner's framework, the negative pole of the breadwinner model was the individual model. The dimensions were the familial and gender ideology, principles of entitlement (basis, unit, and recipient of benefits, unit of contribution), the tax system, employment and wage policies, and the organization of care work. The framework also distinguished between social rights and benefits that were familialized (based on family relations) and those that were individualized.

These dimensions were employed to analyze the policies of the Netherlands, Sweden, the United Kingdom, and the United States (1996). The countries were chosen because they represented a broad array of variations, and the key research question was: What differences do welfare state variations make for women (and men)? The empirical task was not so much to classify the countries as model types but to utilize the dimensions to uncover similarities and differences in the gray zone between the two polar opposites. A chief difficulty of the framework is that it limits policies to two opposite poles. For example, the organization of care work falls between the family and the state, without considering the market or other nonstate providers (Orloff 1996: 71). Nevertheless, the framework proved useful in delineating policy differences and similarities across the four countries; and it revealed a third type: the separate gender role model that celebrates differences between women and men but, as distinct from the male breadwinner model, confers social rights to both sexes on the basis of these differences. The analysis also resulted in quite a different classification of countries compared to mainstream typologies. The most striking difference was that the policies of the Netherlands and Sweden, often bracketed together because of their generous welfare states and high decommodification scores, represented opposite extremes when gender was incorporated into the analysis, especially from the 1950s to the mid-1980s.

In moving beyond the single pole of the male breadwinner model and the polar opposition of male breadwinner and individual models, Rosemary Crompton (1999, 2006), drawing heavily on Birgit Pfau-Effinger (1999), sketches a continuum of gender relations featuring five categories of households with different earner–carer arrangements: (1) male breadwinner / female carer; (2) male breadwinner / female part-time earner; (3) dual earner / state carer; (4) dual earner / marketized carer; and (5) dual earner / dual carer. Other analysts have used these earner–carer arrangements to analyze welfare state policies (Gornick and Meyers 2003) and the intersection between these earner–carer arrangements and welfare state regimes (Pfau-Effinger 2005).

An additional line of development has been to construct gender policy regimes as a counterpart to welfare regimes, which rest on the assumption that a specific state–economy organization produces a policy logic of its own. In a similar fashion, a gender policy regime embodies a given organization of gender relations associated with a specific policy logic. The organization of gender relations is shaped by principles and norms (gender ideologies and practices) that prescribe the tasks, obligations and rights of the sexes. Accordingly, gender policy regimes can be distinguished on the basis of ideologies that describe actual and/or preferred relations between women and men, principles of entitlement, and policy constructions. The typology's dimensions were used to analyze the inscription of gender relations in the policies of the social democratic regime countries – Denmark, Finland, Norway, and Sweden. Sainsbury also examined the interplay between the dimensions of the gender typology and those of the welfare regime typology (1999: ch. 3) and later the dynamics between the policy logics of welfare state regimes and gender policy regimes across countries representing different welfare regimes (1999: ch. 8).

The care dimension

All the analytical constructs discussed above point to the importance of care, and many feminists have sought to elaborate the nature of care and the care dimension, which is missing in the mainstream concept of the welfare state (O'Connor 1996: ch. 2). The dimension has evolved from emphasizing the nexus between unpaid work, paid work, and welfare, where unpaid work was equated with care, as in the original male breadwinner typology (Lewis 1992), to developing an encompassing concept of care.

To elevate the importance of care in welfare state analysis, Lewis (1997) proposed devising caring regimes based on the crucial variations of how unpaid work is valued and how it is shared among women and men. More specifically,

Barbara Hobson suggested two alternative care regimes. The first assumes that all mothers are carers, and single mothers are entitled to a social wage as caregivers. The assumption of the second regime is that mothers are workers; care services are available so that mothers can engage in paid employment, and compensation for care is based on labor market status (Hobson and Takahashi 1996). The construction of caring regimes also centered on the right to care and to receive care (Knijn and Kremer 1997).

In arguing that unpaid work was not synonymous with care, Jane Jenson (1997) was instrumental in bringing about a shift toward a more comprehensive concept of care. She called for making care central in theorizing the gender construction of welfare state policies. According to her, this would entail an analysis of "the gender division of labor among caregivers, gender differences in the capacity or need to pay, and the gender consequences of different institutionalized arrangements for provision" (1997: 187). Later, in a preface to a comparative analysis of childcare across four countries and the European Union, Jenson emphasized the need to rethink the welfare state in terms of its core, arguing that access to care rather than protection against unemployment has been a primary issue. This perspective also highlighted a new set of policy goals: the redistribution of the costs of care, improving the quality of care, and enhancing the autonomy of persons receiving care (Jenson and Sineau 2001).

Finally, Jane Lewis and Mary Daly developed social care as a multidimensional concept for analyzing welfare states and welfare state change (Lewis 1998; Daly and Lewis 2000). As a corrective to the existing fragmented consideration of care, the concept encompasses care services and care-related cash benefits, formal and informal care, public and private care, and focusing on the division of care labor (responsibilities and costs) between the family, the market, the state and the voluntary/community sectors. They further argued that social care involves a dynamic and thus lends itself to the analysis of welfare state change. More precisely, the dynamic relates to the shifting boundary of the welfare state in the provision of care. Although they stressed the concept's capacity to analyze the gender dimension of social policies and differences in benefits received by women and men, a disturbing feature of their discussion is that it devotes no attention to either employment outside the provision of formal care or to work-related benefits.

In conclusion, a major strength of the strategy of highlighting gender separately has been its efforts to conceptualize how gender relations are encoded in welfare state policies. This approach also allows for an analysis of the interaction between gender-sensitive dimensions of variation and mainstream dimensions. A serious shortcoming is that the approach is incomplete to the extent that it adopts an exclusive focus on gender.

Building gender in

Turning to the second broad approach, Ann Orloff's (1993) analytical framework represents the most cogent and systematic effort to build gender into existing mainstream constructs.[2] More generally, her point of departure was the power resources perspective and, more specifically, Esping-Andersen's regime typology. Orloff's strategy entailed both refashioning the key dimensions of variation of the typology by incorporating gender and complementing them with two new dimensions. The dimension – *state, market and family relations* – required elaboration because, as feminist critics observed and Esping-Andersen (1999: 47) later conceded, it was only mentioned and not developed in his analysis. Orloff proposed that this dimension specifically address (1) the role of the family and women's unpaid work in providing welfare, (2) the gendered nature of care provided by other institutions (the market and state), and (3) how state policies affected women's and men's unequal power in the family. The *stratification* dimension was redesigned to examine gender hierarchies in social provision. Orloff stressed retaining *decommodification* because it "protects individuals, irrespective of their gender, from total dependence on the market for survival" (O'Connor 1993: 513, cited in Orloff 1996: 72). However, women's disadvantaged position in terms of commodification necessitated two new dimensions. The first dimension was *access to paid work*, which assigned attention to state policies that promote or discourage women's paid employment. Second, to provide a gauge of the quality of social rights of those who do domestic and care work, she formulated the dimension, *the capacity to form and maintain an autonomous household*.

This framework served as the foundation for an analysis of four most similar countries, representing the liberal welfare state regime – Australia, Canada, Great Britain, and the United States. The choice of countries was dictated by the desire to understand the differences and likenesses of countries of this regime type, the early prevalence of feminist research focusing on most different countries, and a number of specific research questions (O'Connor, Orloff, and

---

[2] In an article published within months of Orloff's, Julia S. O'Connor (1993) proposed a similar framework, and she and Orloff joined forces in refining the framework (Orloff 1996: 71–2). Other scholars who worked to gender Esping-Andersen's regime typology included Anette Borchorst (1994), Siv Gustafsson (1994), and Jet Bussemaker and Kees van Kersbergen (1994, 1999).

Shaver 1999: 37–42). The research questions included how country differences were related to liberalism, notions of equality, and the levels of responsiveness to women's concerns. The analysis focused on three key policy areas: the labor market, income maintenance, and the regulation of reproduction.

Since this important book, scholars building gender into mainstream analysis have analyzed specific types of gender inequality outcomes across welfare regime types. In particular, mainstream analysts of the power resources school have examined how the features of different welfare state regimes shape policy outcomes for women and families (Esping-Andersen 1999; Korpi 2000; Huber and Stephens 2001).

A major strength of this approach, as put by Orloff, is that the advances in the mainstream literature can be incorporated in feminist research, at the same time as mainstream analysis is transformed through the incorporation of gender relations (1993: 305). The framework also focuses on the gender and class effects of welfare state policies. Ten years on, efforts to include both gender and class appear all the more important, since most feminist research on welfare states has privileged gender at the expense of class (see Weldon in this volume). Moreover, the framework and its dimensions have broad applicability, lending themselves to the analysis of countries representing other regime types, across regime types, and countries not included in Esping-Andersen's regime typology, as well as historical case studies and comparative analysis. Finally, by directly engaging mainstream literature, it has promoted a dialogue between feminist and mainstream researchers; and mainstream researchers have recognized the insights and new knowledge generated by the inclusion of gender relations (e.g. Pierson 2000).

Despite the differences in approaches, common denominators exist. At bottom, each approach has focused on gendering the dimensions of the welfare state, which has entailed refashioning and complementing existing dimensions as well as examining the dynamics between old and new dimensions. Similarly analysts representing both approaches have combined feminist and mainstream insights. Initially a shared research problem was whether Esping-Andersen's regime typology would hold up if gender were included in the analysis.

In other respects, the approaches have complemented each other. Several dimensions in Orloff's framework are welfare state outcomes, while the dimensions of the other frameworks are policy attributes. Orloff (1993) and O'Connor (1993) put more emphasis on women's mobilization as a determinant of gendered welfare state outcomes. Lewis and Sainsbury stressed familial and gender ideologies as a determining factor and paid more attention to taxation, or fiscal welfare, as a policy affecting gender relations. Their early studies focused on most different countries, while O'Connor, Orloff, and Shaver (1999) concentrated on most similar countries. Thus each approach has provided insights, and together they have enriched the comparative analysis of welfare states and gender. In sum, both approaches have recast the analysis of welfare states, and the analytical constructs produced by the two approaches clearly demonstrate that gendering the welfare state has been a much more complex conceptual enterprise than merely adding on to the existing concept. It has involved incorporating gender into the existing dimensions of the concept, questioning the necessary dimension of the concept, and developing new concept dimensions.

Concept dimensions and operationalizations

As noted in chapter 2 in the discussion of the Operationalization Guideline, it is better practice to operationalize concept dimensions rather than the entire concept. In gendering the welfare state, feminist researchers developed several dimensions of the concept. This section discusses concept dimensions and their operationalizations, focusing on gender stratification and a variety of dimensions formulated as parallels or complements to decommodification. Its purpose is to illustrate how specifications of the dimensions affect operationalizations and their application in empirical research.

Gender stratification

The gender stratification dimension, according to Orloff, involves gender differentiation and gender inequality. More specifically, gender differentiation is evidenced, first, in separate programs for labor market and family needs and, second, in claiming benefits on the basis of the traditional division of labor between the sexes. Men claim benefits as family providers and workers, while women claim benefits as wives and mothers. Gender inequality refers to differences in benefit levels stemming from the gender division of labor. Benefits tied to participation in the workforce are usually more generous than benefits claimed on the basis of wifely or motherly labor, and women's unpaid work also adversely affects their engaging in paid employment. Orloff's operationalization consists of a comparison of the existence of separate programs for labor market and family failures, the bases for claiming benefits, and the relationship between gender differentiation and gender inequalities in benefits across the four liberal regime countries (O'Connor, Orloff, and Shaver 1999: 141–3).

In analyzing the stratifying effects of welfare policies, Sainsbury (1996) places major emphasis on the principles of entitlement. She uses a wide range of principles, by combining the bases of entitlement in both the feminist and mainstream literature. The three principles of entitlement in the mainstream literature are need, labor market participation, and citizenship/residence, while feminists have noted the importance of wifely and motherly labors as a crucial basis of entitlement for women. Sainsbury distinguishes between women's entitlements as wives (rights via their husband) and as mothers (rights based on the principle of care). Also of special significance to gender stratification is how the principle of care intersects with other bases of entitlement, specifically need, labor market participation, and citizenship/residence. She maps out women's and men's access to benefits, and benefit inequalities between women and men, using statistics on beneficiaries (1996: ch. 6 and 7).

Mary Daly (2000) emphasizes access to benefits, the gender bases of claiming benefits, and the financial returns accruing to different kinds of claims. Thus there are clear parallels to Orloff's stratification dimension. An important innovation in Daly's operationalization is the inclusion of both individuals and households, and she uses survey data on family expenditures and sources of income (2000) and data from the Luxembourg Income Study (Daly and Rake 2003).

Beyond decommodification

Feminist researchers have formulated alternatives or complements to decommodification. As brought out earlier, Orloff has developed the dimension of the capacity to form and maintain an autonomous household as a parallel indicator of the quality of social rights of persons performing domestic and care tasks. She defines autonomous as "without having to marry to gain access to breadwinners' income" (1993: 319). This specification tends to focus on single mothers, although Orloff argues that it potentially pertains to married women by allowing them to exit a bad marriage. Still, it seems to give inadequate attention to the situation of married women who do not want to leave their husbands and especially to those in low-income families. It overlooks the fact that the same policy measure, for example means tested unemployment benefits or tax benefits, such as the USA's federal Earned Income Tax Credit, have very different consequences for single mothers and for married women. Orloff operationalizes this dimension by examining the social benefits available to mothers without access to a male breadwinner's income, primarily social assistance and the eligibility rules of these programs. The rules concern whether assistance is an entitlement program, that is, a guaranteed social right; the existence of work requirements to be eligible for benefits; and child support by fathers. A final crucial aspect is whether the benefits of these programs provide an adequate income (O'Connor, Orloff, and Shaver 1999: 32–3, 148–56, 111).

O'Connor recommends that decommodification be supplemented by the concept of personal autonomy or insulation from personal and/or public dependence. At first glance, this formulation in relation to social provision seems to highlight the importance of social insurance benefits based on labor market participation. However, she further elaborates that a "central element of insulation from dependence is the extent to which public services are available as citizenship rights as opposed to a dependence enhancing income and/or means-tested basis" (1993: 511–12, at 512). These specifications point to an operationalization that involves women's access to work and social insurance benefits, women's benefit levels in these schemes, and the range of public services whose entitlement is based on citizenship or residence. Conversely, to assess dependence the operationalization would center on social rights derived from husbands' rights and means-tested benefits.[3]

The parallel dimension of decommodification proposed by Ruth Lister is defamilialization, which she defines as "the degree to which individual adults can uphold a socially acceptable standard of living, independently of family relationships, either through paid work or social security provision" (1994: 37). Several researchers have utilized this dimension in empirical research, leading to diverse operationalizations.

Among these researchers are Majella Kilkey and Jonathan Bradshaw (1999), who emphasize that a gender-sensitive typology must examine how welfare states structure women's access to both paid employment and caregiving. They adopt defamilialization, taking single mothers as an analytical category

---

[3] O'Connor's dimension of personal autonomy or insulation from personal and/or public dependence is conceptualized in terms broader than social provision (1993: 511–12).

because they are both breadwinner and carer and their situation can elucidate how welfare states construct the relationship between work and care for all women (1999: 154). Their operationalization encompasses access to paid employment, the tax/benefit system (primarily taxation and social assistance), and poverty. Kilkey and Bradshaw also note that they do not measure whether benefits are linked to family status, which is a key component of Lister's formulation. Instead, they assume that since single mothers are living independently of men, the key question is whether they can achieve an acceptable standard of living either through paid employment or through benefits that support caregivers.

In revisiting his regime typology, Esping-Andersen also utilizes the defamilialization dimension, which he paraphrases as "policies that lessen individuals' reliance on the family; that maximize individuals' command of economic resources independently of familial or conjugal reciprocities." He defines the negative pole of defamilialization as assigning a maximum of welfare obligations to the household (1999: 45). His operationalization centers on family policies and policies creating incentives or disincentives for married women to work outside the home. Four indicators related to family policies are used to capture the degree of defamilialization across welfare states: (1) expenditures devoted to family services as a percentage of the GDP, (2) spending on subsidies to families (cash transfers and tax benefits) as a percentage of the GDP, (3) coverage of public childcare for children under three years of age and (4) the percentage of the elderly receiving public home help services (1999: 61). His policy indicators affecting married women's employment are the benefit loss for an unemployed person if the spouse works, and tax increases if the wife works (1999: 72). A problematic aspect of his operationalization, however, is the inclusion of cash transfers and tax benefits for children, since they can support either traditional family roles or unconventional ones. Historically, several countries with generous benefits introduced them to ease the support burden of the male family provider. Other operationalizations of defamilialization that include maternity benefits run into similar problems if the analyst does not introduce additional criteria to distinguish between measures that support mothers as carers and as workers.

To sum up, operationalizations are a crucial link between concepts and empirical research, and two points need to be stressed. First, the specifications of a concept dimension have important ramifications for the empirical analysis, that is, whether the researcher chooses one particular specification in preference to another, for example, selecting the capacity to form and maintain an autonomous household or defamilialization. Second, even if analysts select the same concept dimension, such as defamilialization, our examples reveal quite different operationalizations. Thus it is vital to clarify the steps in operationalizing the dimension so that research findings contribute to the accumulation of generalizable knowledge.

Impact on the concept

The gendering of comparative welfare state research has altered the concept of the welfare state in several ways. Perhaps the most noticeable impact has been a series of dimensions that have broadened the concept with respect to the nature of social provision, social rights, and the bases of entitlements. Social provision is not limited to the major social insurance schemes and the safety net, but also encompasses family benefits, parental/maternity benefits, and other care-related benefits – as well as a wide range of services. Rethinking social rights from a gender perspective has concerned both *what* rights and *whose* rights. Social rights include protection not only against market failures but also against family failures and rights of personhood or bodily integrity, reproduction rights, and the right to care and to receive care. Equally important, a gendered analysis of social rights focuses on whether rights are accorded to families or to individuals. The gendering of welfare state research has involved an analysis of the bases of entitlement of *all* beneficiaries. The bases of entitlement are no longer confined to need, work performance, and citizenship/residence, but also comprise the principle of care, the principle of maintenance, and the derived rights of adult dependants in the family. The underlying dimension of the concept has expanded from state responsibility for welfare to the interlocking activities of the state, market, and family. Ultimately this conceptualization of the welfare state includes not only modifying social and market forces but also ending male domination in society (Orloff 1996: 52).

From the outset, feminist analysis of the welfare state has focused on the policy outcomes for women and on discrepancies between women and men in the impact of policies. Gendering the comparative analysis of welfare states has clarified both the underlying commonalities and scope of variation in welfare state outcomes. The commonalities included gender segregation and inequalities in the labor market, disparities in benefit income, and imbalances in responsibilities for unpaid work. Among the significant cross-national differences are the possibilities of combining employment and family responsibilities, the privileging of different types of families, the familialization versus the individualization of social benefits, and the redistributive impact of transfers and taxes in reducing gender inequalities and women's poverty (cf. Daly and Rake 2003: 153, 155).

A gender lens in welfare state analysis has also brought new determinants of welfare state development into focus. First, mainstream analysts have considered the importance of the "isms" in shaping welfare states and policy outputs, while feminist scholars have attached major weight to gender and family ideologies (see Duerst-Lahti in this volume) or alternatively gender cultures and family values as a determinant of gender policy outcomes. The ideological or cultural factor assumes significance at the societal level but can also influence the ideologies and strategies of women's movements. At the societal level, gender ideologies influence the policy process by providing or denying legitimacy to the policy proposals of various groups.

A second determinant, totally ignored by mainstream analysis, has been women's organizing and the role of women as political actors in the construction of social provision. Women actors seem to have exerted more influence on policies of direct concern to them, such as maternity benefits and child allowances; however, their clout has varied dramatically across countries, time, and issues. Among the variables central to their influence have been movement resources and strategies (see McBride and Mazur in this volume); access to the policy process, the state, and political parties; and alliance-building and the partisan composition of the government. Feminist researchers have also examined women's organizing and demands as a source of welfare state variation across countries and among countries representing the same welfare regime type (Bock and Thane 1991, Skocpol 1992, Koven and Michel 1993, Hobson and Lindholm 1997, O'Connor, Orloff, and Shaver 1999, Sainsbury 1999, 2001, Huber and Stephens 2001, Annesley 2003, Bergqvist 2005, Haussman and Sauer 2007).

Third, feminist analysis has revealed that religion as a political force is a decisive variable. Mainstream analysis has either largely glossed over religion as a determinant of welfare state development or limited its significance to one regime type or type of welfare state – the conservative corporatist regime (Esping-Andersen 1990) or the Christian democratic welfare state (van Kersbergen 1995, Huber and Stephens 2001). Initial studies of gender equality policies found different outcomes in Catholic and Protestant countries (Schmidt 1993, Siaroff 1994, Gardiner 1997). Subsequent analysis questioned the paramount importance attributed to the Catholic–Protestant divide, noting that religious mobilization in the form of political parties, influential party factions, or core constituencies of parties has had a policy impact irrespective of whether the country was Catholic or Protestant (Sainsbury 1999: 268–9). The most compelling and insightful analysis to date is Kimberly Morgan's study (2006) of the determinants of different work–family policies (parental leave, working hours, and childcare) in France, the Netherlands, Sweden, and the United States. Her main research question is: Why are the countries' policies for working mothers so different? A major argument is that church–state relations and religious divisions shaped educational policies and the role of the state *vis-à-vis* the family, producing four distinctive patterns. The policy legacies from this early period subsequently influenced the type of work–family policies adopted in the 1960s and 1970s.

In conclusion, the 1990s saw a breakthrough as mainstream scholars recognized gender and the welfare state as a major area of research. The span of its research agenda (its traveling capacity) has successively included other regions, such as Eastern Europe and the former Soviet Union (Pascall and Manning 2000), East Asia, and the global South (Razavi and Hassim 2006). Despite the many accomplishments of the 1990s onward, a question mark looms large. To what extent will mainstream researchers integrate a gender perspective in their own work? This question is especially pertinent in the case of research on welfare state retrenchment and restructuring. By not incorporating a gender perspective, there is a real danger of inaccurate specification of the dependent variable – welfare state change. While major social insurance schemes have been downsized, care-related benefits represent an area of expansion in several countries. Second, a major thesis in this literature is that retrenchment and cutbacks have produced a different type of politics compared to welfare state expansion. Again, without considering gender, the retrenchment literature might miss a crucial element of the new politics of the welfare state – the greater clout of women as political actors in several countries. Conversely, in countries where women are a weak policy constituency, failure to bring gender into the analysis inflates the picture of welfare state resilience and ignores the large-scale disentitlement of women in the 1990s. In short, future comparative welfare state research would profit from a deeper synthesis of the insights of feminist and mainstream perspectives.

6 Gendering governance

Georgina Waylen

Since the late 1980s, governance has become a central concept used not only by political scientists and other social scientists but also by policymakers and politicians located at the local, national, regional, and global levels. Indeed, Peters and Pierre (2000: 1) argue that "one key reason for the importance of this concept is its capacity – unlike that of the narrower term 'government' – to cover the whole range of institutions and relationships involved in the process of governing." However, the broadening out from the study of government to governance has also resulted in an ambiguous, complex, and all-embracing concept that is both useful and problematic. There is no one definition that all practitioners and social scientists agree upon, and, as a result, the concept is used in many different ways. For example, Bevir and Rhodes (2003) list seven different definitions of governance: governance as new public management; governance as international interdependence; governance as a socio-cybernetic system; governance as the new political economy; governance as corporate governance; governance as good governance; and governance as networks.

But although the term "governance" can be applied to almost any institution or organization, this chapter looks at the ways "governance" is used by political scientists both conceptually and within different subdisciplines. In her overview of the governance literature in political science, Kjaer (2004) outlines the varying uses and definitions that are evident in the three different subfields that have been most interested in governance: public administration and public policy; international relations / international political economy (IR/IPE); and comparative politics. The governance literature in public administration has been primarily concerned with the tasks, organization, management, accountability, and structure of the public sector. IR/IPE

I would like to thank Francesca Gains and particularly Matt Flinders for their helpful comments and advice on earlier versions of this chapter.

has focused more directly on the impact of globalization and the growth of international organizations and nongovernmental organizations and their activities, and particularly on how to establish rules and procedures that can help to lessen the challenges that result from intensified globalization. The literature falling broadly under the heading of comparative politics is, according to Kjaer (2004), often concerned with the formal and informal rules of the game and the exercise of power in setting and implementing rules as well as with the state and social relations. It has also looked at the role of governance within development and particularly the role of "good governance."

Obviously there is considerable overlap between these three areas. Indeed, as evidence of this, Kjaer (2004) cites the example of the burgeoning literature on multi-level governance, much of which has focused on the Europen Union and the different levels – local, national, regional – associated with it, and has drawn on scholarship in the different subfields of public policy, comparative politics, and IR/IPE. Furthermore, much of the governance literature from all subfields uses variants of institutionalist theory and is broadly concerned with the setting and management of the political rules of the game and the search for control, steering, and accountability (Kjaer 2004: 11). However, as already indicated, each of the different subfields tends to place greater emphasis on some characteristics associated with governance rather than others. The concept of governance therefore has a broad remit. It "travels" in geographical, disciplinary, and conceptual terms, which both enhances and detracts from its utility. But overall there is sufficient coherence to allow us to look at the concept as a whole, bearing in mind its different meanings and uses.

Despite its large remit, however, gendered perspectives have been almost entirely absent from any aspect of this growing political science literature on governance. The mainstream work has not considered gender (except occasionally to mention women's organizations outside the state as new policy actors in a cursory way more reminiscent of a tokenistic "adding women in") (Peters and Pierre 2000). But to date, feminist critiques of this mainstream literature are also sparse. There have been virtually none in the subfield of public policy and administration, with the possible exceptions of some research in social policy. There is more feminist scholarship that falls under the rubric of IR/IPE and comparative politics; but there have been few attempts to provide any overarching gendered theories and analyses of governance, particularly from a perspective that can be broadly defined as political science and spans all these subfields (Donovan 2007, Brush 2003, Newman 2005b, Meyer and Prugl 1999, Rai and Waylen 2008).[1]

But this chapter will argue that, despite the lacuna with regard to gender, the move away from government to the newer focus on governance in a large body of mainstream political science literature does open up some possibilities for feminist political scientists that were not present with the old focus on government.[2] Much feminist scholarship already uses ideas and arguments that are compatible with much of this governance work. And the adoption of some other insights of the mainstream governance literature could help feminist theorizing of the state – which has been somewhat stagnant recently – to move forward (Kantola 2006). Conversely, the incorporation of a gendered perspective into the mainstream work will also give those scholars and policymakers a much more rigorous and nuanced concept of governance. Therefore both feminist and mainstream political science have something to gain from each other.

This chapter will focus on those notions of governance that emanate from the disciplines of political science and IR/IPE, in particular on those state-centric variants that still see the state as playing a central role, rather than on those variants that focus on broader concerns such as corporate governance. But the relatively recent rise to prominence of the concept of governance, its broad usage, and the relative lack – except in a few subfields – of a substantial gendered literature, means that this chapter is somewhat different than many of the others in this volume that address concepts, such as representation and participation, that have more clearly fixed definitions and larger bodies of gendered work to draw upon. As such, some of the discussion does not fit this volume's guidelines as clearly as some other contributions.

The chapter will first discuss the "context" of the concept: the current meanings of the term "governance" and how and why the concept came to prominence; before "naming" it: examining the ways in which governance as an analytical framework is open to gender analysis and can itself be gendered. This will entail a discussion of the four key "dimensions" needed to form a gendered concept of governance. The last part of the chapter will examine

---

[1] Lisa Brush (2003) has written perhaps the longest gendered analysis of governance, but it is from a social policy perspective – with some emphasis on the gender and politics literature on women's representation and the state – and often informed by Foucauldian analyses. It does not really address many of the gender issues raised within IR, public administration, and multi-level governance. Claire Donovan (2007) has attempted a very short overview for an encyclopedia.

[2] The concept of governance has existed for a relatively long time, but it has become fashionable only in recent years; see, for example, Low (1904).

some of the efforts to operationalize a gendered concept of governance to date – primarily in the study of global governance in IR/IPE – and discuss the implications of the incorporation of a gendered perspective into areas like multi-level governance.

The context: the origins and meaning of governance

Governance is therefore notoriously "slippery" and remains an essentially contested concept. But despite their many differences, most scholars do agree that the move toward the use of governance is the result of important changes – both in the structures and processes of government and in the emergence of new ways of thinking about governing – that have crystallized over the last few decades.

Because it is possible to make this distinction between (1) governance in practice and (2) how governance is understood and analyzed, there is both a body of work that examines governance as a phenomenon that describes real world changes as well as a growing body of work that is trying to develop governance as a theory or analytic framework (Peters and Pierre 2000). In many ways the remit of this chapter – to look at the concept of governance – would place it in the second camp. But it is not possible to divorce the two strands, as real world changes are inevitably related to these analytical approaches to the concept. Therefore, as part of delineating the context I will briefly consider governance as a phenomenon before I can deal with the conceptual questions that are more central to this chapter. This will allow us to have a better understanding of why the concept came to prominence at the end of the twentieth century and the ways in which it is a product of the complex changes occurring at this time.

Although multiple real world changes have accompanied, resulted in, or been intensified by adoption of the term "governance" with attendant policy implications, I will only consider the most significant. My starting point is to divide the large number listed by Peters and Pierre (2000) into three groupings. First, there have been important changes in the nature of the state, particularly in the developed world, first recognized in the second half of the twentieth century. By the 1970s the financial crisis of the state was considered to be an important problem, and in the 1980s there was a growing perception of state failure. Second, broader social change, increasing social and economic complexity, together with the impact of globalization, also profoundly altered the context in which governing was taking place. Indeed, new sources and institutions of governance – at national, regional, and international levels – emerged. Finally, important ideological shifts took place in the latter part of the twentieth century. As a result, the move to the market, exemplified by the widespread support for the doctrine of neoliberalism, reached its height in the 1980s and 1990s. Indeed the emergence of new public management is often seen as one aspect of this.

These real world changes have impacted on the general ideas that characterize the new thinking about governing within the governance literature (Peters and Pierre 2000: 6). Flinders (2002) has argued that it is possible to extract three primary distinctions or approaches from this large body of work. The first makes a distinction between governance as *structure* and governance as *process*. Governance as structure emphasizes the different arrangements and forms, often of hierarchies, markets, and networks, and their roles in mediating state/society relationships. Increasingly attention has been drawn to the perceived failures of various institutional forms, such as hierarchies and markets; and government and the public sector have come under sustained attack for being overly rigid and bureaucratic. Governance as process emphasizes that governance is about more than institutional design and focuses particularly on steering and coordination. And different aspects of the process of governance are highlighted in different contexts. For example, in Europe it is more associated with the involvement of society in the process of governing, whereas in the USA the term often retains more of its original steering conception. Governance as a process is therefore dynamic and focuses on issues such as accountability and control (Flinders 2002).

That part of the public administration and policy literature most concerned with governance as a structure has emphasized both the move from hierarchy to fragmentation and that the state is not a unitary actor. Therefore, although the state is still considered an important actor with unique powers, it is perceived as increasingly dependent on other societal actors. It is these evolving roles of "government and its changing capacity to pursue collective interests under severe external and internal constraint that are at the heart of governance" (Peters and Pierre 2000: 7). This downplaying of the importance of the state is reflected in the widespread emphasis of many scholars on the importance of networks, new policy actors, and new processes in constituting governance. Indeed, Peterson (2003: 1) argues that as part of modern democratic governance "public policies are made via some hybrid arrangement involving a range of different actors, including some representing private or non-governmental interests. The concept of networks – clusters of actors, each with an interest or 'stake' in a given policy sector and the capacity to determine policy success or failure – has been developed and refined as a way to try to describe, explain and predict the outcomes of policy-making via such hybrid arrangements."

The second distinction delineated by Flinders (2002: 53) is between the "horizontal (across governance networks) and vertical (between different governance levels) dimensions to governing modern states." Horizontal governance is predominantly considered at the level of the nation-state and therefore is primarily a concern of the public policy-focused literature. Because vertical governance emphasizes the growing interdependence between different governmental levels, it has been a much greater focus in the IR/IPE and comparative politics literatures, as evidenced by the literature on multi-level governance. Indeed, according to Bache and Flinders (2004: 1) at the heart of multi-level governance is a critique of the false dichotomy between domestic and international politics. At its broadest, the emphasis on vertical governance also incorporates an analysis of the impact of the global economy and transnational civil society.

Finally, for Flinders (2002), the most significant distinction found in the wider governance literature is that made between state-centric versus society-centric approaches. Although the state-centric approaches accept that the traditional understandings of state power and capacity have been challenged, for them the nation-state remains the key political actor. According to Flinders (2002), much of the national level horizontal governance literature adopts an implicit state-centric approach, whereas the vertical multi-level governance literature is more likely to use a society-centric approach that draws on analyses of the global economy and transnational civil society. By the mid-1990s, some scholars were arguing that the state had been "hollowed out" and state power decentered (Rhodes 1997). But this view has been contested subsequently (Holliday 2000). Now, many would argue that although state power has been transformed, states still remain powerful actors and retain control over critical resources. Indeed, it is claimed that states have attempted to adapt to these changes and "fill in" state power. The "hollowing out" thesis also ignores the differences between different kinds of states. In the same vein the focus on a unidirectional move from government to governance can also obscure the complexity of the often contradictory dynamics of change – including the move towards multi-level governance (Newman 2005a). States therefore continue to exercise coercive forms of power and now play a key role in "metagovernance" that sets the rules of the game within which these networks and policy communities of state and nonstate actors operate. But this divergence of opinion as to how far the changes described in the governance literature (particularly with regard to the actual diminution of state power) have extended underlies much of the skepticism surrounding the concept of governance.

Indeed, some scholars have also made a methodological distinction between the dominant political science approaches to governance that are broadly positivist/modernist and rely on empiricism, and newer interpretive approaches, often influenced by poststructuralism, that seek to decenter governance, emphasizing that beliefs, traditions, and dilemmas play a key part in all "governance stories" (Bevir and Rhodes 2003, 2006). As part of this newer interpretive approach, Bevir and Rhodes (2006: 167) reject a comprehensive idea of contemporary governance, arguing that there are no essential characteristics that are part of the concept of governance, only a set of family resemblances, and that there need be no single feature that is shared by all cases labeled "contemporary governance." But despite this view, the three family resemblances that Bevir and Rhodes (2006: 168–9) use to characterize contemporary Britain do resonate with a number of earlier analyses of governance. These are, first, that reforms that attempted to redefine the role of the state brought something of a shift from hierarchy to markets to networks in many diverse forms. Second, the central state has adopted a less hands-on role and that steering and coordination have taken many diverse forms. Third, these changes challenge the dominant political models; for example, by posing new problems of accountability as the privileged place of representative democracy as a means of channeling citizen interests and government action is eroded (Newman 2005a). So even those who try to adopt different methodological approaches do not necessarily come up with very different conclusions.

To sum up, in recent years governance, rather like globalization, has become a catchall phrase used by academics, politicians, journalists, and business people to describe the processes associated with governing sport, schools, businesses, and indeed any organization in any sector. In trying to isolate the academic kernel and define the key concepts, we find that its relative newness does create challenges for political scientists – which perhaps makes it a good time for feminists to intervene, as it is to be hoped that they will be more able to influence coalescence of these discussions. As recently as 2000, Peters and Pierre (2000) claimed that governance theory was still at the stage of proto-theory as the debates had not moved beyond concepts and theories. But although no consensus has emerged as to one definition, and it is not possible to outline one coherent analytical framework associated with the concept, we can discern some significant commonalities in approach, and identify which issues and approaches predominate in particular subdisciplines.

Overall, the concept of governance does a number of things. It problematizes the notion of the state as a unitary actor. It highlights the fragmentation of state institutions and explores new forms of power through which social and economic life is now coordinated (Newman 2005a). It sees this as no longer hierarchically organized with the state and government at the top. Power is now more dispersed as networks oversee new patterns of coordination. State power, although not necessarily diminished, has been displaced in different directions: upward, downward, outward. Therefore the interrogation of these changing relationships between key dimensions such as the market and the state and the public and private sectors, and the emergence of new policy actors and networks at different levels of governance, form an important part of the concept's remit.

Naming the concept and its dimensions: how does this relate to gender?

What then can we take forward from the preceding discussion of governance to help us with our endeavors? First, rather than create a new concept, this chapter argues that it is possible to gender the existing concept of governance. We will therefore keep the name but change the substance, as the large existing literature has largely ignored gender and is almost without exception gender-blind. In common with much of the political science literature on government, it has no sense of the ways in which processes associated with governing are profoundly gendered, or indeed of the ways in which transformations of governance are explicitly and implicitly gendered. Most governance literature does not mention gender, except in passing, or engage with any of the feminist political science debates and research. At the moment only a few references to women are included within any of the governance literature, whether this comes from the dominant positivist/empiricist perspective or from a more poststructural perspective.

As part of gendering the concept, mainstream scholars therefore need to become aware of the gendered dimensions of governance and to overtly recognize these in their work. But scope to do this does exist within the ways the current concept has developed – for example in its emphasis on the fractured nature of institutions and a new multiplicity of actors involved in processes of governing. As such, our preferred definition of governance encompasses this wide range of phenomena, broadening out from government to include the interrogation of a range of changing relationships. In particular it incorporates the key dimensions of the relationship between market and state, policy communities of state and nonstate actors, and public and private sectors.

We need to consider the implications of each of these interrelated factors in gendered terms. We will therefore focus on producing gendered analyses of institutions, of the actors and the relationships between them, and, particularly, of the changing relationship between the market and state and the role of citizens.

The initial stage in this process is to outline the ways in which mainstream work is gender-blind, before demonstrating how gender could be taken on board in these analyses of governance. Although there exists no sizeable, recognizable, and coherent body of work that both falls under the rubric of gender and governance or of feminist analyses of governance, and that spans the subdisciplines of political science, feminist scholars have already analyzed many of the key themes within the mainstream governance literature. Reflecting the interdisciplinarity of gender research, much of the work that can contribute to the gendering of governance comes from disciplines outside political science and political theory such as feminist economics, gendered political economy, and development studies. This section of the chapter will endeavor to bring this work together. But in comparison to feminist political theory and political science, research in some areas, like feminist economics, is still at a relatively early stage of development. After assessing the gender critiques of the mainstream concepts, I will look at how a gendered version of governance has been operationalized in one subdiscipline of political science: IR/IPE. To do this, I will organize the discussion into four broad but overlapping dimensions – the market; the relationship between public and private; the state; and networks – that are central to the governance literature, and look at how they can be gendered.

The dimensions of the concept

The market

Markets feature prominently in contemporary governance literature. Markets are often presented as the result of abstract relations of supply and demand, of competition and relations of exchange, and, as such, as neutral institutions with outcomes that do not favor any particular groups or individuals. But critics of orthodox economics have long claimed that markets are not natural neutral arenas filled with rational actors exercising their preferences under conditions of perfect competition and needing only to be regulated and adjudicated at the edges. Feminist economists, among others, argue that the economy and the market are socially constructed (Elson 1995). Indeed, markets, as social institutions which embody social norms and practices, are imbued with power relations that include a gender dimension, and roles within market systems are structured by nonmarket criteria. As a result, "the non-market, though clearly not non-economic, criteria lead to gender based distortions of markets" (Rai 2008: 25). Rai (2008: 25) goes on to argue that "participants come to specific markets with unequal capabilities and bargaining capacities and resources as a result of and which inhere in unequal market structures, regulated and stabilised by gendered state formations, and characterised by more or less equal power – class, race and gender are three bases for unequal power relations operating in the market." Labor markets, for example, are highly gendered. Although it varies in different contexts, the sexual division of labor is still crucially important in determining employment patterns. On average, men and women have differential wage levels, and elements of the differences in men and women's employment and remuneration can only be explained by discrimination. Lisa Prugl (2008) has also shown how agricultural markets in the European Union are highly gendered. Therefore, markets themselves are sources of patterns of inequality that are gendered as well as classed, racialized, and aged.

Markets need to be analyzed as gendered institutions, and the introduction of market mechanisms into any institution will not be neutral but will have gendered consequences. As such, the introduction of market mechanisms into the state and the restructuring of the provision of state services, so often advocated in programs of reform, will not happen in an abstract neutral way but will have important gender consequences (Newman 2005b: 8). The introduction of competition, for example through a reduction of regulation, will change labor markets, often leading to a "feminization" of labor as low-paid, flexible, part-time, temporary service sector jobs often associated with women workers grow in importance. As we see in chapter 5 on the welfare state in this volume, the marketizing of care services, for example moving them into the private sector, also has gendered consequences as women are often the majority of workers in this sector.

The public and the private

Any analysis of governance needs to have a better understanding of the gendered nature of the relationship between the public and private. This is a key area that feminist scholars have focused on, whether they are working in political theory, social policy, or feminist economics. To date, much of the governance literature has had quite a narrow economistic view of the public/private relationship. Because of its focus on the economic and the political, the governance literature excludes the social and cultural. As a result it uses a version of the private sphere that sees it as a primarily economic domain, with a very narrow view of what counts as economic. Feminist scholars argue that an extended view of the private that includes households, the "reproductive" economy as well as the "productive" economy, is needed. Without taking into account the social reproduction that takes place in the domestic sphere in the form of unpaid work, economic analysis is flawed and economic statistics are inaccurate (Hoskyns and Rai 2007). If this is done, different concerns will come to the forefront – such as the extent to which the marketizing and privatizing of care are pushing the burden on to women in households and increasing their unpaid labor. This form of analysis has, for example, been used to examine the impact of structural adjustment programs, linked neoliberal economic reforms, and the development of new welfare regimes that have been associated with the era of governance.

Feminist political theorists also claim that not only must the cultural and social be included in the concept of the private sphere, but that it is also necessary to challenge the exclusionary notion of the public sphere as comprising male citizens enjoying rights from which women are excluded, which has long been central to political theory (Pateman 1983, 1989). In this traditional vision, the "political" and the public sphere are therefore implicitly masculine, and women have been analytically relegated to the private sphere that lies outside the domain of the political. However, women have never remained entirely outside of the public sphere, and the boundary between the public and private spheres has not been fixed; but the distinction between the two and the roles ascribed to women in the private sphere have seriously impacted on the ways in which they can participate in the public sphere (Elshtain 1981). For example, the sexual division of labor within the household differentially affects men's and women's access to the public sphere, as women generally undertake the bulk of domestic labor. Feminists have also argued that "private" issues such as rape and domestic violence needed to be politicized and brought into the public sphere. By the same token, notions of citizenship are also gendered, and the question of whether some of the governance literature relies on new forms of citizenship must also be examined using a gender lens.

The state

We have seen from our discussion of the meaning of governance that although many governance theorists think that the power of the state has diminished, it still plays a crucial role within their frameworks. In the same way, as feminist critiques examine the gendered ways in which markets and the public/private divide operate, feminist scholars have also highlighted the ways in which the state is gendered even though this work has been ignored by mainstream analyses. But the early feminist debates on the state tended to be rather simplistic and overhomogenizing in their analyses. One of their main concerns was whether the state could ever be a vehicle for feminists attempting to further women's interests (assumed to be homogeneous). Initially the arguments were polarized between those who claimed that, for women, a homogeneous state was either potentially essentially good (from a liberal/pluralist perspective) or potentially essentially bad (from a radical feminist perspective). Opposing analyses therefore emerged – that feminists should either keep away from the state, as an irredeemably patriarchal and oppressive institution, or engage with it rather uncritically as it was a neutral instrument and could be an arbiter between different interest groups (Waylen 1998) – or, in the case of Nordic feminist writing, that the "women-friendly" Scandinavian welfare state could be a benign instrument for social change enabling women to avoid dependence on individual men (Kantola 2006).

Since the 1980s there has been greater agreement among many feminists that the nature of the state and the relationship between the state and gender relations is not fixed and immutable. Influenced in part by poststructural analyses, the state has been recognized not as a homogeneous entity but as a collection of institutions and contested power relations. Indeed, the state is an arena where interests are actively constructed rather than given (Watson 1990). Battles can therefore be fought in the arena of the state, as it is "an uneven and fractured terrain with dangers as well as resources for women's movements" (Rai and Lievesley 1996: 1). Consequently, while the state has for the most part acted to reinforce gender subordination, the space can exist within the state to act to change gender relations (Alvarez 1990). Within this framework, the state bureaucracy becomes an arena in which feminists can play an active role from within, attempting to change its structure and the ways in which it operates as well as influencing its policies at a number of different levels and areas. These analyses of the differentiated state are therefore in sympathy with the idea of the state as a fractured institution prevalent within the governance literature.

Feminist scholars have also examined other aspects of the state that are relevant to the gendered analysis of governance. They have examined the ways in which different state institutions operate. Louise Chappell (2002) has divided the state into three different arenas – the electoral, the bureaucratic, and the constitutional/legal – arguing that each one plays a key part in processes of governing and is gendered in particular ways. The electoral arena is a key focus for promoting citizen participation, representation, and accountability. It is also an area where women participate at lower levels than men and often in different ways. As we know from other chapters in this volume, much effort has been put into understanding why and how women's participation rates are lower, and into developing strategies – such as the implementation of quotas – that can be adopted to remedy this situation. The bureaucratic arena, as the arena where policies are devised and implemented, has been described as a gendered hierarchy, with large numbers of women employed at the bottom but very few at the top of the pyramid (Savage and Witz 1993). Taking issue with Weberian models, it, too, has been analyzed in terms of its embedded masculine style (Ferguson 1984). Finally, since the late 1990s the consititutional/legal has been recognized as a vitally important one, as legal frameworks and constitutions embody certain gender norms and help regulate and construct gender identities and citizenship (Dobrowolsky and Hart 2003).

Despite this large body of work, some contemporary feminist scholars have asked: Where is feminist state theory today? Kantola (2006: 15) claims that, in comparison to earlier decades, it is now far harder to discern what feminists have to say about the state. In some ways it can be argued that feminist theories of the state are now "everywhere" in so far as many of the ideas that emerged in the 1980s are implicit within a wide range of feminist scholarship. But it can also appear that feminist theories of the state are "nowhere" because the more abstract analytical debates about the nature of the state seem to have ended. Nonetheless, according to Kantola (2006: 16), two contradictory tendencies currently inform much feminist social and political inquiry that looks at the state. And these two tendencies also resonate with much of the governance literature.

First, some feminist work is premised on the assumption that the powers of the state have been transformed and, more specifically, have declined. This is reflected in much of the gender literature that looks at international phenomena such as transnational networks, global human rights, and global production. In the national context, gender scholars have examined the ways in which the reconfigured state offers different opportunities and challenges to women's movements as the political opportunity structure alters (Banaszak, Beckwith, and Rucht 2003). For example, the uploading of state power to institutions such as the European Union has created new, remote structures but also new fora for lobbying. The downloading of state power, for example through devolution, has, in some circumstances, afforded the opportunity to get gender concerns integrated into new constitutional arrangements. And the lateral loading of decision-making towards nonelected state bodies may in fact reduce the opportunities for activists to frame key issues. The second tendency identified by Kantola (2006) within feminist literature on the state reflects the fact that not only does the state remain important, but feminists have increasingly been engaging with it. Often categorized as "state feminism," discussed later in this volume, the state has been the focus of efforts to implement policies and strategies that improve gender equality in a range of locations (McBride Stetson and Mazur 1995, Mazur 2002, Lovenduski 2005a). The establishment of women's policy agencies, gender mainstreaming policies, and the interaction of feminists outside the state with these institutions and strategies that attempt to alter processes of governing, have figured largely in this work. And in a range of contexts, feminists have attempted to get gender concerns incorporated into new constitutional/legal frameworks, for example during devolution in Scotland and in the South African transition to democracy (Mackay, Myers, and Brown 2003, Waylen 2007).

Networks

The perception of the diminution of state power and significance of a wider range of policy actors has meant that the role of networks is emphasized in much of the governance literature. In fact, virtually the only context in which women actors and women's organizations are mentioned within this mainstream work is as potential members of policy networks. However, feminist critics of the governance literature argue that the discussions of the processes of network coordination, and bargaining and the resource dependencies that shape them, often present them in disembodied form without any recognition of the significant role that factors such as gender, class, and race play in the way networks will operate. Newman (2005b), for example, claims that the use of the concept of networks obscures these issues of inequality, differential status and rights bestowed by formal power; and that the operation of networks is overshadowed by flows of influence that operate in interpersonal relationships that are so often gendered in ways that have negative consequences for many women and other excluded groups. Therefore, although the term "policy networks" can be used loosely to describe some of the alliances that women's organizations make with policy actors within state bureaucracies, governments, and other policy actors, it is crucial to be aware of its limitations.

Indeed, feminist scholars have long been interested in women's organizations and their activities and have increasingly examined the interaction between women's organizations and the state, often influenced by a social movement perspective. But there is also a growing feminist literature that explores how gendered policy outcomes come about in particular policy sectors – such as reproductive rights and domestic violence – which does resonate with some of the dominant themes of the governance literature. In a large multi-country study, Laurel Weldon (2002a) looks at the various factors – including the roles of women's movements, women's policy agencies, and key actors within governments – that contribute to whether a government will take on violence against women as a policy issue. She argues that, although women's organizations are crucial to ensure that certain gender issues are articulated, more is needed if those issues are to enter the policy agenda and finally result in a concrete policy outcome, as women's activities on their own are not enough. Alliances between women's movements, actors within governments, legislatures, and women's policy agencies are often crucial. And more recently Durose and Gains (2007) have framed their gendered analysis of New Labour policies in the UK to include the activities of policy advocacy coalitions and networks and their impact on the core executive. Indeed, the role of key actors within various sectors and their alliances is increasingly seen by many feminist political scientists as more significant for the achievement of positive gender outcomes than the presence of a "critical mass" of women, for example within legislatures (Waylen 2007). These developments are clearly in sympathy with the governance literature that focuses on the roles played by policy networks.

Operationalizing the concept: global governance[3]

One way to examine these trends more concretely is to look at global governance, as the area where gendered analyses have gone furthest and attempts have already been made to operationalize a gendered concept of governance. These efforts examine the impact of the changing roles of states, international institutions, markets, and actors in gendered terms as well as interrogating influential notions such as "good governance." Much of this scholarship comes from the subdisciplines of IR and IPE (Rai and Waylen 2008). There is now a huge body of mainstream work on global governance. The key shift underlying the emergence of this literature has, of course, been that from

---

[3] For a more detailed discussion of this theme see Rai and Waylen (2008), on which much of this section is based.

state-based studies of government to the supranational understanding of the regulation of both the economy and the polity. The increased importance of international organizations (which are often, though perhaps erroneously, referred to as global) has therefore engaged the interest of international relations scholars, especially as the reach of these organizations, their institutional profile, and their relations with individual states as well as with nonstate organizations, have changed. However, the changing nature and roles of nonstate organizations and actors in shaping regulatory systems within and from outside increasingly important global institutions have also become important. The literature on global governance covers both the increasingly global language in which epistemic communities influence our political vocabulary and even imagination, and their input into framing and legitimizing policy at the global level (Clark *et al.*, 1998). At the same time new social movements have emerged and become global actors – their interaction with international organizations such as the United Nations, the World Bank, and even the International Monetary Fund is evidence of this (O'Brien, Goetz, Scholte, and Williams 2000). They lobby, challenge, and support specific causes, and also shape what we think about those causes. The environmental and ethical trade and indeed the women's movements have been particularly visible at that level (Bretherton, 1998, Liebowitz, 2002).

Scholars have put forward a number of arguments in favor of addressing the conceptual and institutional framework of global governance. Two of these have been particularly influential: first, instrumental approaches – global economic activity needs regulation at a global level; and second, normative concerns – the democratization of national-level institutions needs to be matched by that of international institutions and underpinned by common norms of human rights as well as of common public goods such as health and food security. Some instrumental approaches have been criticized for being overly technocratic and managerial in ways that attempt to turn governance into a depoliticized policy framework. As such, "global governance" often attracts disapprobation as ideology – "a realignment of elite thinking to the needs of the world market" (Murphy 2002) dressed up as a normative framework for analyzing world institutions. But linked to these approaches is still the analysis of the state, which remains at the heart of the international system but which can often become obfuscated when we speak of global governance. Finally, the critical IPE question of the relationships between states and markets has been examined in the context of the processes of globalization that, too, cannot be ignored in any analysis of global governance (Gill 1995, Murphy 1994, Brodie 2005). Despite this range of issues and approaches, much of the mainstream work on global governance has been rather narrowly associated with policy studies, political science, and international relations, and thus has missed the complexity of many of the processes under consideration. Indeed, in all this growing body of literature marking out the field of global governance, little attention is paid to the way in which both the processes and the institutions of governance are gendered and result in an institutional, discursive, and structural bias in favor of men that leads global governance to take particular forms, which affect different sections of society unequally.

It is, then, not surprising that feminist scholars have begun to challenge this mainstream literature, even if the body of scholarship produced to date has been relatively small in comparison, for example, to the gendered analyses of globalization (Bell 2001). But the mainstream literature on global governance can provide and has provided a useful starting point for these attempts to gender the analysis of global governance. Because its definitions of global governance are broad – it can encompass a range of global rules, regulations, regimes, and institutions – it fits with feminist approaches. Many mainstream analyses of global governance have also usefully interrogated how global governance has developed, its fluid and changing nature, how it might link to the diminishing power of the nation-state, and its relationship to globalization and to the rise of new global actors that can also inform gendered analyses.

The feminist writing on global governance, predominantly from an IR perspective, has already addressed a number of important themes. Its initial focus was on the ways in which women's activism has engaged institutions of governance and attempted to shift their policy parameters as well as opened them to women's membership. The role that women's movements have played in this process, especially through lobbying the UN, international institutions, and conferences, has also been highlighted (Friedman 2003, O'Brien, Goetz, Scholte, and Williams 2000). One early contribution in this area that took this approach was the collection edited by Mary Meyer and Elisabeth Prugl (1999), *Gender Politics in Global Governance*. In their Introduction the editors outline three key themes in the analysis of global governance: the spaces women have carved for themselves inside the institutions of global governance; the interchange between intergovernmental organizations and states, including the international women's movement; and contestation of both formal and informal rules and discursive practices that have global reach.

In recent years, another separate – and more institutionally based – strand has emerged to complement the early concentration on women actors outside of the institutions of global governance in some of the feminist research. In particular, this has examined the struggles around gender mainstreaming within both institutions and policy processes (Hafner-Burton and Pollack 2000, True 2003, Walby 2005). Issues of political participation and representation, as well as the outcome of institutional deliberations, have also been highlighted in this growing literature. Overall, this scholarship demonstrates the importance of gendered analyses of global governance, showing how institutions of global governance often act to reinforce patterns of gender inequality at the global level. But it also demonstrates the striking heterogeneity of these different institutions of global and regional governance. They do not all act in the same ways. For example, the gender regimes, the way issues are framed, and the functioning of the institutions of the United Nations family differ considerably from the international financial and trading institutions. Analyses of the contrasting examples of the International Criminal Court (ICC), World Bank, Asia-Pacific Economic Cooperation (APEC), and the European Union have demonstrated yet again how different global institutions and regimes vary considerably and institutions are not homogeneous and monolithic (Chappell 2008, Bedford 2008, Hoskyns 2008, True 2008). Individual institutions themselves are often made up of complex, fragmented, and sometimes contradictory structures.

Indeed, the contrast between the global human rights regime and the economic governance regime of the World Bank demonstrates this heterogeneity (Waylen 2008). The United Nations human rights regime is seen as a relatively open and favorable institutional context for women activists. The mainstreaming of the discourse of women's rights into human rights conventions and UN institutions is considered an important success of global women's movements. Most of the gender literature on the governance of human rights looks at women's organizing, particularly at UN conferences. Partly as a result of the relative openness of these institutions and effective strategic framing of the issues, relatively coherent networks of women's organizations successfully articulated gender issues and put them on the global human rights agenda. But the little literature that looks at the actual implementation and the extent of institutional change tells a rather different story. Charlesworth (2005) argues that any changes that occurred were largely rhetorical and that institutional inertia and resistance prevented more profound change.

The World Bank offers a very different institutional context (Waylen 2008). It is a relatively closed organization, located in the United States, with few entry points for outside actors such as nongovernmental organizations. Economic issues are framed very differently (in terms of neoliberal economic efficiency) from the framing of human rights issues. There is no coherent global women's movement organizing around World Bank activities (O'Brien, Goetz, Scholte, and Williams 2000). Organizing itself is made more difficult by a lack of expertise and the potential divisiveness of economic issues. The opportunities to form effective policy networks are therefore small. But over the years the World Bank has paid increasing attention to gender issues, particularly around Beijing, and after 2000 it adopted gender mainstreaming, partly due to "gender policy entrepreneurs" such as James Wolfensohn. But it is in the context of the business case for equality, and more recently "gender equality is smart economics." But, again, less has happened in terms of practice. Implementation has not been mandatory. Few resources have been devoted to gender in comparison to other areas such as the environment. But the institution is not monolithic, so more has happened in some parts than in others. Feminist scholarship operationalizing gendered conceptions of markets, states, and networks has therefore begun to produce gendered analyses of some key areas of global governance.

Conclusions: toward a gendered concept of governance

We have seen that the concept of governance is an important and yet indistinct one. In terms of the framework outlined at the beginning of this volume, it is also a continuous concept. There is not one type of governance but many, and no negative concept. All institutions have some form of governance. It is hard to envisage a situation in which an institution exists but has no form of governance. One common way of designating this continuum is with good governance at one end of the spectrum, bad governance at the other end, and a gray zone in the middle. However, although "good governance" is considered almost universally desirable and bad governance is decried wherever it is deemed to occur, what constitutes either is not universally agreed. This has not prevented governments and international institutions such as the World Bank from advocating a range of measures, including facilitating participation, accountability, efficiency, and an end to corruption, to encourage good governance. Although initially gender-free, a gendered dimension has also entered into these discussions of good governance. Women are often seen as somehow less corrupt than men and therefore to be encouraged into institutions (Goetz 2007). Increasing the participation of women in governance institutions, particularly legislatures, is seen as way of widening participation and making these structures more accountable and inclusive. The World Bank therefore now advocates increasing women's participation and gender equality as part of its efforts to promote both good governance and economic growth, most recently under the slogan "Gender equality as smart economics." But these exhortations to improve governance associated with World Bank conditionality have been contentious and have fed into criticism of the general relevance and applicability of World Bank neoliberal-inspired programs in very varied contexts.

We have seen how the broader concept of governance has been used in the analysis of a wide range of institutions and policymaking processes operating at various levels, whether local, national, regional, or global, and how it is utilized in a range of subdisciplines of political science. As such, we have seen that governance is a concept that travels. At the same time, some of these discussions of governance, such as good governance, does raise issues about the extent to which it is legitimate to apply the concept in varied cultural and regional contexts. However, if we set aside the rather loaded term "good governance," the broader concept of governance, as long as it is operationalized in ways that are sensitive to contextual specificity and do not try to fit all cases into one predetermined model, does travel.

But although there is now a large and heterogeneous body of literature on governance, little of the mainstream academic work incorporates gender into its approaches. However, this chapter has shown that a large amount of gendered research that makes a valuable contribution to the gendering of the concept of governance already exists. It focuses on a number of key dimensions: the market, the state, networks, and the relationships between them and the public and the private spheres. It is important to remember that, although little of it is actually regarded as part of the governance literature, a vast array of gender scholarship from a range of disciplines outside political science looks at themes such as the gendered impact of marketization and restructuring, particularly in key policy sectors like welfare provision. Much of this work has come from social policy and development studies. Path-breaking research has also been undertaken on the gendered implications of structural adjustment programs and the creation of "market citizens," and other changes that mark the shift towards processes of governance that took place toward the end of the twentieth century (Elson 1995, Schild 1998). This substantial body of scholarship, which lies outside the fields of public policy, comparative politics, and IR/IPE work, also needs to be incorporated. But, to date, these large and varied existing literatures from both within and outside political science have not been brought together to form a coherent and recognized corpus of work under the rubric of "gender and governance." Indeed, this might be facilitated if some feminist scholars (often political scientists) were to give up their apparent reluctance to use the term "governance."

There are also significant overlaps between recent feminist approaches to the state, institutions, and processes of governing and those utilized in mainstream work on governance. Using these could enable mainstream scholars to go beyond simply talking just about women as policy actors outside the state, thereby improving their understanding of the processes they are examining. Clavero and Gilligan (2007), for example, argue that the studies of the evolution of gender equality policy at the European level can offer useful insights to those scholars seeking to understand the nature of the European Union as a polity and can enhance the literature on multi-level governance. They argue, first, that the explanations for the development of gender equality policies should examine the interaction of women's interests, institutions, and ideas in policy processes, highlighting the roles played by transnational women's advocacy networks that include institutional actors, in articulating interests outside the nation-state. Second, Clavero and Gilligan (2007) argue that the evolution of gender equality policy demonstrates the roles played by governance institutions at different levels – national and supranational – in policy formation and EU decision-making. Citing Van Der Vleuten (2007), they also argue that understanding the EU as a multi-tiered polity (rather than a multi-level one that obscures the hierarchies of power between the different levels), and focusing on a wide range of actors and institutions, allows scholars to see the multiplicity of sites of women's substantive representation in the EU as well as the variety of channels through which this representation might occur. This allows us to gain important insights into how the governance of the EU is gendered.

Therefore, by the same token, the move away from the exclusively state-centric focus that is implied in government, together with an emphasis of the fractured and heterogeneous nature of institutions and the need to look at a broader range of actors and formal/informal networks, could make governance a relatively friendly terrain for feminist scholars. And a move toward governance could take feminist scholars beyond much of the state theorizing that dominated feminist debates in the 1980s. There is also scope to include the discussions around feminist institutionalism emerging within comparative politics in this framework and approach. As a result of all this scholarship, the potential exists to recognize governance as a gendered concept in ways that can only improve its usefulness and create further opportunities for feminist scholars. It would help feminist researchers to develop some of their existing agendas around the interactions between actors and institutions and to make more inroads into relatively "hostile" areas of political science such as public policy and public administration, but in ways that combine specificity with broader analyses.

Gendering development

Kathleen Staudt

What happens when one conceptualizes development with a gender lens? I try to answer this question, focusing on the editors' conceptual guidelines, in order that readers may acquire insights on and pathways toward researchable questions about meaningful issues. In so doing, I hope to sustain readers' interests on a reading/writing journey that addresses people's lives, deaths, and well-being around the world. The journey offers enormous potential for substantive research, action, policies, and outcomes. To my mind, guidelines do not trump substance, but attentiveness to the guidelines should produce better substantive research and outcomes. This chapter addresses the intersection of comparative politics and international relations (IR), bringing in North–South dimensions and thereby adding enormous complexities to this collection. The chapter embraces almost two hundred nations, thousands of cultures, and the institutions within and between them – both governmental and nongovernmental organizations (NGOs). People in transnational institutions and in governments create, implement, resist, and respond to public policies for "development" in "developing countries." The word "development" is highly politicized, traveling (Traveling Guideline) awkwardly in multiple directions, bottom-up, top-down, and sideways from researchers to international organizations (IOs), to governments and multiple agencies therein, to NGOs, and to the people who supposedly benefit from development interventions (but are sometimes burdened instead). For most of history and in the early post-World War II era, analysts had not examined development with a gender lens.

Since the late 1970s, however, once marginal and now more central feminist voices, using the words "women" and/or "gender," have interrogated the conceptualization and measurement of "development," so much so that quotation marks are often placed around the term. As Gustavo Esteva says so

Thanks to Jane Jaquette for commenting on this chapter.

well about the term "development," "[It] appears mostly in jokes... If you live in Mexico City today, you are either rich or numb if you fail to notice that development stinks" (1985: 78, cited in Staudt 1998: 25). Henceforth in this chapter, I will remove the quotation marks around development, but by the time readers reach the conclusion, they may decide to avoid this increasingly loaded and passé term.

At the most basic level, development's core concern is the *quality of life*. Development's many definitions are fed into a process (often in public policy planning and implementation) to enhance different aspects of the quality of life, connected to various direct and indirect short- and long-term outcomes. Most mainstream analysts have assumed that economic expansion is the central issue, measured in terms of national growth, increased per capita income, and investment. Economic expansion, it was also assumed, would lead to better policies at the macro level and wider choices for individual "consumers" at the micro level, whether they "choose" government or market options to meet their needs. Alas, until recently, analysts did not focus enough on specifics about decision-makers, their constituencies, and public power (or powerlessness).

In this chapter, I argue that development studies initially focused on men (not women), an exclusionary approach that made women's well-being and work invisible, especially their informal unpaid work, interests in public policy, and political voices. Such a focus automatically narrowed the concept and lost significance of larger goals. Feminist analysts reconceptualized the field, but had to "master" (Staudt 2002) the language and understand paradigms in the process. I argue, after outlining the shifting context of (Context Guideline), names for (Naming Guideline), and meanings of the term development over the last half century – in units of analysis stuck at the nation-state level – that the development term should be avoided altogether in lieu of specific public policies, economic approaches, global inequality, or governance. The reasons for moving on, away from the use of a general development term, are woven into this chapter. First, let me say something about the geographic scope of this chapter and its challenges for the editors' concept traveling from one nation to another or from capital cities to regions and cultural groups.

Geographic scope

Currently, the world contains approximately 200 nation-states, 192 of them members of the United Nations. Development has long relied on comparative analysis, specifically cross-national studies and longitudinal studies, using the same indicator to compare and rank countries at one point in time, or across time. Much analysis emanates from the USA and Europe (the "West") or uses those areas as models for what development is trying to achieve as well as for how to get there.

Analysis is confined *within* nation-states, some of them minuscule island states (of less than a million people) and others of them huge in geographic and population terms (of over a billion people), with potentially scores to hundreds of linguistic and cultural groups within nation-state boundaries, especially on the African continent. States are the structures from which citizens seek accountability through the democratic political process, but recent estimates from Freedom House indicate that only a third of nations are democracies and another third are semi-democracies (2007). Thus, there may be problems of, or an absence of, accountability in the majority of states. (See other chapters in the volume for how gender might inform terms like "democracy," "representation," and "governance.") Despite real or hoped-for national-level accountability, the global economy shapes nations and their decisions, especially smaller states and weaker economies. Thus, researchers must think about the level at which they focus analysis: local, state, regional, global (or all of these).

Cultural identities are imposed upon or claimed by people. Within many states, multiple cultures shape people's lives, work, and connections to governments. Cultures are notoriously difficult to conceptualize, much less compare at cross-national levels with deeper meanings in grounded contexts (see multiple cultures analyzed in Staudt 1990: ch. 2). Western societies now think of culture in terms of identity politics, but culture means much more for work and life than an "identity." Generic development concepts do not translate or travel well from capital cities and international organizations to subnational or transnational "cultural" groups whose identities may change and shift. And cultures are far from monolithic. As Renato Rosaldo maintains, one cannot plant and impose monolithic cultural constructions in geographic spaces like static and fixed "museum-metaphors"; instead, he suggests that diversity be captured within, through "garage-sale" metaphors (1989: 434).

Another broader agenda posed in this chapter involves the way development requires analysis beyond political science into anthropology, area studies, sociology, economics, and history. The development industry of the last half century produced a growing array of adjectives that precede the term development; these fall into three broad groupings: economic, equitable, and human. Yet even more adjectives are attached to numerous policy areas: urban and rural, industry and agriculture; health, education, and welfare; violence, safety, and crime; among others.

Development studies have always included both theory and practice. A further complexity that I analyze is the effort to bridge the divides between academic researchers, activists, and policymakers. The Association of Women in Development (AWID) was founded in 1982 on the principle of "trialogue" among multiple constituencies and audiences: scholars, practitioners, and advocates (also see Tinker 1990). IOs, many of them affiliated with the United Nations, commission research and/or hire consultants to pursue institutional agendas (for better or worse). IO analysts fish in academia to find policy-relevant research that they distill in their widely disseminated reports. They reach far outside the USA into the policy, practitioner, and research worlds of the non-USA, the other 95 percent of the global population. NGOs, often operating on a shoestring, search for funds from various sources, including IOs and governments, on terms that potentially compromise their autonomy (see Alvarez 1998 on NGO-ization). Perhaps no other chapter of this volume grapples with the "theory/practice" divide or the constant pressure to develop action or policy recommendations from research. The field is highly sensitive to political contexts and historic era, meriting more attention to the editors' Context and Naming Guidelines.

Shifting contexts, changing names: historical perspectives

Historical analyses of changing development concepts make it clear that development is an ideology (i.e. a belief system) linked to economic paradigms (like capitalism and socialism) that have shifted since the late 1950s. Ideologies frame public policy options with real consequences for "who gets what, when, how" (Lasswell, 1936). Issues like violence against women, key to safety, health, and well-being, entered the policy agenda only in recent decades. Power theorists call attention to the "mobilization of bias," "nondecisions," and the ways that the "rules of the game" prevent certain issues from entering the policy agenda (see Lukes's summary, 2005). The mobilization of male privilege in development silenced the identification of "women's interests" or what is now viewed as a gender lens. Feminist activists and researchers politicized this silencing in the 1970s, laying the groundwork for gendered analysis.

In this section, I set the stage and provide a timeline (also see Jaquette and Staudt 2006 on the international and foreign policy contexts). I begin with the postwar and Cold War periods, which were oblivious to women, what they do, and their relations with men. In the 1970s, political and conceptual openings occurred, making women's economic decision-making more visible and challenging the view that "modernization" produced positive outcomes for both men and women. In the 1980s and 1990s, UN-connected global women's networking peaked, creating civil society organizations with high levels of women's participation, but also the end of the Cold War and the "triumph of capitalism" (Heilbroner 1989).

Colonial beginnings: pervasive racism and sexism

To understand the foundations of development requires knowledge of the predecessor colonial paradigm, marked by its ruthless capitalism, "civilizing" mission, white supremacy, and male superiority. That paradigm offered a particularly narrow version of the means and ends of development. Britain, France, Germany, Portugal, the Netherlands, Belgium, Spain, Italy, and the United States gained control over vast amounts of territory in Asia, Africa, Latin America, and the Caribbean. The western powers gained access to resources, markets, and the hearts and minds of mostly male indigenous leaders, who moved toward decolonization and independence, yet retained lingering ties to colonizer countries. A striking example of this is the fact that the most widely read IR journal, *Foreign Affairs*, was originally titled *Journal of Race Development*; the name was changed in 1922.

Development was a concept born in the post-World War II era of new international institutions, decolonization, US–Soviet economic competition, and aspiring US hegemony. In 1947, there were 45 nation-states in the newly created United Nations; with the addition of Soviet satellites that joined later, the body was only a quarter of the current membership. The terms of the capitalist–socialist debate were set by the West.

In the capitalist West, development theory divided the world into two states of being: traditional and modern. A classic example is US economist W. W. Rostow (1960), who defined development as economic growth, and the competition between the USA and the Soviet Union was framed entirely in terms of which system could provide the most effective path to high consumption. Daniel Lerner (1958) assumed the emergence of "modern" societies once economic growth occurred, displacing "traditional" societies and causing them to disappear. If writers mentioned women at all, they saw them through 1950s-style western glasses: economically dependent ("parasites"), or traditional, backward, and tied to customs. Catherine Scott points out that Rostow and

Lerner worried about women's "pervasive boredom," content to watch "soap-operas to fill their days" (1995: 25–6). The population literature was riddled with assumptions of women's ignorance, in bodies "at risk for reproduction" (Jaquette and Staudt 1985). These views would be laughable if they had not determined that resources would be directly almost entirely to men.

The traditional–modern dichotomy has long been passé. With empirical research, beginning in 1970 (Boserup) and thereafter, readers could better understand women's work, paid and unpaid, the time invested in work, their decision-making roles in the household, the benefits derived from work, women's political participation, and their access to resources such as land and money in various global, national, and local contexts. Comparisons began between men and women, first in the name of collecting "sex-differentiated data" and later, in the 1980s, in the name of gender. It became clear that "modernization" theories and intervention practices had enhanced men's power at the expense of women, increasing women's dependency on men and undermining indigenous assets not recognized by "modern" views of property.

In the 1960s, many more colonies moved toward political independence, but often remained economically dependent on the former colonizer country. At that time, Marxist and dependency theorists critiqued historic world capitalist systems and the dependency of countries on former colonizers. The mainstream left had little to say about patriarchy, women, or gender inequalities.

Mainstream economists adopted friendlier-sounding names for categories, now positioned on a continuum. Consider going first from "developed and developing nations" to "more developed and less developed nations," and by the 1970s to "rich and poor nations." Geographic categories came into common use, reinforced by caucuses within the United Nations General Assembly, especially North and South (with Australia and New Zealand part of the North). In *The White Man's Burden*, William Easterly refers to patronizing moralism and racism when he says the century-old phrase "uncivilized countries" was replaced with "developing nations" (2006: 24). The World Bank adopted more neutral language, categorizing countries by per capita income: low, middle, and high.

The absence of negations in all-gray zones

Development is a process of moving from one level to another level, presumably toward well-being, which is defined in numerous ways (see below).

There is no nondevelopment: all countries exhibit partial development. (If well-being was substituted for development, perhaps negation could be conceptualized.) No nations exhibit zero annual per capita income, but several countries in Africa have annual per capita incomes of US$500 or less. Such countries might be labeled *under*developed, that is, places with potential, but that label also implies intentional exploitation on the part of colonizer nations or profiteers in the global economy, especially in critical paradigms such as dependency theory. Critical theorists might shed the exploitation label when economies with resources and products of value become diversified, trading with multiple partners and self-sufficient in their basic food needs. Economists report negative or no-growth rates, say minus 5 percent annually, but these figures do not denote nondevelopment.

As for developed countries, their location is also on a continuum, for their growth and advancement is limitless! Take some of the richest countries in the world, for example. Switzerland's and Luxembourg's annual per capita income currently surpasses US$40,000, but the model suggests they could continue to rise – there are "no limits to growth." In hindsight, this thinking has wrought much environmental destruction.

Economic paradigms

The Cold War competition between the USA and USSR chilled the international atmosphere, aligning countries with either capitalist (market) economic (also called the "First World") or socialist (planned) economic (also called the "Second World") paradigms. This was a difficult context for nations that sought to pursue alternatives (called the "Third World"), mixing capitalism and socialism or forging new paths outside those paradigms altogether. Depending on the ideology, the means and ends of development differed. For example, in one, publicly subsidized health is central, while in another, consumer choice in a health marketplace is considered optimal, excluding those without an ability to pay. Most of the IOs and the English-language development writers aligned with the capitalist and market model, although dependency and left critics levied compelling critiques.

The early analysts used masculine terminology as generic for people – but a gender-undifferentiated people or public. Only in the 1960s did researchers and IOs pursue "sex-differentiated data," that is, data disaggregated to compare men and women. The word "gender" was still stuck in linguistics, not yet invented for social analysis.

Comprehensive research, plus feminist critiques: 1970+

Danish economist Esther Boserup made the pioneering breakthrough that sparked the new field of research initially known as "women in development." Boserup (1970) focused on agriculture, for in many southern countries most people lived in rural areas and relied on farming for their food and livelihood. Boserup criticized agricultural development strategies that not only missed many of the workers and decision-makers in farming – women – but also infused new resources and authority to and for men, thereby increasing resource gaps between women and men. Policy allocated agricultural loans and land title deeds to men, automatically assumed to be "heads of household." Had gender terminology been present, one might argue that Boserup examined agricultural development with a gender lens: she critiqued the focus on men in societies that constructed agriculture as "women's work."

Irene Tinker was another pioneering researcher and policy practitioner associated with the Society for International Development. Tinker's article "The adverse impact of development on women" (1976) became a classic. In it, Tinker criticized measures derived from the *formal* and *regulated* economies of the developed, industrialized western world, such as labor force participation – oblivious to counting women's laborious income-generation or income-substitution work in subsistence agricultural economies and informal markets at a time when the majority of the world's people (especially in Asia and Africa) subsisted in agricultural economies. It was ludicrous to say that women represented just 5 percent of the labor force in East African countries, where women did the bulk of work on farms and in markets, feeding their families and communities. The UN's International Labour Office made breakthroughs in analyzing *informal* economies and unregulated workers in the 1970s. By this time, analysts replaced grandiose terms like development with specific reference to labor or labor policy, including formal and informal labor.

Adding new dimensions and their interdependence: entrées for women and gender

Until the 1970s, development focused on economics, assuming expansion would "modernize" nations. Thereafter, analysts began to expand and fine-tune definitions of development with new language and adjectives. The most important among these included:

Growth with Equity (associated with the Overseas Development Council)

Rural and agricultural change (as discussed above, with Boserup)

Basic human needs (BHN) (predecessor to the human capabilities movement) (associated with Paul Streeten and Shahid Javed and, later, Mahbub ul Haq on "enlarging people's choices"), and

Poverty reduction.

(See overviews in Staudt 1990: ch. 1: Staudt 1998: ch. 2.)

These overlapping approaches offered entrées for feminist and gender critiques of development. Consider a fuller discussion of three below.

The language of equity legitimized routine data collection and reports that differentiated and compared people within nations for research, government documents, and IO reports, such as those produced annually in the World Bank and United Nations Development Programme (UNDP). The principles of equality or equity opened doors to new kinds of questions about policies and programs. What was the extent of women's and of men's access to and receipt of micro enterprise loans? Should access be equal or equitable (the latter allowing normative considerations based on need, historic discrimination, and culture, among other topics)? The language of equity provided entrée to a gender-equity agenda. The word "gender" offered a technical-sounding name for a new type of development "expert," useful to IOs that sought to depoliticize women's and redistributive political demands.

The basic human needs (BHN) approach became the entrée to focus on a whole host of public policy issues: hunger, food, health, housing/shelter, maternal-infant-child mortality, longevity, and literacy. With these basic elements of well-being and quality of life in an expanded development agenda, critics could pose questions about contradictions: why is economic growth associated with massive famine and/or homelessness? These contradictions called attention to failures in democratic governance. BHN provided the rationale for policy attention to food distribution, access to healthcare, and safe working conditions.

Growth with equity and BHN formed the foundation for the United Nations Development Programme's annual *Human Development Report* (*HDR*) which defined development in broad human dimensions (health, literacy, and economic growth) and ranked countries based on a Human Development Index (HDI) and a Gender Development Index (GDI), discussed below under the Operationalization Guideline. BHN preceded the later rise of a human capabilities approach in the 1990s, which focused on freedom, choice, and well-being for both women and men (selections in Nussbaum and Glover 1995) – an approach already in process among some IOs.

To reduce poverty, analysts documented its shocking extent based on both income and basic needs considerations and proposed safety-net intervention strategies. Growth with equity provided entrée for analyzing the concentration of wealth and poverty, using income deciles within and between countries. In a key phrase of the era, women and gender were highlighted with studies on the "feminization of poverty" and the overrepresentation of "female-headed households" in poverty.

Necessity: economic growth and/or redistribution

Whether narrowly or broadly defined, development processes require economic resources. From where do resources come to meet basic human needs, reallocate for equality or equity, and reduce poverty? The answer was and is usually found in one of three broad strategies: resource growth, redistribution of existing resources, or some combination of both. Strategic decisions like these are politically charged. Whether for gender equity or for poverty reduction, the key question becomes: Will decision-makers redistribute the wealth in minor to major ways (with what political costs?) or generate enough additional resources to address equity?

At the bottom line, additional economic resources expand options for government decision-makers and for individual consumers with supposed resources to "choose" to purchase more food, housing, and healthcare. Under conditions of high wealth concentrations, state developers can redistribute the wealth (a costly political strategy) or generate growth to spread additional resources beyond those already privileged. The latter strategy is safer for political elites, albeit not necessarily optimal to enhance human capabilities. One certainty, though, is that neither redistribution nor growth invested in women/gender equality will occur without changing power relations: diverse women's engagement in the political process.

From women's politics to gender and the triumph of capitalism

Gender would be invisible without the rise of the global women's movement and its connection to the United Nations-sponsored conferences, beginning in 1975 with the International Women's Year (Mexico City) conference and turning into subsequent conferences mid-decade and decades thereafter.

Women's visibility signaled growing power (albeit still limited) and the potential for changing gender power relations. The UN conferences hosted not only official delegations from government but also from NGOs, known as the Tribune. Thousands attended high-visibility meetings mid-decade in Copenhagen, Denmark (1980), in Nairobi, Kenya (1985), and in Beijing, China (1995), after which conservative and religious backlash set in (Baden and Goetz 1997).

Before the backlash, however, a breakthrough document emerged from women in the South (Sen and Grown 1987): *DAWN, Development Alternatives for Women in a New Era*. It analyzed women's multiple and diverse realities and called for "common opposition to gender oppression and hierarchy" (Sen and Grown 1987: 19; also see analysis in Staudt 1998). *DAWN* triggered the rise of a gendered approach to development that emphasized empowerment.

Other momentous events affected the move toward a single economic paradigm in a global neoliberal economy. By the late 1980s, the former Soviet Union collapsed and with its aligned countries, moved toward capitalist paradigms or what is now called the neoliberal global economy (with the rest of the world parting ways with how US politics uniquely uses the word "liberal"). Economist Robert Heilbroner wrote a compelling, widely disseminated article titled "Reflections: the triumph of capitalism" (1989). He by no means celebrated the triumph, but rather called for attention to connections between democracy and capitalism in ways that would temper crude, predatory capitalism with regulations and redistributive policies.

Now, nearly 200 countries govern as sovereign and semi-sovereign regimes in a globally linked economy within a neoliberal, capitalist-market economic paradigm – without a seemingly alternative paradigm (though see the World Social Forum program positions). Analysts rarely use the term development alone, for the term has become passé without its descriptor adjectives (like human or equitable), references to public policy, or grand paradigms. More and more, people align with globalization and antiglobalization discourses to augment or displace the generic term development. World Social Forums offer alternatives to global neoliberalism, but contain curiously little analysis of women and gender (George 2004) (see critique in Staudt, Rai, and Parpart 2001; also selections in Eschle and Maiguashca 2005). With an alternative paradigm, will feminist internationalists start their interrogation all over, or build on a better foundation?

Perhaps those in the South, including feminists, will focus attention on global redistribution before gender equity at the national level. An early *Human Development Report* contained a champagne-glass-shaped figure on global inequalities, with the top fifth of the world's population in the wide, shallow glass, and the rest of the world's population along the narrow stem (1994: 63). After all, in a context where the richest 20 percent controlled 85 percent of the wealth (UNDP *HDRs* address figures like these annually in multiple ways; this figure from 1996: 2), and where the gaps have increased, not decreased, it makes sense to prioritize *global* redistribution over gender redistribution *within* the meager scraps of impoverished countries. While nation-states are the usual units of analysis, with governments ostensibly accountable to their inhabitants, the global context may shape well-being as much as or more than national policies.

Let us put this inequality in starker monetary terms in a world where nearly half the world's inhabitants earn the average of approximately US$2 daily. If women and men in country *X* achieve equality, perhaps with enhanced capabilities, at US$3 daily, how does that *national* gender equity square with women and men in country *Y*, where women earn a minimum of US$40 daily (and perhaps gender-expert consultants earn US$100–300 daily)? Is gender equity without global redistribution a smokescreen for sustaining world inequalities? Without a global inequality critique, much current gender analysis lacks a challenging edge.

Furthermore, gender intersects with race, class, caste, and region, requiring political engagement on multiple fronts and in multiple struggles. Let us also put those intersecting issues in stark terms. If a nation-based inverted pyramid shows the majority working poor on top, with a small middle and upper class below, how would augmented opportunities for upper-class women affect the majority of impoverished women? Currently, gender analysis alone offers too modest a challenge for global inequalities.

The gender lens: what difference does/might it make?

By the mid-1980s, the term "gender" was born, and the concept became useful to a variety of constituencies. *Academics* preferred the word, for it opened potential analysis to social constructions of women and men in ethnicity/race, caste, and class terms and of power relations between men and women in everyday lives. *IOs* preferred the word, for it depoliticized women's offices and opened the door for outreach to men, as, for example, in condom distribution or batterers' programs amid gender-based violence epidemics. The word "gender" did not translate into other languages all that well (Jahan 1995), but activists and academics were willing to use it if it legitimized attention and opened the spigots for funding more equitable resource distribution.

Consultants/NGOs used the word to respond to requests for "gender train-ing," a potential way to spread awareness about male privilege among those once resistant to women's programs. Training may last from a few hours to a few days, with participants carrying lifelong baggage of male privilege. As Maitrayee Mukhopadhyay and Franz Wong have so well analyzed (2006), the effectiveness of gender training has rarely been assessed in different con-texts and audiences. Indeed, they argue that the gender training model has been based on a northern, one-size-fits-all approach (Moser 1993), ultimately reducing its effectiveness and depoliticizing its potential.

International organizations (like the World Bank and UNDP) quickly adopted and coopted "gender training" and "gender analysis," though rarely conceptualized gender in its full-blown possibilities. Institutional reorganizers renamed "women's programs" as "gender programs." Feminists debated the merits of discourse on women versus gender with concern for the depoliti-cization of women to accommodate IOs' alleged technical neutrality and the allocation of gender funds to men (see extensive analysis in Jaquette and Staudt 2006). Gradually, the field became known as "Gender and development."

A gender lens applied to expanded and more comprehensive definitions of development approaches documents clearly differentiated experiences between men and women within national and subnational units of anal-ysis. Routinely, researchers, analysts, and program evaluators use gender-disaggregated data to identify development problems and address solutions. Literacy and school enrollment figures are frequently broken down into "gen-der" columns: women and men. Gender experts train personnel to examine agricultural societies with a gender lens, asking, for example: What work do men and women do, with what assets? What benefits do they derive from their labors? Mostly, gender serves as a substitute for "sex" differentiation or for social analysis to design better programs and projects, rather than for the analysis of intersections of race/ethnicity, caste, and class, or of gender power relations and the social constructions of masculinity and femininity in insti-tutions themselves. Despite these modest gains, gender analysis is an advance over earlier conceptions of the generic man as equal to people, without calling attention to difference, equality, equity, and basic fairness or justice.

At minimum, a gender lens acknowledges that the kinds of market, soci-etal, and policy changes associated with generic development affect women and men differently. More substantially, a gender lens could call attention to the changing power relations between men and women in different eco-nomic classes, ethnic and language groups, nations, and the world. To do so in ways that change policies and budgetary allocations would likely require vast increases in visible women's political power. Gender is usually reduced to the disaggregation of data by male and female (formerly named sex differentiation) to identify opportunities for better program and policy intervention.

Many governments and IOs adopted women's programs, later renamed gender program offices, to which there was much internal resistance, marginalized as "political" or as political concessions (Staudt 1985, 1998, Jahan 1995). Such offices allowed potential women/gender advocates inside bureaucracy, nudging modest concessions or redistributions, without necessary connections with outside NGOs (Staudt 1997). Such offices had ambitious mandates to "mainstream" government agencies (Rai 2003a), but feminist institutional analysis has been fruitful in separating realities from rhetorical promises and ambitions (Goetz 1997, Miller and Razavi 1998, Staudt 1997, 2008). Some agencies and governments declared that gender mainstreaming was finished as a rationale to eliminate offices. As such, gender can serve as a tool to eliminate attention to ubiquitous and still lingering gender disparities.

Operationalization Guideline

Deborah Stone, in her insightful analysis of the economy and polis (1997), considers principles and evidence used to move policy analysis into successful broad-based constituencies coalesced for change in the decision-making process. Jane Jaquette (1990) takes principles and applies them to women and development policies. Stone's chapters 6 and 7 examine the use of metaphors, both symbolic and numeric. Quantitative indicators are considered more credible in IOs and governments (not to forget mainstream political science departments) than qualitative analysis. If gender analysts accept the preference for quantitative research, they should interrogate the choices of indicators for the numeric metaphors they choose.

Development studies have tended to use numeric metaphors to compare, contrast, and rank nations in terms of their levels of development. They report data in cross-sectional ways, at single points in time, and in longitudinal ways, across time. Much of the data used come from government reports, of varying quality and reliability, and from independent research. And again, the data are stuck at the nation-state level, rather than the global, the local (including changing cultural groupings within states), or at borders.

In the postwar period, development researchers and IOs adopted numeric indicators from developed nations to capture the means and ends: income, earnings, labor force participation in the formal regulated economy, national and domestic economic growth rates, industrialization, and formal communications, among others. As such, they excluded the majority of southern populations, who work informally or in the subsistence and care economies, such as women (see geographer Jan Monk's exercise in Staudt 1990: ch. 4). Western indicators of men do not travel well to men or women in countries where much income-generating work occurs outside the formal economy.

Numeric indicators portray a partly fictional world that may hardly measure the full scope of trade, income, and work. (For a fascinating account of off-the-books, uncounted economies that begins grounded analysis in southern Africa and goes global to ports around the world, see Nordstrom 2007.) Analysts from northern rich countries would do well to pursue grounded research to determine whether enough confidence exists in official quantitative figures about areas they study.

Development analysts initially neglected uncounted problems that had obvious implications for the quality of life, the seeming core of development's meaning. How can country X's high growth rates be compatible with high rates of infant mortality, maternal mortality, famine deaths, people lacking resources to eat but one meal daily, less than 1,000 calories (and clearly not on western "diets")? Once armed with numbers, these problems began to be counted and reported to critique the contradictions.

Even comprehensive definitions of development bypassed considerations about voice, violence, choice, and governance as difficult to measure and therefore not countable and reportable. If country Y's middling per capita income coexisted with involuntary motherhood, political dictatorship, and forced conscription, could it represent development? There are enormous obstacles to generating, counting, and reporting national-level data that people hide because of painful shame (e.g. domestic violence) or because their actions could subject them to criminal prosecution (self-induced abortions, for example).

Gender-disaggregated data

As development conceptions expanded, with new names in the 1970s and thereafter (growth with equity, poverty reduction, and basic human needs), analysts searched for more indicators to make visible problems *within* nations (again, rather than between nations). Daunting challenges of collecting accurate data existed then and now in nations without transparent governance, resources for data collection, and appropriate indicators. Few nation-states have counting obsessions like those in the United States.

Even if governments made good-faith efforts at counting, inaccuracies arise. The super-rich are often adept at hiding their income and assets despite luxury, overconsumption, opulent homes, and Mercedes Benz cars. The resourceful poor also hide assets (like jewelry) from tax collectors. Yet tools are available, however flawed and speculative the numbers and curves shown on charts. For example, analysts used Gini coefficients to graph income inequalities, with reported earnings for the top decile compared to the bottom decile.

And where would women fit in such graphs? Analysts assume equality within households, but Sen (1990a) and Dwyer and Bruce (1988) put such idyllic notions to rest. How would one accurately calculate women's control over income and assets or the "worth" of their labor in informal earnings, work that substitutes for earnings, or the cost of hiring labor for women's unpaid work? Some IOs, like the International Labour Organization, grappled with these issues. Economist Lourdes Benería, who worked at the ILO for some years, discusses the "underestimation of unpaid work in national and international statistics," mentioning the "typical story about the decrease in GNP [Gross National Product] when a man marries his housekeeper" (2003: 133).

Quantitative figures can reveal much about gender's consequences for quality of life. Some readers believe only numbers. And from superficial figures, one can further explain intersections with figures, rates, and gaps in ethnicity/race, region, caste, and class terms, with both economic and social data – if counted and reported. Pre-1994 apartheid South Africa could never be understood without such data disaggregation.

Analysts regularly use health and education indicators to tap the essence of life quality, capacity, and longevity. Infant mortality rates reveal how many infants, of 1,000, die before age one. In rich countries, rates fall below 20, but in poor countries rates swell to 100–200. Child mortality rates reveal the same, focusing on children who die under age five. Causes of death may be easily treatable health problems that would cost cents per child to cure, but few have access to healthcare and simple medicines in many countries. Longevity rates reveal much about the risks of life in poverty, war, and stingy social funding. Childbirth is a leading cause of death in some nations. Maternal mortality figures on the number of deaths per 100,000 reveal much (the African continent has the highest numbers, over 900) as does Total Fertility Rate (average number of births per female), still averaging as high as 8 per woman in some countries. Figures on adult literacy and the proportion of school-aged children enrolled in school are relatively easy to collect and report. Social indicators like these joined economic indicators to paint a more comprehensive picture of development.

It is relatively easy to disaggregate health and education indicators in female and male columns, called gender disaggregation (but not based on the nuances of social intersections). National figures are available from many IOs, and in annual reports, such as the World Bank and the United Nations Development Programme's *Human Development Report*. In over 20 countries, gender gaps in literacy exceed 15 points, especially in certain countries of Asia and the Middle East. Relative deprivation is on some scholarly, policy, and practitioner agendas. Consider China's "high suicide rates by rural women. Chinese women make up about one-fifth of the world's women, but they comprise half of the female suicides" (Summerfield 2006: 154). Such reports are chilling reminders of systemic structures that devalue women's lives.

It took economist Amartya Sen to make visible the stark consequences of patriarchy and female subordination that take their toll on women's very lives. He used concrete universal numeric indicators from the censuses of Asian countries, quantitative data that are more credible to wider audiences than ethnography and small samples. To a wider audience than academics reading obscure scholarly journals, he titled his article "More than 100 million women are missing" (1990b). The analysis of demographic sex ratios showed selected South and East Asian regions with as few as around 80 females for every 100 men. From Sen, we can infer that the systemic devaluation of women is gruesomely patterned, reflecting the neglect of girls and possible female infanticide. Perhaps we should name this "fem-infanticide."

HDI, GDI, and GEM: numeric advances, yet flaws

Since 1990, the UNDP's annual *Human Development Report* contains comparative analyses of nations using quantitative composite scores of the Human Development Index (HDI). The HDI consists of longevity (life expectancy indicators), educational attainment (adult literacy and enrollment at primary, secondary, and tertiary school levels), and per capita income adjusted with purchasing power formulas. The HDR ranks countries with a Gender-HDI index, called GDI. Given ubiquitous and pervasive gender inequalities, GDI lowers all national rankings and, for countries with large gender gaps, lowers their rankings considerably compared with the HDI. This is a remarkable finding, and one useful for political challenges and pressure.

The HDR also uses a Gender Empowerment Measure, known as GEM, consisting of political and economic participation, the latter the percentage of women in managerial and technical positions. Yet GEM (like GDI) is not unpacked in intersection terms (i.e. in ethnicity/race, class, caste, and region). How does one interpret these "gender equity" data in societies with wealth concentrations and majority impoverished populations? High GEM could reinforce class/caste inequalities and conceal powerlessness for the female majority. The interdependence (Interdependence Guideline) is difficult to operationalize. Also, one can take issue with the choice of indicators, for women's lives are far more complex than what formal positions in politics and the work force reveal. Informal grassroots women's organizations are typically invisible in national-level reporting systems.

For both HDI and GDI, some quantitative figures are scanty, unreliable, and probable undercounts. For example, *HDR* publishes charts on violence, but even the fraction of countries that submit data post official figures for gender violence (sexual assault) that governments report, which are unrealistically low compared to independent research results. Yet both the GDI and GEM rankings make inequalities visible and provide some critical leverage.

A still remaining challenge is the deeper, cross-national, cross-cultural meanings of mostly western-derived concepts amid thousands of cultural, linguistic, and identity groups in the world through grounded analysis.

Traveling Guideline

Once the abstract, grandiose notions about globalization, economic paradigms, and development (along with their numerous numeric metaphors) are considered, some analysts pursue a *grounded* analysis through ethnographies, case studies, participant observation, and conversations with real people who can provide "reality checks." One can thereby analyze the connections, disconnections, and intersections for generic and specialized conceptions of global–local analysis. Herein, the Traveling Guideline raises questions about culture, a term of notorious conceptual challenges.

Cultural studies range from the philosophical-literary wordplay of postmodern studies on the one hand, to art and music on another, and, more commonly, to studies in the "field" of society involving immersion in the languages and undisciplined real worlds of complex realities. In this chapter, I define culture as everyday diverse behaviors, attitudes, and historical legacies that are sustained across generations (Chabal and Daloz 2006). The imposition of a "museum-like" model of static, essentialist values to connect large numbers of people is futile, as noted earlier. Feminist scholar Uma Narayan (1997) warns of the haste in which western feminists paint India with the dowry-death, bride-burning swath, reducing the problem of women (or of men) to culture. She wonders whether western feminists recognize domestic violence and murder – women-hating practices – in their own countries.

Recall the construction of cultures in what were once called "national character" studies of the mid-twentieth century: Russian swaddling practices that supposedly gave rise to authoritarian cultures, Burmese early weaning practices that generated political instability, and so on. Such studies cast shadows on the value of anthropology, a discipline which once reeked of masculinist, patronizing, colonial agendas. Within countries around which colonizer countries imposed boundaries, one might locate hundreds of language and cultural groupings (in Nigeria, for example), *vis-à-vis* other groups and the state.

Causal Relationships Guideline

Analysts often clarify their research with specifications about what is to be explained – the dependent variable (DV) – and the factors that appear to contribute to explanations, known as independent variables (IVs). Quantitative research demands such specifications, particularly for making sense of complex datasets. Development's multiple stakeholders and audiences complicate the attribution of women as the DV or one of the IVs that enhance development. NGO and IO advocates often make their cases about gender to resistant mainstream economists with evidence about the efficiency, instrumentality, and effectiveness of enhancing women's skills, power, and assets for better development.

Some examples are in order. Several UN agencies focus on enhancing girls and boys – children – their survival, growth, and development. Advocates compile data on how increased women's education and/or income (women = IV) enhance children's development. In contexts of high female illiteracy and low school enrollments, such discourse may produce good outcomes for women. But IOs like UNICEF have children as their central concern, not women. Similarly, to tap the often vastly superior amounts of resources available for economic development, like agricultural loans and small business development, advocates may draw on evidence-based research of women farmers' efficiency and innovativeness in agricultural production or their loan repayment rates in micro enterprises.

Yet across the decades of women/gender/feminist research, analysts have often focused on women's power, assets, and rights as the DV. They document the effects of mainstream development strategies and public policies on women, different categories of women, and gender power relations. Researchers often "choose" which side of the equation on which they align.

Concluding reflections

Drawing on historical perspectives regarding context and naming practices, this chapter raises questions about the continued use of the generic word development in national units of analysis. Instead, I argue that researchers should draw on all the conceptual flowering since the late 1950s, whether inserting adjectives before development, focusing on specific public policies, and/or addressing globalization, local grounded realities, or the interdependent linkages between levels.

The chapter also offers realistic insights about the advances associated with politicizing women's issues and the remaining challenges of using discourse like "gender" in an institutional world that prides itself on professionalism yet promulgates economic paradigms and ideologies in the name of fill-in-the-blank development. Gender-disaggregated data (or columns with data on women and men) are essential tools in research, yet gender terminology has not produced much progress in analyzing power relations, intersections, and social constructions in development research. In fact, some institutions have simply coopted the term "gender" and continued past practices.

This chapter has taken on the huge agenda of examining different conceptions of development, their measurements, and feminist/women/gender analyses that speak to multiple constituencies which, I argue, must be kept in mind in conceptualizing multiple versions of development: advocates, practitioners, and researchers. The chapter is probably broader and more interdisciplinary than most others in this volume.

I focused on the changing conceptions of mainstream, overly economist orientations to development and the obliviousness to women and gender until the advent of extensive scholarly and activist attention to and with powerful disciplines, governments, and IO institutions. These scholars and activists move inside and outside the institutions, for better or worse, influencing processes more than disciplinary-specific writers whose work is imbibed only by scholarly specialists and rarely applied in the real world.

Scholars increasingly use a gender lens that certainly represents an advance in previous conceptions, but generates relatively modest impacts. Mostly, "gender" is a substitute for essentialist language like "sex" in the routine data disaggregation to report, compare, and design better policies, programs, and project interventions at the national and subnational levels. At best, gender and development could examine power relations and race/ethnicity, class, caste, and regional social constructions that infect institutions and governments to their very core (Lovenduski 1986). At worst, gender could be used to dismantle women-renamed-gender programs in the name of successful gender mainstreaming.

Gender is no panacea to women's relative political powerlessness (compared with men) at global, transnational IOs, and national levels. As a concept stuck at nation-state levels of analysis, gender equity lenses may mask global, class, and other inequalities. Gender analysts should find better ways to connect the global, national, and local levels of analysis.

The women/gender and development cauldron merits investment and energy, for the urgency of women's very lives are at issue and the terrain of analytic opportunity is huge, covering nearly 200 countries and thousands of cultures. Obstacles are present: analysis confined to nation-states in the global, transnational world; overreliance on quantitative indicators that tap only partial realities about women and gender relations; the interdependence (Interdependence Guideline) of gender and class within nations.

Analysts should bring global-state-local perspectives to their work, dealing with real people in grounded contexts but moving beyond the confines of nation-state analysis in comparative politics. As Lourdes Benería also argues, one should "take a global approach" to the regulation of markets, labor protection, and standards (2003: 68). At the same time, we must recognize that now, accountability in governance rests only in nation-states that are more or less democratic (and more or less masculine, patriarchal, or misogynist). Backlash has set in to the energetic women's world conferences since 1975, so much so that subsequent conferences, including the most recent "Beijing Plus 10" in 2005, have been quiet affairs, designed to affirm and confirm agendas from past meetings (Baden and Goetz 1997; Molyneux and Razavi 2006). Democracy must be woven into global-local perspectives for a fairer and more equitable distribution of global assets, resources, and incomes.

PART II

GENDER-SPECIFIC CONCEPTS

8 Gender ideology: masculinism and feminalism

Georgia Duerst-Lahti

Gender ideology is a concept often used, but seldom interrogated. In distinct contrast to other concepts such as gender identity, its use is so off-hand that it seldom rates an index entry in books related to any topic on gender, feminism, or women, although hegemonic masculinity – a concept that clearly suggests ideology – often is indexed. One suspects the definitional flexibility and multiple meanings associated with ideology more generally to be the source of both its common use and conceptual disregard. In "terminology reshuffling" (Gerring 1997: 960), gender ideology often is used synonymously with concepts such as gender attitudes, gender norms, gender power, gender relations, gender structures, and gender dynamics. It also appears in discussions of feminism, especially when feminism challenges cultural tradition or patriarchal dominance. A quick electronic search of the phrase "gender ideology" from 1980 to 2007 yielded 5,170 results.[1] A nonsystematic examination of random pages from this search suggests that these articles overwhelmingly are concerned either with Bem sex-typing of traits and various psychological attitudes toward gender or with gender roles related to marriage, family, or household arrangements. Similar to the Poole-Rosenthal treatment of the liberal-conservative "political ideology" scale, some studies scaled gender ideology from traditional to egalitarian. Most of the 5,170 studies emanated from sociology or psychology, although anthropology also yielded a strong presence, analyzing the gender ideology underpinning norms for gender roles found in various world cultures. In short, the concept has been used quite loosely, which suggests that the systematic exploration of the topic invited by this book is entirely in order.

In this chapter, I explore the concept of gender ideology and consider gender's ideological dimensions. Particularly, I argue that gender ideology should be conceptualized as a political ideology that has at least two interdependent

---

[1] I used Google Advanced Scholar for the exact phrase anywhere in the text, from 1980 to 2007. Search performed May 30, 2007.

categories of masculinism and feminalism, as well as concepts in the gray zone. While masculinism may be familiar to many readers, the concept of feminalism draws heavily from the ideology of feminism and has emerged from feminist analysis of gender ideology. As will be pursued in this chapter, like many new concepts important to research, it identifies new phenomena – or at least a good way to operationalize hard-to-name phenomena – and moves to areas heretofore not studied. In the process of exploring gender ideology, I also critique the usual disciplinary boundaries of "political ideology" for ways it erases many modes of politics, including gender politics. I try to demonstrate how recognizing gender ideology of masculinism and feminalism, along with the internal complexity of each, leads to different, enriched, and more sophisticated understandings of political ideologies and their consequences.

Getting to masculinism and feminalism via gender ideology

Context

Gender ideology emerged from the study of gender and feminist considerations of political ideology. As will be explicated, gender ideologies are structured beliefs and ideas about ways power should be arranged according to social constructs associated with sexed bodies. It is ideas about how gender and power should be put into action. But why speak of gender ideology instead of just gender?

Following earlier work by J. Scott (1986), Harding (1986) and others, Mary Hawkesworth (1997, 2005, 2006) has eloquently articulated the need to focus on gender as a category of analysis and to avoid slipping into gender as a universal explana. Because of the strong propensity to accord explanatory force to gender, she suggests "a need to interrogate the concept more thoroughly" (1997: 655 n. 2) and hence "to take advantage of crucial distinctions such as sexed embodiedness, sexuality, sexual identity, gender identity, gendered divisions of labor, and gender symbolism, rather than collapsing such diverse notions into the single term *gender*" (1997: 682). In taking up gender ideology rather than collapsing gender's ideological aspects into the single term of gender (or feminism), it is possible to recognize ways usual treatments of political ideology have rendered gender nonpolitical and invisible. It also enables conceptual tightening of the loose use of the concept "gender ideology," which ideally strengthens its scholarly potency, along with fostering more accurate and unbiased research. Such is the project of this book and this chapter. Both parts of the compound noun, gender and ideology, thus require attention.

Gender has conventionally been tied to the human body – male and female, men and women – but cannot be done essentially or exclusively. Human bodies do not fall neatly into two opposite and "given" sexes (Lorber 1987, Fausto-Sterling 2000). Further, the biological category of sex is itself constructed by the human mind as a way of thinking about corporeal bodies, so the neat distinction between sex as biological and gender as socially constructed is also imperfect (Butler 1990). Although gender as binary or dualism is consistent throughout world cultures, the exact makeup of the two genders varies greatly, and some cultures have recognized three and even four genders. Sophisticated gender analysis therefore constantly struggles against the "natural attitude," in which gender is assumed to be ordinary, dichotomous, and rooted in knowable dichotomous sexed bodies. Despite enormous differences traveling across cultures (Tripp 2000), ingrained belief systems, tradition, and other socialization and social control mechanisms place prescribed roles associated with the two "opposite" sexes within a culture, making them very difficult to see as anything but "natural" (Hawkesworth 1997, 2006). Gender ideology, arguably among the most important of all political ideologies, is one key mechanism holding the link to bodies and the naturalness of binary opposites in place (Duerst-Lahti 2002a, 2002b). As a result, conceptualizing gender-related terms such as masculinism and its concomitant feminalism without referring to sexed bodies is difficult (Nicholson 1994).

Yet, feminist scholars have also recognized that gender has been constructed through social and political processes that play out as innumerable performances and practices of masculinity and femininity, which in turn are embedded in and enforced by social and political structures and institutions. These manly and womanly practices and associations need not be tied to human bodies. The military is imbued with masculinity and nursing with femininity, for example, and neither is a human body even if each is associated with them, and perhaps disproportionally preferred by men and women respectively. Such gendering derives from beliefs about masculinity and femininity, and beliefs rest upon ideologies, whether or not most of us are aware that an ideology is operating. The state, for example, controls women's reproduction, sets kinship rules, and enforces gender roles in families in order to ensure its own survival (J. Stevens 1999). Gender can be created through policies that may seem unrelated to gender (Johnson, Duerst-Lahti, and Norton 2007). The centrality of ideas and belief systems to both gender and politics inevitably involves ideology. Gender itself has ideological dimensions through ideas about biological sex and the ways power should be distributed. Despite a tendency to conflate politics with phenomena related to governing, gender ideology is very political.

The definitions of ideology are many, as John Gerring (1997) has ably detailed through an analysis of key social science studies of it (e.g. Adorno *et al.* 1950, Lowenstein 1953, Campbell *et al.* 1960, Minar 1961, Lane 1962, McClosky *et al.* 1964, Converse 1964, Geertz 1964/1973, Nettle 1967, Sartori 1969, Marx and Engels 1970, Mullins 1974, Keohane 1976, Foucault 1979, Hamilton 1987, and Rejai 1991). Gerring identifies five common approaches: a tendency to contrast elite and mass publics; avoiding the term "ideology" and substituting others such as "myth worldview" or "belief systems"; through traditions of usage that lack a definition (Gramsci did not use the term, for example); explaining it without providing a shared general definition; and letting a thousand definitions bloom (1997: 959–64). My reading of common uses of "gender ideology" suggests that usually other terms are substituted – norms, attitudes, expectations, roles, beliefs, and sometimes gender power – or it is used without definition.

Gerring also developed a "comprehensive definitional framework" that involves six related attributes with subattributes of each. For example, he traces the "location" of ideology as authors treat or locate it as thought, behavior, and language or discourse (1997: 966–7). He recognizes that ideology has been considered to be only ideational, what political actors do, and discourse or a set of linguistic symbols, although he also is aware that many scholars find it impossible to separate these, as behavior requires discourse to be comprehended, and ideas usually underpin behavior and arguably are inextricably linked to studying discourse. Certainly gender ideology has been considered to be all of these by various authors.

More important for our purposes is the "subject matter," which Gerring finds divided according to politics, power, or the world-at-large. This categorization, while clearly reflected in studies, reveals a problem long encountered by feminism. "Political" and "politics" remain undefined. Yet, most political science scholars of ideology have considered politics to be related exclusively to government and its processes. For example, "Politics is the 'home turf' of ideology and to move beyond politics – even broadly defined – is to move beyond the generally understood meaning of the term and beyond the sphere to which many of its common attributes properly apply" (Gerring 1997: 968). As a result, feminists needed to discover and then contest the "boundaries of the political" (Benhabib 1996). Discovery took consciousness-raising in order to see beyond the hegemonic norms of "normal" because the government-related conception of politics overlooked elements important to the world-at-large approaches, such as social norms and controls enforced by traditions or "social" institutions such as religion or the family. These forces of ideology, articulated most famously by Geertz (1964/1973 in Gerring, 1997: 969), create individual identities that arise out of related processes, shared meaning, and cultural and symbol-systems. For these reasons, below I will argue that the traditional left–right continuum of political ideology so common in studies of political science should be instead called "governing ideology." Doing so enables more forms of political ideologies, such as gender, race, and class to be analyzed for its politics.

Gerring's subject matter categorization also suggests that many scholars of ideology have similarly overlooked forms of power other than legitimized political power. While entire traditions of usage, such as the structural Marxists, certainly recognize political ideology for its power elements, the influential studies in the early 1960s (e.g. Campbell *et al.* 1960) often began by assuming that ideology was primarily political, suggesting but not defining "political" as related to government. Such studies then went on to broaden ideology to include power found in other realms, such as social institutions, discussed above. This focus particularly considered the distribution of power and the relations of domination it sustained based upon an ideological statement of the human situation. Such positions also include the notion of power in action or that in some way the ideations of an ideology are intended to be enacted. The more successful the ideology, the more successful the enactment. Accordingly, politics is about power relations, regardless of whether they occur in and around government or within social relations.

Nonetheless, readers of this book likely are social scientists interested in politics, especially governmentally related politics. In studying equal representation, congress, and policy I have taken the position that gender as political ideology requires three conceptual dimensions (Duerst-Lahti 2002a, 2002b, Johnson, Duerst-Lahti, and Norton 2007): Ideology involves judgments about human nature (usually based upon some type of constructed group difference), a determination about the way power should be distributed as a result of those judgments (through state institutions, religious doctrine, cultural traditions, legitimized coercion, etc.), and an action plan for enacting that power distribution (through legitimating institutions, law, and belief systems, cultural norms, expectations, and practices, most of which shape human behavior). The context of gender ideology is of this understanding of political ideology.

The emergence of gender ideology: patriarchy and feminism

Throughout much of second wave feminist thinking in western societies, the primary concepts for gender ideology have been patriarchy for men and feminism for women (e.g. Barrett 1980, Coward 1983, G. Lerner 1986, Walby 1990). The alternative concepts of masculinism and feminalism have emerged from these terms as sophistication grew. Particularly, feminist analysis began to theorize gender as a category of analysis itself, rather than merely "a social variable assigned to individual people" (Harding 1986: 17). The notion of a category of analysis sometimes leads to confusion when the terms *variable* and *category* are used synonymously. Such often occurs in sex difference research in which sex is treated as a variable and hence is one category to be analyzed for difference. Usually this type of analysis is done between unproblematized biological males and females; sex, which is often not specified beyond male–female, masculinity–femininity, men–women, is understood to be a static category about which much is already known (Hancock 2007a; Junn 2007). In contrast, to look at gender, Scott influentially argued, was to look at a "constituent element of social relations." It is an element that makes up social relations and which operates in multiple interrelated, overlapping ways that bring meaning, set norms, underpin identities, and more. It also means analyzing "a primary way of signifying relations of power" (J. Scott 1986: 1067–8). This conceptualization, notably, overlaps greatly with various aspects of ideology in social science detailed by Gerring. By this reasoning, one could just study gender rather than gender ideology.[2] But gender scholarship has evolved greatly since 1986, and gender ideology has been studied widely as part of family roles. Further, gender as an analytic category invites a closer interrogation of gender ideology in order to take advantage of crucial distinctions between it and other concepts important to understanding gender.

Western political thinkers have long considered normative aspects of gender, even if it was not conceived as gender ideology (Shanley and Pateman 1991). For example, Plato detailed ways "good men" should behave to be proper

---

[2] Importantly, to move from sex as a variable to gender as a category of analysis means not succumbing to that which is assumed to be known and true. Mary Hawkesworth (1997, 2005) cogently traces the metamorphosis of feminist gender scholarship since 1975, although she and others recognize its earlier use as a binary concept in functionalism (e.g. Levi-Strauss 1969) and as a longstanding and wildly inconsistent aspect of languages. This second wave feminist theorizing grew out of a larger tradition in the English-speaking world that R. W. Connell calls 'gender theory' (Connell 2002: 115–35). He locates these theories as beginning during the Enlightenment period and accelerating during the mid-nineteenth century when "science, suffrage, and empire" figured as dominant influences. Nonetheless, overt analysis of gender is a relatively new undertaking, with Sandra Harding offering a strong defense of gender as an analytic category in 1986.

guardians, and what women could do to be philosopher kings (Saxonhouse 1985). In the West, men's near control of "their" women was institutionalized at least through the Renaissance,[3] at first through religion and then through the state (Morgan 2006: 35–7). Under liberal theory, masculine dominance became simultaneously legitimized and masked in discourse of the individual, which in US practice meant male head of household (Kerber 1980). Universal rights and citizenship for individuals proved not very universal, and men with institutional power had every reason to normalize their masculine advantage (Phillips 1998, Connell 1995). In this context of legitimized masculine dominance, ideas and action for female resistance emerge.

If patriarchy and its ideology, which by the 1990s became widely known as masculinism, had incentive to mask its hegemonic dominance in the discourse and practices of universal individuals and meritorious standards, women had reason to react against their subordination. Those who wrote in opposition to men's domination of women and their unequal treatment have been named feminists, a tradition that begins at least in the twelfth century and certainly takes flight with Christine di Pizan during the late fourteenth and early fifteenth centuries. A classically educated woman in the court for French ruler Charles V, she wrote about the need for women's equality (di Pizan 1999). By the eighteenth century many political thinkers, especially female thinkers, focused upon the need for women's education, as well as the "rebellious" position put forward by Mary Wollstonecraft that women should have the same rights as men (Gunther-Canada 2001). Both di Pizan and Wollstonecraft have been called the first feminist, even though the term did not come into widespread use in English until the late nineteenth century.

Unlike patriarchy – which can be used to mean a system of rule, a way to organize households, an ideology, and more – feminism has always been recognized as a political ideology. It is marked by the suffix "ism," and indisputably has sought more political power for women, two dimensions of ideologies. It also was recognized as ideological because it challenged the ideology of masculinism that was both unnamed and made largely invisible due to its hegemonic position. As the dominant gender ideology, masculinism has been capable of setting the terms of normal, just, and proper arrangements for political and social power. This recognition of masculinism and feminism as

---

[3] Because class and race could override sex, the use of "their" women suggests that elite women could dominate non-elite men, slaveowners dominate slaves regardless of sex, and generally the powerful dominate the less powerful regardless of sex. Nonetheless, laws and practices generally institutionalized elite men's advantages over all women and less powerful men. Even elite women confronted the institutionalized system of male dominance, although they may not have suffered its full effects.

political ideologies is a necessity for understanding these concepts, a point taken up in more detail later. Important here is the evolution of gender ideology, and the development of masculinism along with an even newer concept, feminalism.

On naming, negation, and gray zones

The language of dichotomies, dualisms, and opposites suffuses conceptualizations of sex and gender and carries over into gender ideology. Biological sexes of male and female become cultural constructs of women and men, who perform masculinity and femininity. In terms of anthropological categories, patriarchies have been cast as entirely distinct from matriarchies, in systems of rule by fathers and mothers respectively. Of course, many feminist scholars have long critiqued the notion of such dichotomies. First, humans – regardless of biological genitalia, hormones, morphology, or other markers of sex difference – share much more than they differ. Such construction of differences demonstrates the "givenness" and ideology of biology (Butler 1990, Lorber 1987). Sex differences are opposites not empirically but ideologically. Second, because nurture is so integral to nature – with some estimates that about half of any human is a product of innate biology with the other half a product of human nurture – actually knowing the ontology of males and females becomes impossible. Such confounds knowing what biological humans would be like without cultural ideologies that shape the gender of any given individual, as well as the materiality of human bodies themselves (Jaggar and Bordo 1989). Third, sex and gender differences emerge most clearly in studies that focus on averages and the relatively marginal differences between those who are known as males and those known as females. Lost in such conceptualizations are tomboy girls or sensitive boys, as well as many practices of homosexuals, transsexuals, and transgendered communities. Like the first point, even sex-difference studies find much greater differences among males and among females than between them (Eagly 1987). Finally, bodies come in many biological variations, not just two, as intersexed bodies readily demonstrate. At least five distinct biologically sexed bodies have been identified using the standard markers of biological sex (Fausto-Sterling 2000).

In other words, despite discursive dichotomies, human bodies and the genders that shape and reinforce them run along a continuum and generally overlap extensively. As Judith Shapiro (1991) has demonstrated amply, given sex-change operations and transsexual and transgender processes, the *idea* of two genders appears to be much more fixed and enduring than biological sex.

The power to enforce and make material this ideation, through institutions, cultural practices, and belief systems, creates the two-genders construction. In short, it is gender ideology that holds dichotomies in place, not biology.

Gender, and hence gender ideology, is most commonly understood as manifesting along a continuum, with differently sexed bodies falling variously along it, regardless of discursive practices that dichotomize. Sometimes gender ideologists and analysts posit a continuum with masculine and feminine traits at each pole. Alternatively, another gender concept or gender role ideology can be applied to both males and females. In the case of gender role ideology, the poles run from traditional to egalitarian, with prescriptions for both males and females along the continuum. Regardless of the content of the poles, and whether sexed bodies (gender) serve as dependent or independent variables, discourse matters greatly precisely because it constructs gender "reality," and the reifications that become what we know about government and politics, including gender politics. For gender ideology, many would argue that discourse cannot be separated from ideology – the signs, signifiers, and words – that bring meaning to ideas and enable conceptualization and action. As this book seeks to demonstrate, concepts matter greatly to ontology and epistemology. The methodology we use to know politics in a scientific way also matters greatly.

Table 8.1 helps to illustrate how names matter to the ways in which politics is conceptualized. It juxtaposes important "opposite" concepts and shows concepts that lie in the gray zone of each. An explication of these semantic fields shows how I arrived at the concept of feminalism as the appropriate concomitant to masculinism, as well as touching upon the evolution of these concepts.

Names, negations, and absences

All analysis of gender ideology has originated in relationship to feminist analysis, usually within it, which would make the female pole positive and the male pole negative. More often in practice, however, to ascertain which of the gender poles is positive and which negative depends upon whether the analysis is feminist or not feminist. Political science has been decidedly not feminist (Sapiro 1991), as well as dominated by men and arguably imbued with masculinity, which would leave the female field cast as the negative pole. Alternatively, feminist scholars have challenged the discipline, and more generally what was in the 1970s called male-stream scholarship, to recognize and examine its masculine orientations and privileging. As such, the male field

Table 8.1 Gender ideology: names and negations

Concepts	"Male" field	"Female" field	Gray zone options
Constructed difference: performance, practice, norms, adjectives, ontology	Masculine Manly	Feminine Womanly	Androgyny Gynandry
Classic: political systems	Patriarchy	Matriarchy	Gender egalitarian
Women's and men's movements, early second wave	Masculism	Feminism	Humanism Gender neutral
Feminist analysis, late twentieth century	Patriarchy Masculinism	Feminism	Antifeminism Profeminist men
Other relevant concepts	Viriarchy	Femininism	Gender irrelevant
Research: twenty-first century: ideology	Masculinism	Feminalism	Transgenderism Polygenderism Polyversalism

is the negative pole. According to the Guidelines of this book, the "female" pole functions as the positive pole because it is of greater interest to most gender scholars. With ideologies, which pole is positive or negative arguably is far less important analytically than explicitly recognizing the importance of the starting point for what needs to be explained. Gender analysis – even by feminist scholars – too often is made synonymous with the female field, which naturalizes the male field as the universal norm. While gynocentric analysis certainly has been important for recovering lost knowledge about women and correcting masculinist errors about them (Nelson 1989), gender analysis requires attention to both poles, and more. Men have gender too, and masculinity and masculinism have important political ramifications. These poles have lacked symmetry, which is interesting for analysis and gender ideology.

First, one can note the considerable difference in power and societal value accorded to those things associated with men compared to women, from sex-segregated jobs (e.g. engineers versus elementary school teachers), sports (e.g. football versus figure skating), or cultural productions (e.g. oil paintings versus quilts). To impose gender distinctions within functional equivalents, as suggested by the now famous analysis of the gendered practices "waitering and waitressing" (West and Zimmerman 1987), is usually also to deploy gender power (Duerst-Lahti and Kelly 1995). These asymmetries appear in Table 8.1 and will be discussed later in Figure 8.4. These could be analyzed through value placed upon manly compared to womanly behaviors, or the frequency of patriarchal compared to matriarchal political systems either historically or presently.[4] Such an analysis of power in most instances must at least take into account the ideology underpinning it.

The concept of masculism, a term common to the early days of second wave feminism and especially related to men's movement activities, presents one interesting asymmetry that uses feminism as the positive pole. Most closely associated with men's movement activist Warren Farrell, the concept initially promoted gender egalitarianism and the promise of mutual benefit (http://en.wikipedia.org/wiki/Masculism). Later, many feminists came to see masculism as a threat, an assessment aided by conservative ideologists of the men's movement who decried women's civil rights and family role advantages under the banner of masculism. In many regards, masculism is the concomitant of women's liberation and its ideology of radical feminism. This strand of feminism lacks much traction in US politics today. More important for asymmetry, feminism is widely recognized, whereas masculism arguably is not known outside gender activist circles in the US. More common is the notion of feminist and nonfeminist or even antifeminist, the negative of which could apply to either men or women. A positive alternative might be the notion of "profeminist," a concept that allows men to claim affiliation with or advocate for feminism, but also to sidestep arguments that only women can be feminists.[5] The main distinction between masculinism and masculism is its tie to the men's movement, and, as I will unfold below, the greater political and analytic scope of the former.

The evolution to masculinism

Naming and negation also apply directly to the concepts of masculinism and feminalism. Elsewhere I have discussed in more detail the evolution of these concepts (Duerst-Lahti 2002a). Suffice here to say that use of the term masculinism in political science goes back at least to Christine DiStefano (1983), and the ideas contained by it were featured by Wendy Brown (1988) in *Manhood and Politics*, although Patricia Sykes (2006) has located references in English literature studies as early as the mid-1960s.

---

[4] Although anthropologists offer evidence of matrilocal societies, most still contend that matriarchies are a myth and have never existed. Such presents a prominent asymmetry in political forms and control.

[5] Women can be profeminist as well. The distinction between feminist and profeminist arguably lies in whether one is feminist or one advocates positions held by feminists. The latter has been deemed profeminist.

The term "masculinism" seems to have evolved rather than developed from conscious theorizing or as an identity associated with a movement. Its impetus involved "patriarchal confusions" over a term that could cue at least three potentially overlapping meanings (Pateman 1988: 23): These include patriarchal systems based upon father rule, contemporary feminists' critiques of modern patriarchy, and patriarchal political thought advocated by Sir Robert Filmore, which lost out to John Locke's liberalism (Schochet 1975). Another likely impetus was the lack of the English language marker of an ideology, "ism" or "ist," which is seldom attached to patriarchy. Hence, patriarchy is not readily recognizable as an ideology despite clearly functioning as the guiding thought that advocates rule by men. Accuracy may have been a further impetus for change. The term "patriarchy" also falls short because "patriarchy" derives from the Greek term *pater*, for "father." Despite a distinct language of manhood during the US revolution that promoted the "family man" in governing (Kann 1991), and a US practice of referring to "founding fathers," not all men who rule are fathers (Hearn 1992). The language of both the US and French revolutions was more of fraternity than patriarchy, a "nice conjuring trick" that shifted power from fathers to brothers under the guise of equality but left masculine rule in place (Pateman 1988: 78). Viriarchy, or rule by adult males, is a more accurate term (Waters 1989), although it never has been widely deployed. As any quick electronic search of contemporary scholarship shows, by the early 1990s the term "masculinism" had become commonplace, although I can find no work that theorized the change in terminology from patriarchy to masculinism.

Further, feminists recognized that masculinists had compounded their gender ideology with governing ideologies, but few outside feminist circles recognized this fact. This "invisible" and naturalized masculinist process of giving governing power to men, regardless of what type of "political" thinking was involved, produced a great absence of and for women. This absence perhaps is most clearly demonstrated by foundational feminist political theorists who unearthed patriarchal or masculinist assumptions and flaws of the "great thinkers" (e.g. Saxonhouse 1985, W. Brown 1988, DiStefano 1991, Elshtain 1981, Hartmann 1979a, Ferguson 1993, Zerilli 1994). Yet initially, suitable language was largely absent for naming patriarchal Marxism, patriarchal liberalism, and so on. Even today the concept of liberal masculinism does not really have much cachet, though it should if gender ideology were widely recognized in political science. In essence, masculinist "political" ideologies about governing claimed the space of all political theory, rendering their own internal masculinist debate the complete debate: Which men? For what purposes preferred by men? How best to organize men to govern?

This intra-masculinist construction of political ideology left two absences: gender ideology as political ideology, and women's ideas about the best way to govern and run politics.

Gender ideology as protoideology

Because politics is a far larger concept than government, it would be most accurate to employ the term "political ideology" for any set of ideas or beliefs that offers ideas on how to distribute power and to put that set of ideas into action. By this reckoning, what is commonly called political ideology actually is a subset of political ideology. The term "governing ideology" therefore would better capture what is commonly meant by political ideology. Gender ideology and governing ideology are then both subsets of political ideology. How much they overlap, or whether governing ideology should be subsumed under gender ideology, is a point for debate.

Feminist scholarship of the 1980s made clear that sexual politics preceded governments and governing politics. Men could not have been free to dominate in the public sphere if they did not also control women in the private sphere of home. Masculine political thinkers' awareness of this fact goes back at least to Plato and Aristotle, and the "properness" of this distribution of power persists throughout western political thought (Shanley and Pateman 1991). The dominance of women by men, in the private sphere of the home as well as the public sphere, suggests the need to rethink "political ideologies" also. If, as many foundation theory scholars have argued, gender ideology should be thought of as a political ideology that functions as proto- or parent ideology to governing ideologies (Duerst-Lahti 2002a, 2002b, Johnson, Duerst-Lahti, and Norton 2007), then gender ideology serves as a central foundation for other ideologies important to governing, and governing ideology is a subset of gender ideology.[6]

Whether as the first (coerced) social contract or through some other means (Pateman 1988), gender – masculinity or not masculinity – has been a source of the dominant ideology important to ideas and debates about the organization of power and governing. It also has provided the initial

---

[6] I do not claim that sex-gender is the only possible protoideology. Certainly race and ethnicity are important in most cultures, as is age, (dis)ability, and sexuality. This framework for conceptualizing protoideology as compounded with the "know" or governing ideologies could be adapted for other identity characteristics as well.

distribution of preferences that determine how most contemporary governing institutions work (March and Olsen 1989, Dodson 2006). These preferences' proto source is that which is associated with males and masculinity and which gives role advantages (Chappell 2006). Ideology related to gender provides a root ideology that informs and mutually constitutes other political ideologies. The parent ideology could have been associated with females and the feminine, or equally with both, but it was not.

An alternative view would be that gender ideology and governing ideology overlap, perhaps considerably, but can be analyzed separately and as "cousins" or maybe "siblings" in family relations. Because governing ideology has great influence upon the continual (re)creation and transformation of gender through policies (Johnson, Duerst-Lahti, and Norton 2007), it can be argued that gender ideology cannot subsume governing ideology. So while masculinism's success in achieving men's dominance of women was required for governance at the onset, once it was in place, government and the state could be used to perpetuate dominant gender norms and forms. With the advent of liberalism, its focus on individuals, and discourse of equality, governing ideologies opened space for resistance and change.

Important also is the level of analysis. Much scholarship focuses upon patriarchy or masculinism because it has been the dominant gender ideology. However, gender ideology, which subsumes masculinism, is the protoideology, because masculinity can operate only in conjunction with its positive, femininity/feminality. They are mutually constituted and largely determined by what each is not. Political systems have to a great extent been constructed upon the exclusion or enforced absences of women and the feminine. This awareness provides the opening for ideas in support of women and opposed to masculine advantage – feminism, or perhaps more aptly, feminalism – to challenge as its gender ideological counterpart. Therefore, a clear understanding of gender ideology enables analysis of political action, especially in nonfeminist domains. It also allows openings for gray zones that have existed throughout history through people in variously sexed bodies with ideas about nondominant gender arrangements. Gender ideology is the critical concept. It enables richer analysis of political ideology, especially through use of masculinism and feminalism, its two most prominent strands.

Getting to feminalism

The route to naming feminalism is much more deliberate, and problems with negation, absence, and opposites are fully implicated. First, feminism has dealt with "hyphenated" or adjectivized feminisms since its inception in the second wave (Freeman 1995). Seemingly, feminists have always wanted to demarcate their ideological positions in both governing ideologies (e.g. liberalism, socialism, Marxism) and gender ideology. In other words, they recognized ways in which gender ideology was every bit as much a political ideology as those commonly applied to governing systems, but the compounded feminisms functioned mostly as negations of "regular" political (governing) ideology.

Second, within the female-linked pole, feminism itself creates negations and absences. The very fact that feminism is *not* a single coherent ideology makes it tricky to analyze accurately. Too often the analyst imposes one simplistic definition of feminism. By recognizing the complexity of feminism, the door opens to a host of other conceptual questions and problems. Chief among them is the fact that feminism does not run the full gamut of governing ideology, especially on the right side of the continuum. As a result, conservative women, especially, can only be cast in the negative, either as nonfeminists or, more often, antifeminists. This negation presents a problem for analysis because conservative women often disagree with their male counterparts about priorities affecting women, as well as occasionally disagreeing about what is best for women. As scholars of conservative women know, these women see themselves as very pro-woman even if they disagree with feminists about what is best for women. Analyses of policy agenda and language in political discourse show these differences. Because it is usually feminist scholars and/or ardent opponents of feminism who have framed these debates, such negation makes the intra-woman dispute – whether feminism is positive or negative – a central element of debate rather than the policy or issue at stake. Also, most (feminist) scholarship simply ignores or dismisses women's points of view outside its definition of feminism. In addition, using feminism as the female-linked pole of gender ideology leaves no space for women who do not claim feminism, but act in ways that might be deemed consistent with at least some strands of feminism. The usual hyphenated feminism list cannot deal adequately with the "feminist by any other name" (Katzenstein 1998a: 20), often leaving feminist scholars to impose a label upon these pro-woman nonfeminists that they themselves do not espouse. In other words, feminism remains exceptionally important to gender ideology, but it is incomplete. Another gender ideology concept that does not negate a large portion of women was needed.

Third, and closely related, while feminism has ably critiqued the shortcomings of liberalism, socialism, Marxism, and so on, *from within* that ideological orientation, it can critique the ideological right only from outside. Absent is a parallel way for conservative women to critique from within conservatism (or fascism).

In moving to compare the two main poles of gender ideology, a further absence reflects the first point about feminism. Feminism and masculinism are not parallel concepts, because masculinism incorporates a larger scope of governing and social ideological space.[7] The fact that they are not full concomitants makes conceptually complete comparisons impossible. If we do have not proper concepts for women on the right, then to ascertain their numbers, their impact on policy direction, their influence on male counter-parts, and so on, is difficult. More importantly, as Kathy Ferguson (1993) tells us, the ability to attain full equality requires an ability to theorize about full equality. So, thinking in terms of a theoretically equal concept is a necessary step to achieve equality. A more encompassing term for the female side of gender ideology was needed.[8]

The concept of feminalism resolves the conceptual shortcomings of the female-linked gender ideology pole. *Feminalism is defined here as an ideology that begins from and generally prefers that which is associated with human females, often conferring advantages on them that can include equality with males.* The term "feminality" derives from the old French word, *feminal.* The dictionary defines feminality as "the quality of being female; womanliness" (Funk and Wagnalls 1997: 465). Feminality improves upon feminine and femininity because most feminists question aspects of its definition such as "modesty, delicacy, tenderness, tact, etc., normally characteristic of women" (1997: 465), which many have argued are the product of masculine desire and dictates, not women's agency. "Feminality" is a better term poststructurally for theorizing about pro-woman ideologies because it derives from the body, from female. Although biology is also given by the human mind, feminality is both closer to the body and consistent with masculinity, which derives from male and not the socially constructed concept of man or men.[9] In

---

[7] In many regards, masculism was intended to be the concomitant to feminism, but its conceptual evolution did not match. As is true of all ideologies, the course it takes is out of the hands of its originators once it enters the public realm (Dawson 2000).

[8] Of course, the dictionary definition of feminism speaks mostly to advocating equality for women. Other dimensions of feminism discussed here suggest why theoretically a "stretched" concept of feminalism would be superior in several regards, without diminishing the political force of feminism.

[9] According to Funk and Wagnalls (1997: 782): "1. Having the distinguishing qualities of male sex, or pertaining to males; especially suitable for men; manly; opposed to *feminine* ... *male* is applied to the sex; *masculine* to the qualities, especially to the stronger, hardier, and more imperious qualities that distinguish the male sex."

contrast, femininity derives from woman, which is the cultural construction of female bodies and hence is doubly constructed.[10] Therefore, feminale, feminality, and feminalism provide a broader concept that matches equally masculine, masculinity, and masculinism, and it does so with neither the negatives from the right toward feminism nor the reticence of feminists toward femininity.[11]

One way to conceptualize feminalism and masculinism as gender ideology is to think of them as concomitant ideologies that are inextricably joined together but also capable of analysis within its own adjectivized continuum. For political science, this analysis might commonly be employed in analysis of policy, as in "What gender ideological positions were central to debates over a policy?" While I will argue below that the exact dimensions of any particular gender ideology can change by situation, a basic framework would always include a side-by-side continuum of masculinism and feminalism, with related but distinct positions for each along it. Figure 8.1 presents a visual representation of masculinism and feminalism as they overlay the conventional left–right continuum.[12] It conceptualizes distinctions by two genders (even more complex gray zone arrangements would be possible) and suggests the potential to share many elements of governing ideology at similar points along the continuum, while not being entirely synonymous on gendered aspects.

For example, using comments from floor debates, the congressional record, and other sources for the 1996 US welfare reform, Johnson, Duerst-Lahti, and Norton (2007) developed a framework that identified shared strands and sex-based variants indicated in Figure 8.1. Strands include gender traditionalism and similarism, while variants occur within a strand such as liberal feminism and neofraternalism for similarists, or corporate feminalism and new paternalism for gender universalism. We found that moderate Republican congresswomen usually argued – used words and expressed ideas – from a corporate feminalist position, and that congressmen whose initial positions

---

[10] Funk and Wagnalls (1997: 465): "1. Belonging to or characteristic of womankind; having qualities such as modesty, delicacy, tenderness, tact, etc., normally characteristic of women."

[11] I first used the term "femininism," which is difficult both to say and to distinguish from the written word "feminism." Femininism also extends the problem of masculinity's hand in shaping its root feminine. Of course, cultural feminists especially have fought to revalue the feminine. I would argue that feminality provides an easier route to appropriate valuation of that which is associated with females because it currently carries little cultural meaning.

[12] Note that these are properly conceptualized as within the same ideological space or sphere, and that they compound. Which one precedes the other genealogically or interactively is mostly a separate normative debate.

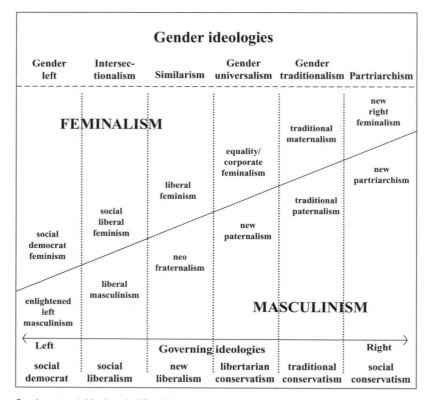

Figure 8.1   Gender as protoideology in US politics

aligned with liberal masculinism or neofraternalism often came to adopt new paternalist arguments.[13] Such analysis is interesting for its nuanced understanding of gender ideology operating in policymaking. It also should prove useful in predicting likely ideological orientations in future reform and could be helpful in political strategy to effect outcomes.

Finally, the definition and dimensions involved in this conception of gender ideology open the door for other kinds of gender politics and different modes of analysis beyond the usual grist of political science. Importantly, because gender is "known" through practices, and roles, it need not be linked directly to bodies. Nonetheless, those who are recognized as females (or males) generally experience mutuality in at least some aspects of life, whether being a

---

[13] For my purposes here, the exact dimensions of each gender ideology strand is less important than illustrating a way to analyze gender ideology as political ideology. See Johnson, Duerst-Lahti, and Norton (2007), for the full argument and details of each ideological variant.

daughter or being "not male." Males and females tend to be channeled by social institutions into same-sex groups and then are subjected to innumerable gendered institutional arrangements. Even if an individual avoids much of this same-sex activity, socialization, and so forth, usually others associate such knowledge and experience with a gendered person regardless. While these lived experiences certainly vary greatly across the roughly 3 billion women on Earth, at least some experiences may be shared at least "serially" (Young 1997). The concept of feminality and feminalism opens options wider for traveling, to find serial similarities and demarcate female-oriented political ideologies.

Gender ideology and complexity

The framework presented in Figure 8.1 should be seen as one approach to inserting gender analysis into other political phenomena, especially ideological ones, rather than the definitive statement of gender ideology compounded with governing ideology. For example, one could imagine (re)examining Black political thought to discover its gendering. In his celebrated work, Michael Dawson (2001: 317) identifies six main "families" or "visions" of ideological categories of Black political thought: community nationalism, disillusioned liberalism, radical egalitarianism, Black feminism, Black social democracy (formally Marxism), and Black conservatism. He carefully and wisely traces relationships among these ideological visions, and finds, among many other things, solid links between Black feminism and both radical egalitarianism and Black social democracy. He also finds somewhat weaker connections with community nationalism that are "maintained mostly by Black women who see themselves as 'womanists'" (2001: 316). While he includes considerable analysis of feminism, and has several questions about gender, men's roles, and women, not surprisingly his focus on gender is largely limited to societal roles (2001: 12). Inserting gender ideology of masculinism and feminalism would move this analysis beyond its focus on feminism as a discrete ideology to ascertain the nuanced distinctions (and similarities) between women and men in each Black ideological family, including Black men who espouse ideas of Black feminism. While a large undertaking, assessing ways Black thought and gender ideology compound or intersect would be as possible as the analysis of gender and governing ideology undertaken by Johnson, Duerst-Lahti, and Norton (2007).

More complex challenges come in trying to identify and either interpret or explain more than two ideological tracks, as those who struggle with meaningful intersectionality know. How gender, race, and governing ideologies overlay

and inform one another, for example, would be enormously complex to dis-
entangle (McCall 2000, 2005). Although sophisticated quantitative analysis
might make this possible, much would be lost in the simplified definitions
such methodologies require. The data would not lend themselves to necessary
nuance, or the nuance and critical meaning would be lost to the methodology
(Junn 2007, Hancock 2007a, 2007b). While ideal, such work is enormously
challenging as Laurel Weldon details in this volume.

Interdependence: a large gray zone

Gender ideology as political ideology goes beyond governing ideology.
Throughout the above analysis, I have linked gender ideology to sexed bodies despite earlier recitations of the problems of fixing sex onto a body and
of the constructed "givenness" of biological bodies themselves. Yet empirically we know that females and women vary greatly, just as males and men
do. Many human bodies fall in the gray zone between "full" (ideal-type)
males and "full" (ideal-type) females constructed by human biologists and
medicine. As such, biological males and females can be considered ideal and
dichotomized types with intersexed and androgynous variations on a continuum between. However, ideas about gender incorporate far more than bodies.
Therefore, any conceptualization of gender ideology that relies upon human
bodies starts from a tenuous empirical foundation, even though bodies matter
(Butler 1993). Guided by gender ideology, bodies are used to organize society
according to two gender identities. Because gender is something people "do"
(West and Zimmerman 1987), most females (and some intersexed humans
and some males) inevitably perform some types of gender practices that are
recognized as associated with women, even "female masculinity" (Halberstam 1998). The converse is true for males and men. In terms of research
and twenty-first-century gender ideology, many gender ideologies and ideas
seek to upset the dualism and add more poles to the equation. Transgenderist
efforts are the best-recognized of these. Further, we can find some areas of
politics that seem gender neutral or for which gender is irrelevant (e.g. certain ways of transferring funds from the federal government to the states),
although a central purpose of gender analysis is to insert gender in order to
discover its importance where none has been commonly thought to be. All of
this speaks both to conceptual interdependence and gray zones and calls for
conceptual clarity in order to analyze them.

To decide whether the concepts should ever be employed as idealized opposites involves questioning the ends to which the research is put along with the consequences of doing so: Is it testing the accuracy of stereotypes or does it seek to develop an ideal in a political concept such as autonomy? Is the research critiquing the masculinist foundation of political phenomena, such as ways legitimacy is conferred or institutions organized? Or mapping out policies that make sharp gender distinctions in gender traditionalist countries? Clearly sociologists and psychologists who use the concept of gender ideology have mainly focused on gender identities and gender roles, especially in families, marriages, or households (e.g. Kroska 2000).

To use a gender continuum also requires careful thought as to which continuum should be used and the consequences of doing so. For example, is gender compounded with the familiar left–right ideology used as shorthand in legislative studies, or should it begin with the categories of Black political thought? Such compounding is ordinary, and adjectives common, because usually masculinism and feminalism are applied to some familiar political topic, and the application is essential in determining both its relevant dimensions and its interdependencies. The notion of hyphenated feminisms, such as liberal feminism or Marxist feminism, are well established and illustrate the point; equally important but less known in political science are concepts such as working-class masculinity and its attending ideological roots. Such conceptual distinctions become critical to studies of public organizations, such as prisons or the presidency. Sound gender methodology should attend to the interdependence of politically relevant dimensions as well as to hegemonic categories important to a specified political location and historical moment. By explicitly recognizing the hegemonic forces at play and incorporating them into methodology, the gender concepts of masculinism and feminalism can travel well with precision and rigor.

Earlier I alluded to the longstanding knowledge that masculinity and femininity are interdependent because, as they are binary "opposites," each is required to "know" the other. Similarly, sex and gender are interdependent, whether sex is used as the base, and gender ideology as the superstructure, or one thinks of a continuum from sex to gender (Lovenduski 2006). Here I suggest one more conceptualization inspired by the gray zone that would be appropriate for analyses of gender transformation in institutions, related social movements, and perhaps public opinion, but certainly for policy surrounding gay, lesbian, bisexual, transgender, and queer (GLBTQ) politics.

I suggest that within gender ideology in all but the most sophisticated feminist understandings, sex might accurately be understood as an ideal-type

Ideal Types	Some gray zones	Transition	(Re)gendered ideations
	→ Polyversalism	→ Respect	→ Diverse humanism
Binary Sex → Gender	→ Crossgenderism	→ Both equal	→ Irrelevant
	→ Transgenderism	→ Gender bending	→ No gender
	→ Transgenderism	→ Switch	→ Change accepted
	→ Polygenderism	→ Transgenderism	→ Infinite options

Figure 8.2   Binary sex-gender, gray zones, alternative gender ideations

construct that moves along a continuum to a more fluid dualistic notion of gender in which a struggle for hegemonic masculinity and femininity (feminality) continually transpires. These dualisms now lead to several gray zones, each of which becomes a branch of the continuum. A few of these dualisms are illustrated in Figure 8.2. Of these, the concept of transgender ideology arguably subsumes most of the gray zone, because its meaning is in great flux, and it has for many activists become an umbrella term in US politics. Its dimensions include challenges to fixed gender dualisms, especially in identities assigned at birth based upon genitalia, and beliefs about unhinging sexed bodies from norms for "gender performances." Its dimensions also include efforts to create gender ambiguity by performing both genders, and/or to attempt human existence by an ideal of no gender. I illustrate them less complexly than they are theorized and enacted as a first attempt to identify elements for analysis within the gray zones of gender ideology.

Other terms also are emerging in the struggle to conceptualize gender ideology accurately. A sampling includes the following concepts. "Polyversal" suggests a diverse whole (Z. Eisenstein 2001: 151), in which bodies are simultaneously different and yet emphasize the similarity of humanity. With "cross-gender" conditions, two distinct genders are present and accepted, but, unlike conditions under masculinism, the two are equally powerful. Although still believed to be distinct, this may be a stage on the way to irrelevance and unhinging gender from bodies entirely. The gender ideological vision of "polygender" conceives of valuing many ways of constructing gender, such that multiple modes of gender expression and identity are fostered and normalized (DiStefano 2006).

In much of the work conceptualizing possible gender options, sex and gender function as one ideal pole, with another concept functioning as the idealized other pole. Alternatively, the research question might instead investigate the distinctions and relationships among these orientations for gender, akin to Dawson's (2001) analysis of Black political thought. Both because scholarship on gender ideology is evolving very quickly and because of the many uses made of the term "gender ideology", whether it is used as an ideal type or a continuum is tied to the research question.

Inserting gender into political ideology: dimensions and necessity

Too often, political science has assumed that to approach gender as an analytic category is to think of gender as the sex variable on most large-N studies. This approach, however, is simple sex difference research, not gender analysis.[14] Gender analysis instead allows researchers to "frame for investigations that are literally inconceivable within traditional disciplines" (Hawkesworth 1997: 708). In the case of masculinism and feminalism, especially without the notion of gender ideology, masculinism was normalized and the feminine was relegated to a subordinate position constructed mostly by hegemonic masculinism. The concept of feminalism suggests an equally valued power counterpart to masculinist dictates. More importantly, feminalism suggests female agency for self-definition. Among the most important aspects of feminalist thought is feminism in its many varieties. Feminist analysis, and its development of the concept of gender ideology, has made possible the insertion of gender into the concept of political ideology.

Gender ideology, especially masculinism and feminalism, has several necessary dimensions. For the gender of gender ideology, a necessary dimension – tautologically – is that it must in some fashion relate to gender. Much of this book has been devoted to trying to unpack what that means, and clearly gender is complex and in many ways problematic. Despite the shortcomings, gray zones, and other disclaimers, an apparently necessary dimension of gender – masculine and feminale – is that it *begins from that which is associated with human males or human females*. This dimension need not be limited to two genders. Even transgenderism cannot currently avoid this dualistic construct in their attempts to subvert it. Gender also need not be tied to human bodies directly, but it must be understood as associated with an origin related to the constructed understandings of male and female.

---

[14] Jane Junn (2007), however, recognizes that sex difference comparisons may constitute an important first and provisional step toward a more sophisticated gender and/or intersectional analysis.

Ideologies are socially constructed out of politically laden language, which is one reason they are so fluid as well as why it is so difficult to pin down the relationships of political concepts within ideologies (Dawson 2001: 7). As a result, fixed and constrained definitions tend not to be particularly helpful, even though some definition is required to communicate meaning. All political ideologies tend to do several things and hence have related dimensions of judging humans, distributing power, and planning for action. *Gender ideologies, then, are structured beliefs and ideas about ways power should be arranged according to social constructs associated with sexed bodies.* Some aspect defensibly related to gender is necessary for the ideology to be gender ideology, but exactly what can be determined only by the situation and context.

Throughout this chapter, gender ideology has been discussed as a *political* ideology and care has been taken to distinguish governing ideologies – the familiar left–right continuum – as a subset of political ideologies. Why? The feminist adage, "the personal is political," highlighted that politics is much more than what happens in, around, and by governments. Anyone who reads this book no doubt also has at least passing familiarity with identity politics. Politics is about who gets what, when, and how, and the authoritative allocation of resources and values.[15] Power is central to politics. Power arrangements occur throughout society, and are usually embedded in and enforced by institutions, which also are very political. It was precisely the insertion of gender ideology into political ideology that enabled us to see masculinism operating, to point out "the problematic nature of the obvious" (Acker 1990: 140), to develop the conceptual tools to analyze masculine power advantages, and to recognize the consequences of masculine beliefs and preferences in politics. That which is associated with males has received a disproportionate share of the resources and has been deemed more valuable than that which is associated with females. Only by feminists inserting gender ideology into political ideology were we able to understand this naturalized masculine power advantage. The concept of masculinism was key to this understanding.

One of the best ways to study ideologies is to try to understand how various concepts have been used (Dawson 2007: 8). What does this mean for masculinism? Inside feminist analyses, the concept remains largely constant with feminist critiques of contemporary patriarchy; men determined that they

---

[15] These familiar definitions were coined by Harold Lasswell and David Easton respectively.

should have power, and that that which is associated with males should be greatly valued. Most (pro)feminist explanations – many of which are made by men who support feminist tenets – highlight masculine advantage, and commonly emphasize female subordination as a necessary element of masculinism. Definitions drawn from the men's movement present alternative perspectives. All include the notion that it is an ideology based upon the experiences of men, and most emphasize multiple masculinities, including various orientations that seek equality between women and men (Messner 1997). Many uses of the term also highlight the dominant or hegemonic masculinity and include critiques of its detrimental effects for nondominant men (e.g. Connell 1995). Much like the gynocentric orientation of much feminist analysis, masculinist analysis tends to concentrate on androcentric foci. This usage could merely reflect the male-stream orientation in which men and masculinity were naturalized as the universal norm. However, most contemporary masculinist thought, inside both the men's movement and the field of masculinity studies, is aware of men's gendering, even if political science largely seems unaware. For some,

to leave masculinity unstudied, to proceed as if it were somehow not a form of gender, is to leave it naturalized, and thus render it less permeable to change. For feminist theorists who recognize the importance of this fact, a "gender studies" that focuses on masculinity need not necessarily entail the depoliticization or betrayal of feminism. Quite the contrary, it can also designate the critical process by which (some) men learn *from* feminism in order to make subversive interventions into reproductions of normative masculinity itself. (Thomas 2002: 61 italics original).

On the other hand, men's rights advocates see women as having unfair advantages and seek redress to attain equality with women. Conservative masculinists espouse positions that include the naturalness of sex difference and the necessity of complementary gender roles, often including natural male authority over women and children (Messner 1997).

In other words, the concept of masculinism can be used across a spectrum of political ideologies. But as a gendered political ideology itself, ideological or analytic use must derive from the ideations of male sexed bodies and reflect beliefs about power arrangements based upon those constructs. A definition for masculinism that captures all of its shared dimensions, yet remains sufficiently nonabsolutist to enable contextual sensitivity is: *Masculinism is a gender ideology that begins from, and generally prefers, that which is associated with human males, usually giving advantages to them, and may include the option of gender equality as advantageous.*

The "that" of "that which": content of operationalization

Throughout, the definitions of masculinism and feminalism have been relatively vague, and that ambiguity has been defended as necessary. What does it mean to derive ideologies from sexed bodies when sex itself is a linguistic construct of human invention? – especially when, as Sylvia Walby (1997) has cogently articulated, gender is continually transformed by human agency – such as activists in the women's movement – through social institutions, the state, and daily practices of individuals. Furthermore, that which is common to males and females varies greatly across world cultures and includes class and ethnic permutations even in the same location. Complicating matters further are differences across time. Pink once was the color for baby boys; before typewriters, men were secretaries; no longer is it considered unladylike for women to vote; and in 2008 we saw for the first time a viable female candidate for the US Presidency join the growing numbers of women who now head countries around the world. As a result, to pin down the "that which is associated" with males and with females can be tricky. Figures 8.3 and 8.4 show two ways the content of gender and its ideological aspects have commonly been studied.

Figure 8.3 takes gendered concepts as the foci, breaking away from the binary approach. For example, gender roles have been measured on a scale from traditional to equality, either by analyzing difference and sameness or by approaching more paradigmatic concepts. Policy can establish and enforce ideological preferences, which can be thought of as gender paradigms. In the USA, the paradigms represent the (binary) sexes as complementary, individuals with choice among gendered options, or attempting to move away from gender's importance entirely (Johnson, Duerst-Lahti, and Norton 2007).

Figure 8.4, in contrast, shows familiar starting points for studies based upon binary opposites, with each possible dimension running from masculine to feminine. It illustrates topics in the family of gender analysis that can be taken up in specific studies. Some are aligned in a continuum, while others focus at the poles. Many second wave feminist studies created these concepts for gender analysis. Usually these studies showed ways that masculinism had masked its operation, such as in the separate spheres doctrine with its accompanying gender roles and power advantages, or by constructing normative differences in traits where only modest ones existed. For physicality, these studies often uncovered normative valuation that greatly favored the masculine and

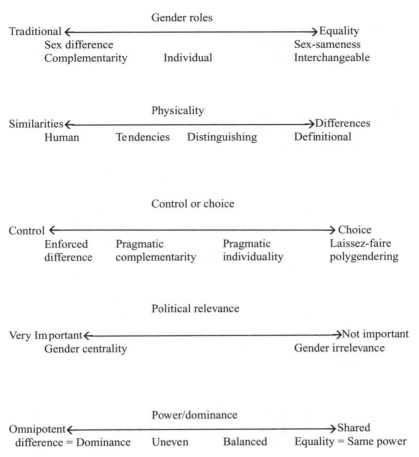

Figure 8.3   Examples of gender content analysis

diminished the feminine. For example, the notion that only men were, and should be, muscular required social controls (e.g. the doctrine that declared that women should not be physically active because it would hinder their reproduction, practices such as styles of clothing that greatly constricted physical movement), or established unequal valuation (e.g. a belief that women and their wombs are mere receptacles for the complete life force of men's sperm). Such research helps to show the difficulty in resuscitating the term "feminine" for positive female ideological purposes; it simply has not been constructed as an equal concomitant to "masculine" under masculinist dominance. This type of research of gender's normative elements is in the genealogy of the concept of feminality.

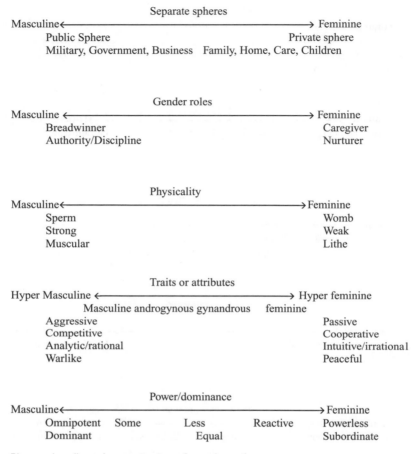

Figure 8.4   Binary poles, dimension constructs, and sample continua

From gender to gender ideology: operationalization

Because gender ideology is one type of political ideology, studies of it must in some way focus upon judgments about human potential according to gender, power distribution, or the way such ideas about potential and power are put into action. The scope of gender ideology is so large, however, that no study could expect to be fully comprehensive. Further, as a concept with a greater affinity for the family resemblance model than definitive and fixed attributes, scholars really can be expected to work on only one part of the larger scheme. One suspects that relatively few studies will grapple with the meaning of gender ideology itself. Instead, studies tend to approach questions related to one or two of the three dimensions of ideology: beliefs about human potential, power, or ways in which plans include or exclude males and females. A few examples about ways to operationalize gender ideology for empirical study illustrate this. The first draws from a recent book by Cathy Johnson, Noelle Norton, and me, *Creating Gender* (2007). Other examples place gender at the poles and consider gendered institutions and campaigns.

For example, Figure 8.1 emerged from a study of gender ideology in policy-making, particularly the 1996 US welfare reform. After defining the six main political positions operating on the standard left–right governing ideology continuum, we began by surveying the Wisconsin state legislators for their liberal–conservative orientation; among other things, for their views on social and fiscal policy, use of state power, and "personal and political beliefs." For the latter, legislators located themselves on a ten-point scale between poles such as:

"traditional gender roles are best" and "women need to support themselves"
"men need to take care of home and children" and "traditional gender roles are best"
"traditional families are best" and "good families come in many forms."

These juxtapositions were combined with responses to questions about taxation, market regulation, social justice, race, and government entitlement. A factor analysis produced two distinct factors. One emphasized the usual governing ideology fiscal and social policy questions, while the other captured family roles and family structures (Johnson, Duerst-Lahti, and Norton 2007: 182). After establishing gender ideology could indeed be teased out of the left–right continuum, we systematically analyzed all amendments to the Personal Responsibility and Work Opportunity Reconciliation Act of 1996 (PRWORA), statements in the congressional record, other direct quotations in news accounts, and the like.

In *Creating Gender*, we placed the gender ideological strands that emerged in Figure 8.1 along the left–right governing ideology continuum so as to not confuse readers who knew little about gender analysis. Alternatively, drawing upon Figure 8.3, we could have constructed the conceptual representation based upon a dimension of gender ideology such as a continuum from control to choice rather than upon left–right governing ideology. In this case, the continuum would follow the gender ideological strands as:

Choice ←————————————————————————————————→ Control
Left ← Universalists ←→ Intersectors ←→ Similarists ←→ Traditionalists ←→ Patriarchalists

That is, the analysis would have moved from the gender ideology that offers the most open choice, free from state coercion (or even perhaps with state incentive for unfettered gender expression) to the ideological strand that most enforced sex difference.

In another example on "knowing Congress as a gender institution," I began with proto attributed gender difference drawn from the expansive sex difference literature (Duerst-Lahti 2002b). These included, for the masculine, such attributes as individuation, instrumental, dominating, power over, competition, and hierarchy; for the feminine, attributes include connection, contextualizing, collaboration, power to, cooperation, and web-centered. With these attributes – which are attributed culturally whether individual males and females actually espouse, prefer, or behave accordingly – I move to analyze two famous organizational theorists, Frederick Taylor and Mary Parker Follette, whose approaches mirror these gender attributes. Drawing upon the influential institutional theory of March and Olsen (1989), I contrast these approaches to aggregative and integrative institutions, again demonstrating the gender correspondence between masculinity, Taylor's hierarchical management style, and the aggregative nature of contemporary Congress and the gender converse for Follette and integrative institutions. The aggregative approach greatly dominates contemporary Congress, perhaps to the grave disadvantage of women in the institution. An analysis of the institution's formal and informal practices (rules, norms, expectations), social demography, and history then followed, demonstrating masculinism's role in its formation and current functioning.

A final example of masculinity in presidential elections also draws upon the gender pole approach. On the premise that "To think explicitly about masculinity in presidential elections is to open the door wider for women," I use 10,000+ newspaper accounts to analyze which normative model of masculinity reigned during the 2000 and 2004 presidential elections (Duerst-Lahti 2006).[16] To do so I searched newspaper articles for words associated with the two most common modes of masculinity according to R. W. Connell (1995), namely technical expertise masculinity and dominance masculinity. According to Connell, these modes of masculinity struggle for the hegemonic position as the most influential and powerful. The expertise words included "technical," "intelligent," "smart," "advocate," and "wonk"; words for dominance included "dominate," "strong," "aggressive," "attack," and "blast." After

---

[16] I also analyzed words associated with femininity and found few. When they were used in 2004, they were usually applied negatively to John Kerry.

eliminating irrelevant uses, I noted the frequency of use. Much to my surprise, given Al Gore's reputation as a smart wonk, dominance words were used twice as often as expertise words in articles about 2000 presidential candidates. Not to my surprise, they were used four times as often in 2004, when contests about masculinity were central. This characterization of candidates in presidential campaigns, and the triumph of dominance masculinity, has consequences for women, given cultural gender prescriptions. Women find entering on expertise much more culturally acceptable than the performance of masculine dominance. I also looked for words that explicitly cued masculinity, including "manly," "masculine," "wimp," "testosterone," and "tough." While explicit references to masculinity were few, I found 3,280 references to "tough." Gender analysis then can question to what extent and in what ways is "tough" gendered toward the masculine compared to the feminale. How will a female candidate need to handle appearing and behaving tough? How have cultural belief systems embraced or rejected tough women? In what ways might associations between feminality and toughness be changing given the triumphs of the feminist movement, and the like? A focus on normative aspects – judgments, power, action – move analysis toward gender ideology.

Feminalism and its utility for studying gender ideology

Above I argued that some aspect defensibly related to gender is necessary for the ideology to be gender ideology, but exactly what can be determined only by the situation and context. In outlining the dimensions and definitions of masculinism and feminalism, I have deliberately developed broad concepts that are intended for analytic use. The notion of power distribution – so central to political ideology – is captured in my definitions by "generally prefers" and "usually giving advantages to." For some scholars, these dimensions will be too weak. Also, for some, not claiming that feminalism is necessarily subordinated to masculinism will be seen as inadequate, naive, or even disloyal feminist analysis. Finally, although the development of masculinism from patriarchy appears to be largely uncontested,[17] some feminists especially will resist the conceptual stretching involved in the concept of feminalism. Beyond a general unwillingness to grapple with a new concept, these resistances include that (1) it is unnecessary because feminism is sufficiently

[17] The only source I know might be found in men's rights activists who continue to prefer masculism, a direct concomitant with feminism.

flexible to handle all female-related gender ideology, (2) feminism should remain as the positive pole and not a diluted version of it, and (3) political thought by nonfeminist women should be cast as the negative or nonfeminist. Many also reject the analytic tone of the concept of feminalism because it could detract from the important political aims of feminism. Although I acknowledge these resistances, I contend that stretching to feminale, feminality, and feminalism remains sufficiently valuable to analysis of women's political thought and gender ideology to warrant the enlargement.

First is the simple and practical matter of feminine and femininity touched upon above. Feminists remain suspicious of the term because of the large hand men had in the construction of feminine characteristics and norms. One need not revisit the enormous review of feminine characteristics as weak or as implicating male desire to highlight this problem. Further, nonfeminist women remain very suspicious of the label "feminism," even many women who espouse several important feminist tenets or who care deeply about women. The concepts of feminality and feminalism provide an opening to join with them or at least understand better their pro-woman ideas.

Second and more importantly, feminism remains integral to much of feminalist ideology. Nothing in the concept of feminalism precludes hearty feminist analysis. One might say that feminism has a privileged place in feminalism due to the evolution of the concept and the purposes to which it has thus far been put. Feminalism provides a means to take seriously pro-woman political thought by women who do not consider themselves feminists. While feminists might resist opening space for conservative women, certainly providing a location for pro-woman political thinking that eschews the term "feminism" has merit. Black womanist thought or postcolonial pro-woman thought from the majority world (i.e. the Third World, the South) is in keeping with the spirit of feminism. The concept of feminalism enables more accurate and full analysis of political ideas that begin from, and are generally preferred by, that which is associated with human females. One reason this concept is particularly valuable is that the concept of feminalism, like masculinism, travels well.

On traveling: feminalism and the positive pole

Feminists have long recognized differences in the ways gender arrangements are structured, and the ways gender expectations, practices, roles, and the like, are manifested throughout history and across cultures. Historians and anthropologists, particularly, have concentrated on such analyses. Little controversy has surrounded such detailing of patriarchy or masculinist arrangements in a variety of context.[18] In contrast, women from nondominant groups in the USA and beyond have also written about these differences, often as challenges to western feminist scholars. As a concept with relatively few necessary dimensions – "begins from and generally prefers that which is associated with human females" – feminalism offers a robust concept that invites analysis of ways gender ideology manifests itself in particular contexts of both space and time. Under the rubric of gender ideology and feminalism, scholars can recognize and analyze such political thought as marianismo, the (supposed) complement to Latino machismo, for its sources in Catholicism, material conditions, merits as a political strategy, mutual constitution of machismo, value and detriment to women, and the like (E. Stevens 1973a, 1973b, Ehlers 1991). Postcolonial political theory can continue to offer feminist critiques and would invite both masculinist and nonfeminist analyses. Womanist theory remains firmly within feminalist thought while it can maintain its "purpleness to the lavender of feminism" (Walker 1983). The very notion of feminalist thought invites a review of all strands of political thought within a culture or historical context as well as careful scrutiny of relationships between and among these strands of thought.

Much as US domestic politics relies on a construct of the liberal–conservative continuum, and international relations relies on realism, liberalism, institutionalism, rationalism, and so on, using these dimensions of gender ideology encourages the belief that dominant (white, professional) US feminism will not translate smoothly to other contexts. Because feminalism does not already have firmly held (and contested) meanings, it opens analytic doors to conceptual traveling.

Causality and conclusions

The move from gender to gender ideology enables scholars "to take advantage of crucial distinctions . . . rather than collapsing such diverse notions into the single term *gender*" (Hawkesworth 1997: 682). Such is the project of this book. Such also is the intent of this exegesis on gender ideology, especially

---

[18] Certainly the biological anthropology work of Lionel Tiger has caused great controversy, but not because he maps different masculinist arrangements across cultures.

masculinism and feminalism. If names give theories, propositions, and causal mechanisms a good deal of their substance, then the names "masculinism" and "feminalism" matter greatly. The apparent reason for moving from patriarchy to masculinism was precisely to broaden its scope and analytic reach, as well as to mark it explicitly as a political ideology. The stretch to feminalism should occur for similar reasons, but, more importantly, the stretch should occur to provide a new concept to study old ideas more clearly and help us identify new phenomena. Critically, it provides the conceptual space for women's agency and self-definition of normative political positions related to gender as a full concomitant to hegemonic masculinism.

With the reach to gender ideology, as political ideology, which has at least two important concomitants of masculinism and feminalism, the concepts can be used in two primary ways. First, analysts can begin by assuming that gender matters to political arrangements and seek out the particular manifestations in a specified time and place. This stance encourages investigations and drives the denaturalization of masculinist power advantages. The stance should foster assumptions that research projects need to discover how gender ideology is used, and what forms it takes in a particular polity or historical moment, rather than to impose preconceived notions upon extant ideological constructions. Second, scholars should be encouraged to insert analysis of gender ideology into studies of all political ideology in order to ascertain what changes once it has been inserted. Much as the process of creating Figure 8.1 forced Johnson, Duerst-Lahti, and Norton (2007) to think seriously about the gendered political ideology of conservative women and all men during welfare reform; this process can be employed for any policy. It also can be used to map out gendered orientations driving an election, and to trace nuanced positions in social movements or normative shifts from the successes of women's movements. With the right questions, the fine work such as that of Michael Dawson on Black political thought might be made even stronger by identifying the gender fault lines in Black conservative thought or among disillusioned liberals.

Most of all, we must recognize gender ideology as political ideology and search for it whenever political ideology is scrutinized. We also must take care with language, so that we focus upon gendered dimensions as causes and do not simply impugn gender itself. The point of gender analysis is to analyze gender. Doing so requires embracing the complex dimensions that construct it. For gender ideology, that means a focus on power arrangements, preferences, and advantages as well as constructions associated with males, females, and the gray zones around them.

9   Intersectionality

S. Laurel Weldon

The concept of intersectionality is an important contribution of feminist theory to the general endeavor of understanding society and politics. The concept is especially valuable for those scholars (such as critical theorists) who aim to critically evaluate social relations, exposing relations of domination, or "speaking truth to power." As I explain below, the concept originates in efforts of Black feminists in the United States to theorize about their experiences and social position, but I argue in this chapter that the concept has great potential to illuminate other national contexts as well. The concept confronts an important dimension of social complexity: the interaction between social structures such as race, class, and gender (among others). Like many important concepts, however, there are multiple ways of understanding and applying the concept of intersectionality. I argue that one of these ways of understanding the concept, an approach I call the *intersectionality-only* approach, makes the concept harder to operationalize and less able to travel, while another possible interpretation, the *intersectionality-plus* version, renders the concept more useful for research, especially cross-national research, and is truer to the core elements of the concept. I use the guidelines for conceptual analysis to highlight these differences.

What is intersectionality? The context of the concept

Intersectionality is a concept that describes the interaction between systems of oppression. The concept grew out of efforts to specify how race *and* gender

I would like to dedicate this chapter to the memory of Iris Young. I would also like to thank those who commented on earlier versions of this chapter and/or otherwise helped refine the thinking in it, including Iris Young, Evelyn Simien, Ange-Marie Hancock, Gary Goertz, Amy Mazur, Rosalee Clawson, Bill Shaffer, Leigh Raymond, Penny Weiss, Pat Boling, Berenice Carroll, Aaron Hoffman, Lisa Baldez, Karen Beckwith, Dorothy Stetson, Simone Bohn, and the students in my comparative social policy graduate seminar at Purdue University.

relations shaped social and political life. Black feminists argued that their problems and experiences could not be described as the problems of black men *plus* the problems of white women. Black women face many problems *as black women*, and their unique perspectives, identities, and experiences, cannot be derived from examination of the experiences and position of either black men or white women.

For example, in *Ain't I a Woman?* bell hooks argues that black women's experience has been obscured by a political movement and theoretical discourse that tend to focus on blacks and women as separate groups. If black women are equally important as women as are white women, oughtn't their experiences to be just as constitutive of our analysis of gender? But black women's experience differs in critical ways from white women's experience (hooks 1981). Similarly, Elisabeth Spelman (1988) has famously argued that "identity" is not like pop-beads: people cannot discern the "woman part" from the "African-American part" or from the "middle-class part." In other words, "As opposed to examining gender, race, class and nation, as separate systems of oppression, intersectionality explores how these systems mutually construct one another" (Collins 1998: 63).

Kimberlé Crenshaw (1991) fleshes out the idea of intersectionality, applying it to violence against women, an issue many think of as cutting across differences of race, class, and disability. Crenshaw argues that women of marginalized race and ethnic groups in the United States confront different structural barriers in trying to address the sexual violence that permeates their lives. For example, non-English-speaking women find themselves barred from women-run shelters because the Anglo women who run these shelters are concerned that they will not be able to understand and adhere to house rules and to participate in support groups. This makes already scarce shelter space even less accessible to such women. Similarly, African-American women confront housing discrimination that makes escape from abusive situations even more difficult. Residential racial segregation means that shelters tend to be located in white communities, not communities of color. The position of African-American women at the nexus of race and gender relations means that their experience of sexual violence is qualitatively different from the experience of either white women or African-American men (Crenshaw 1991).

Another way of putting this is that we cannot characterize African-American women's experiences as being "more of" white women's experience, as being basically the same, only worse (Harris 1990). Nor can we just add the problems of African-American men and white women, as the discourse of "double oppression" suggests, in order to understand the Black female experience. The structures of race and gender *intersect* to create a "matrix of domination" in which each cell defines a position in the race and gender hierarchy (Collins 1990). There is no gender apart from race; there are no race-less women. For *all* women, not just women of color, race shapes the experience and meaning of femininity (Ferber 1998). Of course, race and gender are not the only social structures that intersect: race, gender, class, disability, nation, sexual orientation, and age (among others) are all intersecting systems of oppression (Burnham 2001). Every social position is defined by an interaction between these hierarchical systems. Speaking of gender apart from race, class, ethnicity and other divisions is inaccurate and distorting: there is no such thing as gender apart from race and class, no such thing as race apart from gender, no such thing as class apart from gender or race (Brewer 1999).

Ignoring the intersectional nature of these systems means we systematically overlook the experiences of many different groups of marginalized women, and by default focus only on the most privileged women (white, middle-class, able-bodied, heterosexual), on whom most of our theorizing and research is based. Theoretically, this means we are mis-specifying the ways gender works. Politically, it suggests that feminists who try to organize "as women" are actually excluding those women who are constructed as "different" from whatever it is that unites that particular (probably privileged) subgroup of women who are unaware of the privileges their class, race, heterosexual, national, able-bodied position confers.

It is important to note that "intersectionality" is not just a concept that applies to marginalized groups: It is not a content-specialty in "disadvantaged women." Rather, intersectionality is an aspect of social organization that shapes all of our lives: gender structures shape the lives of both women and men, and everyone has a race/ethnicity. It is also important to note that groups may be advantaged or disadvantaged by structures of oppression: they may be intersectionally marginalized (Black working-class women), intersectionally privileged (white male professionals), or a bit of both. Indeed, social relations are so complex that nearly everyone is privileged in some ways and disadvantaged in others (Note that this does not mean that everyone is *equally* advantaged and disadvantaged.)

"Naming" intersectionality as a new concept: beyond dual systems and triple burdens

Intersectionality, then, is a social-theoretical contribution of feminist theory to efforts to understand and conceptualize social relations. It refers to a form of relationship between social structures, specifically one in which social structures combine to create social categories to which certain experiences and forms of oppression are unique. As a concept, intersectionality is opposed to monism, the idea that each category of social relations (gender, race, class) can be adequately analyzed or understood separately from each other, as a single dimension. Even if the analysis of social relations combines the results of this monistic analysis in some way, we can never grasp the nature of the interaction of social structures by starting with analysis of these axes of social relations as if they operated autonomously. No combination of general features of gender, race, class, and the like will point to the specific nature of oppression of social groups at the nexus of these categories. Focusing on groups defined by the intersection of these social structures reveals *new issues* for political analysis (Smooth 2006). It is important to note that this form of relationship cannot be conceptualized as simply an additive or multiplicative function of the component social structures (gender, race, class, sexuality, nation, etc.). As Fogg-Davis (2006: 71) notes: "Some black feminists working within law and the social sciences rely on the trope of 'multiplication' to convey the intuitive sense that black women's oppression exceeds the sum of their constitutive identifications . . . However, these mathematical metaphors obscure rather than clarify black lesbians' theoretical status within black feminism."

It is worth emphasizing that intersectionality is *not* the opposite of privilege or advantage: it is possible to be intersectionally advantaged or privileged as well as intersectionally marginalized, dominated or oppressed. Indeed, although many (even most) empirical studies of intersectionality do focus on particular disadvantaged groups, there are also studies that focus on the ways that race, class, and gender combine to advantage particular social groups and characteristics (Ferber 1998), as well as studies that use the concept of intersectionality to ground comparisons between advantaged and disadvantaged groups (Strolovitch 2007).

In order to understand the meaning of the concept of intersectionality, it is important to examine how it relates to other concepts in the semantic field: intersectionality is a critical concept, pointing out the limits of previous ways of understanding the relationship between social structures. For example, intersectionality moves beyond the "dual systems" theory once offered (but often criticized) as a way of understanding the coexistence of systems of oppression based on gender and class. Dual systems theory is the idea that patriarchy and capitalism are two distinct systems, with autonomous logics, that nevertheless coexist. Feminist scholars have criticized this approach, for example, arguing that it is not a sufficiently thoroughgoing critique of

Marxism since it assumes that class relations can be understood without reference to gender, and that capitalist exploitation does not have gender-specific forms (Young 1990). The concept of intersectionality offers a way of articulating this critique (that there are effects of gender and class relations that cannot be entirely reduced to the effects of either set of social relations alone) with respect to intersecting social structures more generally, not just the interaction of race and class.

The concept of intersectionality also highlights the limits of the idea that social structures layer on top of each other to create a double or triple or quadruple burden or double oppression. These ways of conceptualizing the interaction among different axes of oppression see distinct results of race, gender, and class (for example) that combine to create "more disadvantage" for those at the nexus of social structures. But the concept of intersectionality rests on a rejection of the idea that the effects of interacting social structures can be adequately understood as a function of the autonomous effects of these social categories. The idea of intersectionality also points out that social structures not only disadvantage particular groups (as the language of burdens suggests); they also privilege certain groups, again, in ways unique to particular gender-race-class groupings. Every person is marked by multiple social structures. So the idea of intersectionality criticizes, improves on, and moves beyond the language of double or triple burdens as well as the concept of "dual systems."

The idea of intersectionality, then, has been very important in pointing out the limitations of existing theoretical approaches to gender analysis. Specifically, the idea of intersectionality has been helpful in showing how thinking in terms of gender *plus* race is incomplete and obscures the experience of women at the interstices of these social relations. But in moving from critique to framework for research, theorists have inadvertently moved away from the core of the idea of intersectionality, developing a version of the concept that the original proponents of the idea would likely reject.

A problem with the contemporary understanding of intersectionality

Young (1994) has pointed out that theoretically, the concept of intersectionality can seem to lead to an infinite regress, an infinite process of splitting of social groups, until one is left with nothing but individuals. For example, the concept of intersectionality requires more than an acknowledgment that gender is modified by race and class: class and race are not stable or unified categories either, since there are many differences among people of color and within class groups (Young 1994; Lugones 1994; MacKinnon 1989; Fogg-Davis 2006). Systems of compulsory heterosexuality cut across all of these categories, as do social divisions of age, disability, and national origin, among others. There are also local and regional variations in the way these structures work. Thus, a myriad structures combine to define extremely specific social positions.

Consider, for starters, a set of axes that we can easily identify (gender, race/ethnicity, class, sexuality, ability, religion, rural/urban, nationality). If each axis involved only two categories (an oversimplification for purposes of discussion), the combination of these axes generates a matrix with 256 cells designating distinct social positions. Clearly, any individual piece of analysis could not examine *all* of these social groups "on their own terms," as if they were the most important group, moving them from margin to center.

Faced with the complexity of this analytic task, scholars of social policy seeking to use the concept of intersectionality in empirical work have followed one of two strategies: (1) focusing on analyzing the experiences of a specific race-class-gender group, and (2) using an additive approach, that is identifying the experiences or interests of each of several broadly defined social collectivities and placing them alongside one another. Neither of these strategies, as I show below, actually operationalizes the idea of intersectionality in its strong version.

First, some scholars aim to take account of the intersectionality of social structures by focusing on the experiences of particular social groups. Misra and Akins (1998), for example, propose focusing on different groups of women as a way of understanding why different women have such different experiences of the welfare state.[1] Examining specific groups of women in their interaction with the state avoids the problems involved in assuming a shared "women's experience." In statistical terms, there is a lot of heterogeneity in the "population" (women, or African-Americans, etc.), that necessitates examining each subgroup separately. This suggests that one is likely to get very different statistical results when doing analyses by subgroup. Indeed, much research in women and politics shows exactly this (Whitaker 1999: 79, CAWP 2000, 2004, Bedolla and Scola 2006). For example, looking at *New York Times* exit poll data

---

[1] In this piece, Misra and Akins (1998) seek to find a way to conceptualize women's diversity while recognizing the importance of both structures and agents. The structure–agency problem is too complex to address in this chapter, but I want to note that contemporary social theorists have mostly moved beyond a debate about whether social structures deny agency or vice versa to a position that acknowledges the mutual constitution of structures and agents (Young 2000, 2005, Wendt 1999).

for the years 1972 to 1996 shows that analyzing the "gender gap" in voting by gender-race groups (instead of just by gender) suggests that the gender gap is slightly (and consistently) larger between black men and women than between white men and women. In addition, it seems the gender gap emerges between black men and women at least as early as 1972 (maybe earlier), while for whites it does not emerge until 1980 (Connolly 1996).[2]

But focusing only on the distinctive problems of narrowly defined groups makes it hard to discern how broader social structures disadvantage people. For example, in a cross-national analysis of variation in class structures, Erik Olin Wright (1997) concludes that "in spite of these variations [in class structure], the fundamental class division based on ownership of the means of production remains a consistently important division" (1997: 42). Similarly, Collins (1998) notes that despite their many differences, "all Black men must in some way grapple with actual or potential treatment by the criminal justice system," and that "whatever their racial/ethnic classification, poor people as a group confront similar barriers for issues of basic survival." Young (1994) notes that in spite of women's many differences, women share a vulnerability to sexual violence. Fogg-Davis (2006: 73) calls for more attention to the connections between the specific forms of oppression to which black lesbians are subject and those which afflict heterosexual black women. On the strong version of intersectionality, which holds that there is no "class," "Black men," "women," or "black women" as such (since these groups are fractured by other social structures), these general statements would be meaningless. If we think there is anything to the observations about class, race, or gender above, then this version of intersectionality obstructs analysis of the similar or at least related effects that social structures have on many people's lives.

On this reading, then, the idea of intersectionality requires that each cell or social position follows its own, autonomous logic and *assumes* that there is *nothing* shared across social positions. Different conditions characterize the different groups defined by each cell, different causal processes produce these distinctive conditions, and there is little or nothing to be gained by examining commonalities across cells (say, grouping people by row or column). Focusing on just one specific social group, just one cell in the matrix, seems like a strategy for adhering to this principle. At the same time, however, theories of intersectionality often emphasize that social structures are mutually

---

[2] Thanks to Rosalee Clawson for directing my attention to this finding.

reinforcing, and that each cell is structurally related to the other cells (Fogg-Davis 2006). These axes are part of a unified system. In order to understand how these cells all fit together, and how these axes combine, we must examine the relations among and between these cells. But examining only one social group or a few groups at a time will hardly be adequate to sort out the complex interactions between so many axes of disadvantage, so focusing on only a particular social group in a very detailed way is not a very satisfying solution to this analytic problem.

Another solution might be to eschew social structural analysis altogether. Recall, though, that the idea of intersectionality grew out of the idea that social structures intersect to shape social positions. The very idea of intersectionality *assumes* that social positions, and corresponding social groups (larger than individuals, or a handful of individuals), are created and delineated by social structures (constellations of norms, laws, institutions, traditions) (Collins 1997, Young 1994). Indeed, the scholars that urge the adoption of the idea of intersectionality usually advocate, in the same breath, the analysis of multiple systems of domination. The exhortation to examine the interstices of structures of gender and race hardly makes sense if there are no such structures to begin with (Zinn and Dill 1996, Burnham 2001, Collins 1998). Examining the intersection of structures suggests that these structures can be identified prior to the focus on the intersections, that they are to some degree or in some sense autonomous of one another. But on the popular understanding of intersectionality, there is no autonomy to gender, race, or class categories, no content (for example) to gender apart from race. So the idea of intersectionality, in this strong version, requires social structural analysis, but makes such analysis difficult (if not impossible) to undertake.

Possible solutions[3]

Some scholars have responded to this problem by suggesting that we think of gender as a category of analysis (Beckwith 2005b, 2000, Hawkesworth 2005; see also J. Scott 1986). But the leverage gained from considering gender as

---

[3] I do not consider the possibility of adopting a position of skepticism towards the category gender as some scholars do (e.g. Butler 1990, Mohanty 1991); nor do I embrace a general skepticism of group-based politics or analysis (Lugones 1994). Because I am convinced by those who argue that progressive politics and structural social analysis depends on group-based politics and analysis (Collins 1998, Young 1990, 1994, 2002), in this chapter I focus on addressing the literature on intersectionality, pointing out that those who advocate using the concept also advocate structural, group-based analysis.

a category of analysis stems from the importance of gender in everyday life, the importance of gender structures, symbols, and identities (Hawkesworth 2005). If gender as a social structure has no independent effects, then it is hard to see what justifies an analytic focus on gender as a category, as opposed to, say, gender-race, or gender-race-class. Indeed, this is the force of some current critiques of feminist scholarship that uses gender "unmodified" as a category: some of these scholars argue that gender as an analytic category has no meaning apart from race, class, and other axes of disadvantage (and that these other categories similarly have no autonomous effects) (Brewer 1999, Harris 1990, Ferber 1998, Collins 1990, Burnham 2001).

Proposing a different sort of solution, Iris Young (2005) has argued that we ought to retain the category of gender for political analysis, arguing that focusing on gender as a social structure abstracts from the complex experience of particular individuals and focuses on the macro politics of social organization. Young argues that "social groups defined by caste, class, race, age, ethnicity, and, of course gender name subjective identities less than axes of structural inequality. They name structural positions whose occupants are privileged or disadvantaged in relation to one another due to the adherence of actors to institutional rules and norms and the pursuit of their interests and goals within institutions" (2005: 21). Social structures are macro-level, not individual-level, phenomena. Taking this approach has the advantage, Young argues, that "we no longer need to ascribe a single or shared gender identity to men and women" (2005: 22). While attributing a shared gender identity to women is problematic, seeing "women" as sharing a structurally defined social position is not: "Thus, membership in the group called 'women' is the product of a loose configuration of different structural factors" (2005: 21). Following Young, Htun (2005) explicitly distinguishes between structure and identity, arguing that scholars ought to focus on large-scale social structures and processes.

For Young, then, gender is a social structure, a mode of social organization, that systematically disadvantages women. Like other social-theoretical work in political science (e.g. Wendt 1999), Young combines structural analysis with a sophisticated account of individual agency, acknowledging that agents and structures are mutually constituted (Young 2000, 2005). The reason for developing such a social structural account of politics, as Young convincingly argues, is that we need to be able to criticize social structures (Young 2005). Moreover, I agree that such macro-level analysis need not imply shared identities across gender, race, or class groups.

But this approach does not obviate the need to think about how to theorize the interaction of different axes of structural inequality, even if we are working at a macro-social, and not individual, level (Wright 1997). Indeed, theorists of intersectionality insist that we cannot understand the ways that women are disadvantaged as women or the ways that people of color are oppressed *unless we examine the ways these structures interact.* Specifically, they claim that certain aspects of social inequality, certain social problems and injustices, will not be visible as long as we focus on gender, race, and class separately (Collins 1990; Crenshaw 1991; Roth 2004; Hurtado 1989, Harris 1990). It is not often recognized that structural analysis is *required* by the idea of intersectionality: it is the intersection of social *structures*, not identities, to which the concept refers. We cannot conceptualize "interstices" unless we have a concept of the structures that intersect to create these points of interaction.

Feminist scholars of color have argued convincingly that an account that focuses only on gender will not be able to provide a full account of the ways that women are disadvantaged: in some ways, women of color are disadvantaged as *women* of color; poor women are disadvantaged as poor *women*. But these marks of the female condition are nevertheless race- or class-specific; they are not shared by all women, and may not even be visible unless we focus on specific race-class-gender groups. Moreover, these group-specific experiences reveal aspects of gender structure that are important to understanding the overall social context (Hurtado 1989; Harris 1990, hooks 1981, 2000, Collins 1990, 1998, Crenshaw 1991). If gender as a principle of social organization cannot be fully understood without an examination of the interaction between social structures, and if women are structurally disadvantaged *as women* in class-and-race-specific ways, then a structural approach to gender analysis requires some account of this structural interaction. The problem remains, then, of how to conceptualize and analyze the interaction between these different structures.

I propose a third sort of solution, one that retains the core aspects of the concept of intersectionality but avoids some of the problematic elements of contemporary usage. Scholars of intersectionality point to the limits of "monism" (or focus on one structure), argue that social structures of race, class, and gender mutually modify one another, and push for scholarship on women "at the interstices" as a way of understanding the ways that these social structures interact (Roth 2004, Collins 1990, 1998, Harris 1990, Crenshaw 1991; Burnham 2001). But a variety of possible relations between axes of domination is consistent with these core ideas. In other words, we could theoretically specify intersectional relationships between gender, race, and class structures in a number of different ways.

For example, as noted, one group of scholars seems to understand the idea of intersectionality as implying that systems of gender, race, and class have *no autonomous effects* (e.g. Harris 1990, Brewer 1999, Ferber 1998). In other words, we really have one social structure called gender-race-class-ability-ethnicity-sexuality, and people occupy one social position as defined by these categories. On this view, it would be nonsensical to suggest that capitalism sometimes reinforced and sometimes undermined gender or race hierarchies (Lipton 1988), that race is a more salient division than class in the United States while the reverse is true in Europe (Wacquant 1995), or that gender is more important than class in explaining some features of women's work (Hartmann 1994, Wright 1997). Making such claims requires the existence of identifiably separate dynamics for each of these axes. Precluding the possibility of autonomous effects assumes that systems of race, class, and gender *always* work together seamlessly as a single system, and never have any significant independent effects. This idea that all effects of gender-race-class systems are intersectional effects, that there are no autonomous effects of these axes, I will call for purpose of discussion the *intersectionality-only* model of social structural interaction.

There are other ways of thinking about how systems of gender, race, and class interact that are consistent with the core of the concept of intersectionality. For example, we might think of gender, race, and class as having some independent effects *and* some intersectional effects. Or we might think of gender and race as being mutually reinforcing while class undermines these systems. Or we might think of all three systems as being mutually reinforcing but analytically separable, and also having some intersectional effects.

Let me try to illustrate by means of an example. One might think of social structures as light shining through multiple layers of colored transparencies on to a patchwork quilt: the color and play of the light shining through depend on the constitution of each layer, but there is no light that shines through just one layer. And the effect of the light will vary based on the patch of quilt it hits. As long as the transparencies map perfectly on to one another, describing the light shining through just one layer of transparency (say, red, green, or purple) would not capture how the light actually falls on any part of the quilt. And the light that shines through will be one color or consistency, although it will fall on different patches differently. The effects are not patches of green *beside* patches of red *beside* patches of purple. The effect is just brown shadows: the transparencies combine to fall on every part

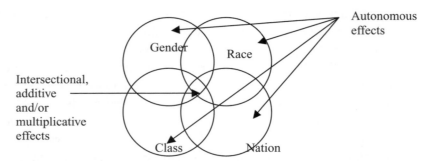

Figure 9.1   Intersectional and autonomous effects of gender, race, class, and nation

of the quilt together. Each slide always modifies the effect of the others, and none has an independent effect. Looking at light shining through just the red slide, or just green, or just purple, will not show us how they will combine. Nor does the light from one slide affect some parts of the quilt and not others; the same color of light falls on all patches. This is the *intersectionality-only* version of how gender, race, and class interact.

Alternatively, the colored slides could be overlapping, but not mapping perfectly on to each other. This would suggest that some areas would be just green, just red, or just purple, while other areas would be brown (as light filtered through all three slides). In order to capture the play of light over the quilt, we would want to describe the areas of green, red, and purple as well as the areas of brown. Indeed, it might even help us to notice the green and red and purple areas, even if most of the quilt is covered in brown-colored shadows, because it might help us to understand that the light that falls on the brown areas is filtered through three slides, not one single slide. In other words, each social structure could have both autonomous and combined effects. Finding that some combined effects (areas patterned brown) cannot be described solely by looking at one element of its composition (say, red) does not preclude the possibility that other areas *are* just red, or green, or purple. So finding that gender, race, and class *sometimes* combine to create effects that are unique to specific gender-race-class groups does not mean that *every* effect of social structures is unique to such groups. Finding intersectionality in *some* effects does not necessarily imply intersectionality in *all* effects (Figure 9.1).

Let me also illustrate this point using a formalization common in quantitative analysis. Sometimes we show additive effects of particular factors using a common formula for regression analysis, where some effect of interest (Y) is produced by a combination of factors (x_1, x_2, $x_3 \ldots$), coefficients that determine the size of the effect of each variable (b_1, b_2, b_3), a constant (c) and some error term (e):

$$Y = a + b_1x_1 + b_2x_2 + c + e$$

Say that the effect (Y) was the degree of freedom or autonomy granted to citizens in a given society. Here, the term x_1 could represent the effects of gender, and x_2 the effects of race. This would be the way to model these effects as being separable from each other and combining in additive ways: gender *plus* race. We might think of this as a sort of "double burden" or "double jeopardy" conceptualization of the interaction between gender, race, and class: each dimension of disadvantage creates some distinct advantages and disadvantages that combine by adding on to each other.

Sometimes, factors combine in mutually reinforcing ways, so that they *magnify* each other's effects. This mutually reinforcing relationship is often modeled as a multiplicative one (also called interaction effects) using the formula for interactions between two variables, x_1 and x_2 (say, gender and race):

$$Y = a + b_1x_1 + b_2x_2 + \boldsymbol{b_3x_1 * x_2} + c + e$$

Here, the mutually reinforcing effect can be captured as a function of the original variables. We might call this the model of gender, race, and class as *separable but mutually reinforcing*.

Note that modeling multiplicative effects does not rule out additive effects: it is possible for social phenomena to have both sorts of effects (Wright 1997). If there are no additive effects, then $b_1x_1 + b_2x_2$ will be equal to zero, leaving only the interaction term ($\boldsymbol{b_3x_1 * x_2}$), constant and error.

Sometimes quantitative researchers seem to assume that *intersectional* effects are the same as multiplicative effects (the convention of calling such effects *interaction* effects probably contributes to this confusion). But it is important to note that theorists of intersectionality have been emphatic that intersectional effects cannot be *generally* defined as some standard mathematical manipulation of the effects of gender, race, and class considered independently: as noted, they are not just "more of" the effects of gender and race considered independently (i.e. not just "more" violence against women, or "more" discrimination) (Harris 1990; Crenshaw 1991). Combinations of gender-race-class (or other axes) produce distinctively different effects, effects of phenomena that other social groups do not even experience. The point is that there are distinctive effects of gender-race-class combined that could be, for example, opposite in direction to the effects of gender or race or class considered separately. So the idea of intersectionality suggests that there is a third type of effect, say, x_4. We would model these effects as follows if x_1 is gender and x_2 is race, and x_4 represents the intersectional effects of a particular gender-race-class configuration:

$$Y = a + b_1 x_1 + b_2 x_2 + b_3 x_1 * x_2 + \mathbf{b_4 x_4} + c + e$$

To return to the earlier example, by way of illustration, if Y represents the degree of autonomy a society grants its citizens, $b_1 x_1$ represents the effect on autonomy stemming from gender inequality, $b_2 x_2$ represents the effect on autonomy stemming from race inequality, $b_3 x_1 * x_2$ represents the effect on autonomy stemming from the mutually reinforcing nature of race and gender inequality, and $b_4 x_4$ represents the effect on autonomy stemming from a specific, qualitatively different effect on autonomy resulting from a particular combination of gender-race, and particular to a particular gender-race group. Consider that it is theoretically possible that while gender and race alone result in reductions of autonomy, the intersectional effects increase autonomy for specific gender-race groups, countering the autonomous effects of gender and race for that specific group.

Note that here I specify this relationship as one incorporating all three types of effects: additive ($b_1 x_1 + b_2 x_2$), multiplicative ($b_3 x_1 * x_2$) and intersectional ($b_4 x_4$). On the *intersectionality-only* hypothesis, though, the first parts of the equation (additive and multiplicative effects) would drop out (be equal to zero), leaving only the intersectional effects (x_4): The *only* effects are intersectional effects.

It is possible, though, that gender, race, and class interact in such a way that there are all three types of effects: additive, multiplicative, and intersectional. It is also possible that the relationship between these different structures varies over space and time. In some times or places, systems of race and class may undermine each other, while in other places they reinforce each other. Insisting that the only version of gender, race, and class is one which sees all effects of social structures as intersectional under all circumstances, it seems to me, wrongly limits the possible configurations of social structures consistent with the observation of some intersectional effects.

I propose allowing the possibility that there are additive and multiplicative *as well as* intersectional effects of gender, race, and class. Let us allow that the transparencies might not map perfectly on to one another, so that the play of light includes some green, red, and purple patches. Let us call this the *intersectionality-plus* version of the interaction of these social structures.

We can use Ragin's (1987) Boolean logic, which is more holistic and qualitatively oriented, to illustrate the same point (Mahoney and Goertz 2006). For this purpose, we can define Y as representing a reduction in the degree of autonomy granted to the citizenry. There may be many paths or sources of this reduction in autonomy: the social structure of race may reduce autonomy on its own (we can define R, appearing by itself, as designating such a causal path); similarly, the social structure of gender alone (G) may also reduce autonomy, as could class (C). On a monistic approach to social structural interaction, reductions in autonomy can stem from race, gender, or class, which we would represent as

$$Y = R + G + C$$

But theorists of intersectionality have pointed out that race, class, and gender combine to produce effects that none produces on its own. The combination is transformational: eggs, nuts, flour, sugar, chocolate, and the like combine to make a cake, and the taste of the final product (cake) is nothing like eating eggs, nuts, sugar, etc., in sequence. Nor can we easily decompose the cake into eggs, flour, chocolate, and so on once it is baked. These combined effects are qualitatively different: every combination of the social structures of race, gender, and class produces qualitatively unique outcomes. We might designate this view as

$$Y = R * G * C$$

– that is, race, class, and gender *combine* to reduce autonomy or freedom; the reduced degree of freedom in a society is a result of the combined effect of social structures of race, gender, and class. This is the *intersectionality-only* approach.

But note that the second claim does not rule out the first: saying that race, class, and gender combine to reduce autonomy does not rule out the possibility that these social structures also reduce autonomy on their own, albeit in different or merely related (not exactly the same) ways. So even if we cannot, for example, take out the nuts, eggs, or chocolate chips from the cake, it might be relevant in some cases (say, for those with severe food intolerances) to know that there are nuts, eggs, or the like in the cake. Some important outcomes could be produced by one ingredient, while different, equally important outcomes might be produced by the combination of ingredients. We could represent this approach, the *intersectionality-plus* approach, as

$$Y = R + G + C + R * G * C$$

That is, for this example, there are (at least) four separate causal paths which lead to a societal reduction in autonomy: those stemming from race, gender, and class alone, and those stemming from combinations of race, gender, and class.

Can the concept of intersectionality "travel"?

The *intersectionality-plus* account of the interaction of social structures has a major advantage over the *intersectionality-only* version when it comes to comparative analysis: it admits the possibility that the ways that social structures affect each other vary over space and time. Some axes might be more salient or politicized in some contexts than in others. For example, most of the writing about intersectionality derives from the work of women of color in the United States. Are gender, race, and class similarly entwined in other national contexts? The *intersectionality-plus* model of social structural interaction is consistent with the idea that different social structures might have different types of effects in different contexts. Observing such variation helps us to identify the distinctive features (and perhaps the causes) of particular national constellations of social structure, perhaps linking such structures to particular historic trajectories. *This makes the intersectionality-plus approach particularly useful for comparative political analysis, and it makes comparative political analysis critical to understanding gender (and race, and class) politics.*

Operationalizing intersectionality

On the *intersectionality-only* view, then, every category of social relations is necessarily equally relevant for every analysis of political phenomena. Empirical studies applying this idea of intersectionality, however, have been few (Bedolla and Scola 2006, Hancock 2006) and have mostly been limited to case studies demonstrating differences among women, studies providing a basis for contesting the use of unitary categories of race, class, and gender (McCall

2005). But merely contesting categories does little to advance our understanding of the complex ways that social structures interact. In order to study the relationships between social structures, rather than treat the intersectional nature of social structures as a background assumption or condition, however, we need a different approach to studying intersectionality (McCall 2005, Weldon 2006a).

I propose the *intersectionality-plus* model as the conceptual basis for a new approach. I have described the conceptual understanding of this idea above: in the sections below, I apply the concept to the study of the welfare state to demonstrate what it means to operationalize this revised idea of intersectionality, and how such a revised concept provides advantages over existing approaches.

Application to study of the welfare state

In order to illustrate the problem with the *intersectionality-only* version of the concept, and the advantages of the alternative approach I suggest here, let us examine one effort to examine race, class, and gender in the area of research on the welfare state. Fiona Williams (1995) offers a framework for the comparative analysis of race/ethnicity, gender, and class in welfare states. Williams argues that "we need to be aware of the variety of structured divisions that affect both people's lives and the development of welfare provisions" (1995: 128). In particular, she argues that relations of gender, race, and class are the most salient social divisions in late twentieth-century industrialized societies. These axes of division are "mutually constitutive: the effects of race, class and gender divisions are interrelated and multifaceted – one element compounds or modifies the others" (1995: 128). With this conceptual background, then, Williams seeks to undertake to analyze how social relations of gender, race, and class shape welfare states.

Williams begins by noting that most analysis of the welfare state is focused on class relations, on state–market relations, rather than on gender or class. Williams convincingly argues that "'class politics' were and are also crucially about gender relations, race and nation" (1995: 131). But even these gender critiques of the class-based literature do not fully take race into account (1995: 135). So we have no theorization of the welfare state that attends to gender, race, and class.

Williams notes that although we could reformulate core concepts of the welfare state literature to take race into account,

There is a danger, however, that in racializing the gender regimes or the gendered dimensions we are simply adding in race to analyses that are following their own gender or class/gender logics. What is necessary first, then, is to spell out the dynamics of a separate "race/ethnicity logic" even though we recognize that this logic does not operate autonomously. (1995: 137)

Williams suggests that studies of race/ethnicity and the welfare state should focus on the concept of *nation*, including nation-state formation, conditions of colonialism and imperialism, systems of migration, and processes of inclusion and exclusion from the nation-state (citizenship). Historical studies of the legacy of ethnic, cultural, or religious conflict and discourses of racism should inform such an analysis, as should studies of mobilization and resistance to the process of welfare state formation (both racist and antiracist). Returning to the welfare state literature, then, Williams argues that the literature's examination of market, state, and family must be expanded to take these aspects of the articulation of *nation* into account. In addition, she suggests some reformulation of our analysis of family and work to include processes of inclusion and exclusion.

This analytic strategy does suggest some interesting and important new areas for social policy research. But analytically, this strategy for devising an approach to comparing welfare states does not recognize the intersectional nature of race, class, and gender, at least on the contemporary, popular understanding of the concept. The effort to articulate a distinct logic of race/ethnicity is itself precluded by the strong version of intersectionality: *on that view, there is no such logic distinct from logics of class and gender.* One cannot separate the "race" part from the "gender" part or the "class" part. The idea of focusing primarily on race and then returning to integrate this logic into the study of welfare states assumes the analytic separability of these dimensions, although they cannot be separated in reality. But the idea of intersectionality denies this analytic separability, and suggests that adopting such a strategy marginalizes those "at the interstices" of gender, race, and class (for example, working-class women of color).

An approach that was truer to the prevailing idea of intersectionality would proceed not by distinguishing axes of race, class, and gender and then combining them, but by constructing a matrix of domination, and examining each position in that matrix on its own terms (see Figure 9.2). Each social

	Whites	People of color
Bourgeois	Women	Women
	Men	Men
Working class	Women	Women
	Men	Men

Figure 9.2   Matrix of domination: race, class, gender. For purposes of illustration only, this figure assumes these categories of race, gender, and class are binary.

position defined by this matrix represents a *unique* instantiation of the intersection of gender, race, and class, and has a particular relationship to the other seven categories. A unique causal story must be told about each cell. One would assume that there is no shared experience across any of the columns or rows. A framework for comparative analysis, then, would have to examine the history of the groups defined by each cell separately, seeking to define the ways that social policies relate to that specific group (see Figure 9.2).

Of course, categories of gender, class, and race are likely multiple, and this table does not even seek to address divisions of sexuality, disability, age, or language (to name a few). To do so would make this table even more unwieldy than it already is. But for now, for the sake of argument, let us examine this simplified table as a way of considering the promise of and problems with the idea of intersectionality.

Williams's approach falls short of even this simplified model of intersectionality because her theoretical approach considers each dimension as separate unities. Williams considers the experiences of those in the cells under "People of color" and asks what aspects of social policy considering these experiences as a group suggests. She does this without considering how the logic of racialization she described likely differentiated women from men, propertied people of color from those without property. For example, do not the concept of family, and efforts to combine family and work, have different ramifications for women of color than it does for men of color? Black feminist theorists in the United States have focused on the unique challenges of motherhood for African-American women (e.g. Collins 1990). Similarly, if she were to confront the experiences of working-class women of color on their own terms, for example, she might find that sexual violence and harassment in the workplace and family, and the proliferation of sweatshops, figured prominently in their experiences. Why is it that working women of color are so particularly vulnerable to these problems? These experiences fall through the cracks of the framework for comparative analysis of gender-race-class and social policy that Williams proposes.

The problem is that it is not clear that anyone could develop a framework for examining the ways that gender, race, and class structure social policy that actually operationalizes the *intersectionality-only* version of the concept. If we take the *intersectionality-only* approach seriously, even a thorough examination of how a particular welfare state affected a particular group of working women of color (leaving aside the other seven categories in the matrix) would not be an analysis of social structural relations of gender, race, and class. It would be an analysis of the particular relationship between the specific social position examined and social policy. For example, examining the impact of the development of TANF (Temporary Assistance for Needy Families) on poor Mexican-American women (and/or their resistance to policy development or change) tells us nothing about how poor African-American or Chinese-American women or middle-class Mexican women were affected by this same policy. And of course, on the *intersectionality-only* view, the unity of the group "poor Mexican-American women" here, is a pernicious fiction, obscuring the ways that disability, sexuality, and age (for example) further fracture this group. Focusing on the group "poor Mexican-American women" pushes the most marginalized members of this group into obscurity. Thus, taking the *intersectionality-only* version seriously makes empirical research on structural social relations and social policy impossible.

An intersectional analysis of the welfare state

In this section, I aim to provide an example of how the *intersectionality-plus* version of the concept can be the basis for empirical research by making use of it in a cross-national analysis of the welfare state. As noted, existing studies of welfare states that aim to confront the diversity among women either focus on the effects of social policy on particular groups of women *or* they add together the effects of social relations of each of gender, race, and class (an additive understanding of the interaction). Intersectional gender analysis requires that we undertake both of these research tasks simultaneously: we must complement an additive analysis with a focus on those at the interstices of social structures. Some scholars have called these groups *intersectionally marginalized* or *intersectionally privileged* groups (Crenshaw 1991, Strolovitch 2004).

From this perspective, then, we should explore both independent or autonomous logics *as well as* intersectional aspects of these major axes of oppression. Indeed, these are not conflicting agendas: as Williams suggests, seeking to confront these axes on their own terms can reveal aspects of group relations that remain obscured when we start by examining the intersection of these categories. For example, Williams points out that taking race into account cannot mean merely reformulating existing conceptualization of the relation between state, market, and family. In addition to such reformulation, the centrality of the idea of "nation" to the development of welfare states should be explored. Similarly, some scholars have criticized the literature on gender and welfare states as focusing too much on motherhood and work and not enough on sexual violence (Brush 2003). Beginning from a focus on women as women illuminates issues important for all women, although the specific nature of this experience may be different for women of different racial/ethnic and class groups. Indeed, as noted, Williams does not mention the importance of sexual violence (as a raced, classed, and gendered phenomenon) for poor women of color. This may be because, as I suggested above, focusing *only* on the intersection of particular categories, rather than sometimes trying to ask what women or people of color or the poor do have in common, can make us focus too much on the distinctive aspects of such experiences and not enough on the experiences that are shared or that follow similar logics.

As a first cut, then, a framework for the analysis of the welfare state should employ various efforts to get at the relationship between welfare state development and class, welfare state development and gender, and welfare state development and race. In each case, the category should be confronted on its own terms as a way of discovering the autonomous logics (if any) that are present. This provides the basis for exploring the relationships between these three sets of social relationships and the welfare state. To explore possible additive effects, one could develop indicators of how the welfare state interacted with each group (treating them as separate). Of course, this additive model does not capture the intersectional (nonadditive, distinct, or unique) effects of social relations. Thus, one would also need to examine particular groups defined simultaneously by race, class, *and* gender to explore their relationship to the welfare state (say, immigrant domestic workers). This focus on particular groups can help illuminate areas of social policy that are obscured by the use of undifferentiated categories (race, class, gender) themselves. This dual approach (both additive and intersectional) should provide a richer picture of welfare state development than analyses that pursue either an exclusively additive or an exclusively intersectional strategy. Such an analysis can never be comprehensive or final: exploring other axes of oppression and other particular groups should suggest refinements and revisions in our analysis. But in this formulation, we can see these refinements as the cumulation of knowledge or the deepening of our understanding.

We can use the existing literature on the welfare state to flesh out what it would mean to employ this approach in a comparative study of social policy. First, we must delineate categories of race, class, and gender, confronting each axis of social relations on its own terms. Then we can ask: What is the relationship between and among these categories? Building on Esping-Andersen's (1990, 1999) analyses of class politics and the welfare state, on F. Williams's (1995) analysis of race/ethnicity and the welfare state, and on a synthesis of gender analyses (Orloff 1993, Lewis 1993, Brush 2003, Elman 2000, 2003, O'Connor, Orloff, and Shaver 1999, Weldon 2002a) we can explore the autonomous logics of each of these dimensions. For example, class analysis will focus on the conditions under which social policy decommodifies workers in the paid labor force (Esping-Andersen 1990). Critical race analysis will focus on whether social policy enforces exclusion or inclusion of marginalized racial and ethnic groups, and whether sameness or assimilation is required for inclusion. An analysis of immigration, citizenship, and cultural policies as well as affirmative action policies for racial/ethnic groups will provide the basis for grouping states as multicultural (inclusive) or assimilationist (internal exclusion) or segregationist (exclusive). Gender analysis will examine the ways that social policies promote or undermine gender equality, focusing on whether such policies equally promote autonomy and responsibility for women and men. This analysis could include analysis of maternity and parental leave policies, policies on violence against women, reproductive rights policies, and antidiscrimination policies among others.

In addition, and importantly, though, *the analysis should also focus on policies of special interest to intersectionally marginalized groups.* Here I suggest three such policy areas as a starting point. The first policy area concerns domestic workers. Domestic workers are mostly working-class women, and are often immigrant women and/or women of color. Thus, examining policies toward domestic workers is one way to get at the relationship between the state and a particular group of intersectionally marginalized women. Are domestic workers covered by general labor laws? How are identified undocumented domestic workers treated? A second area of social policy of particular interest to intersectionally marginalized groups are policies to address violence against women who are noncitizens. What happens to noncitizen women who report violence to the police? Are they deported? Can they apply for residency permits independent of their abusive partner? Third, income assistance is especially important for poor women, but eligibility criteria (such as citizenship, work requirements, and the like) often have discriminatory effects according to race and ethnicity. Thus, examining the eligibility criteria for income assistance for poor women will help illuminate the impact of policy on this intersectionally marginalized group.

Examining the policy areas outlined above would allow an investigation of autonomous effects of race, gender, and class as well as intersectional effects on social policy. It would also be helpful to compare this research with a comparable analysis on policies affecting intersectionally privileged groups. Note that this suggestion constitutes a framework for charting the relationship between different aspects of social relations and social policy outcomes. It does not provide a theoretical account of the relation between different social systems or types of policy. But thinking about social policies along these dimensions allows us to theorize and empirically examine different relationships between different patterns of social relations and social policy.

Summary of evaluation and comparison of the two approaches using the Guidelines

Applying the guidelines for conceptual analysis developed by Goertz and Mazur (chapter 2 above) illuminates the advantages of the *intersectionality-plus* approach and the limitations of the *intersectionality-only* view, especially for comparative research. Leaving aside those Guidelines which do not differentiate between the versions (e.g. Naming, Dimensions, and Context), seven questions distinguish these versions (see Table 9.1). First, what is the opposite or *negation* of intersectionality? Whereas proponents of the *intersectionality-only* approach would point to any analysis that sought to examine gender, race, or class on its own, I propose that the opposite of intersectionality is the absence of any qualitatively unique effects of combinations among social structures. This brings us to the second question, the issue of which elements are *necessary* to the concept of intersectionality. What is necessary for intersectionality is that *some* such distinctive effects must obtain: not *all* effects of social structures must be intersectional, as the *intersectionality-only* approach requires. On the *intersectionality-only* approach, intersectionality is an all-or-nothing affair: *there are no gray zones*. On the *intersectionality-plus* approach,

Table 9.1 Applying the Guidelines to the two versions of intersectionality

Guideline	Intersectionality-only	Intersectionality-plus
Negation Guideline: What is the negation, absence, or opposite of the basic concept?	*Any* autonomous effects of gender-race-class (GRC) are inconsistent with intersectionality.	Absence of distinctive effects of combinations of GRC would indicate absence of intersectionality.
Zones Guideline: Is there a gray zone?	Intersectionality is an all-or-nothing affair; social relations are either intersectional or they are not.	It is possible for effects of social structures to be intersectional as well as autonomous; there may be multiple modes of interaction between social structures.
Necessity Guideline: Are any dimensions necessary?	All conditions are effects of combined social structures that go beyond effects of GRC separately analyzed.	There must be *some* effects of social structures that go beyond effects of GRC separately analyzed for intersectionality to obtain in a relationship.
Interdependence Guideline: What is the interdependence between dimensions?	All social structures are equally important, *a priori*; there can never be a legitimate analytic reason for privileging one axis of social structure.	Social structures may vary in their salience across political contexts (cross-nationally; over time; across groups); they may combine in different ways.
Traveling Guideline: What is the means of empirically connecting cases to the concept?	Travels poorly; does not admit that in some places, gender, race, and class might interact differently. There is already a body of research that suggests this could be the case.	Travels well; allows us to test or explore how social structures interact in different contexts.
Causal Relationships Guideline: How do causal relationships work within and between concepts?	Social structures only have effects that are unique to each cell in the matrix of domination.	It is possible that social structures have both autonomous and intersectional effects.
Operationalization Guideline: How is the concept operationalized?	Not well-operationalized; requires that researchers examine each cell in matrix of domination separately, and *assumes* that there will be no common effects across rows or columns in matrix.	Proposes that there could be unique causal mechanisms for each cell that will not be revealed by examining shared effects across rows and columns, but allows that there *could* also be "row and/or column" effects. It is also possible that studying rows and/or columns in the matrix of domination suggests clues as to where to look for group-specific effects.

some aspects of the interaction between social structures may be intersectional, but some may not be. The core elements of the concept are the same on both views: a rejection of monistic analysis of social structures as adequate for capturing the most important aspects of social and political relations; an insistence that social structures combine in ways that produce effects and experiences that are unique to specific social groups. But beyond this, the *intersectionality-only* approach insists that *a priori*, we know that all social structures are equally important, always, for every research question. The *intersectionality-plus* approach allows that social structures may vary in their salience across political contexts (cross-nationally; over time; across groups); they may combine in different ways. For these reasons, the *intersectionality-plus* approach is more elastic, better suited for cross-national research; it *travels* better.

The *intersectionality-plus* approach is also easier to *operationalize*, and captures what is right and highlights what is wrong with the actual practice of researchers who are trying to examine intersectional social relations empirically. Drawing on the idea of a "matrix of domination," I suggest that the concept of intersectionality directs our analytical attention to the possibility that there are effects or experiences that are unique to each cell, not shared by other groups in the same "row" or "column." The *intersectionality-only* approach demands that we focus on each cell individually, eschewing a broader analysis of each social structure; it mitigates against asking whether structures exhibit any sort of autonomous logic. Thus, each approach suggests different *causal relationships*: the *intersectionality-plus* approach admits that there might be "row and/or column" effects as well as cell-specific effects or experiences.

Implications for political practice: intersectionality as a model for practice

In the feminist activist (as opposed to primarily scholarly) community, there has also been some use of the concept of intersectionality as a normative goal, or preferred mode of organizing. Even in the purely scholarly context, it is clear that the argument is that feminist scholars *ought* to attend to the intersectional nature of social structures of gender, race, class (etc.) inequality. In this more normative sense, "doing intersectionality" often seems to mean attending to differences among women, working to ensure that the unique perspectives of marginalized groups of women are not silenced, excluded, or overshadowed by those of more privileged women.

Of course, noting this normative aspect to the usage of the idea of intersectionality does not make the translation to practice any less troublesome. In theory, activists call for skepticism towards categories such as gender, but in practice, they recommend the use of such categories as a way of teasing out the structural nature of social oppression. In the end, those using "intersectionality" as a guide for advocacy, analysis, and planning actually recommend a practice very similar to the *intersectionality-plus* model that I advocate here: for example, the Association for Women's Rights in Development (AWID) proposes combining categorical analysis employing the more general concepts of gender, race, and class with richly textured studies focusing on those at the intersection of these categories (AWID, 2004). They argue that we need both types of evidence to establish the structural nature of oppression as well as the intersectional nature of many of the effects of these social structures. The proposal to think of intersectionality as "*intersectionality-plus*" actually provides a firmer conceptual footing for such political measures than does the *intersectionality-only* view.

Conclusion

The concept of intersectionality, then, is a contribution of feminist theory to the literature that seeks to understand how social structures such as gender, race, and class work. It provides an important critique of some popular ways of thinking about the interaction of social structures, and is particularly innovative as a way of capturing the *complexity* of the interaction of these social structures (McCall 2005). Attempts to operationalize the concept, however, have brought the potential indeterminacy of the concept into sharp relief. One current way of interpreting the idea of intersectionality, I have argued, needlessly limits empirical investigation employing the concept and obstructs social structural analysis. I propose a different approach to conceptualizing and operationalizing intersectionality, one that recognizes the possibility of multiple types of interactions among social structures, and permits the theorization and investigation of these different types of interactions. This version is truer to the core of the idea of intersectionality and better captures actual analytic and political strategies that activists and scholars have found fruitful.

10 Women's movements, feminism, and feminist movements

Dorothy E. McBride and Amy G. Mazur

"Women's movement" is a term widely used by journalists, activists, politicians, scholars, and citizens alike; most people have a general idea of the concept's meaning. Despite the widespread attention to the term since the 1970s, social science is in the early stages of conceptualization (Beckwith 2005a). A quick glance at scholarly work on women's movements indicates there is agreement on neither a general definition nor how the concept should be used in empirical research. In fact, researchers seldom give an explicit definition of the term. Can we be sure that women's movement scholars are talking about the same thing? If not, studies and theories of women's movements risk being inaccurate and perhaps even unintentionally misleading. Our own research on women's movements and women's policy agencies reveals a debate among scholars that has left unanswered many questions about how to use women's movements as a concept for good research. The more notable ones include:

How can movement characteristics be measured?

How can movement impact be measured?

What distinguishes women participants in government and politics from the movement?

Can men be in women's movements?

Is "women's movement" a singular or collective noun, or are there many movements?

Are women's movements defined by their mobilization of women exclusively, or by their goals, or both? For example, are women's peace movements women's movements?

The absence of a consensus about the conceptual use of "women's movement" is quite similar for the related concept "feminist movement/feminism," but with a controversial twist. Whereas "women's movement" has a benign or nonthreatening connotation, feminism is quite highly charged. Some are even reluctant to set forth a definition of feminism for fear of being labeled ethnocentric or hegemonic for their efforts, particularly when examining feminist issues in different national and cultural contexts. In some situations, identifying a group or a person as feminist may be harmful to the activists being studied and the researcher doing the study. Debate on feminism and its applications to women's movement research continues over whether or not there can be a scholarly definition of feminism applicable by scholars across time and space. Some argue that feminism exists only in the eye of the beholder. Another issue arises because scholars often use "women's movement" and "feminist movement" to mean the same thing. But if they are not the same, what is the difference? How do we reach agreement on such questions as: Can the state be feminist? Can men be feminist?

These debates inform the approach to conceptualization in this chapter; we hope to provide some solutions to the methodological issues raised by the application of the two series of concepts. We use our experience of doing comparative research to lay the groundwork for scientific inquiry about women's movements, feminism, and feminist movements. In building the concepts we follow the Guidelines presented in chapter 2. The first section outlines the theoretical significance of these concepts for social science. The second and third sections describe the levels of conceptualization for the two concepts in women's movement research on postindustrial democracies.[1] The fourth section makes suggestions for research applications of these conceptualizations outside of postindustrial, wealthy, and democratic contexts. The conclusion discusses how the conceptualization presented here helps to solve some of the thornier methodological issues surrounding the use of women's movements and feminism as well as the broader implications of formal conceptualization for gender and politics research and beyond.

Theory and research context (Context Guideline)

Scholars undertake the challenge of conceptualization to build up theory and to design empirical research that will advance knowledge about theory. Concepts are the building blocks of theory (Goertz 2005). It follows that concepts must be grounded in the context of explicit theoretical themes and specific research purposes (Collier and Mahon 1993, Adcock and Collier

---

[1] Postindustrial democracies are the 23 or so countries which have relatively similar levels of high national wealth, similarly large service, or "post-Fordist" economies, a stable nation-state, and a well-established tradition of representative democratic institutions, and/or the emergence of stable democratic institutions since World War II. We use the concept "postindustrial" instead of "advanced industrialized" to avoid normative implications of comparing the "First World" to the "Third World." For more on postindustrial democracies see Esping-Andersen (1993, 1999).

2001, Collier, Brady and Seawright 2004). This theoretical context begins by providing a foundation for the core definition presented in the next section.

In general, the concepts in this chapter – women's movement, feminism, and feminist movements – may be part of the construction of at least five major theoretical domains. What this means is that some significant theoretical propositions in these domains cannot be realized without the use of one or both of these concepts. The following discussion is illustrative, not exhaustive, of the theoretical settings for these concepts.

Democracy and democratization

Central to both the explanation of variations in the operation of democratic institutions and the assessment of patterns of change in democracies is the exploration of representation and participation, both concepts covered in the first part of this book. The fortunes of women's movement activists constitute an indicator of the inclusiveness of democratic institutions in bringing women into power, representing women, and responding to women's demands.[2] Women's movements can also represent women and their perspectives in public arenas, some argue, even more effectively than legislatures and parliaments (Weldon 2002b). Feminism and feminist movements may articulate challenges to any claims often made that particular democracies have achieved the goals of justice and equality.

The state and states

Women's movements, feminism, and feminist movements constitute challenges to the power of states as countries as well as conceptualizations of "the state" as governing institutions and processes (see e.g. Pringle and Watson 1992). There is a long-running debate among feminist and non-feminist scholars alike over whether the state is monolithic or diffuse, self-interested or neutral, patriarchal or penetrable, gendered or universalist. An increasing body of work, to be examined in more detail in chapter 11 on state feminism, shows that states are important sites for women's movement action and can help and hinder the entrance of women's movement demands and actors into the affairs of government. Studies have also identified a new area of government action – feminist policy – that promotes women's status

---

[2] As Pamela Paxton's chapter in this book shows, the empirical definition of democratic institutions remains problematic and contested, especially with respect to gender.

and strikes down gender hierarchies (Mazur 2002). Thus, increasingly, state-centered theories have been put to the test by research that has at its analytical core women's movements and feminism.

Social movements

Because of the widespread assumption that women's movements are a type of social movement, all social movement theory should be amenable to exploration by studying women's movements. Hypotheses about patterns and conditions for mobilization, opportunities, and constraints on collective action, and impacts on social institutions, governments, and culture, can be tested on women's movements along with labor movements, the civil rights movement, the environmental movement, and other "adjectival" movements. Given the extent to which women's movements are motivated by feminist ideologies, looking at feminism could also be a means to examine social movement theories.

Despite the possibility that studies of women's movements and feminist movements may illuminate social movement theory, there are problems that must be addressed before such studies are likely to advance social science knowledge. Later in this chapter we question the assumption that women's movements are easily labeled subcategories of social movements. We argue that conceptualization of social movements for research is underdeveloped and needs to take into account developments in movement activism since the 1970s.

Women and politics

Comparative research on women in politics, as citizens, elected representatives, and public officials, and women in groups, has tended to receive more attention from scholars than taking a gendered perspective where the social construction of men's and women's identities is the major category for analysis (J. Scott 1986). Research on women's political activity is important to developing theoretical propositions about women's movements; at the same time, theoretical work on women and politics must incorporate knowledge about women's movements and feminism. As the concepts are built in the body of this chapter, readers will see that the connections here are extremely close.

Gender and power

A gendered comparative political analysis is in its infancy (Beckwith 2005b, Brush 2003, Lovenduski 1998, Cockburn 1991, Chappell 2002, Mushaben 2005; see Duerst-Lahti and Kelly 1995 for a promising first effort to theorize in the US case). Inquiry on this topic would theorize about the composition, conditions, and effects of gendered power structures and institutions in democracies. Efforts by women's movements, especially those inspired by feminism, to challenge both explicit and implicit gendered institutions would be a key component of theories of gender and power.

Transnational activism and global issues

One of the key examples of growth in transnational networks is the argument that women's movements and feminism have become worldwide phenomena mobilizing across and beyond national borders, often in tandem with global governance (Ferree and Tripp 2006, Naples and Desai 2002, Eschle 2001, Keck and Sikkink 1998). References to global movements and international feminism have so far not yielded rigorous conceptualization; these terms are often used to make more dramatic claims of global challenges to male domination and shifts in women's empowerment, rather than systematically defined and measured (for exceptions see Weldon 2002a and Ferree and Tripp 2006). Nonetheless, the increase in global communication and activism through international and supranational organizations calls for focused attention on development of these research concepts.

The RNGS project

The conceptualizations of women's movements, feminism, and feminist movements presented in this chapter have the potential to be components for theorizing in some of the most important questions in political science. Strengthening the conceptualization of the two concepts, therefore, will help to make better theory in these areas. More immediately, the concepts have served specific research goals on postindustrial democracies, specifically the project of the Research Network on Gender Politics and the State (RNGS). Many of the observations about the state of conceptualization and the proposals made here to address them come out of our work as codirectors of and researchers on the RNGS project.[3] The forty-plus members of this research

---

[3] For information on the entire RNGS project see http://libarts.wsu.edu/polisci/rngs.

network have sought to measure the successes and failures of women's movements in Western Europe and North America in their efforts, since the 1970s, to penetrate state policy arenas. Inspired by social movement literature, the project has looked at the impact of movements in gaining access to policy making subsystems, influencing policy content to reflect their demands, and changing the cultural context for policymaking.[4]

Of special interest to RNGS are the possibilities for movements to develop alliances with women's policy agencies inside the state to advance their goals – *state feminism*. While we will not go into that concept in detail here, the goal of studying state feminism required the group to find a definition of feminism that would enable us to recognize state feminism if we saw it and that would work in a comparative cross-national research project. This was a great challenge, because the meaning of feminism is often contested whenever the term is used to describe an ideology, an individual, an organization or a movement.

The RNGS research plan included a model and a set of research tasks for each researcher to complete for each case study. With respect to the women's movements, this involved gathering evidence about their collective action frames and priorities, cohesion of their strategic frames in specific policy debates, the location and degree of their activism, levels of mobilization and institutionalization, and patterns of change over time. With respect to feminism, the project required that researchers be able to identify feminist ideas and goals, especially within the state. In designing the study, therefore, the network had to develop definitions of the foundational concepts of the study applicable in the countries in the study.

The RNGS study produced over 130 cases of policymaking in 14 countries over 3 decades covering 5 issues: abortion, job training, prostitution, political representation, and several priority issues. Because we published results of debates by issue as soon as the studies were completed, later analyses have benefited from the experience of the first efforts. In other words, the researchers in RNGS learned about conceptualization from experience of hands-on qualitative comparative work. It has been a dynamic process benefiting from the continued interaction between ideas and evidence and learning how to explore and interpret data to achieve the research goals.

Typically, there are two strategies for measurement of complex ideas in diverse cases: (1) set forth the features of the concept that might be measured

---

[4] These three pertain to standard indicators of movement impact: policy content, procedural access, and cultural change (see Gamson 1975, Giugni 1995, Rochon and Mazmanian 1993, and Rochon 1998).

empirically, as Tarrow (1994) does with social movements, and use these in all contexts; or (2) rely on experts in each context (usually a country) to make their own measurements of the concept based on their judgments. In women's movement/feminism research, investigators confronting a large number of cases always opt for the second choice and, initially, RNGS was no exception (Threlfall 1996, Margolis 1993, Basu 1995, Nelson and Chowdhury 1994, B. G. Smith 2000). Yet, as the project moved through its qualitative phase into the development of data for Qualitative Comparative Analysis (QCA) and statistical analysis, the limits of this approach became clear. Unless we could build concepts for both theoretical inquiry and empirical exploration that would yield valid and reliable evidence, the RNGS project would not achieve the overall goal of the endeavor – to be able to contribute to theories of democratization, new institutionalism, and social movements.

The next section turns to the lessons learned from the RNGS study and the subsequent conceptualization of women's movements, feminism, and feminist movements. The first concept is "women's movement" and includes an assessment of the link between "women's movement" and the more general notion of "social movement." The second part of this section covers feminism and feminist movements and builds on the foundation of the women's movement concept and the link between feminism and women's movements.

The conceptualization is directed toward the use of these concepts for comparative theory and empirical research in postindustrial democracies. Given, as we already mentioned, that the process of conceptualization among women's movement scholars is in a preliminary phase, it is too early to search for universal definitions that apply in all settings, if one is even possible. At the same time, we are aware of the urgent need for conceptualization of these important concepts for use in research contexts outside of western democracies, especially in transitional and emerging democracies and in conditions of political instability, revolution, and religious conflict. Thus, in the final section of the chapter, there is a discussion of ways in which the concepts developed here might be reconsidered for application in circumstances found outside of western democracies: in other words, a focus on the Traveling Guideline.

Building the concepts: women's movement and feminist movement

We now map out each concept according to three levels identified by Goertz (2005) – the basic, the secondary, and the operational. The basic, the first level on the concept pyramid, is the level used in theories and typically involves a nominal definition that distinguishes it from other concepts. At this level, it is important to consider not only what the concept *is* or *means* but also what it is *not* or *does not mean* (the Naming and Negation Guidelines), that is, both the positive and negative poles. At the same time, examining the underlying continuum between them at this level determines whether the concept should be considered continuous or dichotomous and whether or not the poles of the concepts are ideal types (the Zones Guideline).

The secondary level moves us closer to using the concept in analysis; it is the crucial step in translating a concept's theoretical meaning into a set of observations by focusing on the dimensions of the concept (Dimensions Guideline), their interactions (Interdependence Guideline) and whether they are essential (Necessity Guideline). Examining the third level involves setting forth empirical indicators for observing the concept (Operationalization and Causal Relationships Guidelines). The goal in this third step is to develop indicators that are both consistent with the basic and secondary dimensions of the concept and suitable to the research context where they will be employed.

Concept 1: women's movement

The basic level

A women's movement means collective action by women organized explicitly as women presenting claims in public life based on gendered identities as women. These claims are derived from a discourse developed by "aspirations and understandings that provide conscious goals, cognitive backing and emotional support among women" (Mansbridge 1996).[5] At the basic level, "women's movement" is a dichotomous concept. The negative pole – *not a women's movement* – means collective action by men (not women), or by women not organized explicitly as women presenting claims other than those based on gendered identities as women. Because of the demographic elements of the positive and negative poles, there is no underlying continuum between the two that could be the basis for empirical observation.

The women's movement means women organizing as women; men cannot organize a women's movement. If there are ways to combine parts of the dimensions of the positive and negative poles – women and men organizing as

---

[5] In addition to Mansbridge, we have developed this definition with a careful reading of Beckwith (2000, 2005a) and Ferree and Mueller (2004).

women or men and women using women's movement discourse – these would no longer have the basic components of the women's movement and would be at the negative pole. The features of the women's movement are both necessary and sufficient; they are not substitutable at this basic level. Also, the two elements of the definition – collective actions by women organized explicitly as women and presentation of gendered identity claims – are necessary and sufficient to identify a women's movement. A women's movement has both of these elements or it is not a women's movement. In other words, there is no gray area at the basic level.

It is likely that "women's movement" is one of the few dichotomous concepts discussed in this book; most, like state feminism, form a continuum. Being dichotomous means that there is no sense of variation in the presence or absence of the components of the concept. The goal of conceptualization is to identify those phenomena that are the women's movement from those that are not. There is no variation implied. To illustrate, compare "women's movement" with another concept such as democracy. In building a definition of democracy there is the implied notion that in empirical observation researchers will be looking for degrees of democracy or, for example, democratization. With "women's movement," researchers do not look for degrees of women's movement. They use the empirical indicators to identify the movement for study. The movement is either there – actors and discourse – or it is not. Certainly, the components have variable qualities – patterns of discourse, types of actors, degrees of mobilization – but they are all part of "women's movement" and variation in those components does not make one movement a "greater" movement or "more" of a movement.

Looking in more detail at the components of the women's movement, it is the ideas that distinguish the women's movement from other forms of collective action. This assumption is at the core of the meaning of "women's movement" and is compatible with the way the term is used in the current literature. Even those who define the movement in terms only of organizations do not claim that the work of these organizations is the whole movement, and admit that just studying these organizations is not grasping the movement (Ferree and Hess 1985). The basic definition does not include any particular set of unconventional or disruptive tactics or the requirement that the movement be contesting the state in making claims as means of identifying the women's movement. Not including tactics as a necessary part of the basic definition avoids the tendency of scholars to try to locate a boundary between the women's movement outside the state and movement activism inside the state (Banaszak 2006, Katzenstein 1998a).

Jenson (1996: 74) offers some insight about the relation between those making claims and the claims themselves: "Politics entails two kinds of representation. First, *representation of the self to others via a collective identity*: Representation of self – that is, a collective identity – involves, among other things, naming oneself since only an actor with a name is recognizable to others. As a consequence, social relations become visible and a range of political strategies emerges."

The second form is *representation of interests*: "A second type, familiar from the language of liberal democracy, is the *representation of interests* – a process which, since the emergence of the modern state, has included presentation to the state through more or less stable organizations (1996: 74). Jenson's conceptual map of the women's movement in France distinguishes between the process of establishing discourses about collective identities and their interests from the actors who present this discourse in public life. Rochon (1998) has a similar approach, by situating social movements in the context of *critical communities*, in other words, the thinkers who develop new values.

Movement leaders take an active role in choosing, bundling together, and shaping the ideas of one or more critical communities in such a way as to maximize the chances of movement success ... Movements are formed by the melding of a critical discourse to collective action. Movement strategies and action are aimed at achieving change in both the political and social arenas (1998: 48).

According to Rochon, movements exist in the relation between the community that produces the discourse and the groups and organizations that advocate them (1998: 48).

The secondary level

What are the fundamental characteristics all women's movements share? Here, there are two: discourse and actors. These two are completely interconnected and, when found together, are necessary and sufficient to constitute a women's movement. The discourse includes ideas, arguments, goals, and claims, all containing language about gendered identity of women. This discourse finds its genesis in *gender consciousness*:

The recognition that one's relation to the political world is at least partly shaped by being female or male. This recognition is followed by identification with others in the "group" of one's sex, positive affect toward the group, and a feeling of interdependence with the group's fortunes. (Tolleson Rinehart 1992: 32)

The varieties of identities, aspirations, ideas, and interpretations of that recognition compose the discourse that distinguishes the women's movement. The form and content of such discourse vary greatly because it can be traced to the experiences of women in many diverse contexts.

A similar notion about the ideas and goals that characterize women's movements was developed in the mid-1980s by Maxine Molyneux when she distinguished between "women's interests" and "gender interests." Unlike the idea of women's interests, which assumes a commonality of concerns among women, gender interests "are those that women (or men for that matter) may develop by virtue of their social positioning through gender attributes" (1985: 232). She separates these into strategic gender interests which are based on deductive analyses of structural positions of women and men and the development of alternatives to this system, and practical gender interests which are derived from the collectivity of individual women reacting to their lived circumstances and needs. The discourse dimension of women's movement includes both types of gender interests.

Although the ideas are the basis of identity of a women's movement, there is no movement without the collective actors who present the discourse in social and public life. The definition of the basic concept sets forth some of the criteria for this dimension: the actors are collective, that is, they are people working in groups, in social and political arenas, but outside the formal state structures. This distinction between the movement and the state is often tricky because the boundaries are not clear. There are many instances of organizations inside the state which act to promote women's movement discourse, including women's policy agencies. Further, some women's movement actors may adopt a strategy of working within a variety of other state institutions (e.g. Katzenstein 1998a, Banaszak 2006). We agree with Ferree and Mueller (2004: 22):

When social movements move into institutions, they move not as individuals trying to 'make it' as tokens for the success of their groups, but as organized collective entities that are trying to change the institution's goals, decision-making or modes of operation, whether or not they end up successful, expelled or co-opted.

At the same time, no state institution would be a women's movement actor. Actors are, therefore, people working through collective means, not part of the formal state structure, presenting claims based on women's movement discourse.

Empirical indicators

Both dimensions of "women's movement" – collective actors and gendered discourse – are necessary and sufficient conditions to compose a women's movement. However, the type of actors and the form of the discourse are likely to be different at various times and between, for example, North America and Western Europe, postindustrial democracies and transitional regimes, predominantly Islamic nations and Hindu nations, revolutionary situations and internationally. Thus, the researcher must think carefully about what empirical indicators are appropriate for the cases of the study. Here we present, as an example, the indicators the RNGS project found appropriate to the comparative study of postindustrial democracies between 1970 and 2000.

The criteria for classifying statements as women's movement discourse are:

1. They express explicit *identity with women as a group*, a form of gender consciousness. Not only must the ideas be based on women's experiences, but the language of the discourse must connect some groups of women together as having a common fate. Thus, one might read the position statement of prostitution rights groups and, at first, assume that they would be presenting women's movement discourse. However, many times, despite the fact that the group represents a group of women, they do not explicitly connect to one another as women. Only if such identity is explicit would the discourse meet this criterion.

2. The language is *clearly and overtly gendered*, referring to women as distinct from men. Gendered references include the following: images of women and what they are like; how women are different from men; how women are different from one another; the ways gender differences shape identities (see Katzenstein 1995). Thus, while a group may have a name like Concerned Women of America or Women for Peace, they would not be using a movement discourse if their language were about moral responsibility or antiwar and not explicitly focusing on, for example, women's moral responsibilities in relation to men or the fact that women are the chief victims of war crimes.

3. The ideas are expressed in terms of *women representing women as women* in public life. Those who are speaking or writing women's movement discourse claim to speak for women as their primary concern. At the same time, they *are* women. This criterion means that those who develop the discourse are women, not men.[6]

To be identified as women's movement discourse, all three of these elements must be present: identity with women as a group; explicitly gendered language about women; and representation of women as women in public life. In other words, these are necessary and sufficient indicators of equal weight. At the

---

[6] Certainly it is possible for men to develop and promote ideas that would help women and advance their status. And, men can articulate women's movement discourse. However, the fact that it is possible does not change these indicators for locating the women's movement empirically.

same time, in studying women's movements, researchers will not observe the processes where this discourse is created by women; what we observe are the statements expressed by actors in public arenas.

To locate the collective actors of the movement, RNGS focuses on organizations active in public arenas in postindustrial democracies. *Organizations* are groups of individuals who share a common structure for action and which are not part of the state. These actors are, broadly, of two types: formal and informal. *Formal organizations* are group activities driven by written rules and policies, such as lobbying organizations, professional organizations, and sections of political parties. *Informal organizations*, sometimes called autonomous groups, are group activities through loosely organized means, such as demonstrations, consciousness-raising groups, and publics. Any organization is a part of the movement as long as it presents women's movement discourse and is not part of the state.[7] Thus a movement may be composed of many organizations or few, small and large, informal or formal, formal and informal. In other words, there is substitutability in the use of these markers for locating the movement collective actors.

Although the dimension of the basic, secondary, and empirical levels of "women's movement" does not identify isolated individuals outside of women's movement groups as a part of the women's movement *per se*, when one gets to looking at women's movement action through discourse in political situations, it may be necessary to include the presentations of individuals without exact knowledge of their connections with collective movement groups. The RNGS case analyses often identified women in parliaments, cabinets, and academia who forwarded a women's movement position in policy debates as women's movement actors, regardless of their position in women's movement organizations. Although individuals may not be permanent members of a women's movement group they are presenting the discourse developed by the movement and, in a sense, representing the goals of collective actors. Looking for the discourse first, then identifying the actors, may be an effective strategy in cultural settings where formal western-style organizations are not the norm.

The following indicators locate the women's movement for empirical observation: the researcher looks for formal and informal organizations which present claims reflecting women's movement discourse – identity with women

---

[7] While there may be women's movement actors who enter state arenas, and individuals in state institutions who articulate movement discourse, official state organizations – bureaucratic agencies, legislative committees, ministries – are not women's movement actors.

as a group; explicitly gendered language about women; and representation of women as women in public life. There is room for a great deal of variation in observations in the pattern of the organizations and the content of the ideas they present. At the same time, one can study characteristics of women's movements and see how they vary, for example, in the content of strategic frames, the degree of institutionalization of organizations, the extent of mobilization of women through movement groups, and the tactics used to promote the goals whether conventional or unconventional or cooperative or confrontational.

These topics – patterns of institutionalization, mobilization, and tactics of women's movements – have been of great interest to scholars of women's movements (e.g. Banaszak, Beckwith and Rucht 2003, Costain 1992, Rosenfeld and Ward 1996). One reason for this is that scholars have been able to observe changes in women's movements since the 1960s and have begun to adapt the traditional notion of "women's movement" derived from social movement literature to help identify, classify, and analyze the changes. The need for a dynamic conceptualization of "women's movement" results from this long-term look and raises questions about the traditional conceptualization of social movements. The next section considers this problem.

Social movement and women's movement: what is the connection?

The conventional wisdom is that the women's movement is a subtype of social movement. The assumption is that women's movements share the basic characteristics of social movements and another characteristic – concern with women – justifies the addition of the adjective "women" to "movement."[8] This way of classifying is implicit among social movement scholars, when they mention women's movements at all, and usually explicit by women's movement scholars engaged in conceptualization.[9] However, there is good reason to step back and reexamine this easy assumption because of the changes in movements and movement scholarship. Another reason for a critique is that if the conceptualization is faulty, social movement theory may have limited usefulness in studying women's movements. Finally, RNGS has discovered the

---

[8] Originally, in the nineteenth century, the adjective used was "woman," as in "woman movement." By making the adjective a possessive form of the noun "women," it makes the name for this movement dependent on the sex of the constituency – women – rather than the goals. Compare with "environmental movement" and "peace movement" to see the subtle but significant difference.

[9] There are many examples, but the inclusion of women's movements as a subcategory of social movements was a major contribution of studies of so-called "new" social movements in the 1990s. See for example Kriesi, Koopmans, Duyvendak, and Giugni (1995), which covers ecology, gay rights, peace, and women's movements. Women's movement scholars, when they look for theory, and definitions, follow suit. Recent examples include Beckwith (2005a) and Grey (2006).

limits of this conceptualization for both research and theorizing in submitting the many cases of movement activism to rigorous analysis.[10] Others engaged in comparative studies of women's movements have also noted the limits of the assumed family relationship between women's movements and social movements (Katzenstein 1998a, Ferree and Mueller 2003).

There is no "official" conceptualization of "social movement," but many are influenced by the work of Sidney Tarrow's book *Power in Movement* (1994); from page 1: "Power in movement grows when ordinary people join forces in contentious confrontation with elites, authorities and opponents. Mounting, coordinating and sustaining this interaction is the peculiar contribution of the social movement." Tarrow's conceptualization continues by locating the secondary dimensions of the concept: collective challenges that are most frequently characterized by disruptive action, common purposes against authorities and elites, solidarity through recognition of common interests; and sustained action turning a contentious episode into a social movement. Are these characteristics necessary and sufficient to constitute a social movement? Is this a continuous concept? Tarrow's conceptualization has both characteristics. The best way to illustrate this is to consider the negative pole opposite the positive concept social movement. This pole – *not a social movement* – may include collective action, such as political parties and interest groups united by a common purpose and groups which have sustained activities against authorities. What distinguishes the negative from the positive concept, however, is that the negative concept lacks the type of tactics that characterize the positive concept, that is, it lacks contentious tactics. The difference between social movements and other forms of collective action is this element of protest. Nevertheless, most scholars recognize that there is a continuum between "social movement" and the negative pole of conventional collective action because social movements can use conventional tactics some of the time; but to be a social movement, collective action must use disruptive tactics as well – it is a necessary dimension. One can imagine sorting various forms of collective action along this continuum and then deciding that when disruptive tactics outnumber the conventional ones, the social movement comes into being and can be classified as such. At the same time, when a social movement goes along the continuum all the way to the negative pole – using only conventional tactics – it is not a social movement any more.

---

[10] For example, concepts from social movement theory, such as political opportunity structure, resource mobilization, and stage, have proved difficult to conceptualize and measure cross-nationally and over time. This may account for the fact that social movement theories of movement success have been of limited use in explaining findings in the RNGS study of women's movements.

Some women's movement scholars consider the use of protest as the defining feature of a movement in comparison with other forms of collective action such as interest groups and political parties (e.g. Grey 2006). Beckwith (2005a: 585) agrees that it is the difference between contained and "transgressive" contention that distinguishes interest groups from women's movements. However, most studies of women's movements do not in practice apply such a condition to their observations. Some challenge it. For example, Katzenstein (1998a) has argued that this necessary condition when applied to women's movements has led social movement scholars and others to equate growing use of conventional means to challenge authority, a sign of the decline of the women's movement and feminism. She contends that the assumption that only protest in the streets challenges power does not apply to the women's movement:

Constrained by traditional gender role stereotypes and by political choice, feminist activists' arsenal of political activism has drawn only fleetingly on demonstrative protest activities and even more rarely on violent activism. This raises the question of whether the very definitional distinction of conventional and unconventional political forms, then, is situated in the experience of freedom movements and, most particularly, of the 1960s male-dominated new left and civil rights movements. (Katzenstein 1998a)

The conceptualization of "women's movement" in this chapter avoids this problem by making the dimension of contention versus disruptive tactics a variable in the study of women's movements, not a necessary dimension. One could study this variation to develop a typology of women's movements that would compare the autonomous protests of the 1970s to the institutionalized movements of the 1990s. In light of these arguments and the experiences and contributions of women's movement scholars, it seems time for an update of the conceptualization of "social movement" to make the concept applicable to the wide range of change-oriented collective action. A way to do this would be to start with the women's movement definition and move up the ladder of generality to define "social movement" (Sartori 1970, Collier and Mahon 1993). Making social movement a dichotomous concept would align its use with the approach to women's movement conceptualization in this chapter.

Concept 2: feminism and feminist movement

Basic and secondary levels

Many scholars have used the terms "women's movement" and "feminist movement" interchangeably (Bull, Diamond, and Marsh 2000, Mansbridge

1996, Weldon 2002a, Mazur 2002, Kaplan 1992, Lovenduski 1986, Katzenstein and Mueller 1987, Gelb 2003, Chapell 2002, Banaszak 2006). This approach does not work effectively for comparative research because women's movement discourse has become so diverse that the concept of feminism is sometimes hotly contested among movement thinkers and actors alike. Further, with the growing political participation of women throughout the world, it is increasingly likely that women's movement actors will seek to promote ideas that no one would agree are feminist.[11] For comparative research, the problem is exacerbated by the resentment of some activists in the global South against what they see as a hegemonic effort by western activists to promote western feminism that neglects local women's own perspectives of their situations and what to do about them (Tripp 2006). Efforts at conceptualization can be further complicated by the political status of feminism in various research contexts and the strong beliefs held by both researchers and activists about what is "true" feminism.[12]

Many scholars use the term "feminist" without any explicit definition, especially when labeling individuals and organizations as "feminist." Others make their meaning clearer by referring to specific ideas. Among these ideas there is some agreement on the basic features of feminism. The writers who distinguish between women's movement and feminist movement do so in terms of the aims: women's movement aims involve women and women's issues while feminist movements involve specific challenges to patriarchy and the subordination of women (Beckwith 2004, 2005a, Ferree and Mueller 2003, Ferree 2006). In any case, the difference between the women's movement and the feminist movement ultimately relates to differences in the ideas, aspirations, and identities presented by collective actors. The feminist movement is a variant of the secondary dimensions of the basic concept of women's movement.

The feminist movement is composed of women's movement actors presenting a particular women's movement discourse, feminism, in social and public arenas. At the basic level, it has the same components of the women's

---

[11] This became especially clear in the RNGS project when activists promoting what they claimed were women's interests opposed proposals such as liberalized abortion laws or sexual harassment policies. Part of the women's movement? Yes, by definition. Feminist? No, but we needed a definition to know for sure.

[12] Claiming that one's definition of a concept captures the true meaning and trumps others' approaches is one of the three measurement validity traps noted by Adcock and Collier (2001). It is wise to remember that definitions always pertain to specific research contexts, and other choices are likely to be just as defensible.

movement in terms of discourse: "claims in public life based on gendered identities as women." At the secondary level, however, the additional dimensions of feminist discourse distinguish the feminist movement as a particular kind of women's movement – what Ferree (2006) calls the "feminist women's movement." The secondary-level dimensions of women's movement discourse are identities, aspirations, ideas, and interpretations based on gender consciousness, such as strategic and practical gender interests. We use the terms "feminist discourse" and "feminism" interchangeably here. (Note the differences between the usage here and Duerst-Lahti's discussion of feminism as a gender ideology in this book). They both refer to a subcategory of women's movement discourse that can be the basis of claims and strategic frames put forth by movement actors. Feminist discourse or *feminism* is characterized by a specific kind of women's movement discourse, one that adds three components:

1. The goal of changing the position of women in society and politics
2. Analysis that seeks to challenge and change women's subordination to men through gender equity
3. Analysis that seeks to challenge and change the structures of gender-based hierarchies

For use in research on the feminist movement in postindustrial democracies, then, feminist discourse includes the elements of women's movement discourse plus these three components of feminist discourse. Together, they are necessary and sufficient dimensions of feminist discourse at the secondary level. The negative pole of feminist discourse would be women's movement discourse without the three feminist components. While, at the secondary level, feminist discourse is a dichotomous concept, there is a potential gray area that becomes evident when we turn to the indicators of feminist discourse. The overlap pertains to the extent to which feminist ideas are presented by feminist movement actors.

Empirical indicators

Again, we use the indicators developed for the RNGS project because they are useful for the study of feminism in postindustrial democracies. The core begins with the necessary empirical markers of women's movement discourse, which are identity with women as a group, explicitly gendered language, and being expressed in terms of representing women as women in public life. RNGS is less comprehensive in linking the secondary dimensions of feminist discourse to its empirical indicators. In research, we rarely observe actors using complex feminist theory; it is much more likely, since we are looking at activists in society and politics, that actors use fragments of feminist thought, often through shorthand references and slogans. Based on these, we can assume these partial ideas are derived from a more complete feminist analysis. As a result, each of the indicators described here is sufficient to signify feminist discourse; it is not necessary to observe all of them and they are substitutable. To be feminist, then, the women's movement discourse must include at least one of following ideas:

1. The claim that there is something wrong with the current status of women or groups of women because they are, for example, poor, powerless, under-paid, mistreated, harassed, or exploited. Thus, the means and goals are justified because they will *advance the status of women and help them over-come their condition*. For example, the argument that family violence goes unpunished would include a feminist element with the claim that govern-ment action should help women confront the violence against them and become self-sufficient. A demand for more shelters to help women victims does not alone contain a feminist component.

2. The ideas seek to *overcome the subordination of women and achieve justice and equality* for women and men. Thus, rhetoric about gender equality and gender equity becomes an indicator of feminist discourse. Note that this is a different notion than just trying to provide more opportunities for women, for example for job training, in gaining custody of children in divorce, or running for office. To be feminist, this indicator includes the idea of attaining an equal status with men that removes the subordination of women, including groups of women as well as women as a whole. Other indicators of this idea of overcoming subordination include *emancipation, autonomy,* and *choice*. They all imply freeing women from an authority that keeps them from equal status and development.

3. Finally, researchers can look for views that explicitly or implicitly *recognize or challenge gender hierarchies*. Feminism contains the idea that the reasons for women's inequality are found in the gender-based hierarchies of society and government: something must be done to change these hierarchies and permanently improve the condition of women. Sometimes this is expressed in terms of challenges to traditional religious notions of family roles or sexual double standards. We look here, not just for the improvements of women's status, but for the challenge to the mechanisms that maintain inequalities. For example, the widespread women's movement demand to bring more women into public office, into the fields of science and engineering or on to corporate boards becomes a feminist demand when it is connected to ideas and proposals that undermine the privileges afforded men to maintain their dominance, such as positive action.

To recap: the feminist movement is a subcategory of "women's movement" that uses feminist discourse or feminism. Feminist discourse is a subcategory of women's movement discourse. As such, it includes all the dimensions and indicators of the root concept and adds special features that distinguish it. Thus, the secondary dimensions of feminist discourse include all of the following: identity with women; being explicitly gendered; representing women; improving the position of women; challenging the subordination of women to men; and challenging gender hierarchies. To be located empirically, the following are examples of ideas that are sufficient to mark feminist discourse in public life: proposals to help groups of women change their position in society; demands for choice, autonomy, gender equality, and gender equity; or claims that would undermine the structures that maintain male privilege.

Research application of "feminism" and "feminist movement": will the RNGS concepts travel?

This chapter has presented conceptualizations of "women's movement" and "feminist movement" that have been developed in the RNGS research project on postindustrial democracies. The definitions described in the previous section are now being used to analyze the cases and classify state responses to women's movement demands with a special focus on the role of women's policy agencies. In RNGS, we use the definition of feminism – the most contested concept – to answer the question: To what extent do women's policy agencies act inside the state to further feminist goals?

Conceptualization work is never done; we will continue to fine-tune the definitions of the systematized concepts as our research goes on. But we are keen to know if the RNGS solutions would be useful to scholars studying feminism in other cases and contexts (Traveling Guideline). To what extent can these concepts developed for one research context be used for other research goals without altering their meaning? In other words, will this conceptualization travel? This section offers some suggestions to scholars considering using or adapting the RNGS construction of the concepts of women's movement, feminist movement, and feminism in other parts of the world.

It is our view that the conceptualization of "women's movement" has great extension (applicability to a wide variety of cases) because its intension (specificity of meanings) is limited (Sartori 1970, Collier and Mahon 1993). It does not require that movement discourse include a specific set of women's interests or policy goals, and thus allows for the women in the movements themselves to define the specific ideas, aspirations, and goals from their own experiences. The extent to which these discourses agree across nations and cultures is a question for empirical research, not something assumed in the definition. It also includes a wide range of collective action, not necessarily only structures that are found in postindustrial democracies. By analytically separating the actors from the discourse, it allows for an array of actors and locations that may constitute the women's movement in a particular place and time. Nevertheless there are limits; our conceptualization of "women's movement" would not pertain to what Molyneux (1998) describes as *directed mobilization*, sometimes observed in left-wing and right-wing revolutionary settings, for example the USSR, Cuba, Bolivia, and Iran. There the so-called women's movement is formed by party or government leaders who provide both the discourse and the organizational forms that mobilize women.

The applicability of the definition of feminism and thus feminist movement is not as straightforward. As noted earlier, it is a very contentious concept within and outside women's movements. Its use in international processes has often led to resentment, for example where "western feminists" are seen as unfeeling ethnocentric, hegemonic interlopers offending the dignity of home-grown women activists. Further, its meaning has often been defined by its opponents ("man-hating, bra-burning, antifamily bitches"), causing those who support its goals to deny any association with the label. Researchers who live and work in political contexts where feminism is so controversial find it difficult to label groups as "feminist" when the groups themselves deny the affiliation.

Apply indicators of feminism in the research context

We propose that the secondary dimensions of the concept "feminist discourse" include three necessary and sufficient dimensions: changing the condition of women, challenging and changing the subordination of women, and analyzing and challenging structures of gender hierarchy. However, in a particular research context, a choice of one or more of several indicators can be sufficient to locate feminism, and these will not be the same in all contexts. In the western postindustrial democracies, such indicators as gender equity, sex equality, choice, autonomy, self-determination, and sexual exploitation were indicators in debates on issues of job training, abortion, prostitution, and political representation. It is unlikely, however, that one would look for similar indicators in other countries. One must be aware of the women's movement discourses that are in the public arenas.

To examine whether scholars of nonwestern countries are offering indicators of feminism that are consistent with the secondary dimensions of feminist discourse set forth in this chapter, we looked at studies in two edited books purporting to cover feminism around the world: Amrita Basu, *The Challenge of Local Feminisms* (1995) and Myra Marx Ferree and Aili Mari Tripp's *Global Feminism* (2006). All the authors in each book who offered a definition of feminism included at least one of the basic dimensions of our concept: changing the condition of women, challenging the subordination of women, or challenging gender hierarchies. But what was interesting was that these conceptualizations often amended these dimensions to include ideas developed from the specific research contexts. Thus, the meanings or intension of feminist discourses can become more specific due to the responses of women to the context of their struggle against the status quo. These may become forms of feminism modified with adjectives.

When challenges to gender hierarchies are combined with challenges to capitalist systems, the result has been called socialist feminism. Many women discover feminist goals while getting involved in other movements such as labor, peace, or environmental (Ferree 2006: 6–8). Feminism during processes of transition to democracy may focus on justice and equality for women in the new system (Frohmann and Valdés 1995, Bagiç 2006). In India, feminist discourse focuses on the specific oppressions stemming from Hindu patriarchy (Kumar 1995), while Islamic feminism uses the Qu'ran to challenge the patriarchal elements of Shar'ia law. Combining ideas, aspirations, and goals for liberation from oppressions due to race and gender is the hallmark of Black feminist discourse. None of these are "official" feminisms that can be applied by researchers; they are the findings of empirical research projects. Thus, researchers must look in the contexts of their own research goals and venues for those ideas developed from within the women's movement that reveal connections with the secondary-level dimensions of feminist discourse and not assume any particular content or analysis *a priori*.

Look for the women's movement, not the feminists

Many writers describe women's movement actors – individuals and groups – as feminists. The conceptualization offered in this chapter will not help researchers to find such "feminists." It does help in finding feminist discourse and women's movement actors who use that discourse in particular times and places. Since this conceptualization analytically separates the discourse from the actors, it removes the possibility of its use to identify anyone as a feminist. There may be people who can be identified as feminists, but to locate them, one would need a separate conceptualization that provides indicators of beliefs, identities, and ideologies.

In principle, although feminist discourse comes from the women's movement, the ideas and goals can be articulated by anyone. At the same time, it is not possible to label any women's movement actors as feminist apart from the discourse they use in specific contexts. Actors can use feminist discourse strategically or refuse to use it, despite their own beliefs, if it will serve their immediate goals. Thus, to locate feminism in any particular research site, it is first necessary to locate the women's movement actors and discourse used to present their claims; the next step is to see what elements of those claims have feminist indicators and which actors are using it at a particular time and place. There the researcher will find the feminist movement.

Can men be feminists?

Whether men can be or are feminists is a hotly debated question whenever feminists gather. Many claim to know feminist men, to have campaigned with them, or even married them. But the conceptualization here does not help a scholar answer this question. Since, however, anyone can articulate or vote for feminist ideas and goals, it follows that men can be allies of the feminist movement. However, the conceptualization offered in this chapter requires researchers who want to locate and observe the feminist women's movement in a particular place and time to start with finding the women's movement discourse and actors and then see if any of that discourse indicates feminist discourse as defined. Feminist discourse is, by definition, derived from women's movement discourse; a necessary component of that is the expression of women representing women. Whether men, or women for that matter, are feminists is a separate research question requiring another conceptualization.

Conclusion

This chapter represents an effort to provide a comprehensive conceptualization of women's movements, feminism, and feminist movements. While clearly bounded by the parameters of the research context from which they came, these conceptualizations still have the potential to provide researchers and students with useful and accurate tools to measure and analyze women's movements and to put to test the various theories where women's movements and feminism are important. We have also made an attempt to extrapolate this research approach to conceptualization to cases outside of the western world.

It is our hope that, in mapping out these concepts, we have addressed many of the conceptual questions that have confronted women's movement research posed at the beginning of the chapter. We have suggested a way that women's movement characteristics can be measured through providing a precise operational definition for women's movement and feminist movement actors. Through better identification of the boundaries of the women's movement, researchers can trace the impact they have on the state, policies, and society. By establishing the articulation of women's movement discourse as a necessary and sufficient condition, researchers can now differentiate between women as participants and women's movement actors. Similarly, forms of female mobilization such as women's peace organizations are only women's movements if they advance women's movement discourse. This conceptualization also points to the existence of a single movement composed of a multitude of actors and groups outside of the state who act together.

With respect to the contested concept of feminism, our RNGS colleagues and we hope to have laid to rest the notion that social science cannot use the term "feminism" in scholarly studies. RNGS is by no means the first to make this claim; most scholars who are interested in feminist comparative policy have come to agree on operational definitions of feminism (Mazur 2002: 30–1). Feminism should be used not just in studying women's movements but also in research on the state, public policy, participation, political parties, and interest groups that cuts across all areas of political science. We hope that researchers see the need to differentiate between women's movements and feminism movements, and no longer insist on using the two interchangeably or stick to "women's movement" as a way of avoiding the word "feminist."

Conceptualization must be a part of every research design and a continuous part of the dialogue between ideas and evidence. Others must try out the concepts built here and put them to rigorous tests in future studies. To get things started, we suggest the following agenda for women's movement research within the purview of political science:

Systematize the study of women's movements in postindustrial democracies.

Improve and promote the use of feminism as an analytical concept.

Determine whether the new conceptualizations can be applied to studies outside of the West.

Develop studies that examine women's movements as entities distinct from social movements.

Use "women's movements," "feminist movements," and "feminism" in testing hypotheses derived from theories of democracy, state, gender and power, women and politics, and transnational activism and globalization.

11 State feminism

Amy G. Mazur and Dorothy E. McBride

State feminism captures the emergence of a new set of state–society relations and introduces a gendered view of state action to empirical and comparative analysis. It is based on the expectation that democratic governments, to be successful, can and should promote women's status and rights in relation to men's, however those rights are defined in specific cultural contexts, and should work to undermine the gender-based hierarchies that contribute to enduring sex-based inequities. In other words, the concept is based on the premise that democracies can and should be feminist. As we argue in this chapter, since the mid-1990s, scholars throughout the world have increasingly used state feminism to study the relations between women's movements and women's policy agencies (WPAs) – "state-based mechanisms charged formally with furthering women's status and gender equality" (RNGS 2006: 1).[1] In this view, WPAs are a potential conduit for women's movement actors and ideas to enter the affairs of government and to influence the process of policy formulation and implementation. Such access thus increases the chances to realize the highly transversal and difficult-to-achieve feminist agenda. In its current usage, therefore, state feminism implies a focus on women's policy agencies in relation to women's movements and a complex process that may or may not produce a certain set of explicitly feminist outcomes.

State feminism has not always been associated with WPAs, or, as the United Nations calls them, "national machineries for the advancement of women" (UN 2006). Researchers have used the notion to refer to a variety of state-based phenomena in both democratic and nondemocratic contexts. Many study the same issues without mentioning the concept, while others reject state feminism as an analytical tool altogether. In other words, when scholars do use the term, they do not always agree on its core meaning. Both women's

[1] We provide a more precise working definition of "women's policy agency" in the third section of the chapter. The acronym WPA is used throughout to indicate the generic term.

movements and women's policy agencies – the concept's components – are broadly conceived entities that can be studied separately.

State feminism is an all-encompassing concept; its operationalization in empirical research and use in theory development touches upon or even incorporates most of the concepts in this book, with a particular focus on feminism, the state, and women's movements. Assessing women's policy agencies and whether they achieve state feminism addresses one of the most perennial questions in the study of politics – the democratic capacity of the state to include underrepresented groups into the affairs of government. In this chapter, we map out the definition, analytical structure, and operationalization of this complex concept using this book's ten Guidelines for concept formation.

Given the concept's broad scope, our first task is to trace the development of the meaning of state feminism since it was first used to its current focus on the relations between WPAs and women's movements – the Naming Guideline. The next section shows how applying the concept in research brings in gender and addresses a wide range of theoretical issues in political science – the Context Guideline. We then present the structure of the concept; its positive and negative poles (the Negation Guideline); whether it is dichotomous or continuous with a "gray zone" and whether it has an ideal type (the Zones Guideline); and the major dimensions – their interactions, the causal relationships between certain dimensions, and whether they are necessary (the Dimensions, Necessity, Interdependence, and Causal Relationships Guidelines). Next, we turn to how state feminism is used in the RNGS project – the Operationalization Guideline and a further examination of the Causal Relationships Guideline. Finally, we examine the issue of whether the concept can be used in analysis outside of western postindustrial democracies (the Traveling Guideline).

Naming state feminism: toward a focus on WPA–WM relations

Understandably, state feminism may be a controversial and confusing concept for political analysts. On one hand, political scientists often have difficulty defining precisely what the state is and is not – a single entity? a set of institutions? processes? power relations? – and determining where it begins and ends in relation to society. On the other hand, as the previous chapter showed, gender and politics researchers have had difficulty pinpointing a single core meaning of women's movements and face controversies that swirl around the concept of feminism. Moreover, some feminist theory assumes that the state is part of patriarchy and thus tainted by the dynamics of gendered power relations and male domination. As Lovenduski asserts, "To some, [state feminism] is an oxymoron" (2005b: 4).

Despite this minefield of obstacles, state feminism is an analytical concept commonly used by researchers, in western countries for the most part, becoming in some circles "extremely popular" (Berqvist *et al.* 1999). Since the term first appeared in studies of Nordic gender politics in the early 1980s, state feminism has gone through three phases of development, each reflecting the specific national/regional settings of the phenomena under study as well as developments in feminist theories of the state at the time, at least in scholarly circles in the West (e.g. McBride Stetson and Mazur 1995: 1–21; Lovenduski 2005b, Chappell 2002, Zheng 2005, Baldez 1997, Berqvist *et al.* 1999). The current usage builds on and is a refinement of these earlier phases and brings more operational clarity and specificity. It is important to note, nevertheless, that there is little agreement on how state feminism in its most recent form should be operationalized.

Phase 1: Nordic state feminism in the 1980s

Analysts began turning toward the state as a potential arena for feminist action in the early 1980s with the decline of the new women's movements in Europe, North America, and Australia (Dahlerup 1986a). The younger and more grassroots autonomous movements found in western postindustrial democracies had tended to avoid working with state-based actors or even looking to government as an arena for social change. Feminist theorists, especially in the UK and continental Europe, took the lessons of the new women's movement and developed an aversion to what they saw as a patriarchal state systemically opposed to the feminist project.[2] It is no coincidence, therefore, that the term "state feminism" began to be used for the first time in the Nordic context, where the autonomous feminist movements and their antisystem stances were less prevalent and feminists were much more willing to "engage with the state" (Chappell 2002) through political parties, trade unions, and parliament (Christensen and Raaum 1999). In addition, the particular arrangement of state–society relations in the Nordic countries made state feminism salient.

---

[2] For a discussion of the critiques of the state made by feminist theorists, see McBride Stetson and Mazur (1995: 6–10).

Not only was the state seen as an important site of social justice that produces redistributive welfare policies, but state–society relations followed a highly corporatist model, where sectional interests were represented through tripartite negotiations between the state, labor, and management to produce extensive social policies. Comparative work on feminism and public policy coming out of other countries in the 1980s did not use the term "state feminism", although, to be sure, women's policy agencies were on the radar (e.g. Lovenduski 1986 and McBride Stetson 1987).

Helga Hernes is usually credited with coining the term in her 1987 book *Welfare State and Woman Power: Essays in State Feminism*. From the Nordic context with active social policies where women were both clients and practitioners, Hernes identified state feminism as both a product and a driver of a woman-centered approach to state–society relations that produced a model of how states could be feminist in terms of actions and impact. Thus, from the beginning, state feminism was associated with a complex causal process. Taken by itself, according to Hernes, state feminism is "a variety of public policies and organizational measures, designed partly to solve general social and economic problems, partly to respond to women's demands." The concept not only implied these state-based actions; it also covered the outcome of a process – "the interplay between agitation from below and integration from above" – and also potentially a driving force in the production of a "woman-friendly polity" that "would enable women to have a natural relationship to their children, their work, and public life" (1987: 15).

Hernes was not clear on whether women needed to be feminists or to have connections to women's movement groups or ideas. She also did not provide a definition of feminism, opting instead for the term "woman-friendly." Other Nordic scholars, in particular Siim (1991), specified that Hernes's "feminism from above" meant the presence of women in elected and appointed offices in various government structures. "State feminism is a visible result of the integration of women in political and administrative institutions. The expression then refers to both feminists employed as administrators and bureaucrats in positions of power and to women politicians advocating gender equality policies" (Siim 1991: 189).

Here, we see the focus ranging from women in the state to women advocating feminist positions; Siim did not provide a definition of feminism either. The Scandinavian scholars writing on state feminism in this first period did not for the most part identify "feminism from above" specifically with the government gender equality bodies created to oversee the new equality policies, although they were assumed to be a part of these policies. Dahlerup (1986b) and Nielsen (1983) were some of the few Nordic scholars to equate "state feminism" with WPAs in this early period.

Thus, the Nordic research laid some of the foundations for our current use of the term: a focus on interactions between individual feminists inside and outside of the state and their connection to women-friendly / feminist policy and, to a lesser degree, a focus on agencies and their ability to promote the ideas of gender equality/feminism. But these terms were still imprecise, and little empirical work applied the concept or developed testable propositions; as much of the literature pointed out, state feminism was still an undeveloped question needing further investigation and analysis.

Phase II: Australian femocracy in the early 1990s

Building from the notion of state feminism as the activities of individual women in the state, Australian scholars in the early 1990s developed a new term, *femocrat*, that was taken up by feminist analysts in Europe (e.g. Outshoorn 1992, 1994, Van der Ros 1995). Here too, we can see the influence of the specific context of Australian feminist theorizing of the state on this new effort to study state feminism empirically. Pringle and Watson (1992) and Franzway, Court, and Connell (1989) put into question the notion of a monolithic patriarchal state by defining the state as a set of arenas divided by policy sector, level of government, and functional role. Australian feminist theorists asserted that feminist actors had the potential to operate from within these different arenas given that states are complex entities. Therefore, the theoretical stage was set for identifying not just individuals who could promote a feminist agenda, but also arenas within the state where the overall patriarchy of the state could be challenged and perhaps even eliminated.

There was a link between theory and context in Australian feminist theorizing similar to the one that produced the Nordic approach to state feminism. Australians assumed the importance and prevalence of state-based agencies on gender equality and women's policy units at all levels of the federal government. Rather than focusing on infrastructure, however, Australian analysts concentrated their attention on the individual state actors associated with the government's feminist agenda either through agencies or policies – the femocrats (Watson 1990, H. Eisenstein 1990, 1996, Sawer 1990, Franzway, Court, and Connell 1989). They identified the general presence and activities of these femocrats as "official feminism" or "femocracy." While the Australians rarely referred to state feminism in their studies of femocracy, Joyce Outshoorn, a Dutch scholar inspired by both Australian and European work on state feminism, situated her study of femocrats in the Netherlands explicitly in the context of state feminism with a focus on WPAs – " the new structures and positions set up to develop women's equality policy and the policies themselves" (1994: 143).

Beyond the consensus that femocrats worked in bureaucratic, appointed positions, throughout the government hierarchy, the Australian scholars were not clear about how to identify who were and were not femocrats. Were they bureaucrats throughout the government who espoused feminist ideas in their jobs (H. Eisenstein 1990)? Or the staff of women's policy agencies (Watson 1990)? Could femocrats be men? Departing from the absence of any clear discussion of the role of women's movements or organizations outside of the state, a major issue for research on Australian femocrats was their allegiance to feminist and women's movement ideas in general and to the specific demands of the women's movement actors. Many activists had seen the professionalized and bureaucratic femocrats in a highly critical light, before they trusted them as allies, "sisters in suits" (Sawer 1990). While research on femocrats did not provide a precise operational definition of femocrat, it did draw scholarly attention to the importance of the bureaucratic agencies at all levels of the state as potential sites for explicitly feminist action. In addition, it posited that state-based actors have the potential to advance a feminist agenda inside the state as allies of women's movement actors outside of the state.

Phase III: A cross-national approach to WPA–WM relations from 1995 to the present

The work of the Nordic and Australian scholars led to a more favorable view of the state as an arena for feminist action and the notion of state feminism associated with a complex process involving femocrats, the achievement of gender equality policy, and alliances between state actors and women's movements. A growing international community of researchers interested in gender, politics, and the state in a comparative perspective then shifted attention to the women's policy agencies as the prime object of analysis for state feminism.[3]

---

[3] In 1999, there were over 80 members of the community of scholars who were studying feminist comparative policy (FCP) issues in western postindustrial democracies. Controlling for country population, FCP scholars were evenly spread across these countries (Mazur 2002: 17).

The mid-1990s was also the heyday of worldwide mobilization around the United Nations women's policy process through the International Women's Policy Conferences to produce Plans of Action on women's rights and gender equality for member states.

The 1995 women's conference in Beijing was a major focal point for feminist mobilization at all levels, local, subnational, and transnational (Rai 2003a, Lycklama à Nijeholt, Swibel, and Vargas 1998, Zwingel 2005). Women's policy agencies were at the center of the UN process: within member states to oversee the process of presenting national reports often at subnational and national levels, at the UN level through its own policy machinery, and as the appointed agents of gender mainstreaming in the final program of action. As Rai and others assert, since the first Women's World Conference in 1975, the UN process had been a driving force in the establishment of women's policy offices in many member states; by the end of the 1990s, 127 member states had set up WPAs at the national level (Rai 2003b: 1). Given the unprecedented attention to and central role of WPAs in the development of what appeared to some to be a transnational women's movement around the UN's efforts in 1995, it was logical that researchers turned their attention to WPAs and that state feminism became a hot topic.

It was in this context of political attention and scholarly interest that we proposed the edited book project, *Comparative State Feminism* (*CSF*). We had each studied the active women's policy agencies in France (Mazur 1995, McBride Stetson 1987). Working with a group of scholars who had already studied these agencies (e.g. Ferree, Outshoorn, and Sawer), or wanted to study WPAs in their countries, we easily assembled researchers, with deep cultural expertise of their countries, to write on state feminism in thirteen postindustrial countries. Due to the importance of the agencies, the absence of any systematic studies of WPAs, and their interest in conducting systematic cross-national analysis, contributors to *CSF* agreed to use a common theoretical framework to select, map out, and analyze one national-level agency in each country.

The framework focused on the issue of whether, how, and why the agencies actually pursued state feminist goals through a focus on policy impact and access provided to women's movement actors in policymaking arenas.[4] To explain the dependent variable, degree of state feminism, we asked contributors to provide information on the establishment and organizational form

---

[4] The two dimensions were based on Skocpol's (1985) research agenda for state-centered research.

of the WPA, the national conception of the state, and the type of women's movement activism – factors that might explain the state feminist record of the WPA within each country. We then used these values as independent variables to sort through cross-national patterns of WPA activities in promoting feminist equal employment policy, based on admittedly vague criteria for determining what constituted a high level of feminist success. It turned out that the resulting typology of state feminism had a low level of external validity due to the focus on a single policy area as the one indicator of policy success (Skjeie 1997).

The methodological problems of this initial study, especially weaknesses in conceptualization and research design, limited its theoretical contributions and spurred some of the book contributors to form the Research Network on Gender and Politics and the State (RNGS) in 1995, to design a more systematic cross-national study of the impact of WPA–WM alliances and state feminism that would apply to all western postindustrial democracies. Despite its theoretical and methodological limitations, *CSF* provided the first systematic cross-national study of state feminism in terms of women's movement–WPA relations and is recognized as an indicator of the analytical turn toward WPAs in comparative gender research.[5]

The work of forty scholars through RNGS (five books devoted to issues [Mazur 2001, McBride Stetson 2001, Outshoorn 2004, Lovenduski 2006, Haussman and Sauer 2007], a quantitative dataset, a capstone book, and a book that maps out WPAs ten years after *CSF* [Outshoorn and Kantola forthcoming]) has contributed to the standardization of state feminism in terms of WPA–WM relations. At the same time, other studies, both inside and outside of postindustrial democracies, also have used the concept to map out relations between women's movements and WPAs in terms of impact on feminist goals.[6] As Krook, an observer of cross-national research on gender and politics, recently noted, the focus on women's policy agencies as purveyors of feminist action within the state "embodies the most common usage of the term today" (2005: 8).

---

[5] Ironically, it is often the 1995 book that is cited as a source on this approach to state feminism rather than the ensuing RNGS books that came out of the larger study.

[6] For a list of the country chapters and authors in all of the RNGS books, go to http://libarts.wsu.edu/polisci/rngs. For nonRNGS studies that take this approach to state feminism, see, for example, Baldez (1991), Zippel (2006), Bergqvist *et al.* (1999), Chappell (2002), Zheng (2005), Dahlerup (1993), Mushaben (2005), Revillard (2007), and Revillard and Bereni (2007). The edited volume by Outshoorn and Kantola (2007) came out of the RNGS project, but did not use the RNGS framework, and many of the contributing authors were not part of the RNGS.

The theoretical context for state feminism

Although the state feminism concept does not contain the term "gender", it is a highly gendered concept. Approaching state feminism in terms of women's policy agencies' ability to bring women's movement ideas and actors into the affairs of government and policy development to achieve feminist goals places gender as a process – the social construction of men's and women's identity in relation to each other – and a set of ideas about men's and women's roles at the center of analysis. The promotion of feminist goals necessarily entails addressing gender-biased hierarchies that contribute to sex-based inequities across all spheres. Examining state feminism in action, therefore, can become an exercise in determining whether WPAs actually gender policy discussions to reflect a feminist approach to framing policy questions by first identifying the causes of women's and men's equality and then providing suitable policy solutions. As Dahlerup first pointed out in 1986, the very essence of WPAs is to "institutionalize gender conflict" (1986a: 17). Moreover, women's policy agencies that promote feminist goals are an institutional counter to the gender-biased/patriarchal features of the state; rather than a tool for furthering the masculinist state, they are a means to bring it to an end. Thus, studying state feminism has great potential to contribute to theories that already have a gendered component as well as to those that have neglected to take on gender.

In this section, we examine three areas of theory which have informed the conceptualization of state feminism and which would benefit from research on state feminism. It is important to note that these are by no means the only bodies of theory to which scholarship on state feminism can make a contribution. Knowledge about the patterns of WM–WPA relations in various countries and contexts can speak to other theories in comparative politics and gender and politics research, such as the formation of feminist public policy (Mazur 2002, Weldon 2002b), the effectiveness of women elected officials through the triangle of women's empowerment (Vargas and Wieringa 1998), the impact of women/femocrats in the bureaucracy (Banaszak 2006), whether welfare states are women-friendly (O'Connor, Orloff, and Shaver 1999), the gendered nature of political institutions (Brush 2003), feminist efforts to "engage" with the state (Chappell 2002, Mushaben 2005, Kantola 2006), and efforts to mainstream gender in public policy at both the national and international levels (Rai 2003a, True and Mintrom 2001).

Democracy, representation, and participation

Asking whether WPAs bring women's movement actors and ideas into the state pertains to questions of participation, representation, and democracy, already discussed in Karen Celis's and Pamela Paxton's chapters in this volume. Does the introduction of feminist ideas into policy discussions increase the substantive representation of women's interests? Will bringing in women's movement actors who speak for feminist ideas expand women's descriptive representation inside the state? As Weldon (2002a) asserts, both women's movements and women's policy agencies are potential representatives of women and their interests, just as much as elected members of governmental bodies. WPAs themselves expand women's participation in the state as well, because they tend to employ women, with some exceptions. In countries where there is extensive policy machinery at all levels of government, this can amount to a significant number of women in government positions.[7] Thus, through facilitating women's representation and participation, WPAs contribute to the process of democratization whether the country is undergoing transitions to democracy, struggling to maintain a stable democracy, or looking to make a stable democracy more democratic. In this light, studying state feminism can contribute to understanding the processes of democratization within and across nation-states. Given that achieving state feminism means that a formally excluded group and its interests have been brought into policy discussions and the affairs of the state, theories of democratic development could include the achievement of some level of state feminism as a necessary and/or sufficient condition of democracy or at least be considered as an independent variable in explaining democratic stability (e.g. Przeworski, Alvarez, Zhebub, and Limongi 2000).

New institutionalism

Needless to say, a focus on state feminism brings bureaucratic institutions to the fore and hence responds to the call of scholars of new institutionalism to focus on institutions as causal mechanisms and as objects of analysis in historical and comparative contexts (March and Olsen 1984, Thelen 2003).

---

[7] In France, for example, the WPA structures, since the mid-1980s – including national-level ministry, central administrative agencies, regional delegations, departmental offices, and the national and territorial network of women's rights information centers – employ 500 people, most of whom are women (Mazur 2007b).

Examining state feminism also highlights the role of long-established practices and rules identified in terms of to what degree, and how, WPAs become players within state arenas – another focus of the new institutionalists. It also implies a state-centered approach that fits into the movement to "bring the state back in" in political analysis, often drawing directly from theories of the state (Skocpol 1985). Given that state feminism suggests a significant shift in activities of the state, studying this new form of state–society relations allows analysts to better understand "the issue of how . . . institutions are themselves shaped and reconfigured over time," an issue that has only recently become an important object of study (Thelen 2003: 208). Clearly, designing research that assesses the prevalence of state feminism helps analysts to answer the question of whether institutions matter in terms of representation, democracy, and achieving feminist goals. The systematic study of WPAs also permits students of politics to "shed light on democracy's critical processes" (Kettl 1993) and to fill the empirical gap on "the role of bureaucracies in making policy" (Peters 1992: 285).

Social movements

Research on social movements and women's movements has been an important source for conceptualizing and analyzing state feminism. As the previous chapter shows, the conceptualization of women's movement and feminism in RNGS research on state feminism has contributed to more precise definitions of women's movements and their relation to social movements more broadly speaking as well as to operationalizing a precise definition of feminism in policy analysis. Social movement theory has often neglected the questions of the institutional impact of social movements (McAdam, McCarthy, Zald 1996, Rochon 1990, Rochon and Mazmanian 1993, Quadagno 1994, Giugni 1995; Giugni, McAdam, and Tilly 1999). Most rare in this literature are studies of links between movement activists and agencies inside the state. Thus, state feminism research has the potential to shore up this theoretical gap as well.

A search for the drivers of state feminism through comparative analysis

In recent years, a major goal in the study of state feminism, and in studies on gender and politics issues as well, has been to identify the conditions that are conducive for WPAs and women's movements to achieve feminist success. In other words, what are the ingredients for successful state feminism? A host of contextual factors have been examined. To name a few: WPA structure and capacity, characteristics of the women's movements, state–society relations, state configurations, regime type, gender regimes, political will, and cultural factors. Analysts have used the tools of comparative analysis to determine the relative importance of factors through single nation case studies, comparisons of state feminism in several countries, or in groups of countries, both within regions and across regions. The RNGS project takes a mixed methods approach using the comparative case study method, qualitative comparative analysis, and statistical analysis to identify the various drivers of state feminism, sorting through explanations by comparing policy sectors and countries (McBride and Mazur 2006). Scholarship on state feminism, therefore, also has the potential to make a methodological contribution to political science by applying and refining the full array of methodological tools available to social science researchers.

The structure of state feminism as a concept

Thus far we have looked at state feminism as an analytical approach that focuses on WPA–WM relations and whether WPAs promote women's movement issues and actors within state arenas. Here we turn to a discussion of state feminism as a basic concept, providing a nominal definition, and, at the secondary level of concept development, present its general structure in terms of the Negation, Zones, Dimensions, Necessity, Interdependence, and Causal Relationships Guidelines. In the following section, we move to a more concrete level, showing dimensions and an operational definition used by the RNGS project as one way of dealing with the thorny operational issues inherent in the application of state feminism in research.

The nominal definition of state feminism is *the actions by women's policy agencies to include women's movement demands and actors into the state to produce feminist outcomes in either policy processes or societal impact or both.* This definition is the positive pole of a continuum between state feminism and no state feminism where cases can be placed in terms of the degree to which they display the different dimensions of the concept ranging from full to none. Thus, the concept is continuous rather than dichotomous, with the positive pole as an ideal type. State feminism has five necessary and sufficient dimensions:

1. The presence of a women's policy agency or an agency with a formal remit to improve women's status and promote sex-based equality within the context under study – e.g. local, subnational, national, international, etc.
2. The presence of a women's movement (discourse and actors) within the context under study – e.g. local, subnational, national, international, etc.
3. WPAs include women's movement demands into the state.
4. WPAs include women's movement actors (WMA) into the state.
5. The WPA/WMA interplay produces feminist outcomes.

To complete this secondary level, we set forth the dimensions of "feminist outcomes." There are two, *either* of which is sufficient to constitute a feminist outcome:

5.1 The WPA/WMA interplay produces feminist political processes.
5.2 The WPA/WMA interplay produces feminist social impacts.

Thus, to constitute state feminism, WPAs must be present and channel women's movement demands and women's movement actors, which also must be present, into the state to produce either feminist processes or feminist social impacts. The concept contains *causal relationships* between the dimensions, that is, in order for state feminism to exist the WPA/WMA interplay must produce feminist outcomes. Cases are placed toward the positive end of the continuum only when the WPAs effectively bring both women's movements demands and actors into the state and produce outcomes that can be clearly identified as being feminist; in other words, when they display all five dimensions. When none of these conditions occurs, there is no state feminism. The fewer key dimensions displayed, the closer the case is placed toward the "no state feminism" end of the continuum. The way the key characteristics of the concept are operationalized determines the precise placement of the cases. Cases can be of WPA–WM relations in entire countries, in specific policy areas, for a single agency at any level of government, or subagencies, bureaus, sections, within larger ministries or other types of agencies, as well as women's commissions/caucuses based in legislatures.

Given that the presence of a WPA is the first necessary and sufficient condition, it is important to clarify our definition of the principal agent of state feminism. *Women's policy agency or machinery* has come to mean any state-based agency, at all levels of government – (national, subnational or local) or in any type of organ (elected, appointed, administrative, or judicial) that has been officially assigned the responsibility of promoting the advancement of women and gender equality. In countries where political parties have a central role in government, in single party states or parliamentary democracies, for example, quasi WPAs (QUAWPAs) may act partially outside of the state parameters in the same manner as WPAs.[8]

Experts agree that the shift from women's interests to gender equality as the focus of most WPAs throughout the world occurred in the late 1980s and early 1990s (Staudt 2003, Rai 2003b).[9] Today, the names of many WPAs do not mention women, as in the cases of Scandinavian countries which focus on gender equality. We use the adjective "women's" rather than "gender equality" to identify all forms of these units, even when their official names do not include the specific term when they primarily focus on sex-based equality. This word choice is in part for expediency – it is easier to say "women" rather than "gender equality" – in part to include a broader range of machineries that may not have as their explicit focus gender equality, but rather the advancement of women's status, and in part due to the difficulty of translating "gender equality" into many languages. For this last reason, the United Nations terminology continues to use the word "women" to identify the policy machineries. This word choice, however, is not without critics; many argue that the gender equality moniker would be a much more accurate choice.

A new form of "diversity agency," first introduced in the USA (Equal Employment Opportunity Commission [EEOC]) in the mid-1960s, where different forms of discrimination (sex-based, race-based, against the disabled, etc.) are dealt with under one rubric – "one-stop-shops" (Lovenduski 2005c) – have become more common in Western Europe since the adoption of a new European Union directive on discrimination. Although there is some debate over whether these combined agencies should be considered WPAs, current research suggests that they have the potential to contribute to state feminism (Lovenduski 2005c). In this conceptualization of state feminism, as Dimension 1 shows, agencies that have a formal remit of sex equality among others may be potential partners in the state feminist process; whether they achieved feminist outcomes, however, remains a question for research. Thus, it is important that students of state feminism turn their attention to these new combined agencies in the context of intersectionality. Given the different ways in which

---

[8] The notion of QUAWPAs was first developed in the context of the RNGS study to discuss women's commissions in political parties in parliamentary systems.

[9] The use of "gender" in the formal title of WPAs in many countries, however, is not about gender as a complex notion, but rather about gender as a synonym for biological sex. In many languages it is more comfortable to say "gender" rather than "sex"; hence in many contexts gender equality is used to mean sex-based equality. This is particularly the case in many of the official documents of the European Union and the United Nations.

different systems of domination are dealt with by these new agencies and the need to situate the treatment of gender equality in relation to the other target areas of these agencies, Weldon's complex approach to "intersectionality-plus" in this book would provide an excellent analytical tool.

It is important to note that dimensions of state feminism do not include women in government or the rather vague notion of the women-friendliness of states, although knowledge of them can contribute to theorizing about these issues. Reflecting current scholarship, women's movement actors speak for women as a group and not just for individual women; to be considered a women's movement ally of WPAs in the state feminist process, individuals must clearly be affiliated with the women's movement in some way, through their discourse or their organizational position. In addition, because women's movements are composed of discourse and actors, it is crucial that WPAs include the individuals that come from women's movements, or actors, as well as the ideas and demands advanced by women's movement actors, for pure state feminism to be achieved.

The inclusion of both actors and ideas also indicates that women's interests have been represented both substantively through the inclusion of women's movement ideas and descriptively through the inclusion of individuals from the movements. As Karen Celis points out in this book, for many analysts it is not enough to achieve numerical representation of women; women representatives need to bring women's interests into the political arena as well. This caveat also applies for the study of state feminism.

When looking at feminist outcomes, there are two dimensions. The first – feminist processes – focuses on the extent to which WPA activities bring feminist movement actors and ideas into institutions and policymaking processes in government and the extent to which WPA interventions result in policies that reflect aspects of feminist ideas. The second – feminist social impacts – refers to the results of the WPA/WMA partnerships in changing the social condition of women along feminist lines: improving women's position, promoting equality between the sexes, and striking down gender-based hierarchies. If feminist results are operationalized in terms of such a major impact on society, complete feminist outcomes in both process and social impact are likely to be impossible in any setting and are best thought of as ideal types.

Given that feminist discourse is inherently gendered – striking down the subordination of women, the promotion of women in relation to men, and addressing gender-based hierarchies – the inclusion of feminist movement ideas involves gendering political discussions, agendas, and policy content. WPAs that are contributing to state feminism, therefore, help to gender the affairs of government. This may or may not include a fully fledged gender mainstreaming approach, where considerations of gender equality are systematically introduced across all policy sectors with the goal of developing policy that effectively strikes down the causes of gender-based discrimination and promotes equality between the sexes. Indeed, many WPAs with portfolios and remits formally assigned to a single policy area are not allowed to take a mainstreaming approach, for example commissions that focus on women's work issues. Nonetheless, while gender mainstreaming is not defined as a dimension of state feminism, WPAs are potentially the major purveyors of gender mainstreaming strategies (Rai 2003b). Thus, gender mainstreaming policies can be an arena for feminist outcomes of WPA–WM alliances where processes and impacts can be assessed. At the same time, state feminism can occur in cases where WPAs introduce a gendered perspective into the formation of discrete areas of policy, rather than systematically across all policy areas.[10]

Operationalizing state feminism in the RNGS project

As the old adage "the devil is in the details" indicates, moving to the application of state feminism in actual research is a challenge, reflecting in part the early stages of systematic conceptualization of women's movements and feminism. The issues to solve here include: How do we identify women's movement actors and their demands? What does it mean for WPAs to include women's movement demands and ideas into the state? And what is meant by feminist outcomes? We present the operationalization of state feminism from the RNGS study as *one* solution to the problem of locating empirical indicators of these dimensions. At the same time, this approach has a high level of external validity and reliability, given the process RNGS used to develop the study's research design.

At regular research meetings the forty members of the network collectively defined, elaborated, and refined all the concepts used in the RNGS project. Testing these concepts in the context of their own case analyses, these experts in gender and politics nevertheless kept an eye toward constructing concepts that could travel across national boundaries. At the same time, it is important to note the particular analytical choices that the network made in the context of the RNGS project may limit the use of the concept for other projects;

---

[10] For more on the concept of gender mainstreaming, its basic definition and literature, see the website on gender concepts that are not covered in this book, introduced in the Appendix.

by no means do we claim that we have come upon the "true" meaning of state feminism. In fact, we invite researchers to test and criticize the RNGS conceptualizations and propose alternative ways to tackle this tough concept. We accept the distinct possibility that many researchers will choose other ways of studying the core issues of gender politics and the state that are raised by state feminism (e.g. Chappell 2002, Mushaben 2005, Kantola 2006). Understanding the logic of these choices, therefore, also suggests the limits of the study.

The first RNGS choice to highlight is the decision to study only western postindustrial democracies.[11] Second, the RNGS study focuses on the political process and policy outputs as the dimension of feminist outcomes, not the social impact of policy. The effectiveness of WPAs is evaluated not in terms of whether the policy actions pursued by the WPAs actually promote women's rights and strike down gender hierarchies through policy implementation and impact evaluation, but in terms of whether the frame of debates about policy and the content of their decisional end points were affected and whether women's movement actors were included in the process. Thus, the argument can be made here that the RNGS study of state feminism is just a first step, as the task will be completed only when we can study whether the changes in the state actually made a concrete difference in society.

Third, to better focus on the policymaking process, the network decided to use the policy debate and move away from the nation-state as the unit of analysis. A policy debate is one that leads to some sort of government decision or nondecision. We sought to examine the WPA–WM alliances in areas of the state action that touched upon core gender relations: (1) the division of labor in the home and workplace; (2) human reproduction; (3) sexuality; and (4) citizenship rights and selected specific issues from each – job training, abortion, prostitution, and political representation. The group also wanted to assess state feminism in an area of top national priority – the "the hot issue" – and agreed on a set of criteria to select such issues in each country. The goal for each country team was to study three policy debates in each policy area (one for the hot issue); not all of the areas were covered in each country, nor were all western postindustrial democracies covered.[12] The results were published

---

[11] From the beginning, the RNGS agreed to take a "most similar systems" approach and not examine state feminism in countries outside of the West, in large part due to the similarities of the processes of political development and women's movement mobilization shared by western postindustrial democracies and their distinctiveness when compared to other regions of the world.

[12] The original intent was to recruit teams for all western postindustrial democracies and at the EU level and to cover all areas for all countries. In the end we covered all issues in Italy, France, the USA, and Spain; analyses of some of the issues areas were provided for Austria, Belgium, Sweden, Australia, Great Britain, Germany, Ireland, the Netherlands, and Canada. Individual issue analyses were also conducted in Japan for the hot issue and in Israel for prostitution.

in five separate issue books with country chapters (Mazur 2001, McBride Stetson 2001, Outshoorn 2004, Lovenduski 2006, Haussman and Sauer 2007).

Given the dimensions of the concept and RNGS research decisions, the following are the concrete steps by which to observe and measure state feminism.

1. To determine *whether WPAs included women's movement demands in state processes*, researchers compared the positions, called micro-frames, taken by women's movement actors (WMA) in the topic of the debate with the WPA micro-frames on the issue to see the extent of agreement.[13]

2. To determine *whether WPA's action brought women's movement actors (WMA) into the state processes*, researchers investigated the effectiveness of the WPAs in introducing gendered ideas into the issue frame used by policymakers. Based on the assumption that when the policy debates are defined to be of interest to an outside group, such as women, representatives of those groups will have access to the decision-making arenas.[14]

Researchers must provide information about the six questions presented below for each policy debate that was studied in the RNGS project. The first two questions cover Dimensions 3 and 4 of state feminism at its basic level – the inclusion of WM demands by the WPA and the inclusion of WM actors by the WPA. The next four questions addressed whether the WPA/WM interplay produced feminist outcomes in terms of process, but not impact – Dimension 5.1. (Since the RNGS research design selected only debates where WPAs and WMAs were present, Dimensions 1 and 2 are not included here.)

1. To what extent did the WPA promote a micro-frame that matched the feminist movement micro-frame?

2. Was the WPA successful in incorporating the feminist movement micro-frame into the dominant frame of the policy subsystem?

3. Did the policy content match micro-frames of the feminist movement actors?

4. To what extent were women's movement actors in the policy process presenting feminist micro-frames?

---

[13] From the literature, we developed a hierarchy of policy definitions at three levels: general frames, issue frames, and micro-frames. At the general level, the definition of policy problems and the actors that are involved occur in the national or even extranational arenas; its dynamics affect action and policy content on a wide range of policy issues. An issue frame is the definition of meaning of a specific policy area, e.g. employment, health, environment, etc., used by actors in that policy subsystem in a given policy debate. A micro-frame is the position specific actors seek to insert into the issue frame to change the definition of the issue and policy content.

[14] This is similar to the idea of "mobilization of bias" outlined in Schattschneider (1960).

Table 11.1 Categories for the state feminism continuum

SF	Full	Partial	Unsuccessful	Absent	None
a. WPA micro-frame matched WMA feminist micro-frame	X	X/O*	X/O[a]	O	O
b. WPA gendered debate with feminist frame	X	X/O*	X/O*	O	O
c. Policy content contained feminist micro-frames	X	X/O*	O	X/O*	O
d. Feminist WMAs participate in subsystem	X	X/O*	O	X/O*	O

[a] A score of X for either c or d places a given case in this category.

Based on the definition of the women's movement as actors presenting women's movement discourse, we agreed that any individual would be considered a women's movement actor, regardless of their affiliation, as long as they advanced a position that corresponded to women's movement discourse, defined by our three criteria. To be feminist, the women's movement discourse must also include the three feminist criteria. Thus, women's movement actors are defined not in terms of their organizational location, but from what their programs are or what they say at a given moment, which means that actors may not necessarily be speaking for the feminist women's movement all of the time. Women's movement actors (WMAs) can be individuals, formal organizations, or informal organizations with locations in a variety of sites – freestanding women's movement groups and within non-women's movement organizations, such as political parties. Men were not considered as women's movement actors, and whether a WMA was feminist or not was based on determining whether the content of the positions advanced in the policy debate by the individual actor was feminist or not.[15]

Table 11.1 presents the examples of five categories of state feminism produced from answering the four questions about WMA–WPA relations in individual policy debates. An X indicates the presence of a given attribute, an O indicates its absence, and XO indicates that either attribute *a* or *b* must be present to fit into that category.

These five categories are not discrete; rather, they should be considered as points on a continuum ranging from full to no state feminism, and specific cases may or may not fall precisely in each category. Cases that have different

[15] For a more detailed discussion of the RNGS approach to women's movement, see chapter 10.

combinations of values would be placed on the continuum according to how close they come to one of the five categories. Next, we present the dimensions of each category with an example from the RNGS findings. We also present one case that does not perfectly fit a category and suggest a placement on the continuum.[16]

1. Full state feminism: reimbursement of abortion expenses in France, 1981–3. In this category, women's policy agency (WPA) / women's movement actor (WMA) micro-frames match during the policy debate. The WPA genders the frame of the debate and full feminist outcomes are achieved in the policy process, including the WPA micro-frame matching the WMA feminist frames; the WPA incorporating the feminist micro-frame in dominant policy frame; the policy content fitting the WMA feminist micro-frame; and WMAs with feminist demands participating in the policy debate.

For the abortion policy debate in France in the early 1980s, feminist women's groups worked with Minister of Women's Rights, Yvette Roudy, to get lawmakers to discuss the abortion issue in terms of women's rights and gender-based inequities and to successfully provide state-funded reimbursement for two-thirds of abortion costs, a demand that had been at the core of the feminist agenda within the women's movements for many years.

2. Partial state feminism: social insurance amendment on private enterprise in Austria, 1997. In this second category, WPA/WMA micro-frames match and the WPA genders the frame of the debate as well, but there is not a full feminist outcome. Either feminist movement actors participate in the debate or the policy contains feminist micro-frames. Thus, while the WPAs achieve a feminist success, movement actors have only partial success. In the case of 1997 Social Insurance Law in Austria, the Ministry of Women's Affairs consulted feminist researchers and produced several reports that defended prostitute rights as sex workers. The ministry forwarded recommendations of the feminist report in cabinet-level deliberations on the law and in that formulation process gendered the cabinet discussion on the social insurance law. Representatives of feminist prostitute rights groups were consulted directly in the elaboration of the draft law as well. The final amendment, however, did not advance the feminist approach to prostitutes as sex workers; instead it included a statement that prostitution was immoral and coercive rather than a legitimate form of work.

---

[16] These cases were selected for illustrative purposes to represent all five issue areas and a range of countries covered in the study. None of the examples is representative of any general pattern of state feminism in the countries covered or the issue areas.

3. Unsuccessful state feminism: parity reform in France, 1995–2000. Here, WPA/WMA micro-frames still match and the WPA still genders the frame of the debate as well, but the policy content *does not* fit the WMA feminist micro-frame, and feminist WMAs *do not* participate in the policy debate. The WPA, thus, tried to represent feminists but failed to produce a feminist outcome. In the momentous debates that led up to the parity laws in 2000, where a range of feminist and non-feminist groups mobilized around demands to address women's low levels of political representation, the newly created Observatory for Parity was a major arena for feminist groups to articulate their demands. The groundswell of mobilization and public support amazingly did not translate into a feminist success. The final law did not even mention the French term for sex equality in political office, *parité*, and it contained key stipulations that severely limited the ability of the new quota law to authoritatively promote women in elected office. Although feminist groups presented testimony to the Observatory – one of several WPAs at the time – they were not given access to the parliamentary deliberations where many of their demands were ignored or watered down.

4. Absent state feminism: defeat of proposal to restrict abortion services in Great Britain, 1975–9. In this fourth category of state feminism, the WPAs are not feminist but the policy content fits the WMA feminist micro-frames and feminist WMAs participate in the policy subsystem. In this case, the WPA was the Women's National Commission, an advisory council to the British Cabinet. Although the WNC had taken a feminist position on the abortion issue in an earlier debate, it remained silent with respect to this new proposal to turn back the clock and prohibit legal abortion. Nevertheless, the women's movement was well represented by several feminist members of parliament as well as mobilized autonomous groups who formed strong coalitions against changes in the Abortion Act of 1967. The feminist lobbies were closely involved in the debate and were successful in their goal of preventing any restrictions on the right to abortion.

5. No state feminism: change in the electoral law in Finland, 1972–5. In this last category of state feminism, WPAs take no part in the debate and the policy content fails to fit the WMA feminist micro-frame, or any WMA micro-frame for that matter, and WMAs, feminist or not, are not present in the debate.

In the Finnish political representation debate in the 1970s, there seemed to be little interest among women's movement activists or the agencies in the government's bill to return nominating processes to independent electoral associations which had traditionally been players in this arena. Most saw the barriers to women's representation as being in the social and economic factors, not the electoral law, which they viewed as favorable.

6. A case of almost full state feminism in the Bill on trafficking in the Netherlands, 1983–9. For all categories, except for the "no state feminism" category, it is possible to fit cases in that do not exactly match the values on all four dimensions. In the case of a prostitution debate, on a Bill on trafficking from 1983 to 1989 in the Netherlands, the debate was not a complete state feminist success, but displayed enough of the attributes that it could be placed close to the "full state feminism" end of the continuum. While the feminist women's movement actors gained access to the debate through feminist members of parliament and feminist lawyers participating in the parliamentary debate, and the final law reflected quite closely the feminist demands, the department that coordinated the Emancipation Council, a Dutch WPA, took a pro-women's movement stance but was unable to actually influence the debate.

Does state feminism travel?

Most of the work on state feminism covered in this chapter thus far has been by scholars from and studying western postindustrial democracies. In large part, the approach to state feminism stems from the particular way in which women's movements form and interrelate with state actors as well as the particular state–society dynamics that exist in countries with established democracies and wealthy postindustrial economies. Yet women's policy agencies now exist in many other types of countries. In this section we consider some of the factors that will affect the use and usefulness of the concept across the globe.

Silences on state feminism

There is a growing body of work on gender and the state outside of the West, mapping, both empirically and theoretically, the dynamics of gender and politics within nation-states at all levels and at the international and transnational levels; yet this work rarely mentions state feminism. For example, the concept is absent in Mala Htun's recent review of current scholarship on nonwestern processes related to gender and the state (2005). Similarly, most research that explores regional patterns of gender politics and state change, for example in the post-socialist regimes, Latin America, and Asia, does not use state feminism as a major object of analysis or as a potential key influence (e.g. Nelson and Chowdhury 1994, Craske and Molyneux 2002, Htun 2002, Gal and Kligman 2000, Howell and Mulligan 2005).

This silence on state feminism is not due to lack of interest in either women's movements or women's policy agencies. In fact, there is increased attention to women's policy agencies in non-Western regimes and their role in economic and social development, democratization and gender mainstreaming. Nevertheless, the authors have not posed the existence of state feminism as a central research question (e.g. Rai 2003a, Staudt 1997, Parpart, Rai, and Staudt 2002, True and Mintrom 2001). One study advances a useful notion – the triangle of women's empowerment – that examines relations between femocrats, women elected officials, and women's movement actors; the authors do not connect the triangle to the subject of state feminism (Lycklama à Nijeholt, Vargas, and Wieringa 1998).

One reason for these silences may be the history of the use of the concept we reviewed earlier. The term originated in research on Nordic countries and later in Australia. There had been little agreement on the meaning of the term and little work on conceptualization until the RNGS project took it up as a central focus. So far, the explicit study of state feminism as complex alliances between movements and WPAs has been used almost exclusively in research on the established democracies. For use in other contexts, it is necessary to consider whether the conceptualization could be useful to study women's movements and WPA alliances with different economic and political systems.

A major limitation on the usefulness of state feminism to study nonwestern gender politics is the tainted nature of the term "feminism." To many non-westerners, feminism as an ideology is associated with a specific ethnocentric approach that imposes a narrow view, without asking the people involved, on what changes for women are feminist and what strategies will achieve gender equality. In this same perspective, for some analysts the concept is associated with western imperialism and cultural domination. This double-edged nature of feminism – the fact that it is not culturally meaningful in certain settings and the fact that it may bring a great deal of political baggage with it – explains its unpopularity with both scholars and practitioners outside of the West. Indeed, the policy of all United Nations women's policy machineries is to simply not use the term at all. As a result, none of the UN policy documents, UN-funded studies, or UN reports mention feminism; rather, "gender equality," "equality between men and women," and "the advancement of women" are the accepted and acceptable terms.

Much of the global literature tends to be silent about state feminism rather than overtly criticizing it, with the exception of work on postcommunist countries in the former Soviet Union and East Central Europe (Gal and Kligman 2000, Rueschemeyer 1998). Here the argument is that western state feminism does not travel to the postcommunist context. The socialist states officially supported sex equality, but separate women's federations in the communist parties rallied women together to support the regime and the party instead of taking action to improve women's lot.[17] For women in these countries, associating "feminism" with the "state" is not a desirable outcome. Women's movement actors in the postcommunist context are suspicious of the state and its women's policy agencies as potential partners in pursuing a feminist agenda; thus state feminism as a women's movement strategy is delegitimated.

Making state feminism travel

The conceptualization of state feminism offered in this chapter derives from the RNGS research. The nominal definition of the basic concept locates the term in the actions of women's policy agencies to include women's movement demands and actors into the state to produce feminist outcomes in either policy processes or societal impact or both. The dimensions assume the possibility of women's movement actors' ability to penetrate the state, a condition mostly likely found in democratic systems. Thus the concept has potential for uses in democratic regimes outside of the West. For use in other types of systems, those that are authoritarian or in transition to democracy, researchers would need to consider revising the dimensions in the second level of conceptualization to fit the realities of society–state relationships in the countries studied. One might, for example, consider other links between WPAs and feminist ideas in the women's movement, such as through leadership by feminist women or connections through CEDAW (the Convention on the Elimination of All Forms of Discrimination against Women) and the United Nations. Similarly, the assessment of "feminist outcomes" in terms of policy processes would not be appropriate in many systems. At the same time, assessing the outcomes in terms of impact of policies on society may be a useful approach in assessing WPAs in closed regimes.

---

[17] For specific studies of communist party women's federations, see, for example, J. Robinson (1995) or Zheng (2005). Zheng's study argues that the All-China Women's Federation is no longer a tool of the Communist Party, but is operating more like a western state feminist actor in Chinese politics.

Finally, as discussed earlier, researchers in nonwestern systems have to come to grips with the meaning of feminism in their research areas. In the chapter on women's movements in this volume, we consider ways of using the concept outside of the West. The substitutability of the indicators of feminism – changing women's condition, gender equality, and attacking gender hierarchies – makes the term more flexible in research applications. Similarly, looking at these demands in specific cultural contexts permits analysis of Islamic feminism, socialist feminism, transitional feminism, and so on.

We argue that attention to state feminism cross-nationally would provide a useful tool for assessing the effectiveness of women's policy agencies as points of entry to the state for feminist women's movement ideas as well as actors. There are some scholars who have already tackled the issue in quite different nonwestern contexts. In research on authoritarian regimes, particularly in the Middle East and communist countries, scholars have expanded their studies of state agencies to look beyond the WPAs. In these studies, state feminism is seen as a product of decisions made by male elites who develop policies and structures to gain the support of women, with the help of individual female leaders, usually not affiliated with any broad-based movement. Policies may in the short term help advance women's status, particularly at moments of political change – revolution, *coups d'état* – but as the authoritarian leaders tighten control, these rights and benefits that may help women become less prominent or disappear altogether. In addition to the research on state feminism in communist regimes mentioned above, this authoritarian variant is mapped out by researchers in countries in the Middle East or with a significant Islamic influence in politics, including Turkey, Egypt, and Greece (Bodur and Franceschet 2002, Hatem 1992, 1994, Cacoullos 1994, Abadan-Unat and Tokgöz 1994).

Secondly, there are studies that apply the notion of state feminism as WM–WPA relations for feminist ends in theory-building analyses of gender and the state, most notably in Latin America, where women's policy agencies have been important allies with the women's movement for improving women's rights within countries and across countries (Lycklama à Nijeholt, Vargas, and Wieringa 1998). Baldez 1991 argues that in the case of Chile, state feminism is more effective when there is a competitive party system. Franceschet 2003 also examines evidence of state feminism in the context of Chile by focusing on the Servicio National de la Mujer. Thus, more than the biases of western feminism, it may be that state feminism is a more salient and meaningful conceptual tool for stable democracies or countries where democratization is an ongoing process.

Conclusion

State feminism developed from research on gender, politics, and states in the postindustrial western democracies. It is the central focus of the RNGS project. The core meaning of the term is the relation between feminist women's movements and women's policy agencies inside government and the effects of those alliances on politics and society. Rigorous conceptualization of the term for research is in the early stages and is likely to develop as more scholars focus attention on the topic. The proliferation of combined/diversity agencies throughout the West presents new challenges to the state feminism research agenda – challenges that researchers can meet through new developments in conceptualizations of intersectionality presented in this book. The dataset from the RNGS project can provide a tool for those interested in pursuing questions of state feminism in Europe and North America.[18] With better conceptualization, those who study nonwestern movement–state relations may have a powerful tool to consider in their analyses.

In this process, the dimensions and the operationalization levels of the concept structure are bound to change. It is likely that the term will not travel widely without a major shift in these components. As scholars consider and share ideas and experiences in their research, it may turn out that state feminism is too close to its western origins to be useful across the globe. Or, its use may result in the development of new concepts that are more effective in comparing and assessing the work of the ubiquitous women's policy agencies.

[18] The RNGS dataset and codebook may be downloaded from the project website, http:/libarts.wsu.edu/polisci/rngs.

Appendix
A website for additional gender and politics concepts

Since it is impossible for us to cover all the key concepts that have been modified or created by gender scholars, we have a created a modest website for this book that presents additional concepts not covered in this book. We see this in particular as a service to teachers and students. The website briefly lists each concept and then allows the reader to download a pdf file with more information, references, etc. The pdf file describes briefly each concept and gives some suggestions about what is interesting (to us at least) about this concept from the point of view of gender scholars or from the point of view of the ten Guidelines.

We see the development of the website as responsive to the readers and users of the book. We encourage people to propose concepts along with text and suggested readings. We will establish an email list to notify interested scholars of additions or modifications to the site.

The website for this book can be accessed via the link on the Cambridge University Press webpage for this Book: www.cambridge.org/goertzandmazur. We welcome people to email us – ggoertz@u.arizona.edu or mazur@wsu.edu – with comments or suggestions.

References

Abadan-Unat, Nermin, and Oya Tokgöz. 1994. "Turkish women as agents of social change in a pluralist democracy." In Nelson and Chowdhury, *Women and Politics Worldwide*, pp. 705–20.

Acker, Joan. 1990. "Hierarchies, jobs, and bodies: a theory of gendered organizations." *Gender & Society* 4, pp. 139–58.

1992. "Gendered institutions: from sex roles to gendered institutions." *Contemporary Society* 21, pp. 565–9.

Ackerly, Brooke A., Maria Stern, and Jacqui True (eds.). 2006. *Feminist Methodologies for International Relations*. Cambridge: Cambridge University Press.

Adcock, R. 1998. "What is a 'concept'"? Paper presented at the American Political Science Association Meetings.

Adcock, Robert, and David Collier. 2001. "Measurement validity: a shared standard for qualitative and quantitative research." *American Political Science Review* 95/3 (September), pp. 529–46.

Adorno, Theodore, Else Frenkel-Brunswik, Daniel J. Levinson, and R. Nevitt Sanford. 1950. *The Authoritarian Personality*. New York: Harper.

Alcoff, L. 1991–2. "The problem of speaking for others," *Cultural Critique* (Winter), pp. 5–32.

Alvarez, Mike, Jose Antonio Cheibub, Fernando Limongi, and Adam Przeworski. 1996. "Classifying political regimes." *Studies in Comparative International Development* 31, pp. 2–36.

Alvarez, Sonia E. 1990. *Engendering Democracy in Brazil: Women's Movements in Transition Politics*. Princeton: Princeton University Press.

1998. "Latin American feminisms 'go global': trends of the 1990s and challenges for the new millennium." In Sonia E. Alvarez, Evelina Dagnino, and Arturo Escobar (eds.), *Cultures of Politics, Politics of Cultures: Re-visioning Latin American Social Movements*. Boulder: Westview Press, pp. 293–324.

Annesley, Claire. 2003. "Transforming welfare and gender regimes: evidence from the UK and Germany". *Comparative European Politics* 1/2, pp. 129–47.

Ashford, Douglas. 1986. *The Emergence of Welfare States*. Oxford: Blackwell.

Association for Women's Rights in Development (AWID.) 2004. "Intersectionality: a tool for gender and economic justice." *Women's Rights and Economic Change* 9 (August), pp. 1–7.

Bache, Ian, and Matthew Flinders. 2004. "Themes and issues in multi-level governance," in Ian Bache and Matthew Flinders (eds.), *Multi-level Governance*. Oxford: Oxford University Press.

Baden, Sally, and Anne Marie Goetz. 1997. "Who needs [sex] when you can have [gender]? Conflicting discourses on gender at Beijing." In Staudt, *Women, International Development and Politics*, pp. 37–58.

Bagić, Aida. 2006. "Women's organizing in post-Yugoslav countries." In Myra Marx Ferree and Aili Mari Tripp (eds.), *Global Feminism: Transnational Women's Activism, Organizing, and Human Rights*, pp. 141–65. New York: New York University Press.

Baldez, Lisa. 1991. "Coalition politics and the limits of state feminism in Chile." *Women and Politics* 22/4, pp. 1–28.

Banaszak, Lee Ann. 2006. "Who are movement insiders? The ideological and biographical characteristics of feminist activists inside the state." Paper presented at the American Political Science Association meetings, Philadelphia.

Banaszak, Lee Ann, Karen Beckwith, and Dieter Rucht (eds.). 2003. *Women's Movements Facing the Reconfigured State*. Cambridge: Cambridge University Press, pp. 10–28.

Barnett, Bernice McNair, Rose M. Brewer, and M. Bahati Kuumba. 1999. "New directions in race, gender and class studies: African-American experiences." *Race, Gender and Class* 6, pp. 7–28.

Barrett, Michelle. 1980. *Women's Oppression Today: Problems in Marxist Feminist Analysis*. London: Verso.

Basu, Amrita (ed.). 1995. *The Challenge of Local Feminisms: Women's Movements in Global Perspectives*. Boulder: Westview Press.

Beasley, Chris. 1999. *What is Feminism? An Introduction to Feminist Theory*. Thousand Oaks and New Delhi: Sage.

Beckwith, Karen. 2000. "Beyond compare? Women's movements in comparative perspective." *European Journal of Political Research* 37, pp. 431–68.

  2005a. "The comparative politics of women's movements." *Perspectives on Politics* 3/3 (September), pp. 583–96.

  2005b "A common language of gender?" *Politics and Gender* 1/1, pp. 128–36.

Bedford, Kate. 2008. "Governing intimacy at the World Bank." In Shirin M. Rai and Georgina Waylen (eds.). *Global Governance: Feminist Perspectives*. Basingstoke: Palgrave, pp. 84–106.

Bedolla, Lisa Garcia, and Becki Scola. 2006. "Finding intersection: race, class and gender in the 2003 California recall vote." *Politics & Gender* 2, pp. 5–28.

Beetham, D. 1992. "Liberal democracy and the limits of democratization." *Political Studies* 40/5, pp. 40–53.

Bell, Emma. 2001. *Gender and Governance: A Bibliography*, (BRIDGE bibliography) Institute for Development Studies, University of Sussex.

Benería, Lourdes. 2003. *Gender, Development, and Globalization: Economics As If All People Mattered*. New York: Routledge.

Benhabib, Seyla (ed.). 1996. *Democracy and Difference: Contesting the Boundaries of the Political*. Princeton: Princeton University Press.

Bergqvist, Christina. 2005. "Gender equality politics: ideas and strategies." In PerOla Öberg and Torsten Svensson (eds.), *Power and Institutions in Industrial Relations Regimes*. Stockholm: The National Institute for Working Life, pp. 25–47.

Bergqvist, Christina, *et al.* (eds.). 1999. *Equal Democracies: Gender and Politics in the Nordic Countries*. Oslo: Scandinavia University Press.

Bevir, Mark, and R. A. V. Rhodes. 2003. *Interpreting British Governance.* London: Routledge. 2006. *Governance Stories.* London: Routledge.

Birch, A. H. 1971. *Representation: Key Concepts in Political Science.* London: Pall Mall Press. 1993. "Political representation." In A. H. Birch (ed.). *The Concepts and Theories of Modern Democracy.* London and New York: Routledge, pp. 69–79.

Bock, Gisela, and Pat Thane (eds.). 1991. *Maternity and Gender Policies: Women and the Rise of the European Welfare States, 1880–1950s.* London: Routledge.

Bodur, Marella, and Susan Franceschet. 2002. "Movements, states and empowerment." In Parpart, Rai and Staudt, *Rethinking Empowerment: Gender and Development in a Global/Local World*, pp. 112–32.

Bollen, Kenneth A. 1980. "Issues in the comparative measurement of political democracy." *American Sociological Review* 45 (June), pp. 370–90.
1990. "Political democracy: conceptual and measurement traps." *Studies in Comparative International Development* 25, pp. 7–24.
1998. "Cross-national indicators of liberal democracy, 1950–1990." Codebook. University of North Carolina, Chapel Hill, NC.

Bollen, Kenneth. A., and Robert Jackman. 1989. "Democracy, stability and dichotomies." *American Sociological Review* 54 (August), pp. 612–621.

Bollen, Kenneth A., and Richard Lennox. 1991. "Conventional wisdom on measurement: a structural equation perspective." *Psychological Bulletin* 110/2, pp. 305–14.

Bollen, Kenneth A., and Pamela Paxton. 2000. "Subjective measures of liberal democracy." *Comparative Political Studies* 33, pp. 58–86.

Borchorst, Anette. 1994. "Welfare state regimes, women's interests and the EC." In Sainsbury, *Gendering Welfare States*, pp. 26–44.

Borchorst, Anette, and Birte Siim. 1987. "Women and the advanced welfare state: a new kind of patriarchal power?" In Anne Showstack Sassoon (ed.), *Women and the State: The Shifting Boundaries of Public and Private.* London: Hutchinson, pp. 128–57.

Bordo, Susan. 1993. *Unbearable Weight: Feminism, Western Culture, and the Body.* Berkeley: University of California Press.

Boserup, Esther. 1970. *Woman's Role in Economic Development.* New York: St. Martin's Press.

Bowman, Kirk, Fabrice Lehoucq, and James Mahoney. 2005. "Measuring political democracy: case expertise, data adequacy, and central America." *Comparative Political Studies* 38, pp. 939–70.

Bradshaw, Jonathon, *et al.* 1993. "A comparative study of child support in fifteen countries." *Journal of European Social Policy* 3, pp. 255–71.

Brady, Henry E., and David Collier (eds.). 2004. *Rethinking Social Inquiry: Diverse Tools, Shared Standards.* Boulder: Rowman & Littlefield.

Bratton, Kathleen. 2002. "The effect of legislative diversity on agenda setting: evidence from six state legislatures." *American Politics Research* 30/2, pp. 115–42.
2005. "Critical mass theory revisited: the behavior and success of token women in state legislatures." *Politics & Gender* 1, pp. 97–125.

Braud, Pierre. 1985. "Théories de la représentation: introduction." In François d'Arcy (ed.), *La représentation* Paris: Economica, pp. 33–7.

Brennan, Geoffrey, and Alan Hamlin. 1999. "On political representation." *British Journal of Political Science* 29/1, pp. 109–27.

Bretherton, Charlotte. 1998. "Gobal environmental politics: putting gender on the agenda?" *Review of International Studies*, 24/1, pp. 85–100.

Brewer, Rose. 1999. "Theorizing race, class and gender: the new scholarship of black feminist intellectuals and black women's labor." *Race, Gender and Class* 6, pp. 29–47.

BRIDGE (bridging the gaps between research, policy and practice with accessible and diverse gender information). www.bridge.ids.ac.uk

Briggs, Asa. 1961. "The welfare state in historical perspective." *Archives of European Sociology* 11, pp. 221–58.

Brodie, Janine. 2005. "Globalization, governance and gender: rethinking the agenda for the twenty-first century." In Louise Amoore (ed.), *Globalizing Resistance*. London: Routledge, pp. 244–56.

Brown, Carol. 1981. "Mothers, fathers and children: from private to public patriarchy." In Lydia Sargent (ed.), *Women and Revolution: A Discussion of the Unhappy Marriage of Marxism and Feminism*. Boston: South End Press, pp. 239–67.

Brown, Wendy. 1988. *Manhood and Politics*. Totowa: Rowman & Littlefield.

1992. "Finding the man in the state." *Feminist Studies* 18/1 (Spring), pp. 7–34.

Brush, Lisa D. 2003. *Gender and Governance*. New York: Altamira (Rowman & Littlefield).

Bryson, Valerie. 2003. *Feminist Political Theory: An Introduction*. Houndmills and New York: Palgrave Macmillan.

Bueno de Mesquita, Bruce, Alastair Smith, Randolph M. Siverson, and James D. Morrow. 2003. *The Logic of Political Survival*. Cambridge, MA: MIT Press.

Bull, Anna, Hanna Diamond, and Rosalind Marsh (eds.). 2000. "Introduction." In Anna Bull, Hanna Diamond, and Rosalind Marsh (eds.), *Feminisms and Women's Movements in Contemporary Europe*. New York: St. Martin's Press, pp. 1–18.

Burger, Thomas. 1987. *Max Weber's Theory of Concept Formation: History, Laws, and Ideal Types*. Durham, NC: Duke University Press.

Burkhart, Ross E., and Michael S. Lewis-Beck. 1994. "Comparative democracy: the economic development thesis." *American Political Science Review* 88, pp. 903–10.

Burnham, Linda. 2001. "Introduction." In Maylei Blackwell, Linda Burnham, and Jung Hee Choi (eds.), *Time to Rise: US Women of Color – Issues and Strategies*. A Report to the UN World Conference Against Racism, Racial Discrimination, Xenophobia and Related Intolerance, Durban, South Africa, Aug. 28–Sept. 7, 2001. Berkeley: Women of Color Resource Center Press, pp. 1–17.

Burrell, Barbara C. 1994. *A Woman's Place is in the House: Campaigning for Congress in the Feminist Era*. Ann Arbor: University of Michigan Press.

Bussemaker, Jet, and Kees van Kersbergen 1994. "Gender and welfare states: some theoretical reflections." In Sainsbury, *Gendering Welfare States*, pp. 8–25.

1999. "Contemporary social-capitalist welfare states and gender inequality," In Sainsbury, *Gender and Welfare State Regimes*, pp. 15–46.

Butler, Judith. 1990. *Gender Trouble: Feminism and the Subversion of Identity*. New York: Routledge.

1993. *Bodies that Matter: On the Limits to Discursive "Sex."* New York: Routledge.

Cacoullos, Ann R. 1994. "Women confronting party politics." In Nelson and Chowdhury, *Women and Politics Worldwide*, pp. 311–25.

Cameron, David. 1978. "The expansion of the public economy." *American Political Science Review* 72, pp. 1243–61.

Campbell, Angus, Philip E. Converse, Warren P. Miller, and Donald E. Stokes. 1960. *The American Voter*. New York: Wiley.

Carroll, Susan. 1984. "Women candidates and support for feminist concerns: the closet feminist syndrome." *Western Political Quarterly* 37/2, pp. 307–23.

2001. "Representing women: women state legislators as agents of policy-related change." In Susan Carroll (ed.), *The Impact of Women in Public Office*. Bloomington and Indianapolis: Indiana University Press, pp. 3–21.

Caul, Miki. 1999. "Women's representation in parliament. The role of political parties." *Party Politics* 5/1, pp. 79–98.

Celis, Karen. 2006. "Substantive representation of women: the representation of women's interests and the impact of descriptive representation in the Belgian Parliament (1900–1979)." *Journal of Women, Politics and Policy* 28/2, pp. 85–114.

Celis, Karen, Sara Childs, Johanna Kantola, and Mona Lena Krook. 2008. "Rethinking women's substantive representation." *Representation: Special Issue on the Substantive Representation of Women* 44/2.

Center for the American Woman and Politics (CAWP). 2000. "Gender Gap in the 2000 elections." Eagleton Institute of Politics, Rutgers University. www.cawp.rutgers.edu/Facts/Elections/gg2000.html, accessed October 31, 2007.

2004. "Gender gap in the 2004 Presidential race is widespread." Eagleton Institute of Politics, Rutgers University. www.cawp.rutgers.edu/Facts5.html, accessed October 31, 2007.

Chabal, Patrick, and Jean Pascal Daloz. 2006. *Culture Troubles: Politics and the Interpretation of Meaning*. Chicago: University of Chicago Press.

Chafetz, Janet Saltzman, and Anthony Gary Dworkin. 1986. *Female Revolt: Women's Movements in World and Historical Perspective*. Totowa, New Jersey: Rowman & Allanheld.

1989. "Action and reaction: an integrated, comparative perspective on feminist and antifeminist movements." In Melvin Kohn (ed.), *Cross-National Research in Sociology*. Newbury Park, CA: Sage.

Chappell, Louise A. 2002. *Gendering Government: Feminist Engagement with the State in Australia and Canada*. Vancouver: UBC Press.

2006. "Comparing political institutions: revealing the gendered 'logic of appropriateness.'" *Politics & Gender* 2 (2 June): 223–34.

2008. "Governing international law through the International Criminal Court: a new site for gender justice?" In Rai and Waylen, *Global Governance: Feminist Perspectives*. Basingstoke: Palgrave, pp. 160–84.

Charlesworth, H. 2005. "Not waving but drowning: gender mainstreaming and human rights in the United Nations." *Harvard Human Rights Journal* 18 (Spring), pp. 1–18.

Childs, Sarah. 2001. "In their own words: New Labour women and the substantive representation of women." *British Journal of Politics and International Relations* 3/2, pp. 173–90.

2004. *New Labour's Women MPs*. London and New York: Routledge.

Childs, Sarah, and Mona Lena Krook. 2005. *The Substantive Representation of Women: Rethinking the Critical Mass Debate*. Paper presented at the 2005 APSA Annual Meeting, Washington.

2006. "Gender and politics: the state of the art." *Politics* 26/1, pp. 18–28.

Chodorow, Nancy. 1978. *The Reproduction of Mothering: Psycho-analysis and the Sociology of Gender.* Berkeley: University of California Press.

Christensen, Ann-Doret, and Nina C. Raaum. 1999. "Models of political mobilization." In Bergqvist *et al., Equal Democracies,* pp. 17–26.

Cingranelli, David L., and David L. Richards. 2007. The Cingranelli-Richards (CIRI) Human Rights Dataset. www.humanrightsdata.org.

Clark, Anne Marie, Elisabeth Friedman, and Kathryn Hochstetler. 1998. "The sovereign limits of global civil society: a comparison of NGO participation in UN world conferences on the environment, human rights and women." *World Politics* 51/1, pp. 1–35.

Clavero, Sara, and Yvonne Gilligan. 2007. "Women's substantive representation in the multi-level Euro polity: towards a framework for analysis." Paper presented at the ECPR joint sessions, Helsinki, May 2007.

Cockburn, Cynthia. 1991. *In the Way of Women: Men's Resistance to Sex Equality in Organizations.* Ithaca: ILR Press.

Collier, David, and Robert Adcock. 1999. "Democracy and dichotomies: a pragmatic approach to choices about concepts." *Annual Review of Political Science* 2, pp. 537–65.

Collier, David, Henry E. Brady, and Jason Seawright. 2004. "Critiques, responses, and trade-offs: drawing together the debate." In Brady and Collier, *Rethinking Social Inquiry,* pp. 195–227.

Collier, David, and Steven Levitsky. 1997. "Democracy with adjectives: conceptual innovation in comparative research." *World Politics* 49 (April), pp. 430–51.

Collier, David, and James E. Mahon, Jr. 1993. "'Conceptual stretching' revisited: adapting categories in comparative analysis." *American Political Science Review* 87/4 (December), pp. 845–55.

Collins, Patricia Hill. 1990. *Black Feminist Thought: Knowledge, Consciousness, and the Politics of Empowerment.* Boston: Unwin Hyman.

1994. "Shifting the center: race, class, and feminist theorizing about motherhood." In Donna Bassin, Margaret Honey, and Merle Mahrer Keplan (eds.), *Representations of Motherhood.* New Haven: Yale University Press, pp. 56–74.

1997. "Comment on Hekman's 'Truth and method: feminist standpoint theory revisited': Where's the power?" *Signs* 22, pp. 375–9.

1998. "Its all in the family: intersections of gender, race and nation." *Hypatia* 13, pp. 62–82.

Connell, R. W. 1995. *Masculinities.* Berkeley: University of California Press.

2002. *Gender.* Cambridge: Polity Press.

Connolly, Marjorie. 1996. "After the election: the numbers: portrait of the electorate," *New York Times,* November 10, 1996, Section 1, P. 28, Col. 1.

Converse, Philip E. 1964. "The nature of belief systems in mass publics." In David E. Apter, ed., *Ideology and Discontent.* London: Free Press of Glencoe, pp. 206–61.

Copi, Irving M., and Carl Cohen. 1990. *Introduction to Logic.* London: Macmillan.

Costain, Ann. 1992. *Inviting Women's Rebellion: A Political Process Interpretation of the Women's Movement.* Baltimore: Johns Hopkins University Press.

Coward, Rosalind. 1983. *Patriarchal Precedents: Sexuality and Social Relations.* London: Routledge & Kegan Paul.

Cramer Walsh, Katherine. 2002. "Female legislators and the women's rights agenda." In Cindy Simon Rosenthal (ed.), *Women Transforming Congress.* Norman: University of Oklahoma Press, pp. 370–96.

Craske, Nikki, and Maxine Molyneux (eds.). 2002. *Gender and the Politics of Rights and Democracy in Latin America.* London: Palgrave.

Crenshaw, Kimberlé. 1991. "Mapping the margins: intersectionality, identity politics and violence against women of color." *Stanford Law Review* (Special Issue: Women of Color at the Center: Selections from the Third National Conference on Women of Color and the Law), No. 6 (July), pp. 1241–99.

1993. "Demarginalizing the intersection of race and sex." In D. Kelly Weisberg (ed.), *Feminist Legal Theory*, vol. 1: *Foundations.* New York: New York University Press, pp. 383–95.

1994. "Mapping the margins." In Martha Albertson Fineman and Roxanne Mykitiuk (eds.), *The Public Nature of Private Violence.* New York: Routledge, pp. 93–118.

Crompton, Rosemary (ed.). 1999. *Restructuring Gender Relations and Employment: The Decline of the Male Breadwinner.* Oxford: Oxford University Press.

2006. *Employment and the Family: The Reconfiguration of Work and Family Life in Contemporary Societies.* Cambridge: Cambridge University Press.

Dahl, Robert A. 1956. *A Preface to Democratic Theory.* Chicago: University of Chicago Press.

1971. *Polyarchy: Participation and Opposition.* New Haven: Yale University Press.

1989. *Democracy and Its Critics.* New Haven: Yale University Press.

1998. *On Democracy.* New Haven: Yale University Press.

Dahlerup, Drude. 1986a. "Introduction." In Dahlerup, *The New Women's Movement*, pp. 1–26.

Dahlerup, Drude (ed.). 1986b. *The New Women's Movement.* Bristol: Sage.

1988. "From a small to a large minority: women in Scandinavian politics." *Scandinavian Political Studies* 11/4, pp. 275–98.

1993. "From movement protest to state feminism: the women's movement and unemployment policy in Denmark." *NORA: Nordic Journal of Women's Studies* 1, pp. 4–21.

2006. *Women, Quotas and Politics.* London and New York: Routledge.

Daly, Mary. 2000. *The Gender Division of Welfare.* Cambridge: Cambridge University Press.

Daly, Mary, and Jane Lewis. 2000. "The concept of social care and the analysis of contemporary welfare states." *British Journal of Sociology* 51/2, pp. 281–98.

Daly, Mary, and Katherine Rake. 2003. *Gender and the Welfare State.* Cambridge: Polity Press.

Dawson, Michael C. 2001. *Black Visions: The Roots of Contemporary African-American Political Ideologies.* Chicago: University of Chicago Press.

di Pizan, Christine. 1999. *The Treasure of the City of the Ladies.* London: Penguin.

Diamond, Irene, and Nancy Hartsock. 1981. "Beyond interests in politics: a comment on Virginia Sapiro's "When are interests interesting? The problem of political representation of women." *American Political Science Review* 75/3, pp. 717–21.

Diamond, Larry J., Juan J. Linz, and Seymour M. Lipset (eds.). 1988. *Democracy in Developing Countries.* Boulder: Lynne Rienner.

(eds.). 1990. *Politics in Developing Countries: Comparing Experiences with Democracy.* Boulder: Lynne Rienner.

Diani, Mario. 1992. "The concept of social movement." *Sociological Review* 40 (February), pp. 1–25.

Diaz, Mercedes Mateo. 2005. *Representing Women? Female Legislators in West European Parliaments.* Oxford: Oxford University Press.

DiStefano, Christine. 1983. "Masculinity as ideology in political theory: Hobbesian man reconsidered." *Women's Studies International Forum* 6 (1983), pp. 633–44.

1991. *Configurations of Masculinity*. Ithaca: Cornell University Press.

2006. Personal conversation. August 30. Philadelphia.

Dobrowolsky, Alexandra, and Vivien Hart (eds.). 2003. *Women Making Constitutions: New Politics and Comparative Perspectives*. Basingstoke: Palgrave.

Dodson, Debra. 2006. *The Impact of Women on Congress*. New York: Oxford University Press.

Dodson, Debra, *et al.* 1995. *Voices, Views, Votes: the Impact of Women in the 103rd Congress*. New Jersey: Rutgers.

Dolan, Julie. 1997. "Support for women's interests in the 103rd Congress: the distinct impact of congressional women." *Women & Politics* 18/4, pp. 81–94.

Donovan, Cynthia. 2007. "Gender and governance." In Mark Bevir (ed.), *Encyclopedia of Governance*. Thousand Oaks, CA: Sage, pp. 545–51.

Dovi, Suzanne. 2002. "Preferable descriptive representatives: will just any woman, black, or Latino do?" *American Political Science Review* 96/4, pp. 729–43.

2007. *The Good Representative*. Oxford: Blackwell.

Duerst-Lahti, Georgia. 2002a. "Knowing Congress as a gendered institution: manliness and the implications of women in Congress." In Cindy Simon Rosenthal (ed.), *Women Transforming Congress*. Norman, OK: University of Oklahoma Press.

2002b. "Governing institutions, ideologies, and gender: toward the possibility of equal political representation." *Sex Roles* 47/7–8 (October), pp. 371–88.

2006. "Presidential elections as gendered space". In Sue Carroll and Richard Fox (eds.), *Gender and the 2004 Election*. Cambridge: Cambridge University Press.

Duerst-Lahti, Georgia, and Rita Mae Kelly (eds.). 1995. *Gender Power, Leadership, and Governance*. Ann Arbor: University of Michigan Press.

Duncan, Simon. 1995. "Theorizing European gender systems." *Journal of European Social Policy* 5/4, pp. 263–84.

1996. "The diverse worlds of European patriarchy." In Maria Dolors Garcia-Ramon and Janice Monk (eds.), *Women of the European Union: The Politics of Work and Daily Life*. New York: Routledge, pp. 74–110.

Durose, Catherine and Francesca Gains. 2007. "Engendering the machinery of governance." In Claire Annesley, Francesca Gains and Kirstein Rummery (eds.), *Women and New Labour*. Bristol: Policy Press, pp. 93–115.

Dwyer, Daisy, and Judith Bruce (eds.). 1988. *A Home Divided: Women and Income in the Third World*. Stanford: Stanford University Press.

Eagly, Alice H. 1987. *Sex Differences in Social Behavior: A Social Role Interpretation*. Hillsdale: Lawrence Erlbaum Associates.

Easterly, William. 2006. *The White Man's Burden: Why the West's Efforts to Aid the Rest Have Done So Much Ill and So Little Good*. New York: Penguin.

Ehlers, Tracy Bachrach. 1991. "Debunking marianismo: economic vulnerability and survival strategies among Guatemalan wives." *Ethnology* 30/1, pp. 1–16.

Eisenstein, Hester. 1990. "Femocrats, official feminism and the uses of power." In Sophie Watson (ed.), *Playing the State: Australian Feminist Interventions*. London: Verso, pp. 87–103.

1996. *Inside Agitators: Australian Femocrats and the State*. Philadelphia: Temple University Press.

Eisenstein, Zillah. 2001. *Manmade Breast Cancers*. Ithaca: Cornell University Press.

Elman, R. Amy. 1996. *Sexual Subordination and State Intervention: Comparing Sweden and the United States*. Providence and Oxford: Berghahn Books.

2003. "Refuge in reconfigured states: shelter movements in the United States, Britain and Sweden." In Banaszak, Beckwith, and Rucht, *Women's Movements facing the Reconfigured State*, pp. 94–113.

Elshtain, Jean Behtke. 1981. *Public Man, Private Woman*. Princeton: Princeton University Press.

Elson, Diane. 1995. "Male bias in macro economics: the case of structural adjustment." In Diane Elson (ed.), *Male Bias in the Development Process*. Manchester: Manchester University Press.

Epstein, Julia, and Kristina Straub. 1995. *Body Guards: The Cultural Politics of Gender Ambiguity*. New York: Routledge.

Eschle, Catherine, 2001. *Global Democracy, Social Movements, and Feminism*. Boulder: Westview Press.

Eschle, Catherine, and Bice Maiguashca (eds.). 2005. *Critical Theories, International Relations, and "The Anti-Globalisation Movement.": The Politics of Global Resistance*. London: Routledge.

Esping-Andersen, Gøsta. 1985. *Politics Against Markets*. Princeton: Princeton University Press.

1990. *The Three Worlds of Welfare Capitalism*. Cambridge: Polity Press.

(ed.). 1993. *Changing Classes: Stratification in Postindustrial Societies*. London: Sage.

(ed.). 1996. *Welfare States in Transition: National Adaptations in Global Economies*. London: Sage.

1999. *Social Foundations of Postindustrial Economies*. Oxford: Oxford University Press.

Esping-Andersen, Gøsta, and Walter Korpi. 1987. "From poor relief to institutional welfare states: the development of Scandinavian social policy." In Robert Erikson, Erik Jørgen Hansen, Stein Ringen and Hannu Uusitalo (eds.), *The Scandinavian Model*. Armonk, NY: M. E. Sharpe, pp. 39–74.

Esteva, Gustavo. 1985. "Development: metaphor, myth, threat," *Development: Seeds of Change* 8, p. 78.

Eulau, Heinz. 1967. "Changing views of representation." In Ithiel de Sola Pool (ed.), *Contemporary Political Science: Toward Empirical Theory*. New York: McGraw-Hill, pp. 53–85.

Eulau, Heinz. *et al*. 1978. "The role of the representative: some empirical observations on the theory of Edmund Burke." In Heinz Eulau and John C. Wahlke (eds.), *The Politics of Representation. Continuities in Theory and Research*. Beverly Hills: Sage, pp. 111–26.

Farrell, David. 2006. "Inclusiveness of electoral systems." Paper presented at the seminar Inclusive Politics, Radboud University, Nijmegen, May 29.

Fausto-Sterling, Anne. 2000. *Sexing the Body: Gender Politics and the Construction of Sexuality*. New York: Basic Books.

Fenno, Richard E. 1978. *Home Style: House Members in Their Districts*. Boston: Little, Brown.

Ferber, Abby, 1998. "Deconstructing whiteness: the intersections of race and gender in white supremacist thought." *Ethnic and Racial Studies* 21, pp. 48–62.

Ferguson, Kathy E. 1984. *The Feminist Case against Bureaucracy*. Philadelphia: Temple University Press.

1993. *The Man Question: Visions of Subjectivity in Feminist Theory*. Berkeley: University of California Press.

Ferree, Myra Marx. 1991–2. "Institutionalizing gender equality: feminist politics and equality offices." *German Politics and Society*. 24–5 (Winter), pp. 53–66.

2006. "Globalization and feminism: opportunities and obstacles for activism in the global arena." In Ferree and Tripp, *Global Feminism*, pp. 3–23.

Ferree, Myra Marx, and Beth B. Hess. 1985. *Controversy and Coalition: The New Feminist Movement*. Boston: Twayne Publishers.

Ferree, Myra Marx, and Carol Mueller. 2004. "Feminism and the women's movement: a global perspective." In David A. Snow, Sarah A. Soule, and Hanspeter Kriesi (eds.), *The Blackwell Companion to Social Movements*. Oxford: Blackwell, pp. 576–607.

Ferree, Myra Marx, and Aili Mari Tripp (eds.). 2006. *Global Feminism: Transnational Women's Activism, Organizing, and Human Rights*. New York: New York University Press.

Finkel, Steven E., Anibal S. Pérez Liñan, and Mitchell A. Seligson. 2007. "The effects of US foreign assistance on democracy building 1990–2003," *World Politics* 59/3, pp. 404–40.

Flinders, Matthew. 2002. "Governance in Whitehall." *Public Administration* 80/1, pp. 51–75.

Flora, Peter (ed.). 1986. *Growth to Limits*, vols. I, II, IV. Berlin: Walter de Gruyter.

Flora, Peter, and Arnold Heidenheimer (eds.). 1981. *The Development of Welfare States in Europe and America*. New Brunswick: Transaction Publishers.

Fogg-Davis, Hawley. 2006. "Theorizing black lesbians within black feminism: a critique of same race street harassment." *Politics & Gender* 2, pp. 57–76.

Foucault, Michel. 1979. *Discipline and Punish: The Birth of the Prison*. New York: Vintage Books.

Franceschet, Susan. 2003. "'State feminism' and women's movements: the impact of Chile's Servicio Nacional de la Mujer on women's activism." *Latin American Research Review* 38/1, pp. 9–41.

2005. *Women and Politics in Chile*. Boulder: Lynne Rienner.

Franceschet, Susan, and Mona Lena Krook. 2005. "State Feminism and Gender Quotas in the 'North' and 'South': Comparative Lessons from Western Europe and Latin America." Paper presented at the International Studies Association Annual Meetings, March 22–5, 2005, San Diego.

Franzway, Suzanne, Dianne Court, and R. W. Connell (1989). *Staking a Claim: Feminism, Bureaucracy and the State*. Sydney: Allen & Unwin.

Fraser, Nancy. 1989. "Struggle over needs: outline of a socialist-feminist critical theory of late capitalist political culture." In Nancy Fraser (ed.), *Unruly Practices: Power, Discourse and Gender in Contemporary Social Theory*. Cambridge: Cambridge University Press.

Fraser, Nancy, and Axel Honneth. 2003. *Redistribution or Recognition? A Political-Philosophical Exchange*. London: Verso.

Frederickson. George. "Reflections on the comparative history and sociology of racism." In Leonard Harris (ed.), *Racism*. Amherst: Humanity Books.

Freedom House. 2007. www.freedomhouse.org (map from 2006).

Freeman, Jo. 1995. "From seeds to harvest: transformations of feminist organizations and scholarship." In Myra Marx Ferree and Patricia Yancey Martin (eds.), *Feminist Organizations: Harvest of the New Women's Movement*. Philadelphia: Temple University Press.

Friedman, Elisabeth Jay. 2003. "Gendering the agenda: the impact of transnational women's rights movements at the UN conferences of the 1990s." *Women's Studies International Forum* 26/3, pp. 1007–39.

Frohmann, Alicia, and Teresa Valdés. 1995. "Democracy in the country and in the home: the women's movement in Chile." In Amrit Basu (ed.), *The Challenge of Local Feminisms: Women's Movements in Global Perspectives*. Boulder: Westview Press, pp. 302–23.

Funk and Wagnalls, 1997. *Funk and Wagnalls' New International Dictionary of the English Language*, Comprehensive Edition. Chicago: Ferguson Publishing Co.

Furniss, Norman, and Timothy Tilton. 1977. *The Case for the Welfare State*. Bloomington: Indiana University Press.

Gal, Susan, and Gail Kligman (eds.). 2000. *The Politics of Gender After Socialism: A Comparative Historical Study*. Princeton: Princeton University Press.

Galey, Margaret E. 1995. "Forerunners in women's quest for partnership." In Anne Winslow (ed.), *Women, Politics, and the United Nations*. Westport: Greenwood Press, pp. 1–10.

Galligan, Yvonne, Sara Clavero, and Marina Calloni. 2007. *Gender Politics and Democracy in Post-Communist Europe*. Leverkusen: Barbara Budrich Publishers.

Gamson, William A. 1975. *The Strategy of Social Protest*. Homewood, IL: Dorsey Press.

Gardiner, Frances (ed.). 1997. *Sex Equality Policy in Western Europe*. London: Routledge.

Gasiorowski, Mark J. (1996). "An overview of the political regime change dataset." *Comparative Political Studies*, 29/4, pp. 469–83.

Gastil, Raymond D. 1978. *Freedom in the World: Political Rights and Civil Liberties 1978*. Boston: G. K. Hall.

Gauthier, Anne Hélène. 1996. *The State and the Family: A Comparative Analysis of Family Policies in Industrialized Countries*. Oxford: Clarendon Press.

Geertz, Clifford. 1973. "Ideology as a Cultural System." In *The Interpretation of Cultures*. New York: Basic Books, pp. 193–233.

Gelb, Joyce. 2003. *Gender Policies in Japan and the United States: Comparing Women's Movements, Rights and Politics*. New York: Palgrave Macmillan.

George, Susan. 2004. *Another World is Possible if . . .* London: Verso.

Gerring, John. 1997. "Ideology: a definitional analysis." *Political Research Quarterly* 50/4, pp. 957–94.

Giddens, Anthony. 1982. "Action, structure, power." In *Profiles and Critiques in Social Theory*, Berkeley: University of California Press.

Gill, Stephen. 1995, "Globalization, market civilization and disciplinary neoliberalism." *Millennium* 23/3, pp. 399–423.

Gilligan, Carol. 1982. *In a Different Voice. Psychological Theory and Women's Development*. Cambridge, MA: Harvard University Press.

Girvetz, Harry K. 1968. "Welfare state", in David L. Sills (ed.), *International Encyclopedia of the Social Sciences*, vol. XVI. New York: Macmillan and Free Press, pp. 512–21.

Giugni, Marco. 1995. "Outcomes of new social movements." In Kriesi *et al.* (eds.), *New Social Movements in Western Europe*, pp. 207–37.

Giugni, Marco, Doug McAdam, and Charles Tilly. (eds.). 1999. *How Social Movements Matter*. Minneapolis: University of Minnesota Press.

Goertz, Gary. 2005. *Social Science Concepts: A User's Guide*. Princeton: Princeton University Press.

Goetz, Anne Marie (ed.). 1997. *Getting Institutions Right for Women in Development*. London: Zed.

2007. "Political cleaners: women as the new anti-corruption force?" *Development and Change* 38/1, pp. 87–105.

Goldstein, Joshua. 2001. *War and Gender: How Gender Shapes the War System and Vice Versa*. Cambridge: Cambridge University Press.

Gornick, Janet, and Marcia Meyers. 2003. *Families that Work*. New York: Russell Sage Foundation.

Gornick, Janet C., Marcia K. Meyers, and Katherin E. Ross. 1997. "Supporting the employment of mothers: policy variation across fourteen welfare states." *Journal of European Social Policy* 7, pp. 45–70.

Grey, Sandra. 2002. "Does size matter? Critical mass and New Zealand's women MPs." *Parliamentary Affairs* 55/1, pp. 19–29.

2006. "Out of sight, out of mind: the New Zealand women's movement in abeyance." Paper presented at the IPSA World Congress, Fukuoka, Japan, July 9–13.

Griffiths, A. Phillips. 1960. "How can one person represent another?" *Aristotelian Society* supplementary volume 34, pp. 187–208.

Guinier, Lani. 1994. *The Tyranny of the Majority: Fundamental Fairness in Representative Democracy*. New York: Free Press.

Gunther-Canada, Wendy. 2001. *Rebel Writer: Mary Wollstonecraft and Enlightenment Politics*. DeKalb, IL: Northern Illinois University.

Gustafsson, Siv. 1994. "Childcare and types of welfare states." In Sainsbury, *Gendering Welfare States*, pp. 45–61.

Hafner-Burton, Emilie, and Mark A. Pollack. 2002. "Mainstreaming gender in global governance." *European Journal of International Relations* 8/3, pp. 339–73.

Halberstam, Judith. 1998. *Female Masculinity*. Durham, NC: Duke University Press.

Hamilton, Malcolm B. 1987. "The elements of the concept of ideology." *Political Studies* 35, pp. 18–38.

Hancock, Ange-Marie. 2007a. "When mulitiplication doesn't equal quick addition: examining intersectionality as a research paradigm." *Perspectives on Politics* 5 (March 1), pp. 63–80.

2007b. "Intersectionality as a normative and empirical paradigm." *Politics & Gender* 3/2, pp. 248–53.

Hantrais, Linda. 1999. *Gendered Policies in Europe: Reconciling Employment and Family Life*. New York: St. Martin's Press.

Harding, Sandra. 1986. "The instability of the analytical categories of feminist theory." *Signs* 11/4, pp. 645–64.

Harris, Angela P. 1990. "Race and essentialism in feminist legal theory." *Stanford Law Review* 42 (February), pp. 581–616.

Hartmann, Heidi I. 1979a. "Capitalism, patriarchy and job segregation by sex." In Zillah Eisenstein, (ed.), *Capitalist Patriarchy and the Case for Socialist Feminism*. New York: Monthly Review Press.

1979b. "The unhappy marriage of Marxism and feminism: towards a more progressive union." *Capital and Class* 8 (Summer), pp. 1–33.

1994. "The family as the locus of gender, class and political struggle: the example of housework." In Anne C. Hermann and Abigail J. Stewart (eds.), *Theorizing Feminism: Parallel Trends in the Humanities and Social Sciences*, Boulder: Westview Press, pp. 171–97.

Hartsock, Nancy C. M. 1983. *Money, Sex, and Power*. Boston: Northeastern University Press.

Hatem, Mervat F. 1992. "Economic and political liberation in Egypt and the demise of state feminism." *International Journal of Middle East Studies.* 24, pp. 231–51.

1994. "The paradoxes of state feminism in Egypt." In Nelson and Chowdhury (eds.). *Women and Politics Worldwide,* pp. 226–42.

Haussman, Melissa, and Birgit Sauer (eds.). 2007. *Gendering the State in the Age of Globalization: Women's Movements and State Feminism in Post Industrial Democracies.* New York: Rowman & Littlefield.

Hawkesworth, Mary. 1997. "Confounding gender." *Signs* 22/3, pp. 649–85.

2005. "Engendering political science: an immodest proposal." *Politics & Gender* 1 (1 March), pp. 141–56.

2006. *Feminist Inquiry: From Political Conviction to Methodological Innovation.* New Brunswick: Rutgers University Press.

Hearn, Jeff. 1992. *Men in the Public Eye.* London: Routledge.

Heclo, Hugh. 1974. *Modern Social Politics in Britain and Sweden.* New Haven: Yale University Press.

Heidenheimer, Arnold. 1973. "The politics of public education, health and welfare in the USA and western Europe: how growth and reform potential have differed." *British Journal of Political Science* 3, pp. 313–42.

Heilbroner, Robert. 1989. "Reflections: the triumph of capitalism." *The New Yorker* (January 23).

Hernes, Helga. 1987. *Welfare State and Woman Power: Essays in State Feminism.* Oslo: Norwegian University Press.

Hirst, Paul. 1990. *Representative Democracy and Its Limits.* Cambridge: Polity Press.

Hobson, Barbara. 1994. "Solo mothers, social policy regimes, and the logics of gender." In Sainsbury, *Gendering Welfare States,* pp. 170–86.

Hobson, Barbara, Jane Lewis, and Birte Siim. 2002. *Contested Concepts in Gender and Social Politics.* Cheltenham: Edward Elgar.

Hobson, Barbara, and Marika Lindholm. 1997. "Collective identities, women's power resources and the making of welfare states." *Theory and Society* 26, pp. 475–508.

Hobson, Barbara, and Mieko Takahashi. 1996. "Care regimes, solo mothers and the recasting of social citizenship rights." Engendering Citizenship, Work and Care, Seminar 1 of the EC Program "Gender and Citizenship: Social Integration and Social Exclusion in European Welfare States." Netherlands Institute for Advanced Studies, Wassenaar, The Netherlands (July).

Holliday, Ian. 2000, "Is the British state hollowing out?" *Political Quarterly* 71/2 pp. 167–77.

hooks, bell. 1981. *Ain't I a Woman? Black Women and Feminism.* Boston: South End Press.

2000. *Feminist Theory: From Margin to Center.* Boston: South End Press.

Hoskyns, Catherine 2008. "Governing the European Union: gender and macroeconomics." In Rai and Waylen (eds.), *Global Governance,* pp. 107–28.

Hoskyns, Catherine, and Shirin Rai. 2007. "Recasting the global political economy: counting women's unpaid work." *New Political Economy* 12/3 pp. 297–317.

Howell, Jude, and Diane Mulligan (eds.). 2005. *Gender and Civil Society: Transcending Boundaries.* London and New York: Routledge.

Htun, Mala. 2002. *Sex and the State: Abortion, Divorce, and the Family Under Latin American Dictatorships and Democracies.* Cambridge: Cambridge University Press.

2005. "What it means to study gender and the state." *Politics & Gender* 1, pp. 157–65.

Htun, Mala, and Mark Jones. 2002. "Engendering the right to participate in decision-making: electoral quotas and women's leadership in Latin America." In Craske and Molyneux, *Gender and the Politics of Rights and Democracy in Latin America*, pp. 432–56.

Huber, Evelyne, and John D. Stephens. 2001. *Development and Crisis of the Welfare State.* Chicago: University of Chicago Press.

Humana, Charles. 1992. *World Human Rights Guide.* 3rd edn. Washington, DC: Oxford University Press.

Huntington, Samuel. 1991. *The Third Wave: Democratization in the Late 20th Century* Norman: University of Oklahoma Press.

Hurtado, Aida. 1989. "Relating to privilege: seduction and rejection in the subordination of white women and women of color." *Signs* 14, pp. 833–55.

Inglehart, Ronald, and Pippa Norris. *Rising Tide: Gender Equality and Cultural Change Around the World.* New York: Cambridge University Press.

Jaggar, Alison M., and Susan R. Bordo (eds). 1989. *Gender/Body/Knowledge: Feminist Reconstructions of Being and Knowing.* New Brunswick: Rutgers University Press.

Jaggers, Keith, and Ted Robert Gurr. 1995. "Tracking democracy's third wave with the Polity III data." *Journal of Peace Research* 32, pp. 469–82.

Jahan, Rounaq. 1995. *Women and Development: The Elusive Agenda.* London: Zed.

Jaquette, Jane. 1990. "Gender and justice in economic development." In Tinker, *Persistent Inequalities* pp. 70–82.

Jaquette, Jane, and Kathleen Staudt. 1985. "Women as 'at risk' reproducers: biology, science, and population in US foreign policy." In Virginia Sapiro, ed., *Women, Biology and Public Policy*, Beverly Hills: Sage, pp. 235–68.

Jaquette, Jane, and Kathleen Staudt. 2006. "Women, gender and development." In Jaquette and Summerfield, *Women and Gender Equity*, pp. 17–52.

Jaquette, Jane, and Gale Summerfield (eds.). 2006. *Women and Gender Equity in Development Theory and Practice.* Durham, NC: Duke University Press.

Jayawardena, Kumari. 1986. *Feminism and Nationalism in the Third World.* London: Zed.

Jenson, Jane. 1996. "Representations of difference: the varieties of French feminism." In Threlfall, *Mapping the Women's Movement: Feminist Politics and Social Transformation in the North*, pp. 73–114.

1997. "Who cares? Gender and welfare regimes." *Social Politics* 4/2, pp. 182–7.

Jenson, Jane, and Mariette Sineau. 2001. *Who Cares? Women's Work, Childcare, and Welfare State Redesign.* Toronto: Toronto University Press.

Johnson, Cathy Marie, Georgia Duerst-Lahti, and Noelle Norton. 2007. *Creating Gender: The Sexual Politics of Welfare Policy.* Boulder: Lynne Rienner.

Jónasdóttir, Anna G. 1988. "On the concept of interests, women's interests and the limitation of interest theory." In K. B. Jones and A. G. Jónasdóttir (eds.), *The Political Interests of Gender.* London: Sage.

Judge, David. 1999. *Representation: Theory and Practice in Britain.* London and New York: Routledge.

Junn, Jane. 2007. "Square pegs and round holes: challenges of fitting individual-level analysis to a theory of politicized context of gender." *Politics & Gender* 3 (March 1), pp. 124–34.

Kann, Mark E. 1991. *On the Man Question: Gender and Civic Virtue in America*. Philadelphia: Temple University Press.

1998. *A Republic of Men: The American Founders, Gendered Language, and Patriarchal Politics*. New York: New York University Press.

1999. *The Gendering of American Politics: Founding Mothers, Founding Fathers, and Political Patriarchy*. Westport: Praeger.

Kanter, Rosabeth M. 1977. "Some effects of proportions on group life: skewed sex ratios and responses to token women." *American Journal of Sociology* 82/5, pp. 965–91.

Kantola, J. 2006. *Feminists Theorize the State*. Basingstoke: Palgrave.

Kaplan, Gisela. 1992. *Contemporary Western European Feminism*. London: Allen & Unwin.

Karam, Azza (ed.). 1998. *Women in Parliament: Beyond Numbers*. Stockholm: IDEA.

Katzenstein, Mary Fainsod. 1995. "Discursive politics and feminist activism in the Catholic Church." In Myra Marx Ferree and Patricia Yancey Martin (eds.), *Feminist Organizations*. Philadelphia: Temple University Press, pp. 35–52.

1998a. *Faithful and Fearless: Moving Feminist Protest Inside the Church and Military*. Princeton: Princeton University Press.

1998b. "Stepsisters: feminist movement activism in different institutional spaces." In David S. Meyer and Sidney Tarrow (eds.), *The Social Movement Society: Contentious Politics for a New Century*. Boulder: Rowman & Littlefield, pp. 195–216.

Katzenstein, Mary Fainsod, and Catherine Mueller (eds.). 1987. *The Women's Movements of the United States and Western Europe*. Philadelphia: Temple University Press.

Keck, Margaret E., and Kathryn Sikkink (eds.). 1998. *Activists Beyond Borders: Advocacy Networks in International Politics*. Ithaca: Cornell University Press.

Kelber, Mim. 1994. *Women and Government: New Ways to Political Power*. Westport, CT: Praeger.

Keohane, Nannerl O. 1976. "Philosophy, theory, ideology: an attempt at clarification." *Political Theory* 4, pp. 80–100.

Kerber, Linda K. 1980. *Women of the Republic: Intellect and Ideology in Revolutionary America*. Chapel Hill: University of North Carolina Press.

Kettl, Donald F. 1993. "Public administration: the state of the field." In Ada Finifter (ed.), *Political Science: The State of the Discipline*. Washington, DC: American Political Science Association, pp. 176–91.

Kilkey, Majella, and Jonathan Bradshaw. 1999. "Lone mothers, economic well-being and policies." in Sainsbury, *Gender and Welfare State Regimes*, pp. 147–84.

King, Gary, Robert Keohane, and Sidney Verba. 1994. *Designing Social Inquiry: Scientific Inference in Qualitative Research*. Princeton: Princeton University Press.

Kjaer, Anne Mette, 2004. *Governance*. Cambridge: Polity Press.

Knijn, Trudie, and Kremer, Maria. 1997. "Gender and the caring dimension of welfare states: towards inclusive citizenship." *Social Politics* 4, pp. 328–61.

Kooiman, Jan (ed.). 1993. *Modern Governance: New Government–Society Interactions*. Thousand Oaks, CA: Sage.

Korpi, Walter. 1980. "Social policy and distributional conflicts in the capitalist democracies." *West European Politics* 3, pp. 296–316.

1989. "Power, politics and state autonomy in the development of social citizenship." *American Sociological Review* 54, pp. 309–28.

2000. "Faces of inequality: gender, class and patterns of inequalities in different welfare states." *Social Politics* 7, pp. 127–91.

Koven, Seth, and Sonya Michel (eds.). 1993. *Mothers of a New World: Maternalist Politics and the Origins of Welfare States.* New York: Routledge.

Kriesi, Hanspieter, Ruud Koopmans, Jan Willem Duyvendak, and Marco G. Giugni (eds.). 1995. *New Social Movements in Western Europe: A Comparative Analysis.* Minneapolis: University of Minnesota Press.

Krook, Mona Lena. 2004. "Gender quotas as a global phenomenon: actors and strategies in quota adoption." *European Political Science* 3/3, pp. 59–65.

2005. "Quota laws for women in politics: a new type of state feminism?" Paper presented at the European Consortium for Political Research. Granada, Spain.

Kroska, Amy. 2000. "Conceptualizing and measuring gender ideology as an identity." *Gender & Society* 14/3 (June), pp. 368–94.

Kumar, Radha. 1995. "From Chipko to Sati: The Contemporary Indian Women's Movement." In Basu, *The Challenge of Local Feminisms*, pp. 58–86.

Lakoff, G. 1987. *Women, Fire and Dangerous Things: What Categories Reveal about the Mind.* Chicago: University of Chicago Press.

Lane, Robert. 1962. *Political Ideology: Why the American Common Man Believes What He Does.* New York: Free Press.

Lasswell, Harold. 1936. *Politics: Who Gets What, When, How.* New York: McGraw Hill.

Laver, Michael, Monique Leyenaar, Kees Niemöller, and Yvonne Galligan. 1999. *Electoral Systems in Europe: A Gender Impact Assessment.* Brussels: European Commission.

Lerner, Daniel. 1958. *The Passing of Traditional Society: Modernizing the Middle East.* New York: Free Press.

Lerner, Gerda. 1986. *The Creation of Patriarchy.* New York: Oxford.

Levi-Strauss, Claude. 1969. *The Elementary Structures of Kinship.* Boston: Beacon.

Lévy, Martine. 1988. *Le féminisme d'État en France, 1965–1985: 20 ans de prise en charge institutionelle de l'égalité professionelle entre hommes et femmes.* Institut d'Études Politiques, Paris.

Lewis, Jane. 1992. "Gender and the development of welfare regimes." *Journal of European Social Policy* 2, pp. 159–73.

1997. "Gender and welfare regimes: further thoughts." *Social Politics* 4, pp. 160–77.

Lewis, Jane, and Ilona Ostner. 1991. "Gender and the evolution of European social policies." Paper presented at the CES Workshop "Emergent Supranational European Social Policy: The EC's Social Dimension in Comparative Perspective," Center for European Studies, Harvard University, November 15–17.

1994. "Gender and the evolution of European social policies." Working Paper No. 4/94, Centre of Social Policy Research, University of Bremen.

Lewis, Jane (ed.). 1993. *Women and Social Policies in Europe: Work, Family and the State.* Brookfield: Edward Elgar.

1998. *Gender, Social Care and Welfare State Restructuring in Europe.* Brookfield, USA: Ashgate.

Leyenaar, M. 1997. *How to Create a Gender Balance in Political Decision Making: A Guide to Implementing Policies for Increasing the Participation of Women in Political Decision Making.* Luxembourg: European Commission.

Liebowitz, Debra J. 2002. "Gendering (trans)national advocacy: tracking the Iollapalooza at 'home.'" *International Feminist Journal of Politics* 4/2, pp. 173–96.

Lijphart, Arend. 1977. *Democracy in Plural Societies: A Comparative Exploration.* New Haven: Yale University Press.

1984. *Democracies: Patterns of Majoritarian and Consensus Governments in Twenty-one Countries.* New Haven: Yale University Press.

Lipset, Seymour Martin. 1959. "Some social requisites of democracy: economic development and political legitimacy." *American Political Science Review* 53, pp. 69–105.

Lipton, Merle. 1988. "Capitalism and apartheid." In John Lonsdale (ed.), *South Africa in Question.* Cambridge: University of Cambridge African Studies Centre and Heinemann Educational Books, pp. 25–37.

Lister, Ruth. 1994. "'She has other duties' – women, citizenship and social security." In Sally Baldwin and Jane Falkingham (eds.), *Social Security and Social Change: New Challenges to the Beveridge Model.* New York: Harvester Wheatsheaf, pp. 111–28.

1997. *Citizenship: Feminist Perspectives.* London: Macmillan.

Lorber, Judith. 1987. "Believing is seeing: biology as ideology." *Gender & Society* 2, pp. 125–51.

Lovenduski, Joni. 1986. *Women and European Politics: Contemporary Feminism and Public Policy.* London: Wheatsheaf.

1998. "Gendering research in political science." *Annual Review of Political Science* 1, pp. 333–56.

2005a. *Feminizing Politics.* Cambridge: Polity Press.

2005b. "Introduction: state feminism and the political representation of women." In Lovenduski, *State Feminism and Political Representation,* pp. 1–19.

2005c. "One stop equality or state feminism?" Paper presented at the ECPR Meeting, Granada, Spain.

Lovenduski, Joni (ed.). 2006. *State Feminism and Political Representation.* Cambridge: Cambridge University Press.

Lovenduski, Joni, Claudie Baudino, Marila Guadagnini, Petra Meier, and Diane Sainsbury. 2006. "Conclusions: state feminism and political representation." In Lovenduski, ed., *State Feminism and Political Representation,* pp. 260–93.

Lovenduski, Joni, and Pippa Norris. 2003. "Westminster women: the politics of presence." *Political Studies* 51/1, pp. 84–102.

Low, Sidney. 1904. *The Governance of England.* London: Unwin.

Lowenstein, Karl. 1953. "The role of ideologies in political change." *International Social Science Bulletin* 5/1, pp. 51–74.

Lugones, Maria. 1994. "Purity, impurity and separation." *Signs* 19, pp. 458–79.

Lukes, Steven. 2005. *Power: A radical view.* 2nd edn. London: Palgrave Macmillan.

Lycklama à Nijeholt, Geertje, Joke Swiebel, and Virginia Vargas. 1998. "The global institutional framework: the long march to Beijing." In Lycklama à Nijeholt, Vargas, and Wieringa, *Women's Movements and Public Policy in Europe, Latin America, and the Caribbean,* pp. 25–48.

Lycklama à Nijeholt, Geertje, Virginia Vargas, and Saskia Wieringa (eds.). 1998. *Women's Movements and Public Policy in Europe, Latin America, and the Caribbean.* New York: Garland.

McAdam, Doug, John D. McCarthy, Mayer N. Zald. 1988. "Social movements." In Neil J. Smelser, ed., *Handbook of Sociology.* Newbury Park: Sage, pp. 695–737.

1996. *Comparative Perspectives on Social Movements: Political Opportunities, Mobilizing Structures, and Cultural Framings*. Cambridge: Cambridge University Press.

McBride Stetson, Dorothy. 1987. *Women's Rights in France*. Westport: Greenwood Press.

McBride Stetson, Dorothy (ed.). 2001. *Abortion Politics, Women's Movements and the Democratic State: A Comparative Study of State Feminism*. Oxford: Oxford University Press.

McBride Stetson, Dorothy, and Amy Mazur. 1995. *Comparative State Feminism*. Thousand Oaks: Sage Publications.

2006. "Building a (data) bank while crossing the bridge: RNGS strategies to integrate qualitative and quantitative methods." Submitted to *Perspectives on Politics*. Summer.

McCall, Leslie. 2000. "Gender and the New Inequality: Explaining the College/Noncollege Wage Gap." *American Sociological Review* 65, pp. 234–55.

2001. *Complex Inequality: Gender, Class, and Race in the New Economy*. New York: Routledge.

2005. "The complexity of intersectionality." *Signs* 30, pp. 1771–800.

McCammon, Holly J., and Karen E. Campbell. 2001. "Winning the vote in the West: the political successes of the women's suffrage movement, 1866–1919." *Gender & Society* 15, pp. 55–82.

McCammon, Holly J., Karen E. Campbell, Ellen M. Granberg, and Christine Mowery. 2001. "How movements win: gendered opportunity structures and US women's suffrage movements, 1866 to 1919." *American Sociological Review* 66/1, pp. 49–70.

McClosky, Herbert, Paul J. Hoffmann, and Rosemary O'Hara. 1960. "Issue conflict and consensus among party leaders and followers." *American Political Science Review* 54 (June), pp. 406–27.

McFate, Katherine, Roger Lawson, and William Julius Wilson (eds.). 1995. *Poverty, Inequality and the Future of Social Policy*. New York: Russell Sage.

Mackay, Fiona 2004. "Gender and political representation in the UK: the state of the discipline." *Journal of Politics and International Relations* 6/1: pp. 99–120.

Mackay, Fiona, Fiona Myers, and Alice Brown, 2003. "Towards a new politics? Women and the constitutional change in Scotland." In Alexandra Dobrowolsky and Vivien Hart (eds.), *Women Making Constitutions: New Politics and Comparative Perspectives*. Basingstoke: Palgrave.

MacKinnon, Catharine A. 1983. "Feminism, Marxism, method and the state: toward feminist jurisprudence." *Signs* 8, pp. 635–58.

1987. "Difference and dominance: on sex discrimination." In *Feminism Unmodified: Discourses on Life and Law*, Cambridge, MA: Harvard University Press, pp. 32–45.

1989. *Toward a Feminist Theory of the State*. Cambridge, MA: Harvard University Press.

McLean, Iain 1991. "Forms of representation and systems of voting." In David Held (ed.), *Political Theory Today*. Cambridge: Polity Press, pp. 172–96.

McLean, Iain (ed.). 1996. *The Concise Oxford Dictionary of Politics*. Oxford: Oxford University Press.

Mahoney, James, and Gary Goertz. 2006. "A tale of two cultures: contrasting quantitative and qualitative research." *Political Analysis* 14, pp. 227–49.

Mainwaring, Scott. 1993. "Presidentialism, multipartism, and democracy." *Comparative Political Studies* 26, pp. 198–228.

Mainwaring, Scott, Daniel Brinks, and Aníbal Pérez-Liñán. 2001. "Classifying political regimes in Latin America, 1945–1999." *Studies in Comparative International Development* 36, pp. 37–65.

Mansbridge, Jane. 1996. "What is the feminist movement?" In Myra Marx Ferree and Beth B. Hess (eds.), *Feminist Organizations: Harvest of the New Women's Movement*. Philadelphia: Temple University Press, pp. 27–33.

1998. *The Many Faces of Representation: working papers*. John F. Kennedy School of Government, Harvard University.

1999. "Should blacks represent blacks and women represent women? A contingent 'yes.'" *Journal of Politics* 61/3, pp. 628–57.

2003. "Rethinking representation." *American Political Science Review* 97/4, pp. 515–28.

Mansbridge, Jane, and Katherine Tate. 1992. "Race trumps gender: the Thomas nomination in the black community." *PS: Political Science and Politics* 25, pp. 488–92.

March, James G., and Johan P. Olsen. 1984. "The new institutionalism: organizational factors in political life." *American Political Science Review* 78, pp. 734–49.

1989. *The Organizational Basis of Politics*. New York: Free Press.

Margolis, Diane Rothbard. 1993. "Women's movements around the world: cross-cultural comparisons." *Gender & Society* 7/3 (September), pp. 279–99.

Marin, L. 2001. *On Representation*. Stanford: Stanford University Press.

Marshall, Monty G., Ted Robert Gurr, Christian Davenport, and Keith Jaggers. 2002. "Polity IV, 1800–1999: comments on Munck and Verkuilen." *Comparative Political Studies* 35, pp. 40–5.

Marshall, T. H. 1950. *Citizenship and Social Class*. Cambridge: Cambridge University Press.

Marx, Karl, and Frederick Engels. 1970. *The German Ideology*. New York: International Publishers.

Matland, Richard. 1995. "How the election system structure has helped women close the representation gap." In Lauri Karvonen and Per Selle (eds.), *Women in Nordic Politics: Closing the Gap*. Brookfield: Dartmouth.

Matland, Richard, and Kathleen Montgomery. 2005. *Women's Access to Political Power in Post-Communist Europe*. Oxford: Oxford University Press.

Matthews, Nancy. 1993. "Surmounting a legacy: the expansion of racial diversity in a local anti-rape movement." In Pauline B. Bart and Eileen Gail Moran (eds.), *Violence Against Women: The Bloody Footprints*. Newbury Park: Sage, pp. 177–92.

Mazur, Amy G. 1995. *Gender Bias and the State: Symbolic Reform at Work in Fifth Republic France*. Pittsburgh: University of Pittsburgh Press.

2002. *Theorizing Feminist Policy*. Oxford: Oxford University Press.

2007a. "Comparative feminist policy" In Jack Rabin (ed.), *Encyclopedia of Public Administration and Public Policy*. London: Taylor & Francis, vol. I/1, pp. 1–6.

2007b. "Women's policy agencies, women's movements and a shifting political context: toward a gendered republic in France?" In Joyce Outshoorn and Johanna Kantola (eds.), *Changing State Feminism: Women's Policy Agencies Confront Shifting Institutional Terrain*. New York: Palgrave/MacMillan, pp. 102–23.

Mazur, Amy G., and Dorothy McBride. 2006. "The RNGS dataset: women's policy agencies, women's movements and policy debates in western post industrial democracies." *French Politics* 4/2, pp. 209–236.

Mazur, Amy (ed.). 2001. *State Feminism, Women's Movements, and Job Training: Making Democracies Work in the Global Economy*. London and New York: Routledge.

Meier, Petra. 2002. "Guaranteeing Representation: Democratic Logic or Deficit? A Qualitative Comparative Analysis of Techniques Enhancing Representativeness and the Argumentation on Their Behalf in a Plural Society." Unpublished doctoral thesis, Vrije Universiteit Brussel.

Messner, Michael. 1997. *The Politics of Masculinities: Men in Movements*. Thousand Oaks: Sage.

Meyer, Birgit. 2003. "Much ado about nothing? Political representation policies and the influence of women parliamentarians in Germany." *Review of Policy Research* 20/3, pp. 401–21.

Meyer, Mary K., and Elisabeth Prugl (eds.). 1999. *Gender Politics in Global Governance*. Lanham: Rowman & Littlefield.

Miller, Carol, and Shahra Razavi (eds.). 1998. *Missionaries and Mandarins: Feminist Engagement with Development Institutions*. London: Intermediate Technologies, with UNRISD.

Minar, David W. 1961. "Ideology and political behavior." *Midwest Journal of Political Science* 5 (November), pp. 750–67.

Mink, Gwendolyn. 1990. "The lady and the tramp: gender, race and the origins of the American welfare state." In Linda Gordon (ed.), *Women, the State and Welfare*. Madison: University of Wisconsin Press, pp. 92–122.

    1995. *The Wages of Motherhood: Inequality in the Welfare State, 1917–1942*. Ithaca: Cornell University Press.

Mishra, Ramesh. 1977. *Society and Social Policy*. London: Macmillan.

Misra, Joya, and Frances Akins. 1998. "The welfare state and women: structure, agency and diversity." *Social Politics* (Fall), pp. 259–85.

Mkandawire, Thandika. 2004. "Social policy in a development context: introduction." In Thandika Mkandawire (ed.), *Social Policy in a Development Context*. Basingstoke: Palgrave, pp. 1–33.

Mohanty, Chandra Talpade. 1991. "Under western eyes: feminist scholarship and colonial discourses." In Chandra Talpade Mohanty, Lourdes M. Torres, and Ann Russo (eds.), *Third World Women and the Politics of Feminism*. Bloomington: Indiana University Press, pp. 51–80.

Molyneux, Maxine. 1985. "Mobilization without emancipation? Women's interests, the state, and revolution in Nicaragua." *Feminist Studies* 11/2 (Summer), pp. 227–54.

    1998. "Analysing women's movements." In Cecile Jackson and Ruth Pearson. (eds.), *Feminist Visions of Development*. London: Routledge, pp. 65–88.

Molyneux, Maxine, and Shahra Razavi. 2003. *Gender Justice, Development and Rights*. Oxford: Oxford University Press.

    2006. *Beijing Plus 10: An Ambivalent Record on Gender Justice*. Geneva: UNRISD Occasional Paper 15.

Moore, Barrington. 1966. *The Social Origins of Dictatorship and Democracy*. Boston: Beacon Press.

Morgan, Kimberly J. 2003. "The politics of mothers' employment: France in comparative perspective." *World Politics* 55, pp. 259–89.

    2006. *Working Mothers and the Welfare State: Religion and the Politics of Work–Family Policies in Western Europe and the United States*. Stanford: Stanford University Press.

Moser, Caroline O. N. 1993. *Gender Planning and Development: Theory, Practice and Training*. London: Routledge.

Moses, Johnathon W., and Torbjorn L. Knutsen. 2007. *Ways of Knowing: Competing Methodologies in Social and Political Research*. New York: Palgrave/Macmillan.

Mukhopadhyay, Maitrayee, and Franz Wong (eds.). 2006. *Revisiting Gender Training: The Making and Remaking of Gender Knowledge.* Amsterdam: KIT (Royal Tropical Institute).

Muller, Edward. 1988. "Democracy, economic development and income inequality." *American Sociological Review* 53 (February), pp. 50–68.

——— 1995. "Income inequality and democracy revisited: reply to Bollen and Jackman." *American Sociological Review* 60, pp. 990–6.

Mullins, Willard A. 1974. "Sartori's concept of ideology: a dissent and an alternative." In Allen R. Wilcox (ed.), *Public Opinion and Political Attitudes.* New York: Wiley, pp. 223–37.

Munck, Gerardo L., and Jay Verkuilen. 2002. "Conceptualizing and measuring democracy." *Comparative Political Studies* 35, pp. 5–34.

Murphy, Craig 1994. *International Organization and Industrial Change: Global Governance since 1850.* Cambridge: Polity Press.

——— 2002. "Global governance: poorly done and poorly understood." *International Affairs* 76/4, pp. 789–804.

Mushaben, Joyce. 2005. "Girl power, mainstreaming and critical mass: women's leadership and policy paradigm in Germany's red-green coalition, 1998–2002." *Journal of Women, Politics and Policy* 27/1–2, pp. 135–161.

Naples, Nancy A. 1998. "Toward a multiracial, feminist, social-democratic praxis: lessons from grassroots warriors in the US war on poverty." *Social Politics* (Fall), pp. 286–313.

Naples, Nancy A., and Manisah Desai (eds.). 2002. *Women's Activism and Globalization: Linking Local Struggles and Transnational Politics.* New York and London: Routledge.

Narayan, Uma. 1997a. "Cross-cultural connections, border-crossings, and "death by culture."" In Narayan, *Dislocating Cultures: Identities, Traditions, and Third World Feminism,* pp. 81–118.

——— 1997b. *Dislocating Cultures: Identities, Traditions and Third World Feminism.* New York: Routledge.

Nechemias, Carol 1994. "Democratization and women's access to legislative seats: the Soviet case, 1989–1991." *Women & Politics* 14/3, pp. 1–18.

Nelson, Barbara J. 1989. "Women and knowledge in political science: texts, histories, and epistemologies." *Women & Politics* 9/2. pp. 1–25.

Nelson, Barbara J., and Najima Chowdhury (eds.). 1994. *Women and Politics Worldwide.* New Haven: Yale University Press.

Nettl, J. P. 1967. *Political Mobilization: A Sociological Analysis of Methods and Concepts.* New York: Basic Books.

Newman, Janet. 2005a. "Introduction." In Janet Newman (ed.), *Remaking Governance: People, Politics and the Public Sphere.* Bristol: Policy Press.

——— 2005b. "Regendering governance." In Janet Newman (ed.), *Remaking Governance: People, Politics and the Public Sphere.* Bristol: Policy Press.

Nicholson, Linda. 1994. "Interpreting gender." *Signs* 20/(Autumn), pp. 79–105.

Nielsen, Ruth. 1983. *Equality Legislation in a Comparative Perspective: Towards State Feminism.* Copenhagen: Women's Research Center in Social Sciences.

Nordstrom, Carolyn. 2007. *Global Outlaws: Crime, Money, and Power in the Contemporary World.* Berkeley: University of California Press.

Norton, N. 1995. "Women, it's not enough to be elected: committee position makes a difference." In Georgia Duerst-Lahti and Rita Mae Kelly (eds.), *Gender Power, Leadership, and Governance.* Ann Arbor: University of Michigan Press, pp. 115–40.

2002. "Transforming policy from the inside: participating in committee." In C. Rosenthal (ed.), *Women Transforming Congress*. Congressional Studies Series 4. Norman: University of Oklahoma Press, pp. 316–40.

Norton, Philip. 1993. *Does Parliament Matter?* London: Harvester Wheatsheaf.

Nussbaum, Martha C. 1992. "Human functioning and social justice: in defense of Aristotelian essentialism." *Political Theory* 20/2, pp. 202–46.

1993. "Non-relative virtues: an Aristotelian approach." In Martha C. Nussbaum and Amartya Sen (eds.), *The Quality of Life*. Oxford: Oxford University Press.

Nussbaum, Martha C., and Jonathan Glover (eds.). 1995. *Women, Culture, and Development: A Study of Human Capabilities*. Oxford: Clarendon Press.

O'Brien, Robert, Anne Marie Goetz, Jan Aart Scholte, and Marc Williams. 2000. *Contesting Global Governance*. Cambridge: Cambridge University Press.

O'Connor, Julia S. 1993. "Gender, class and citizenship in the comparative analysis of welfare state regimes." *British Journal of Sociology* 44, pp. 501–18.

1996. "From women in the welfare state to gendering welfare state regimes." *Current Sociology* 44/2, pp. 1–124.

O'Connor, Julia S., Ann Shola Orloff, and Sheila Shaver. 1999. *States, Markets, Families: Gender, Liberalism and Social Policy in Australia, Canada, Great Britain and the United States*. Cambridge and New York: Cambridge University Press.

O'Donnell, Guillermo, and Philippe C. Schmitter. 1986. *Transitions from Authoritarian Rule: Tentative Conclusions About Uncertain Democracies*. Baltimore: Johns Hopkins University Press.

Offen, Karen 2000. *European Feminisms 1700–1950: A Political History*. Stanford: Stanford University Press.

O'Neill, Brenda, and Elisabeth Gidengil (eds.). 2006. *Gender and Social Capital*. New York: Routledge.

O'Regan, Valerie. 2000. *Gender Matters. Female Policymakers' Influence in Industrialized Nations*. Westport and London: Praeger.

Orloff, Ann Shola. 1993. "Gender and the social rights of citizenship: the comparative analysis of state policies and gender relations." *American Sociological Review* 58, pp. 303–28.

1996. "Gender in the welfare state." *Annual Review of Sociology* 22, pp. 51–78.

Outshoorn, Joyce. 1992. "'Femocrats' in the Netherlands: mission or career?" Paper presented at the European Consortium for Political Research. Limerick.

1994. "Between movement and government: 'Femocrats' in the Netherlands." In Hanspeter Kriesi (ed.), *Yearbook of Swiss Political Science*. Bern, Stuttgart and Vienna: Paul Haupt Verlag, pp. 141–65.

(ed.). 2004. *The Politics of Prostitution: Women's Movements, Democratic States and the Globalisation of Sex Commerce*. Cambridge: Cambridge University Press

Outshoorn, Joyce, and Johanna Kantola (eds.). 2007. *Changing State Feminism: Women's Policy Agencies Confront Shifting Institutional Terrain*. London: Palgrave/MacMillan.

Paolino, Phillip. 1995. "Group-salient issues and group representation: support for women candidates in the 1992 Senate elections." *American Journal of Political Science* 39/2, pp. 294–313.

Parks, Robert. 1982. "Interests and the politics of choice." *Political Theory* 10/4, pp. 547–65.

Parpart, Jane L., Shirin M. Rai, and Kathleen Staudt. 2002. *Rethinking Empowerment: Gender and Development in A Global/Local World.* London and New York: Routledge.

Pascall, Gillian, and Nick Manning. 2000. "Gender and social policy: comparing welfare states in central and eastern Europe and the former Soviet Union." *Journal of European Social Policy* 10, pp. 269–96.

Pateman, Carole. 1983. "Feminist critiques of the public-private dichotomy." In Stanley I. Benn and G. F. Gaus (eds.), *The Public and the Private in Social Life.* London: Croom Helm.

1988. *The Sexual Contract.* Cambridge: Polity Press.

1989. *The Disorder of Women: Democracy, Feminism and Political Theory.* Cambridge: Polity Press.

Paxton, Pamela, and Melanie Hughes. 2007. *Women, Politics and Power: A Global Perspective.* Thousand Oaks, CA: Pine Forge Press.

Paxton, Pamela, Melanie Hughes, and Jennifer Green. 2006. "The international women's movement and women's political representation, 1893–2003." *American Sociological Review* 71, pp. 898–920.

Paxton, Pamela. 2000. "Women's suffrage in the measurement of democracy: problems of operationalization." *Studies in Comparative International Development* 35, pp. 92–111.

Pennock, Rowland. 1968. "Political representation: an overview." In J. Rowland Pennock and John W. Chapman (eds.), *Representation: Nomos X.* New York: Atherton Press, pp. 3–27.

Peters, B. Guy. 1992. "Public policy and public bureaucracy." In Douglas Ashford (ed.), *History and Context in Comparative Public Policy.* Pittsburgh: University of Pittsburgh Press.

Peters, B. Guy, and Jon Pierre. 2000. *Governance, Politics and the State.* Basingstoke: Macmillan.

Peterson, John. 2003. "Policy networks." Political Science Working Paper Series 90, July, University of Vienna, available at www.his.ac.at/publications/pol/pw˙90.pdf

Pfau-Effinger, Birgit. 1999. "The modernization of family and motherhood in western Europe." In Crompton *Restructuring Gender Relations and Employment*, pp. 60–79.

2005. "Development paths in care arrangements in the framework of family values and welfare values." In Birgit Pfau-Effinger and Birgit Geissler (eds.), *Care and Social Integration in European Societies.* Bristol: Policy Press, pp. 21–45.

Phillips, Anne. 1991. *Engendering Democracy.* University Park: Pennsylvania State University Press.

1995. *The Politics of Presence.* Oxford: Clarendon Press.

1998. "Democracy and representation: or, why should it matter who our representatives are?" In Anne Phillips (ed.), *Feminism and Politics.* New York: Oxford University Press, pp. 224–40.

Pierson, Paul. 2000. "Three worlds of welfare state research." *Comparative Political Studies* 33, pp. 791–821.

Pitkin, Hanna F. 1969. *Representation.* New York: Atherton Press.

1972. *The Concept of Representation.* Berkeley and Los Angeles: University of California Press.

Piven, Frances Fox. 1990. "Ideology and the state: Women, power and the welfare state." in Linda Gordon (ed.), *Women, the State and Welfare.* Madison: University of Wisconsin Press, pp. 226–49.

Piven, Frances Fox, and Richard Cloward. 1971. *Regulating the Poor: The Functions of Public Welfare.* New York: Random House.

Pringle, Rosemary, and S. Watson, 1992. "Women's interests and the post structuralist state." In Michele Barrett and Anne Phillips (eds.), *Destabilizing Theory: Contemporary Feminist Debates*. Cambridge: Polity Press, pp. 53–73.

Prugl, L. 2008. "Gender and the institutions of global markets: an exploration of the agricultural sector." In Rai and Waylen (eds.), *Global Governance: Feminist Perspectives*, pp. 43–63.

Przeworski, Adam, Michael Alvarez, José Antonio Zhebub, and Fernando Limongi. 2000. *Democracy and Development: Political Institutions and Well-Being in the World, 1950–1990*. Cambridge: Cambridge University Press.

Purdy, Elisabeth R. 1991. *The Representation of Women and Women's Issues: Differences in Voting Patterns of Male and Female Members of the House of Representatives*. Ann Arbor: University of Michigan Press.

Quadagno, Jill. 1994. *The Color of Welfare: How Racism Undermined the War on Poverty*. New York: Oxford University Press.

Ragin, Charles C. 1987. *The Comparative Method: Moving Beyond Qualitative and Quantitative Strategies*. Berkeley, Los Angeles, and London: University of California Press.

Rai, Shirin. (ed.). 2003a. *Mainstreaming Gender, Democratizing the State? Institutional Mechanisms for the Advancement of Women*. Manchester: Manchester University Press.

    2003b. "Institutional mechanisms for the advancement of women: mainstreaming gender, democratizing the state?" In Rai, *Mainstreaming Gender, Democratizing the State?*, pp. 15–39.

Rai, Shirin. 2008. "Analysing global governance." In Shirin Rai and Georgina Waylen (eds.), *Global Governance: Feminist Perspectives*. Basingstoke: Palgrave, pp. 19–42.

Rai, Shirin, and Geraldine Lievesley (eds.). 1996. *Women and the State: International Perspectives*. London: Taylor & Francis.

Rai, Shirin, and Georgina Waylen. 2008. "Introduction: feminist perspectives on analysing and transforming global governance." In Shirin Rai and Georgina Waylen (eds.), *Global Governance: Feminist Perspectives*. Basingstoke: Palgrave, pp. 1–18.

Rainwater, Lee, Martin Rein, and Joseph Schwartz. 1986. *Income Packaging in the Welfare State: A Comparative Study of Family Income*. Oxford: Clarendon Press.

Ramirez, Francisco O., Yasemin Soysal, and Suzanne Shanahan. 1997. "The changing logic of political citizenship: cross-national acquisition of women's suffrage rights, 1890–1990." *American Sociological Review* 62 (October), pp. 735–45.

Razavi, Shahra, and Shireen Hassim (eds.). 2006. *Gender and Social Policy in a Global Context: Uncovering the Gendered Structure of "the Social."* Basingstoke: Palgrave/ Macmillan.

Reich, Gary. 2002. "Categorizing political regimes: new data for old problems." *Democratization* 9, pp. 1–24.

Reingold, Beth. 1992. "Concepts of representation among female and male state legislators." *Legislative Studies Quarterly* 17/4, pp. 509–37.

    2000. *Representing Women: Sex, Gender and Legislative Behavior in Arizona and California*. Chapel Hill: University of North Carolina Press.

Rejai, Mostafa. 1991. *Political Ideologies: A Comparative Approach*. Armonk, NY: M. E. Sharpe.

Remmer, K. (1991). "New wine or old bottlenecks? The study of Latin American democracy." *Comparative Politics* 23, pp. 479–95.

Revillard, Anne. 2007. "La cause des femmes dans l'état: une comparaison France–Quebec (1965–2007)." Doctoral thesis, École Normale Supérieure de Cachan.

Revillard, Anne, and Laure Bereni. 2007. "Des quotas à la parité: 'féminisme d'État' et représentation politique (1974–2007)." *Genèses* 2/67, pp. 5–23.

Rhodes, Rod. 1997. *Understanding Governance: Policy Networks, Governance and Accountability*. Buckingham: Open University Press.

Rich, Adrienne. 1976. *Of Women Born: Motherhood as Experience and Institution*. New York: Bantam Books.

RNGS. 2006. Project description. Available at http://libarts.wsu.edu/polisci/rngs.

Robinson, Jean. 1995. "Women, the state, and the need for civil society: the Liga Kobiet in Poland." In McBride Stetson and Mazur (eds.), *Comparative State Feminism*, pp. 203–20.

Robinson, Richard. 1950. *Definition*. Oxford: Oxford University Press.

Rochon, Thomas R. 1990. "Political movements and state authority in liberal democracies." *World Politics* 42 (January), pp. 299–313.

1998. *Culture Moves: Ideas, Activism, and Changing Values*. Princeton: Princeton University Press.

Rochon, Thomas R., and Daniel A. Mazmanian. 1993. "Social movements and the policy process." *Annals of the American Academy of Political and Social Science* 528, pp. 75–87.

Rosaldo, Renato. 1989. *Culture and Truth*. Stanford: Stanford University Press.

Rosenfeld, Rachel A., and Kathryn B. Ward. 1996. "Evolution of the contemporary US women's movement." *Research in Social Movements, Conflict and Change* 19, pp. 51–73.

Rostow, W. W. 1960. *The Stages of Economic Growth: A Non-Communist Manifesto*. Cambridge: Cambridge University Press.

Roth, Benita. 2004. *Separate Roads to Feminism: Black, Chicana and White Feminist Movements in America's Second Wave*. Cambridge: Cambridge University Press.

Rueschemeyer, Dietrich, Evelyne Huber Stephens, and John D. Stephens. 1992. *Capitalist Development and Democracy*. Chicago: University of Chicago Press.

Rueschemeyer, Marilyn. 1998. *Women in Access to Political Power in Post-Communist Europe*. Oxford: Oxford University Press.

Ruggie, Mary. 1984. *The State and Working Women: A Comparison of Britain and Sweden*. Princeton: Princeton University Press.

Sainsbury, Diane (ed.). 1994. *Gendering Welfare States*. London: Sage.

1996. *Gender, Equality and Welfare States*. Cambridge: Cambridge University Press.

(ed.). 1999. *Gender and Welfare State Regimes*. Oxford: Oxford University Press.

2001. "Gender and the making of welfare states: Norway and Sweden." *Social Politics* 8, pp. 113–43.

Sapiro, Virginia. 1981. "When are interests interesting? The problem of political representation of women." *The American Political Science Review* 75/3, pp. 701–16.

1991. "Gender politics, gendered politics: the state of the field." In William J. Crotty (ed.), *Political Science: Looking to the Future*. Evanston, IL: Northwestern University Press, pp. 165–87.

Sartori, Giovanni. 1969. "Politics, ideology, and belief systems." *American Journal of Political Science* 63, pp. 358–411.

1970. "Concept misformation in comparative politics." *American Political Science Review* 64, pp. 1033–53.

1984. "Guidelines for concept analysis." In Giovanni Sartori (ed.), *Social Science Concepts: A Systematic Analysis.* Beverly Hills: Sage, pp. 15–85.

1987. *The Theory of Democracy Revisited.* Chatham, NJ: Chatham House Publishers.

Savage, Michael, and Anne Witz (eds.) 1993. *Gender and Bureaucracy,* Oxford: Blackwell.

Saward, Michael. 2006. "The representative claim." *Contemporary Political Theory* 5/3, pp. 297–318.

Sawer, Marian. 1990. *Sisters in Suits: Women and Public Policy in Australia.* Sydney: Allen & Unwin.

2000. "Parliamentary representation of women: from discourses of justice to strategies of accountability." *International Political Science Review* 21/4, pp. 361–380.

Saxonhouse, Arlene. 1985. *Women in the History of Political Thought: Ancient Greece to Machiavelli.* New York: Praeger.

Scharpf, Fritz, and Vivien A. Schmidt (eds.). 2000. *Welfare and Work in the Open Economy,* I: *From Vulnerability to Competitiveness.* Oxford: Oxford University Press.

Schattschneider, E. E. 1960. *The Semisovereign People: A Realist's View of Democracy in America.* New York: Holt, Rinehart & Winston.

Schild, V. 1998. "Market citizenship and new democracies: the ambiguous legacies of contemporary Chilean women's movements." *Social Politics* 5/2, pp. 232–305.

Schmidt, Manfred G. 1993. "Gendered labour market participation." In Francis G. Castles (ed.), *Families of Nations: Patterns of Public Policies in Western Democracies.* Aldershot: Dartmouth Publishing Company, pp. 179–237.

Schmitter, Philippe. 1974. "Still the century of corporatism." *Review of Politics* 36/1, pp. 85–131.

Schmitter, Philippe C., and Terry Lynn Karl. 1991. "What democracy is . . . and is not." *Journal of Democracy* 2 (Summer), pp. 75–88.

Schochet, Gordon J. 1975. *Patriarchalism in Political Thought: The Authoritarian Family and Political Speculation and Attitudes Especially in Seventeenth-Century England.* Oxford: Blackwell.

Schumpeter, Joseph. 1942. *Capitalism, Socialism and Democracy.* New York: Harper & Row.

Scott, Catherine. 1995. *Gender and Development: Rethinking Modernization and Dependency Theory.* Boulder: Lynne Rienner.

Scott, Joan. 1986. "Gender a useful category of historical analysis." *American Historical Review* 91, pp. 1053–75.

Sen, Amartya. 1990a. "Gender and cooperative conflicts." In Tinker, *Persistent Inequalities,* pp. 123–49.

1990b. "More than 100 million women are missing." *New York Review of Books,* December 20.

Sen, Gita, and Caren Grown. 1987. *Development, Crises, and Alternative Visions: Third World Women's Perspectives.* New York: Monthly Review Press.

Shanley, Mary Lyndon, and Carole Pateman (eds.). 1991. *Feminist Interpretations and Political Theory.* University Park: Pennsylvania State University Press.

Shapiro, Judith. 1991. "Transexualism: reflections on the persistence of gender and the mutability of sex." In Epstein and Straub, *Body Guards,* pp. 248–79.

Siaroff, Alan. 1994. "Work, welfare and gender equality: a new typology." in Sainsbury, *Gendering Welfare States,* pp. 82–100.

Siim, Birte. 1991. "Welfare state, gender politics and equality policies: women's citizenship in the Scandinavian welfare states." In Elizabeth Meehan and Selma Sevenhuijsen (eds.), *Equality Politics and Gender*. London: Sage, pp. 175–92.

2000. *Gender and Citizenship: Politics and Agency in France, Great Britain and Denmark*. Cambridge: Cambridge University Press.

Singh, Rina. 1998. *Gender Autonomy in Western Europe*. Basingstoke: Macmillan.

Sivard, R. 1985. *Women: A World Survey*. Washington, DC: World Priorities.

Skjeie, Hege. 1997. "Review of *Comparative State Feminism*." *Contemporary Sociology* 26/3, pp. 339–41.

1998. "Credo on difference: women in parliament in Norway. In Karam, *Women in Parliament*, pp. 183–9.

Skocpol, Theda. 1985. "Bringing the state back in: strategies of analysis in current research." In Peter B. Evans, Dietrich Rueschemeyer, and Theda Skocpol (eds.), *Bringing the State Back In*. Cambridge: Cambridge University Press, pp. 3–37.

1992. *Protecting Soldiers and Mothers: The Political Origins of Social Policy in the United States*. Cambridge, MA: Belknap Press of Harvard University Press.

Skocpol, Theda, and Edwin Amenta. 1986. "States and social policies." *Annual Review of Sociology* 12, pp. 131–57.

Smith, Andrea. 2001. "Violence against women of color." In Maylei Blackwell *et al.* (eds.), *Time to Rise: US Women of Color: Issues and Strategies*. Berkeley: Women of Color Resource Center, pp. 89–102.

Smith, Bonnie G. (ed.). 2000. *Global Feminisms since 1945*. London: Routledge.

Smooth, Wendy. 2006. "Intersectionality in electoral politics: a mess worth making." *Politics & Gender* 2, pp. 400–14.

Sobolewski, M. 1968. "Electors and representatives: a contribution to the theory of representation." In J. Rowland Pennock and John W. Chapman (eds.), *Representation. Nomos X*. New York: Atherton Press, pp. 95–107.

Spelman, Elizabeth. 1988. *Inessential Woman*. Boston: Beacon Press.

Squires, J. 1996. "Quotas for women: fair representation?" *Parliamentary Affairs* 49/1, pp. 71–88.

Squires, Judith. 1999. *Gender in Political Theory*. Malden: Blackwell.

Squires, Judith, and Mark Wickham-Jones. 2004. "New Labour, gender mainstreaming, and the Women and Equality Unit." *British Journal of Politics and International Relations* 6/1, pp. 81–98.

Staudt, Kathleen. 1985. *Women, Foreign Assistance and Advocacy Administration*. New York: Praeger.

1990. *Managing Development: State, Society, and International Contexts*. Newbury Park, CA: Sage.

(ed.). 1997. *Women, International Development and Politics: The Bureaucratic Mire*. Pittsburgh: Temple University Press.

1998. *Policy, Politics and Gender: Women Gaining Ground*. West Hartford: Kumarian Press.

2002. "Dismantling the master's house with the master's tools? Gender work in and with powerful bureaucracies." In Kriemild Saunders (ed.), *Feminist Post-development Thought: Rethinking Modernity, Post-colonialism and Representation*. London: Zed, pp. 57–68.

2003. "Gender mainstreaming: conceptual links to institutional machineries." In Rai, *Mainstreaming Gender, Democratizing the State?*, pp. 40–66.

2008. *Violence and Activism at the Border: Gender, Fear, and Everyday Life in Ciudad Juárez.* Austin: University of Texas Press.

Staudt, Kathleen, Shirin Rai, and Jane Parpart. 2001. "Protesting world trade rules: can we talk about empowerment?" *Signs*, 26/4, pp. 1251–7.

Stephens, John D. 1979. *The Transition from Capitalism to Socialism.* London: Macmillan.

Stevens, Evelyn. 1973a. "Machismo and marianismo." *Society* 10, pp. 57–63.

1973b "Marianismo: the other face of machismo." In *Female and Male in Latin America.* Pittsburgh: University of Pittsburgh Press, pp. 90–101.

Stevens, Jacqueline. 1999. *Reproducing the State.* Princeton: Princeton University Press.

Stoffel, Sophie. 2008. "Does state feminism contribute to state retrenchment in the field of women's rights? The case of Chile since the return of democracy." *Representation: Special issue on the Substantive Representation of Women* 44/2.

Stokes, Wendy. 2005. *Women in Contemporary Politics.* Cambridge: Polity Press.

Stone, Deborah. 1997. *Policy Paradox: The Art of Political Decision Making.* New York: W. W. Norton.

Strolovitch, Dara Z. 2004. "Affirmative representation." *Democracy & Society* 1 (June), pp. 3–5.

2007. *Affirmative Advocacy: Race, Gender and Class in Interest Group Politics.* Chicago: University of Chicago Press.

Summerfield, Gale. 2006. "Gender equity and rural land reform in China." In Jaquette and Summerfield, *Women and Gender Equity in Development Theory and Practice*, pp. 137–58.

Sunstein, Cass. 1991. "Preferences and politics." *Philosophy and Public Affairs* 20/11, pp. 156–73.

Swers, Michele L. 2002a. *The Difference Women Make: The Policy Impact of Women in Congress.* Chicago and London: University of Chicago Press.

2002b. "Research on women in legislatures: what have we learned, where are we going?" *Women & Politics* 23/1–2, pp. 167–85.

2002c. "Transforming the agenda: analyzing gender differences in women's issue bill sponsorship." In Cindy Simon Rosenthal (ed.), *Women Transforming Congress.* Congressional Studies Series 4. Norman: University of Oklahoma Press, pp. 260–83.

Sykes, Patricia. 2006. Personal conversation. July 11, Fukuoka, Japan.

Tamerius, K. 1995. "Sex, gender, and leadership in the representation of women." In Georgia Duerst-Lahti and R. Kelly (eds.), *Gender Power, Leadership, and Governance.* Ann Arbor: University of Michigan Press, pp. 93–112.

Tarrow, Sidney. 1994. *Power in Movement: Social Movements, Collective Action and Politics.* Cambridge: Cambridge University Press.

Taylor-Robinson, Michelle M. 2005. "Women on the sidelines: women's representation on committees in Latin American legislatures." *American Journal of Political Science* 49/2, pp. 420–36.

Taylor-Robinson, Michelle M., and Roseanna Michelle Heath. 2003. "Do women legislators have different policy priorities than their male colleagues? A critical case test." *Women & Politics* 24/4, pp. 77–100.

Thelen, Kathleen. 2003. "How institutions evolve: insights from comparative historical analysis." In James Mahoney and Dietrich Rueschemeyer (eds.), *Comparative Historical Analysis in the Social Sciences.* Cambridge: Cambridge University Press, pp. 208–241.

Thomas, Calvin. 2002. "Refleshing the bright boys: or, how male bodies matter to feminist theory." In Judith Kegan Gardiner (ed.), *Masculinity Studies and Feminist Theory: New Directions*. New York: Columbia University Press, pp. 60–89.

Thomas, Sue, and Susan Welch. 2001. "The impact of women in state legislatures: numerical and organizational strength." In Susan Carroll (ed.), *The Impact of Women in Public Office*. Bloomington and Indianapolis: Indiana University Press, pp. 166–81.

Thomassen, Jacques 1994. "Empirical research into political representation: failing democracy or failing models?" In M. Kent Jennings and Thomas E. Mann (eds.) *Elections at Home and Abroad: Essays in Honor of Warren E. Miller*. Anne Arbor: University of Michigan Press, pp. 237–64.

Threlfall, Monica (ed.). 1996. *Mapping the Women's Movement: Feminist Politics and Social Transformation in the North.*. London: Verso.

Tickner, Ann J. 2006. "Feminism meets international relations: some methodological issues." In Ackerly, Stern, and True, *Feminist Methodologies for International Relations*, pp. 19–41.

Tinker, Irene. 1976. "The adverse impact of development on women." In Irene Tinker and Michele Bo Bramsen (eds.), *Women and World Development*. Washington, DC: Overseas Development Council.

Tinker, Irene (ed.). 1990. *Persistent Inequalities: Women and World Development*. New York: Oxford University Press.

Titmuss, Richard M. 1958. *Essays on "the Welfare State."* London: Allen & Unwin.

1968. *Commitment to Welfare*. New York: Pantheon.

1974. *Social Policy: An Introduction*. New York: Pantheon.

Tolleson Rinehart, Sue. 1992. *Gender Consciousness and Politics*. New York: Routledge.

Tremblay, Manon. 1998. "Do female MPs substantively represent women? A study of legislative behaviour in Canada's 35th parliament." *Canadian Journal of Political Science* 31/3, pp. 435–65.

Trimble, Linda. 1993. "A few good women: female legislators in Alberta, 1972–1991." In Cathy Cavanaugh and Randy Warne (eds.), *Standing on New Ground: Women in Alberta*. Edmonton: University of Alberta Press, pp. 87–118.

1997. "Feminist policies in the Alberta legislature, 1972–1994." In Jane Arscott and Linda Trimble (eds.), *In the Presence of Women: Representation and Canadian Governments*. Toronto: Harcourt Brace, pp. 128–54.

2000. "Who's represented? Gender and diversity in the Alberta legislature." In Manon Tremblay and Caroline Andrew (eds.), *Women and Political Representation in Canada*. Women's Studies Series 2. Ottawa: University of Ottawa Press, pp. 257–289.

Tripp, Aili Mari. 2000. "Rethinking difference: comparative perspectives from Africa." *Signs* 25/3 (Spring), pp. 649–76.

2006. "The evolution of transnational feminisms: consensus, conflict, and new dynamics." In Ferree and Tripp, *Global Feminism*, pp. 51–75.

True, Jacqui. 2003. "Mainstreaming gender in global public policy." *International Feminist Journal of Politics* 5/3, pp. 368–96.

2008, "Trade governance and gender mainstreaming in the Asia-Pacific Economic Cooperation Forum." In Rai and Waylen, *Global Governance*, pp. 129–59.

True, Jacqui, and Michael Mintrom (2001). "Transnational networks and policy diffusion: the case of gender mainstreaming." *International Studies Quarterly* 45, pp. 27–57.

UN. 2006. "Directory of National Machineries for the Advancement of Women." DAW – DESA. April.

UNDP (United Nations Development Programme). 1990–2006. *Human Development Report*. New York: Oxford University Press.

USAID. 1997. *Strategic Plan*. New York: US Agency for International Development.

Uusitalo, Hannu. 1984. "Comparative research on the determinants of welfare states: the state of the art." *European Journal of Political Research* 12, pp. 403–22.

Van der Ros, J. 1995. "'Femocrat', you said? What kind of bird is that?" Paper presented at the European Consortium for Political Research, Bordeaux.

Van Der Vleuten, Anna. 2007. *The Price of Gender Equality: Member States and Governance in the European Union*. Aldershot: Ashgate.

van Kersbergen, Kees. 1995. *Social Capitalism: A Study of Christian Democracy and the Welfare State*. London: Routledge.

Vanhanen, Tatu. 2000. "A new dataset for measuring democracy, 1810–1998." *Journal of Peace Research* 37, pp. 251–65.

Vargas, Virginia, and Saskia Wieringa (1998). "The triangles of empowerment: processes and actors in the making of public policy." In Lycklama à Nijeholt, Vargas, and Wieringa (eds.), *Women's Movements and Public Policy in Europe, Latin America, and the Caribbean*, pp. 10–28.

Wacquant, Loic. 1995. "The comparative structure and experience of urban exclusion: "race", class and space in Chicago and Paris." In Katherine McFate, Roger Lawson, and William Julius Wilson (eds.), *Poverty Inequality and the Future of Social Policy*. Russell Sage: New York, 1995.

Walby, Sylvia. 1990. *Theorizing Patriarchy*. Cambridge, MA: Blackwell.

1997. *Gender Transformations*. London: Routledge.

2005. "Comparative gender mainstreaming in a global era." *International Feminist Journal of Politics* 7/4, pp. 453–70.

Walker, Alice. 1983. *In Search of Our Mother's Garden*. New York: Harcourt.

Wängnerud, Lena. 2000. "Testing the politics of presence: women's representation in the Swedish riksdag." *Scandinavian Political Studies* 23/1, pp. 67–91.

Waters, Malcolm. 1989. "Patriarchy and viriarchy." *Sociology* 23/2 (May), pp. 193–211.

Watson, Sophie (ed.). 1990. *Playing the State: Australian Feminist Interventions:* London: Verso.

Waylen, Georgina. 1994. "Women and democratization: conceptualizing gender relations in transition." *World Politics* 46, pp. 327–54.

1998. "Gender, feminism and the state: an overview." In Vicky Randall and Georgina Waylen (eds.), *Gender, Politics and the State*. London: Routledge, pp. 1–10.

2007. *Engendering Transitions: Women's Mobilization, Institutions and Gender Outcomes*. Oxford: Oxford University Press.

2008. "Transforming global governance: challenges and opportunities." In Rai and Waylen (eds.), *Global Governance: Feminist Perspectives*, pp. 254–75.

Weber, M. 1952. "The essentials of bureaucratic organization: an ideal-type construction." In Robert K. Merton (ed.) *Reader in Bureaucracy*. New York: Free Press, pp. 1–17.

Weir, Margaret, Ann Shola Orloff, and Theda Skocpol (eds.). 1988. *The Politics of Social Policy in the US*. Princeton: Princeton University Press.

Weldon, S. Laurel. 2002a. *Protest, Policy, and the Problem of Violence Against Women: A Cross-National Comparison.* Pittsburgh: University of Pittsburgh Press.

2002b. "Beyond bodies: institutional sources of representation for women in democratic policymaking." *Journal of Politics* 64/4, pp. 1153–74.

2006a. "Inclusion, solidarity and transnational social movements: the global movement against gender violence." *Perspectives on Politics*, 4/1, pp. 55–74.

2006b. "Women's movements, identity politics and policy impact: a study of policies on violence against women in the 50 US states." *Political Research Quarterly* 59, pp. 111–22.

Wendt, Alex. 1999. *Social Theory of International Politics.* Cambridge: Cambridge University Press.

West, Candace, and Don Zimmerman. 1987. "Doing gender." *Gender & Society* 1, pp. 125–51.

Whip, Rosemary. 1991. "Representing women: Australian female parliamentarians on the horns of a dilemma." *Women & Politics* 11/3, pp. 1–22.

Whitaker, Lois Duke. 1999. *Women in Politics: Outsiders or Insiders?* Upper Saddle River: Prentice-Hall.

Wikipedia. 2007. "Masculism." http://en.wikipedia.org/wiki/Masculism, accessed June 3.

Wilensky, Harold L. 1975. *The Welfare State and Equality.* Berkeley: University of California Press.

Wilensky, Harold L., and Charles N. Lebeaux. 1965. *Industrial Society and Social Welfare.* New York: the Free Press. First published 1958.

Williams, Fiona. 1995. "Race, ethnicity, gender and class in welfare states" *Social Politics* 127–159.

Williams, Melissa. 1998. *Voice, Trust and Memory: The Failings of Liberal Representation.* Princeton: Princeton University Press.

Wolbrecht, Christina. 2002. "Female legislators and the women's rights agenda." In Cindy Simon Rosenthal (ed.), *Women Transforming Congress.* Norman: University of Oklahoma Press, pp. 170–94.

Wright, Erik Olin. 1997a. *Class Counts: Comparative Studies in Class Analysis.* Cambridge: Cambridge University Press.

1997b. "Deferring group representation." In Ian Shapiro and Will Kymlicka (eds.), *Ethnicity and Group Rights. Nomos 39.* New York: New York University Press: pp. 349–76.

Young, Iris Marion. 1990. *Justice and the Politics of Difference.* Princeton: Princeton University Press.

1994. "Gender as seriality: thinking about women as a social collective." *Signs* 19, pp. 713–38.

1997. *Intersection Voices: Dilemmas of Gender, Political Philosophy, and Policy.* Princeton: Princeton University Press.

2000. *Inclusion and Democracy.* Oxford Series in Political Theory. Oxford: Oxford University Press.

2002. "Lived body vs. gender: reflections on social structure and subjectivity." *Ratio: An International Journal of Analytic Philosophy* 15/4 (December), pp. 410–28.

2005. "Lived body versus gender: reflections on social structure and subjectivity." In Iris Marion Young, *On Female Body Experience: "Throwing Like a Girl" and Other Essays.* New York: Oxford University Press, pp. 12–26.

Zald, Mayer N. 1996. "Culture, ideology, and strategic framing." In Doug McAdam, John D. McCarthy, and Mayer N. Zald (eds.), *Comparative Perspectives on Social Movements: Political Opportunities, Mobilizing Structures, and Cultural Framings.* Cambridge: Cambridge University Press, pp. 261–74.

Zerilli, Linda M. G. (1994). *Signifying Women: Culture and Chaos in Rousseau, Burke, and Mill.* Ithaca: Cornell University Press.

Zetterberg, Pär. 2008. "Gender quotas and political effectiveness. Women's experiences in Mexican state legislatures." *Representation. Special issue on the Substantive Representation of Women* 44/2.

Zheng, Wang. 2005. "State feminism? Gender and socialist state formation in Maoist China." *Feminist Studies* 31/3, pp. 519–44.

Zinn, Maxine Baca, and Bonnie Thornton Dill. 1996. "Theorizing difference from multiracial feminism." *Feminist Studies* 22, pp. 321–31.

Zippell, Katrin. 2006. *The Politics of Sexual Harassment: A Comparative Study of the United States, the European Union, and Germany.* Cambridge: Cambridge University Press.

Zwingel, Susanne. 2005. "How do women's rights norms become effective? An analysis of the Convention on the Elimination of all Forms of Discrimination against Women and its domestic impact." PhD dissertation, Ruhr University Bochum, Germany.

Index